Long Island Women
Activists and Innovators

Papers presented at the Conference on
Long Island Women: Activists and Innovators
March 22-23, 1996
sponsored by
Hofstra University
Long Island Studies Institute and the
Hofstra Cultural Center

The illustration above and on the paperback cover are images from
Women: A Pictorial Archive from Nineteenth-Century Sources, selected
by Jim Hartner, 2d ed. (New York: Dover Publications, 1982).

Long Island Women
Activists and Innovators

Edited by

Natalie A. Naylor

and

Maureen O. Murphy

Prepared under the auspices of
Hofstra University

Empire State Books
Interlaken, New York
1998

"Baseball and Writing," copyright © 1961 Marianne Moore, © renewed 1989 by Lawrence E. Brinn and Louise Crane, executors of the Estate of Marianne Moore; "Hometown Piece for Messrs. Alston and Reese," copyright © 1956 by Marianne Moore; "The Camperdown Elm," copyright © 1967 by Marianne Moore. First appeared in *The New Yorker,* from *The Complete Poems of Marianne Moore* by Marianne Moore. Used by permission of Viking Penguin, a division of Penguin Books USA Inc.

Library of Congress Catalogue Number: 98–70015
ISBN: 1–55787–150–7 (paper)
ISBN: 1–55787–151–5 (cloth)
Manufactured in the United States of America

A *quality* publication from
Heart of the Lakes Publishing
Interlaken, New York 14847

Contents

Creating and Sustaining Community Organizations

Expanding Women's Work

Achieving National Fame

Engaging in Feminist Activism

Appendices

Illustrations

1. Introduction

Natalie A. Naylor

Until recent decades, women usually have been nearly invisible in most historical accounts. Since the 1970s, women's history has developed on the national scene into a vibrant, dynamic field, but progress has been slower in local history. Older accounts of Long Island history occasionally refer to Heather Flower, a Montaukett rescued by Lion Gardiner, a few women accused (but acquitted) of witchcraft, and Anna (or Nancy) Strong who aided the spy ring during the Revolution.[1] However, this virtually exhausts the treatment of half the population in most of the traditional histories of Long Island.

As an initial step, I identified more than 150 nationally notable women who had some connection with Long Island. I subsequently narrowed the list to focus on those who lived or worked on Long Island during their years of achievement (see Appendix, "Long Island's Nationally Notable Women"). In an article discussing these women a dozen years ago, I concluded: "Even this brief review of the accomplishments of notable Long Island women indicates that the contributions of most have been overlooked in Long Island history. This survey may assist in the recovery of this lost part of our heritage. Of course, many thousands of unheralded women also were part of Long Island's history, and their role still remains to be explored."[2]

Hofstra University has a distinguished record of conferences, and the Long Island Studies Institute, since its formation in 1985, has conducted twenty conferences on various aspects of Long Island history. A conference on "Long Island Women: Activists and Innovators" was held in March 1996. A call for papers had been circulated, and the conference directors, Maureen O. Murphy, Professor of Curriculum and Teaching, and Natalie A. Naylor, Director of the Long Island Studies Institute, also sought out papers. The two-day conference was a stimulating exchange of ideas. This conference volume includes many of the papers presented, supplemented by material distributed to those attending the conference: a list of Long Island's Nationally Notable Women and a bibliography on Long Island Women, which has been expanded and updated for this publication.[3]

The arrangement of the essays here varies from the organization at the conference. Marilyn Goldstein was the featured opening speaker; her essay is presented towards the end of this volume which is organized chronologically within thematic parts.

The first part of this book, "Women Challenging Boundaries," includes articles that range from the early colonial period to the mid-twentieth century. In diverse ways, these women challenged the conventional boundaries limiting women of their day. Quaker women enjoyed a more equalitarian position than most colonial women. Mildred Murphy DeRiggi discusses three Friends from Oyster Bay in "The Wright Sisters: Seventeenth-Century Quaker Activists." In an era when Quakers were persecuted, these indomitable women each travelled to Massachusetts at different times where they protested the treatment of Quakers and stood up for their religious beliefs. Two nineteenth-century Long Island historians claimed Mary Wright was accused of witchcraft, but DeRiggi indicates there is no evidence of such charges in Oyster Bay records.

John Strong has explored the history of Long Island's Native Americans in two recent books published under the auspices of the Long Island Studies Institute.[4] In his essay, "The Role of Algonquian Women in Land Transactions on Eastern Long Island, 1639–1859," he documents the significant role that Long Island Indian women played in the notorious land sales. Women often assumed positions of authority in Native communities and were known as sunksquaws. Strong identifies a number of legal transactions with the English where Algonquian women were signatories. Their presence was often obliterated, however, by European Americans who did not acknowledge the possibility of women owning property, and when the New York legislature imposed a governance system on the Shinnecock in 1792, it excluded women. In 1994, Shinnecock men granted women the right to vote in trustee elections, and Shinnecock women have regained their traditional role as tribal leaders.

Long Island was America's Cradle of Aviation. Joanne Lynn Harvey gave a slide presentation documenting Long Island's "First Women in Aviation."[5] Many of the pioneer women pilots, including Blanche Stuart Scott, Bessica Faith Raiche, Matilde Moisant, Viola Gentry, Elinor Smith, Fay Gillis Wells, and Jackie Cochran, learned to fly and set aviation records from the many airfields on the Hempstead Plains. Harvey explains how these and other women aviators "challenged the status quo and expanded the boundaries that hindered them" in the 1910s and 1920s.

Henry M. Holden focuses on another pioneer aviator in his article on "The Life and Times of Harriet Quimby." Quimby was a journalist working in New York City who "challenged and confronted existing norms of behavior for women." She learned to fly on the Hempstead Plains in 1910, and wrote about her experiences for *Leslie's Illustrated Weekly*. Quimby flew a monoplane at a time when bi-planes were more common and wore a distinctive purple satin flying suit. She was the first woman to fly across the English Channel, but her career was cut short when, tragically, she was killed in an airplane accident. Those early years of flight were dangerous for women and men. The women who broke barriers in aviation were courageous heroines.

Lucinda Mayo's essay, "'One of Ours': The World of Jeannette Edwards Rattray," takes its title from the byline Rattray used in her weekly column for the *East Hampton Star* for fifty years. Rattray had deep roots in East Hampton, wrote several important histories of the town, and founded a newspaper dynasty, but it is her world travels that Mayo explores and sees as a fulcrum for her life. From her first voyages to Turkey and China in the 1920s, through her European travels in the 1960s, she always found "East Hampton reminders everywhere" and expanded her hometown's geographic boundaries to the wider world.

Traditionally, women's sphere was in the home. The published diaries of Mary Cooper of Oyster Bay (1768–1773) and Helen Rogers of Cold Spring Harbor (1843–1850) have provided useful glimpses of women's day-to-day lives, centering on their domestic responsibilities.[6] The articles in part two of this book focus on women who spent much of their lives in domestic and traditional roles, but broadened them into new arenas.

In her essay, "Women's Lives at the William Floyd Estate and the Poosepatuck Indian Reservation, 1800–Present," Bernice Forrest Guillaume deals with interactions between white and Native American women over several generations. On Mastic Neck, many Poosepatuck women worked for the Floyd family. In their private and published writings, the Floyd women reveal their own cultural biases and stereotypes about the Poosepatucks. Professor Guillaume describes how Poosepatuck women have functioned as tribal leaders and have been involved in land transactions and court challenges to land holdings. By focusing on a few individuals—Martha Mayne, her granddaughter Mary Brackett, and Red Corn Woman— she documents how Poosepatuck women have maintained and transmitted their Native culture and consciousness. The Floyd Estate is now a historic site under the National Park Service; the Poosepatuck Reservation, though considerably reduced in size and officially recognized only by the state and not the federal government, continues to be home to the Unkechaug Nation.

Kathryn Curran, in her essay "'To Blush Unseen': A View of Nineteenth-Century Women," reminds us that, "It is in the common place and daily occurrences that a society is built." Drawing on letters, diaries, and journals, as well as samplers, quilts, and other cultural artifacts women created, she weaves a portrait of the daily lives of these "keepers of the home." Curran explains how the documentary evidence gives life and substance to the material culture they created. Their needlework often reflected patriotic images and, during the Civil War, they used their domestic skills to provide clothing and raise money for the Union troops, thus broadening into wider spheres.

Alice Ross focuses on "Long Island Women and Benevolence: Changing Images of Women's Place, 1880–1920." Donation parties, church suppers, convention dinners, fundraising cookbooks, women's exchanges, and fairs raised money for religious and benevolent purposes by drawing on women's domestic skills. Ella Smith's activities illustrate the centrality of religion, benevolence, and community service in her life—and, by extension, the lives of thousands of other women. A eulogy to Ella Smith doubtless applies to countless other women, "No one can measure the good she has done not alone in her own home village but reaching far out in places we little know of."

Three other "ordinary" and "exemplary" Smith women are the focus of Norma Cohen's essay, "The Forebears Were Women: Three Smith Sisters." Born between 1884 and 1890, Josephine, Mildred, and Dorothy Smith were very conscious of their family heritage and male forebears, the Smiths who founded Smithtown. It was World War I which first precipitated the Smith sisters into wider spheres: raising Liberty Loans, preparing kits for the Red Cross to send abroad, raising food as Farmerettes, serving as canteen workers on Long Island and in France. Beginning in the 1930s, Mildred and Josephine were using domestic skills to supplement their income. They operated tea rooms, and Dorothy was selling home-baked goods. During World War II, Josephine and Mildred were among the "Janes who made the Planes." As Cohen concludes, these Smith women "quietly but irrevocably stretched out the boundaries that defined women's roles in their communities."

Two of the first professions open to women, or rather created by women, were nursing and social work, growing out of a long tradition of women's volunteer charitable work. Catholic nuns have long labored unheralded in these fields (as well as in education), and several papers at the conference focused on the work of religious orders. In the opening article in the section on "Meeting Social Needs and Services," Sister Edna McKeever, archivist of the Sisters of St. Joseph in Brentwood, focuses on "Mother de Chantal Keating, CSJ: A 'Notable, Noble American.'" Born in Ireland, Jane Keating spent some years in Westbury before joining the Sisters of St. Joseph in 1857. She first taught at St. Joseph's Academy in Flushing. During the Civil War, she was in charge of a hospital in West Virginia which served wounded soldiers as well as orphan children. Mother de Chantal returned to Long Island in 1876, and was in charge of an orphanage in Brooklyn which served thousands of young boys. They donated the stained glass window in the Convent of St. Joseph, Brentwood as a memorial to her. As Sister Edna concludes, "It is a reminder of the many talents and abilities of womankind who, when unhampered, are capable of great achievements for all of human-kind."

Floris Barnett Cash points out that African American women have been doubly invisible in historical studies. Her article, "Gender and Race Consciousness: Verina Morton-Jones Inspires a Settlement House in Suburbia," describes the role of African American women in founding the Harriet Tubman Community Club in Hempstead in 1928. Dr. Morton-Jones had been a physician in Brooklyn and involved in women's clubs. After she moved to Hempstead in the 1920s, she practiced medicine and directed the Harriet Tubman Community Center, a social settlement house which provided lodging for women as well as programs for the community. Dr. Cash relates some of the broader context of these activities and themes that deserve further attention from other historians.[7]

Today, St. Francis Hospital in Roslyn is one of the leading heart centers in the state. Sister Lois Van Delft relates the history of this institution in "Women of Faith: The Spiritual Legacy of the Founders of St. Francis Hospital." The Franciscan Missionaries of Mary received property in Roslyn and opened a summer camp in 1921 that evolved into a sanatorium for children with rheumatic fever in the late 1930s. Adults with heart disease were admitted in 1954; by the 1960s, St. Francis had become a general hospital with a cardiac specialty.

Homelessness has become a significant problem in recent years. Huntington is one Long Island town which has an enviable record of coping with this problem. Cynthia J. Bogard analyzes Huntington's response to the homeless in "Homeless in Huntington: Struggling Mothers and Their Care Givers." Although she includes government agencies, her focus is on religious and private charitable organizations. Significantly, women make many of the policy decisions and are the "hands-on service delivery personnel. . . . These women charity workers in Huntington have decided to help other women." Bogard notes that there is a "common bond of motherhood" for both the providers and recipients of care.

By the late nineteenth century, many women were participating in civic activities and taking a leading role in creating the essential infrastructure of their communities, often initiating activities later assumed by government. The articles in part four, "Creating and Sustaining Community Organizations," discuss individuals or organizations involved in such good works.

The Ladies' Village Improvement Society (LVIS) in East Hampton has indeed, been "A Century of Force," as long-time LVIS member Eunice Juckett Meeker explains in her article. Beautification projects include flower beds, the town pond and greens, the railroad station, and loving care for more than 7,000 street trees. Fundraising is accomplished with fairs, cookbooks, and now year-round shops. The LVIS also monitors government activities and is active in landmarks preservation, to mention only a few of the activities of this important local women's organization.

East Hampton's LVIS inspired the organization of a similar group in Sayville in 1914, the Women's Village Improvement Society. Norma White, in "Civic Minded Women: The Sayville Village Improvement Society," describes how it, too, has been involved with beautification projects, including flowers and trees; however, it also introduced proper garbage disposal and public safety (hiring a policeman). The society was the impetus for formation of the local public library and responsible for acquiring shore-front land subsequently donated to the town for a park. These and other activities helped improve the quality of life in Sayville and certainly demonstrate, as White concludes, the "power of women working unselfishingly together to make their community a desirable village in which to live."

Women's clubs proliferated throughout the country beginning in the late nineteenth century. Dorothy B. Ruettgers focuses on the life of "Abigail Eliza Leonard: Quiet Innovator," to demonstrate the influence of one woman's leadership in her local women's club for civic improvement. Leonard was one of the founders of Farmingdale's Women's Club and served as its president for ten years (1915–1925). Although she apparently was not too successful in getting her fellow members involved in the suffrage movement, she was a major impetus in the Women's Club's formation of the Farmingdale Free Public Library. Other civic activities during her term included purchasing street signs; encouraging the village to pave streets, collect garbage, and have mail delivery; and working to secure a school nurse and business courses in the high school. Abigail Leonard "affected many lives in positive ways," as Ruettgers points out, as "she worked for the good of her community."

Hofstra University's history usually focuses on William Hofstra and its first presidents, Truesdel Peck Calkins and John Cranford Adams, but women were important, too. Hofstra's archivist, Geri Solomon, traces their significant role and contributions in "Kate Mason Hofstra and Alicia Patterson: Founding and Building Hofstra University." Although Kate Mason Hofstra did not originate the idea of starting a college, it was her 1933 legacy for a public benevolent purpose as a memorial to her late husband that enabled the formation of Hofstra as an institution of higher education. Alicia Patterson, the first woman on the Hofstra board of trustees, played an important role in the expansion of the college during her two decades of service (1943–1963), and her money and dedication aided the college in significant ways. As Solomon notes, they both shared a "commitment to creating something permanent on the Long Island landscape," and today's Hofstra University is the beneficiary of their creating and sustaining what was initially a community educational institution.

In "Energizer and Actualizer—The Nassau County League of Women Voters," Arlene B. Soifer chronicles the history and role of the League. Like the national League, Nassau's was organized in 1920, by suffrage leaders after the Nineteenth Amendment had been achieved. Over the years, the Nassau League, a nonpartisan organization devoted to the study of public policy issues, has provided information and resources in fields such as international cooperation, voter's service, county charter, child labor, education, and other civic issues. Soifer explains how the League nurtured women to become "leaders, activists and innovators" in government and non-profit organizations, as well as in professions and business.

Part five, "Expanding Women's Work," focuses on various women who helped broaden opportunities for women in the work force. Candace Thurber Wheeler, a needlework artist and textile designer, worked with Louis Comfort Tiffany, formed her own Associated Artists firm of women, and directed the Applied Arts exhibit at the Chicago Columbian Exposition in 1893. Martha Kreisel, in "Candace Thurber Wheeler and the New York Exchange for Woman's Work," argues that the Exchange that Wheeler helped organize in 1878, was "one of her most enduring legacies to women." The New York Exchange provided training and an outlet for women to bring their handiwork to be sold while maintaining their dignity.

Christine Frederick was a household efficiency expert who lived in Greenlawn from 1912 to 1939, where she operated Applecroft Experiment Station. She tested household products and wrote articles for the *Ladies' Home Journal* and other magazines, three books, and numerous advertising booklets, as well as maintaining an extensive speaking schedule—all devoted to modernizing and easing household tasks. These activities, while she was raising her four children, were possible with household help. Janice Williams Rutherford, in her essay "Christine Frederick: Barometer of Conflict," concludes that "Frederick's career paradoxically exemplified the opportunities for participating in the public sphere that were newly available to women, while it flourished on the old prescription that would have them remain in their traditional roles."

During World War II, new opportunities opened up to women on Long Island and throughout the nation. "Long Island Women Go to War" is in two parts. Alan Singer recounts how "Local Newspapers Report on the Changing Roles of Women, 1941–1946," and Christine Kleinegger discusses "The Janes Who Made the Planes" at Grumman Aircraft Engineering Corporation. Women's work expanded as the labor shortage during the war opened opportunities for women in aviation plants and other non-traditional occupations. Subsidized nurseries facilitated work outside the home for some women. Women were praised for their patriotism and skills. The end of the war, however, brought layoffs and the closing of child care facilities. Now, women were encouraged to be full-time mothers and homemakers, but this "return to normalcy" proved to be only temporary.

By the 1970s, women were making greater inroads into non-traditional occupations, but it was never easy for those who were among the first in a field. Linda Keller, in her article, "Kathryn Dudek: Breaking Barriers in the World of Sports Photojournalism," explains how this talented young sports photographer gained acceptance from male sports editors and in the male-dominated world of thoroughbred racing. Tragically, her life and career were cut short by an automobile accident in 1992. Her photographs survive, and exhibitions have brought them to new audiences.

Long Island has been home to women who have become nationally famous. Many of these women are listed in the Appendix. Several of these women are discussed in part six, "Achieving National Fame."[8] Frances Hodgson Burnett was a very prolific author in the late nineteenth and early twentieth centuries. Born in England and raised in Tennessee, she spent the last decades of her life on Long Island, where she wrote her classic, *The Secret Garden.* Bea Tusiani traces Burnett's many connections with Long Island in "Last Stop Plandome: Francis Hodgson Burnett." Burnett spent a brief time in Long Beach in the summer of 1880, rented a cottage for two summers in East Hampton in 1902–1903, and rented a house in Sands Point in 1907, before building a home in Plandome in 1908.

For more than thirty-five years, the reknowned poet Marianne Moore lived in the Fort Greene section of Brooklyn at the western end of geographic Long Island. She had a love affair with the borough's most famous baseball team, which another Brooklyn and baseball aficionado, Joseph Dorinson, recounts in "Marianne Moore and the Brooklyn Dodgers." Dodger fans will revel in her poem, "Hometown Piece for Messrs. Alston and Reese," and all baseball enthusiasts will enjoy her poem, "Baseball and Writing." Brooklyn and its baseball, Dorinson concludes, "both served as Muses for Marianne Moore."

Alicia Patterson's service as a trustee of Hofstra is discussed in Chapter 18, but Robert Keeler's essay, "Alicia Patterson and the Shape of Long Island," focuses on Patterson as editor of *Newsday,* which is what gained her national fame. Although Patterson had a family heritage in the newspaper business, her early life was spent as a rich playgirl. She found her life work when her husband, Harry Guggenheim, established a new newspaper for her in 1941. Patterson was a working editor who really created *Newsday.* Keeler also explains how she—and *Newsday*—significantly influenced the development of Long Island.

Barbara McClintock spent the most productive years of her life on Long Island. Janice Koch, in "Barbara McClintock: An Overview of a Long Island Scientist," traces her years growing up in Brooklyn, studying at Cornell

University, and facing the difficulty of a woman scientist finding positions in academe. McClintock pursued her research at the Cold Spring Harbor Laboratory from 1942 until she died in 1992. She received a Nobel Prize in 1983 for her work in genetics. Koch explores some of the feminist analyses of her science, though McClintock herself declined to discuss being a female scientist. Koch concludes, "The reality of Barbara McClintock's life is that she rejected categories and labels and lived her own scientific life," and science for her was "pure pleasure."

Artist Lee Krasner spent most of her life in the shadow of her husband, Jackson Pollock, but in recent years, her art has received its due recognition. Helen A. Harrison, Director of the Pollock-Krasner House and Study Center, treats the work and life of this East Hampton artist in "Lee Krasner 'From There to Here.'" Krasner was a native of Brooklyn and did some of her early work in Huntington, where her parents had moved, but her most innovative work was done on eastern Long Island after she moved, in 1945, to The Springs. There, Harrison notes, the "landscape was a fruitful source of raw material for her compositions." After Pollock's death in 1956, her work brought her to the front rank of modern American artists.

The final section, "Engaging in Feminist Activism," focuses on women who have been active in the contemporary women's movement. *Newsday* columnist Marilyn Goldstein was the invited featured speaker at the conference. In "Reflections on Long Island Women," she discusses a myriad of feminist activities on Long Island, focusing on the 1970s: women ran for political office and some were elected; others challenged differential requirements for women police officers, exclusion from Little League, and school district regulations requiring pregnant teachers to leave in their fourth month; Nassau NOW became one of the largest chapters in the United States; Long Island women played an important role in getting women's rights laws passed in Albany. Drawing on her own workplace, Goldstein describes a sex discrimination class-action suit against *Newsday* in the 1970s, which resulted in some better opportunities for women, though gains slowed in the 1980s. Goldstein deplores betrayal by "neo-feminists" of feminist traditions in the 1990s, and offers some explanations for the turn of the feminist tide.

One of the prominent feminists on the national scene has roots on Long Island. Linda F. Burghardt discusses "On the Frontiers of Feminism: The Life and Vision of Letty Cottin Pogrebin." Pogrebin grew up in Jamaica, Queens, and since 1968, has had a summer home on Fire Island. She was one of the founding editors of *Ms.* magazine in 1971, and has written a number of feminist books including titles on child-rearing and Judaism. Pogrebin feels she is a "bridge builder" between "family women and more radical women, and . . . [enables] Jewish identified women to be feminists and feminist women to take part fully in Jewish life."

The National Organization for Women (NOW) has been one of the premier groups in the feminist movement since its organization in Washington, D.C., in 1966. Linda Lane-Weber, an activist in both the South Shore NOW and its successor, the South Suffolk NOW (which she helped organize), relates "Significant Moments in the Evolution of the Southern Suffolk NOW Chapters." She contrasts some of the differences between the two chapters and how concerns and issues have changed over the years with increasing emphasis on political activities. NOW members often have been the impetus in initiating other feminist organizations, including the Long Island Women's Coalition, NOW Alliance Political Action Committee (PAC) of Long Island, and the Long Island Fund for Women and Girls.

The dictionary defines feminism as the "movement to win political, economic, and social equality for women." Equal pay and pay equity have wide support, even from women who may not identify themselves as feminists. In "Long Island's Grassroots Action for Pay Equity: Women on the Job," Charlotte Shapiro describes a local equal employment project organized by women. Beginning with a feasibility study in 1982, and aided by a grant from the Unitarian Universalist Society Veatch Program, coalitions and task forces were developed. Shapiro explains how Women on the Job provided advocacy, technical assistance, and support for pay equity complaints filed by school office workers and public health nurses. Although full pay equity has not yet been achieved for so many Long Island women, progress has been made. This group of women activists has provided a blueprint for achieving pay equity through grassroots coalition-building.

The scope of this collection is broad, extending from the seventeenth century to the recent past and from Brooklyn to the East End. However, it is but a sampling of aspects of Long Island's women's history and the coverage inevitably is incomplete. We do hope it will encourage women's organizations to pay attention to their history, to record it, and to deposit it in an appropriate library or archive. We urge local historians to give more attention to women so they are not as invisible in the historical record as they have been in the past.

The Hofstra conference and this collection are a significant beginning in documenting and recovering the history of Long Island women, particularly some of the unheralded women who have contributed much to their communities. Historian Gerda Lerner has suggested that we should ask, "What were women doing? How were they doing it? What was their own understanding of their place in the world? What would the past be like if women were placed at the center of inquiry?"[9] We trust such questions will continue to intrigue women and historians in the future. Long Island women have been important in many aspects of our history.

Acknowledgments

Athlene Collins was conference coordinator, and the Hofstra Cultural Center staff provided essential expertise and logistical support for the conference. Many of the contributors assisted the publishing process by providing their papers on disk; all responded to what sometimes were numerous queries as we "fine tuned" the articles. Maureen O. Murphy did initial editing. Victoria Aspinwall, Long Island Studies Institute secretary, not only entered changes, but was a valuable editorial assistant, proofreading and providing editing suggestions. Dorothy B. Ruettgers was an indispensable grammatical consultant. Many individuals and organizations have provided photographs. We are grateful to Hofstra University for its continued support of the Long Island Studies Institute which makes possible our conferences and publications.

Notes

1. The story of Nancy Strong's clothesline has been often told; its origins are with a descendant. See Kate Wheeler Strong, "Nancy's Magic Clothesline," *Long Island Forum* 2 (November 1939): 13; reprinted in the *Forum* 15 (March 1952): 49 and 18 (February 1955): 37-38. Strong published more than three hundred articles in the *Forum;* her papers are in the Local History Collection of the Three Village Historical Society housed at the Emma S. Clark Library in Setauket.

2. "Long Island's Notable Women," parts 1 and 2, *Long Island Forum* 47, no. 6 (June 1984): 104-109; no. 7 (July 1984): 135-41; quotation from p. 139.

3. Papers presented at the conference but not included in this volume are: "Long Island Collections at Work: The Floyd Women," by Steven Czarniecki; "Taking Back Childbirth: Birth Wisdom and Its Membership," by Angela D. Danzi; "Molloy College: A Proud Tribute to Dedicated Women," by Sister Dorothy Anne Fitzgibbons; "By Choice or by Chance: Single Women's Lives in Nineteenth-Century Suffolk County," by Sherrill Foster; "Margaret Olivia Slocum Sage: Local, Regional, and National Philanthropy," by Susan Kastan; "Bridget in Brooklyn: The Irish Servant Girl at the Turn of the Century," by Maureen O. Murphy; "Dorothy Whitney Elmhirst, The Life of a Philanthropist," by Deirdre Hurst du Prey; "Daughters of Wisdom: Heeding the Call to Service," by Sr. Margaret Quigley, D.W.; "The Sisters of St. Dominic on Long Island: Meeting Needs Since 1853," by Sr. Joan Staudohar, O.P.; "Marianne Moore and Brooklyn," by Jon Sterngass; "Women Who Made a Difference," by Gaynell Stone; "Mentors in Flight: Encouraging Women in Aviation," by Mary Ann Turney and Diana Santiago; and the Workshop for Teachers on "Changing Roles in World War II," by Jennifer Evans, Melissa Sorgin, Diane Tully, and Pamela Booth. Audiotapes of most of these and other sessions (including questions and answers following the presentations) are in the Long Island Studies Institute collections (Hofstra University West Campus, 619 Fulton Avenue, Hempstead, NY 11549; 516-463-6411).

There were other features of the conference which deserve mention. Laura Schofer, a Long Island playwright, wrote *Silent History: tales my mother never told me,* in conjunction with the conference. Her play featured such famous Long Island women as Heather Flower, Lady Deborah Moody, Elizabeth "Goodie" Garlick; Anna Strong,

Rachel Hicks, Alva Vanderbilt Belmont, Elinor Smith, Irene Castle, Alicia Patterson, and Barbara McClintock. Produced by Hofstra USA under the direction of Bob Spiotto, there were six performances of this dramatic presentation during the weekend of the conference. Two exhibitions also were on display in conjunction with the conference. "Memories of Kathryn: Photographs of Kathryn Dudek" was in the Rochelle and Irwin A. Lowenfeld Exhibition Hall of the Axinn Library. Linda Keller gave a slide presentation on Ms. Dudek at the conference, and her essay is included in this volume (Chapter 23). An exhibit guest-curated by Kathryn Curran, "'To Blush Unseen': Nineteenth-Century Long Island Women," was in the David Filderman Gallery of Hofstra's Axinn Library. Curran's essay, revised and expanded from the exhibit catalog, is included herewith (Chapter 8), together with a few illustrations of the many artifacts which were in the exhibition.

4. *The Algonquian Peoples of Long Island from Earliest Times to 1700* (Interlaken: Empire State Books, 1997); and *"We Are Still Here!": The Algonquian Peoples of Long Island Today* (Interlaken: Empire State Books, 1996; revised and expanded, 1998).

5. At the Long Island Studies Institute's first conference in 1986, Joanne Lynn discussed Curtiss Field, Valley Stream, as the "Cradle of Women's Aviation," primarily because it was the location for the birth of the Ninety-Nines. See "Women's Cradle of Aviation, Curtiss Field, Valley Stream," in *Evoking a Sense of Place,* edited by Joann P. Krieg (Interlaken, NY: Heart of the Lakes Publishing, 1988), pp. 85-95. The plaque to the Ninety-Nines she described on p. 92 of that article was subsequently donated to the Cradle of Aviation, Mitchel Field, Garden City.

6. Harriet G. Valentine, *The Window to the Street: A Mid-Nineteenth-Century View of Cold Spring Harbor, New York, Based on the Diary of Helen Rogers,* 1981 (Reprint; Cold Spring Harbor: Whaling Museum, 1991); and Field Horne, ed. *The Diary of Mary Cooper: Life on a Long Island Farm, 1768-1773* (Oyster Bay: Oyster Bay Historical Society, 1981).

7. On the history of Long Island's African Americans, see also Lynda R. Day, *Making a Way to Freedom: A History of African Americans on Long Island* (Interlaken, NY: Empire State Books, 1997).

8. Candace Thurber Wheeler (Chapter 20) and Christine Frederick (Chapter 21) are also listed in *Notable American Women,* but are included here in part five, Expanding Women's Work, rather than in part six. McClintock and Krasner are not listed in the Appendix because they do not yet appear in *Notable American Women;* they will surely be in a future supplement. (Only women who died before 1976 are included in the four volumes published to date.)

9. Gerda Lerner, *The Majority Finds Its Past: Placing Women in History* (New York: Oxford University Press, 1979), pp.xxv, xxxi.

2. The Wright Sisters: Seventeenth-Century Quaker Activists

Mildred Murphy DeRiggi

In mid-seventeenth-century England, a charismatic movement emerged inspired by a central belief that God had provided each man or woman with an "Inner Light" to direct him or her in the way of truth. The members of this movement called themselves Children of the Light or simply Friends. They were soon known to the world as Quakers, a reference to the trembling that Friends sometimes displayed as an emotional response during prayer.

Quakers recognized women and men as spiritual equals and encouraged women to give public witness to their faith. By so doing, Quakers broke with the Christian tradition advocated by the apostle Paul. He had admonished his followers in these words: "Let the woman learn in silence, with all subjection. But I suffer not a woman to teach, nor to usurp authority over the man, but to be in silence" (1 Timothy 2: 11–12). Quakers were the one Christian group who offered women a worship that was without rituals performed by a ministry of men.

The first Quaker missionaries arrived on Long Island from England in 1657, when the movement was hardly a decade old and filled with millennial hopes and missionary zeal. Half of the Quakers who came to Long Island as missionaries in the seventeenth century were women. They found on Long Island men and women who were receptive to their message.

This essay considers the example of three sisters from the Town of Oyster Bay, Mary, Hannah, and Lydia Wright, who found empowerment in their role as Quaker witnesses to demand an end to religious persecution. Each sister in turn demonstrated a willingness to risk danger and endure slander by publicly protesting the policy of persecution by the Massachusetts authorities against the Quakers. Assertively and independently, each questioned the authority of ministers and magistrates taking a course of action not considered appropriate for women in a paternalistic society. This article addresses both their public actions defying the political leadership in Massachusetts and what is known of their private lives in Oyster Bay.

The Wright family were among the first settlers of Oyster Bay. Peter, father of the sisters, had arrived on the initial voyage of settlement in 1653 with Captain Samuel Mayo from Cape Cod and the Reverend William Leverich. Peter and his family were joined by his two brothers, Nicholas with his family and Anthony. The Wrights had originally settled in Salem,

Massachusetts and later moved to Sandwich on Cape Cod before making Long Island their home.

Salem and Sandwich inhabitants were known to include many individuals who dissented from the religious views of the more orthodox Massachusetts settlers. When members of the Wright family became convinced Quakers is uncertain, but soon they were among the most ardent Friends on Long Island. Anthony, the bachelor uncle of the sisters, held Quaker meetings in his home. Later, part of his homestead became the Quaker burial ground and the site of the meeting house.[1]

Mary, the eldest of the Wright sisters, was the first to appear in the public records when she traveled to Massachusetts to protest the hanging of Mary Dyer, which took place on June 1, 1660. Mary Dyer had been a friend and supporter of Anne Hutchinson, who was accused of heresy and exiled from Massachusetts in 1637. One of the chief complaints against Hutchinson was that she had endeavored to explain Scripture in a series of meetings at her Boston home, thus she stood accused of having attempted to usurp the role of minister. Mary Dyer lived in Rhode Island but she had visited Long Island during the winter before her death and it is probable that the Wrights knew her personally.

It is a reminder of the danger that Mary Wright faced to recall that Mary Dyer herself had been executed because she returned to Massachusetts, after being expelled, to protest the hanging of two other Quaker men. As a result of her protest, Mary Wright was thrown into prison along with several Quakers from Salem, Massachusetts who had accompanied her.

Fortunately for Mary Wright and other Friends, Charles II, restored to the throne of England in 1660, had demanded an end to executions of Quakers in Boston.[2] The new law in Massachusetts provided that any person convicted of being a Quaker would be stripped naked to the waist and tied to the back of a cart. The person would then be whipped through the town to its border. The process would be repeated until the boundary of the colony was reached.[3]

Mary Wright was about eighteen years old when she demonstrated at Boston and endured her resulting punishment. A few years later, her younger sister Hannah made the trek from Long Island to Massachusetts. Hannah was only about thirteen years of age when she appeared before the Boston Court and demanded an end to the persecution of Quakers. The magistrates were startled to be challenged by someone who was only a child. According to a witness, they were silent at first until an official exclaimed: "What shall we be baffled by such a one as this? Come. Let us drink a Dram."[4]

Hannah's youth may have saved her from the consequences that could have resulted from her boldness. A merchant, John Richbell, brought her back to Oyster Bay where she lived with her mother. Hannah, who never married, assumed a role as a public Friend, preaching and visiting meetings. While on a mission to Maryland in 1675, Hannah drowned when her boat capsized.[5]

Two years after Hannah died, the third sister, Lydia, travelled to Boston. Lydia came to the attention of the authorities as a result of an incident at South Church on Sunday, July 8, 1677.

Lydia had entered the church during service in the company of a woman Friend, Margaret Brewster of Barbados. It was the appearance of Margaret Brewster that caused the disturbance. She was barefoot with her hair loose and with ashes on her head, her face blackened, and with sackcloth covering her garments. Brewster was following a practice of some early Quakers who would make a visual statement by dressing or acting in ways that referred to Biblical sources for meaning.

The authorities arrested Lydia along with Brewster and several Quaker companions. On August 4, 1677, Lydia appeared in Court with the other Quakers to be tried before the governor and the magistrates. The testimony of Lydia is significant and deserves examining because it indicates how remarkably poised she was in the face of hostile questioning by magistrates who possessed all the power of office.

When Governor John Leverett began by asking Lydia if she were one of those who came into the meeting house to disturb the minister at his worship, Lydia denied that she had disturbed anyone since she had not spoken a single word. The governor asked why, if that were the case, had Lydia come to the service. Lydia reminded the governor that it was the law in Massachusetts that everyone attend religious service on Sunday and that the magistrates did not recognize the validity of Quaker worship.

Magistrate Simon Bradstreet then interrupted by demanding to know if Lydia had gone to the service to hear the Word of God. Lydia's response was that if the Word of God were there, she had been ready to hear it. Noting that she was alone, the governor asked Lydia if she had her parents' permission to come to Boston. Her father had died, but Lydia assured the governor that she had her mother's permission. When asked to produce a proof of permission, Lydia answered that she did not have a note from her mother, but if they would wait, she would send home a request that her mother write one. Since Lydia's mother was living in Long Island, it would have meant a long pause in the proceedings.

Exasperated, one of the magistrates, named Juggins, exclaimed to Lydia, "You are led by the spirit of the Devil, to ramble up and down the country, like whores and rogues a cater-wawling." Lydia's response to the outburst was: "Such words do not become those who call themselves CHRISTIANS, for they that sit to judge for God in Matters of Conscience, ought to be sober and serious." Magistrate Juggins later accused Lydia, saying: "You are led by the spirit and light within you, which is of the Devil: There is but one God, and you do not worship the God which we worship."[6]

Lydia's final comment was that he was certainly correct in saying that they did not worship the same God, for if the magistrates worshiped the God revealed in the Bible whom the Quakers worshiped, they would not persecute His people. The Court's decision was that Lydia be tied to a cart along with Margaret Brewster and dragged out of town. From Boston, Lydia traveled to Sandwich, Cape Cod, to Rhode Island, and finally home to Oyster Bay.[7]

What do we know of the private lives that followed after Mary and Lydia had so dramatically asserted their opposition to policy in Massachusetts and demanded freedom of religion for Friends? A Quarterly Meeting of Friends in Flushing in 1682 issued a certificate to Quakers in the Caribbean islands of Barbados, Antigua, and Jamaica declaring that Lydia Wright had movings within her heart and mind in the love of the Lord to visit with them. Interestingly, at the same meeting notice was given of the intention of marriage between Lydia Wright and Isaac Horner, a Quaker from Oyster Bay.[8]

Lydia Wright had time to make her intended mission to the Caribbean, because her marriage to Isaac Horner was not solemnized until February 1684. Among the witnesses to the ceremony, were Lydia's sister Mary and her husband, Samuel Andrews. Mary had married Quaker Andrews in 1663 and had become the mother of eight children.[9]

Alice Wright, mother of Mary, Hannah, and Lydia, had remarried after the death of their father. Her second husband was Richard Crabb, a Quaker from Oyster Bay. Alice and her daughters remained active in the Friends meeting at Oyster Bay, and Mary and her husband acted as overseers of the meeting house.

In the 1670s and 1680s, the Quakers in the Oyster Bay area were disturbed by a group of individuals who disrupted meetings by singing and making noises and who caused scandal by rejecting the need for traditional marriages. The names of Mary and her mother appeared among those who signed a Testimony in 1675 against a "People who Stiled themselves New or Young Friends." In doing so, Mary supported the social values traditional in the Quaker community.

Alice Wright Crabb died in 1685. Her will was significant because it gave freedom to a man known as "Black Tom," granting him in the words of the document "1 calf, 1 iron skillet, one mare and Liberty." Mary Andrews confirmed the terms of the will of her mother, making the transaction probably the earliest manumission of a slave on Long Island.[10]

In the fall of 1685, Mary and Lydia with their husbands and children left Oyster Bay and moved to Springfield Township, Burlington County, West Jersey.[11] The families were part of a movement in the late seventeenth

century of Long Island residents who resettled in the Quaker colonies of the
Jerseys. Several months before the move, Samuel Andrews, one of the
wealthiest men in Oyster Bay, assigned to his wife a power of attorney. He
expressed his confidence in Mary to sell property and settle affairs as he
himself would do if he were personally present.[12]

In all, the evidence is scant concerning the way in which the Wright
sisters lived their everyday lives in Oyster Bay. The few references which
do exist suggest that they fulfilled traditional roles within their families and
in their community. It is really the documents that record their public protests
in Boston, the court transcripts that present their ideas, that define the Wright
sisters as exceptional. Mary, Hannah, and Lydia traveled considerable dis-
tances as young women, unaccompanied by either parent or spouse, at a time
when most women lived their lives in confined domestic spheres. In an age
when women lacked legal status, each proved able to represent herself
competently and to express her demands forcibly before a legal tribunal.

Finally, Mary Wright's name has been associated with the charge of
witchcraft in some Long Island histories, including those of Nathaniel Prime
and Benjamin Thompson.[13] According to Thompson's account, after being
accused of witchcraft in 1660, Mary Wright was sent to Massachusetts for
trial. When there was insufficient evidence for conviction for witchcraft,
Thompson concluded that Mary was convicted of Quakerism and banished.

The Wrights, however, were a leading family in Oyster Bay, and there
is no evidence of any incident or charge concerning witchcraft originating in
that settlement. Furthermore, the Court at Boston had no jurisdiction over
Long Island. It is much more plausible that Mary Wright went to Boston of
her own accord to protest the hanging of Mary Dyer. Mary Wright's
association with witchcraft is understandable: many of Mary's contemporaries connected witchcraft with Quakerism. Quaker women were routinely
stripped naked and searched by authorities who were looking for unusual
marks on their bodies that would identify them as witches and servants of
the Devil.[14] When Mary went to Boston to protest a policy of persecution,
she was outspoken and did not defer to the authority of magistrates and
ministers. Recent research has emphasized the connection between assertive
or insolent speech, or lack of deference by women and resulting charges of
witchcraft.[15]

Mary Wright was no witch. She was just ahead of her time.

Notes

1. The will of Anthony Wright (August 15, 1672), granting the land to the Quakers,
is copied in the *Oyster Bay Town Records, 1653-1878,* edited by John Cox (New York:
T. A. Wright, 1916-1940), 1: 687.

2. English Friends had presented accounts of the persecution of Quakers in New England. In 1661, the English government ordered that Quakers condemned to death be released or sent to England.

3. William Sewel, *History of the Rise, Increase and Progress of the Christian People Called Quakers,* 1722 (Reprint, Philadelphia: Friends' Book Store, 1856), 1: 281.

4. Ibid.

5. Matthew Prior, a neighbor, recorded his account of the accident in the Minutes of the Friends Meeting at Oyster Bay, Matinecock, and Flushing, Haviland Records Room, New York City. These and other Quaker records are now at Swarthmore College in Pennsylvania; microfilm copies are available at Columbia University and the Long Island Studies Institute, Hofstra University.

6. Testimony quoted in Joseph Bessie, *Sufferings of the People Called Quakers, For the Testimony of a Good Conscience* (London: Luke Hinde, 1753), 2: 263.

7. Howland Delano Perrine, *The Wright Family of Oysterbay, L.I.: With the Ancestry and Descent from Peter and Nicholas Wright, 1423-1923* (New York: privately printed, 1923).

8. Entry in the Friends Quarterly Meeting, copied in Perrine, *The Wright Family of Oysterbay,* p. 56.

9. The certificate of the marriage of Lydia Wright and Isaac Horner is copied in the Flushing Monthly Meeting Records, Haviland Records Room, now at Swarthmore College.

10. *Oyster Bay Town Records,* 2: 702; John Cox, Jr., *Quakerism in the City of New York, 1657-1930* (New York: privately printed, 1930), p. 55.

11. Perrine, *The Wright Family,* p. 57.

12. *Oyster Bay Town Records,* 1: 303.

13. Nathaniel Scudder Prime, *A History of Long Island, From its First Settlement by Europeans to the Year 1845, With Special Reference to Its Ecclesiastical Concerns* (New York: Robert Carter, 1845), p. 89; Benjamin Thompson, *History of Long Island from Its Discovery and Settlement to the Present Time,* edited by Charles J. Werner, 3d ed. (New York: Robert H. Dodd, 1918), 2: 45.

14. Carol F. Karlsen, *The Devil in the Shape of a Woman* (New York: Norton, 1987), p. 13.

15. Jane Kamensky, "Words, Witches, and Woman Trouble: Witchcraft, Disorderly Speech, and Gender Boundaries in Puritan New England," *Essex Institute Historical Collections,* 128 no. 4 (Oct. 1992): 286-307; Christine Leigh Heyrman, "Specters of Subversion: Societies of Friends: Dissent and the Devil in Provincial Essex County, Massachusetts," in *Saints and Revolutionaries: Essays on Early American History,* ed. David D. Hall, John M. Murrin, and Thad W. Tate (New York: W. W. Norton, 1984), p. 68.

3. The Role of Algonquian Women in Land Transactions on Eastern Long Island, 1639–1859

John A. Strong

One of the more heated contemporary controversies in archaeology and anthropology concerns the role of women in the political and economic affairs of their communities. At the annual meeting of the Massachusetts Archaeological Society in 1992, a panel entitled "Recognizing Gender in Historical and Archaeological Contexts" charged that the role of women in traditional societies has been undervalued by male scholars, who tend to focus on the men in a given society (Spencer-Wood 1994; Handsman 1992; Ward 1992). This critique was voiced two decades earlier by anthropologist Eleanor Leacock who challenged the widely held premise that male dominance was a universal characteristic shared by all human societies. Leacock raised the issue in a paper she read at the 1974 meeting of the American Anthropological Association and further developed the argument in a collection of essays she edited, *Myths of Male Dominance: Collected Articles on Women Cross-Culturally* (1981).

Prior to the arrival of the Europeans in the seventeenth century, argues Leacock, the women were independent, autonomous participants in community affairs (Leacock 1981: 133–61). Many scholars have supported Leacock's charge that the existing anthropological data on the status of women in hunting and gathering societies was biased because the research was done by male anthropologists who talked to the male members of the groups they were investigating. (See also Slocum 1975; Foster 1993; and Rohrlich-Leavitt, Sykes, and Weatherford 1975.) A similar issue has been raised by Elizabeth Chilton, an archaeologist who reviewed reports from Paleo-Indian sites in the Northeast. Chilton argued that some male archaeologists tended to romanticize *man as hunter* and ignore the female role as a food procurer and community provider (Chilton 1994: 12–13).

Several anthropologists criticized Leacock's conclusions, beginning a debate which continues today (Goldberg 1973; Friedl 1975; Reiter 1975; Bonvillain 1989; Devens 1992; Kidwell 1992). Although most of Leacock's critics did not take the extreme position argued by Steven Goldberg that male dominance was both universal and inevitable, many noted that they could find no convincing evidence of any human societies, past or present, which were not ruled by males. Some agreed that sweeping generalizations about universal male dominance "must always be questioned," but that, while women might be autonomous and have some power, they did not hold positions of *authority* in precontact hunting and gathering bands (Cohen 1981).

Much of the discussion focused on two questions: were preconquest societies dominated by males, and, if not, was male dominance imposed by colonial powers or did it evolve with the introduction of horticulture as a means of controlling the distribution of surplus material goods? Although some disagreed about the proper criteria for determining "dominance" and "authority" in a given society, most scholars agreed that such factors as control over the production and distribution of surplus goods, over inheritance rights, over major community decisions such as warfare and trade, and over religious rituals and ceremonial gatherings must be carefully examined (Schlegel 1977: 7–37).

Unfortunately the data base for evaluating these factors in preconquest societies is very sparse. The primary sources include archaeological reports, seventeenth-century European records, and the contemporary studies of the few remaining hunting and gathering societies. One of the first scholars to examine the data for Coastal Algonquian societies was Robert Grumet, who studied the role of women as sunksquaws, shamans, and tradeswomen during the first century of contact with Europeans. He concluded "that women played a key role in all phases of traditional Coastal Algonquian economic life," and that this role continued during the colonial period (Grumet 1980: 59). Martha Harrow Foster, who studied the role of women in Hidatsa and Crow societies in the eighteenth century, came to similar conclusions (Foster 1993: 143–45).

Grumet also noted that modern scholars have also tended to overlook the presence of females in the ethnographic record. "Ethnohistorians have traditionally assigned male gender to native figures in the documentary record unless otherwise identified. . . . This practice has successfully masked the identities of a substantial number of Coastal Algonquian leaders of both sexes" (Grumet 1980: 52–53). Responding to the growing awareness that more research on the role of Native American women was needed, Nancy Shoemaker edited a collection of essays on this theme entitled *Negotiators of Change: Historical Perspectives on Native American Women* (1995). The essays examined the involvement of women in the process of social changes which threatened the survival of traditional values.

Shoemaker concluded that while it was true that females lost power and influence in the early decades following European conquest, they frequently regained that power in the twentieth century. Wilma Mankiller, for example, became principal chief of the Cherokee, one of the largest and most influential tribes in North America. The scholars in Shoemaker's book demonstrate that native women, "actively, creatively, and often successfully resisted marginality" (Shoemaker 1995: 20). The seventeenth-century documents for Long Island clearly suggest that during the post contact period, women continued to play an important role in transactions involving tribal lands.

Women and the Land

The special relationship between women and the land began with their role as collectors of medicinal and nutritional plants which were vital to the survival of the community. These women were the custodians of a storehouse of knowledge about the ecosystem around them. As the women foraged for the daily meals they studied the characteristics of the wild plants, their growth cycles, and their interrelationships and they passed this information along to their daughters. When horticulture was gradually introduced, the role of planting and harvesting remained with the women. They determined when a field should be abandoned to lie fallow and where to open up a new planting ground.

Although we have very limited documentation about the inner workings of northeastern Algonquian societies, there is general agreement that most had ambilocal residence and ambilineal inheritance patterns, village level political systems, and exogamous kinship networks (Salwen 1978: 166–67; Williams 1973: 114–29, 201–9; Rainey 1936: 33–38). The Lenape people of western Long Island, however, may have had a matrilocal residence pattern. Zeisberger reported that among the Delaware, who are closely related to the Lenape, a married couple usually moved in with the bride's mother until the husband completed a separate bark house for his family (Kraft 1986: 134–35; Zeisberger 1910: 81–82).

There is also a general consensus that women often assumed positions of authority over their communities (Strong 1995). According to Roger Williams, these women were called "sauncksquuaog," which he translated to mean "Queens" (Williams 1973: 201). The term has been spelled several different ways, but the more common form is "sunksquaw." Some of the women who became sunksquaws were the wives of widows of sachems, but others were married to men who had no position of authority in the tribe (Grumet 1980: 49; Lamb-Richmond 1988; Menta 1988). The widows may have assumed the status of their husbands when there was no acceptable male candidate available.

The sunksquaws often took over their deceased husband's role in negotiations with the English over land sales and whaling rights (DSBD, 2: 156–57). The whales, which frequently beached themselves on the South Shore of Long Island, were a lucrative source of whale oil for the English settlers. This oil was a primary source of hard currency for the settlers during the seventeenth century. The right to whale carcasses, therefore, was as important as land titles in the relations between Indians and the English.

Women as Proprietors

The sunksquaws were not the only women who had a voice in land transactions. Wives of sachems and other women in the community were often called upon to take part in the negotiations or endorse a deed. The first deed signed by the English on Long Island was a transaction in 1639 between Aswaw and her husband Yovawam and Lion Gardiner (Gardiner 1890: 58). The Algonquian couple, in exchange for ten cloth coats, granted Gardiner the right to settle on Manchonat, an uninhabited island at the entrance to Peconic Bay on the eastern end of Long Island. Gardiner promptly renamed the island after himself and moved his family there. Gardiner's wife, of course, was not a party to the deed because in European society, property was in the male domain. (See Appendix, p.36 for list of this and other land transactions involving Algonquian women.)

Subsequent deeds for land in Southampton (1640) and East Hampton (1648) do not appear to have any female signatures. There may have been some women among the twelve who are named in the Southampton deed, but none of them were so identified. In 1649, however, Governor Eaton of New Haven purchased a tract of land called Aquebanck (Aquebogue, near the present-day boundary between the towns of Riverhead and Southold), from an Indian named Occomboomaquus and a woman identified as the wife of Mahahannuck, who were the "true Indian owners" of the land (DSBD, 2: 210–11; Tooker 1962: 16–17, 263–64). The Indians were paid three coats, two fathoms of wampum, four hatchets, four knives, and four tobacco pipes.

This is the first reference to an Indian woman who held title to land independently from her husband. Unfortunately her name is not entered on the deed, perhaps because the English did not accord their own women any legal status in such matters. It is clear from the documents, however, that Mahahannuck's wife held authority over the territory. According to the deed, she was a woman of "sachem's blood. It was the constant custom of all Indians to ask her leave to gather wurtleburyes and flaggs for mats" (DSBD, 2: 210–14). When a confirmation of the deed was negotiated in 1660, Mahahannuck's wife was identified this time as the "daughter of Ockenmungan," (DSBD, 2: 212–13). Unfortunately the document does not mention whether Ockenmungan was the mother or the father.

It is clear, therefore, that some women played an important role in decisions about the ownership and transfer of land. Although the English never mentioned the woman by name, they did acknowledge that she was "of the sachem's blood," and "sole heir and legal proprietor of Accabogue" (DSBD, 2: 212). Ockenmungan had only two children, a daughter and a son who died in infancy. Upon his death, the daughter inherited the property and retained control after her marriage to Mahahannuck. Under English law, in contrast, a woman's property became her husband's after she married.

In 1658, a group of twelve Indians in what is now the town of Oyster Bay sold a parcel of property to a settler named Francis Weeks (DSBD, 2: 90–91). Five of them are identified as women by the English clerk who recorded the deed. Three of them, Awena, Ramoth, and Nonos are mentioned by name, and two more are simply referred to as "squaws." These women certainly played a role in the important decisions made by the community. The Oyster Bay deed is similar to the one for Southampton where several Indians, perhaps community leaders, negotiated and approved the transaction.

Other women, such as the wife of Mahahannuck, inherited property rights and maintained control over large parcels of land. When Wyandanch, the Montaukett sachem, died, his widow became sunksquaw and proprietor over all the Montaukett lands. She took over her husband's role in negotiations with the English over land sales and whaling rights. Although the woman was a principal party in five major transactions between 1660 and 1663, the English clerks never identified her by name (DSBD, 2: 119; RTEH, 1: 172–74; Smith 1926: 25–29; DSBD, 2: 156–57; RTEH, 1: 199–200). Her son, Wyancombone, however, was always named. This is a noteworthy omission because it again reflects English attitudes about the status of women, and it once more demonstrates that Indian women were underrepresented in the colonial documents.

When her young son died during an outbreak of smallpox, the Montaukett sunksquaw continued to lead the tribe. She met with Lion Gardiner, a prosperous English settler, to endorse the sale of whale rights made by her husband shortly before his death. The borders of Gardiner's lease had apparently been challenged by another settler in one of the frequent land squabbles which characterized the European scramble for Indian land in the seventeenth century. The sunksquaw resolved the dispute by defining the boundaries of the lease and, in return, demanding that she be paid according to the terms set by her husband (RTEH, 2: 199–200). This agreement bears no other Indian signature. Clearly, she was the authority to negotiate without the supervision of any of the male elders of the tribe. When she died, she passed along the title of sunksquaw to her daughter, Quashawam (Strong and Karabag 1991).

When Quashawam became sunksquaw in 1664, the English scramble for Indian land was chaotic. Individual English entrepreneurs, town officials, and private companies pressed local sachems to sell them tracts of land. The Indians, who tended to view these transactions as temporary leases, frequently sold the same land twice, or sold land claimed by a rival sachem. If the land was not occupied in a reasonable time by the new owner, the local sachem assumed that the tract could be "sold" again. To further complicate matters, the children of these sachems and sunksquaws often demanded to be paid again for the same land. English entrepreneurs, of course, were quick to step in and attempt to manipulate the unstable market. The English were somewhat uncomfortable in dealing with women about real estate because, as we have noted, such transactions were in the male domain in their society. They were forced, however, by the realities of Indian customs to negotiate with Algonquian women. (See also Strong 1983, 1997.)

In the fall of 1665, following the English conquest of the Dutch on Long Island, Richard Nicholls, the new English governor of New York, called a three-day meeting of all the prominent sachems on Long Island. Nicholls met with Quashawam and the East Hampton town officials to negotiate several controversies which had emerged since the death of her mother (DSBD, 2: 123–27; Strong and Karabag 1991: 197–98). The issues were very similar to those raised throughout Long Island: damage done by English livestock to Indian planting grounds, damage done to English livestock by Indians and their dogs, the use of Indian planting fields after the harvest and before spring planting by the English for grazing, controversies over boundary lines, and English objections to the seasonal burning of planting grounds and the lands around the Indian villages.

Quashawam reached an agreement with East Hampton, marking her western border with East Hampton, agreeing to stop the Montaukett seasonal burnings, and allowing the English to graze their cattle on Montaukett lands from October to March. In return, the English agreed to pay for damage done by their cattle to Indian crops, and abandoned a claim they had made to the ownership of all of the Montaukett lands.

Quashawam and her mother were not the only women who were recognized as the owners of large parcels of land. In 1663, a woman named Assurs, who resided in Setauket, sold a parcel of land in the town of Hempstead to Robert Williams, an English settler (DSBD 2: 167–68). Apparently Assurs came into possession of the property as a member of the Matinecock community and later moved east to Setauket, perhaps to reside with her husband. Even though Assurs changed her residence, she retained proprietorship over lands in Oyster Bay. A few months later, Assurs sold a second tract to Williams (DSBD, 2: 165). In 1664, three other women, a sunksquaw from Setauket (RTBH Book A: 11; RTBH Hutchinson: 12–13), Haxxowooke, from Matinecock (DSBD, 2: 79–80), and Sawase from Jamaica (DSBD, 2: 235), all were named in deeds as parties to the negotiations.

The newly established English colonial government required that all of the previous land purchases be reviewed, in part, to bring some semblance of stability to the real estate market. Quashawam was called upon to endorse several deeds, which her father had signed, in an attempt to protect them from challenges in court. The court records for seventeenth-century Long Island are full of lengthy cases involving conflicts over boundary lines, questions of original ownership, and outright fraud.

One such contentious case involved three sunksquaws. Soon after Quashawam's mother had taken over control of Montaukett affairs, Weany, a Shinnecock sunksquaw, sold land to a man named Thomas Topping that had been included in a larger tract which the Montaukett had previously sold to another English settler named John Scott (Strong 1983: 53–63). Weany was identified in a related document as "Pametsechs' squaw" (RTSH, 2: 27–28). A second Shinnecock sunksquaw, the widow of a former sachem, protested the sale, charging that Weany had no right to sell the land in question (DSBD, 2: 200–202). The widow and her supporters proceeded to sell the same land to the Town of Southampton, pending the investigation of the colonial governor.

The governor examined the documents and ruled that the town of Southampton was the rightful owner and that the widow should be paid twenty-four feet of wampum, the same amount received by Weany.[1] Both sunksquaws signed an agreement accepting the governor's decision. The agreement was endorsed by twenty-four Shinnecock men. These sunksquaws clearly had the full authority of their followers to negotiate these transactions with the English.

The role of women in matters related to the control of territory and boundary lines is demonstrated in the court records involving boundary disputes. In 1657, the town of Southampton called upon the Shinnecock sachem and his wife to testify about their eastern boundary with the town of East Hampton (RTSH, 1: 114). The controversy, however, continued for nearly two hundred years. In 1667, Southampton had a similar problem about the location of its northwestern boundary with the town of Southold. (The area in contention is now in the town of Riverhead.) Two Montaukett women, Aquabacack and Impeagwam, who had lived in the disputed areas as children, were called in to testify. The women had both left their home village, probably to live with their husbands, but they were still considered the best sources of reliable information about the land (NYCD, 14: 600–602; RTSH, 1: 157–60). The women also testified that the land was owned, at that time, by the Shinnecock sunksquaw, who was the sister of the Montaukett sachem (RTSH, 3: 110–11).

In the eighteenth century, Indian women continued to play important roles in land transactions. In 1703, Massarokan, an Indian woman identified in an earlier deed as the "chief proprietress" of land in the present-day town of Islip (Bailey 1938: 51–52), her daughter, Onepape, and their family were granted a tract of land by William Nicoll "for ever hearafter" (Bailey 1938: 55). That same year, when the town of Southampton purchased all of the remaining lands in their jurisdiction from the Shinnecock and the Unkechaug, Suomo, the sister of Wiangonhut, the Unkechaug sachem, was called upon to endorse the deed (RTSH, 2: 179–80). Suomo was married to Pomgumo, a Shinnecock sachem, and moved to her husband's village where she was recognized as a sunksquaw. Suomo and her brother testified that her husband, Pomgumo, and the Shinnecock sachems had the authority to sell a tract of land on the border between the two tribes.

The conclusions by Grumet and Foster about the uninterrupted persistence of women's roles during the colonial period is also true for Long Island. There is evidence that women retained their positions of influence long after contact with whites. Individual Shinnecock, primarily women, leased small parcels of reservation land to whites for grazing and planting. Apparently the informal procedure resulted in frequent squabbles over who had the right to collect revenues from a given parcel. The controversies were very similar to the ones which plagued the land sales in the previous century on Long Island. The white farmers undoubtedly attempted to manipulate the unstable situation, adding to the chaotic state of affairs.

In 1764, the town of Southampton negotiated a temporary settlement with the Shinnecock, which called for the lease system to be brought under the control of the tribe as a whole, prohibiting individual Shinnecock from leasing land without tribal approval. The agreement stated that:

> Indians and squaws belonging to Shinnecock do mutually agree that for the future no Indian or squaw shall hire out any land to plant or sow upon in any cases whatsoever without the consent of the whole . . . the money arising from such hires shall be equally divided among the whole, and if any Indian or squaw shall hire out any land contrary to the intent of this agreement then he or she or they shall forfeit forty shillings for every acre.

The agreement was endorsed by twenty-nine women and eight men (SHTA: "Indian Papers").

The problem with this arrangement was that the whites had so thoroughly undermined the traditional system of leadership, that there was no consensus among the Shinnecock about the procedures for making tribal decisions. Finally, in 1792, the town petitioned the New York State legislature to impose a system of governance on the tribe modeled after the English system of elected trustees (Strong and Holmberg 1983: 226–27). The majority of Shinnecock apparently did not oppose the law, entitled "An Act for the Benefit of the Shinnecock Tribe of Indians," although there is no evidence that they were consulted in the matter. The new procedures called for annual tribal elections for three trustees on the first Tuesday of April. The Indian women, following the practice among the whites, were not allowed to vote. Although the trustee system was established primarily to deal with the leasing system, which was traditionally within the female domain, the women were excluded. In spite of this exclusion from the electoral process, the women continued to control the use of the planting grounds on the reservation. A few months after the new system was imposed, Uriah Rogers, a local farmer, leased twenty-one and one-half acres from fifteen Shinnecocks, eleven of whom were women (Papageorge 1983: 145–46).

Ironically, the tribal trustee system served the Shinnecock well in their struggles to preserve Indian land and tribal integrity over the next two centuries. In 1967, however, the women protested the disenfranchisement to the local Human Relations Council. The men charged that the trusteeship system was part of their "ancient Indian traditions" and refused to make any changes. Beginning in the 1960s, a disproportionate number of Shinnecock women completed college degrees. Two women went on to become lawyers, and one earned her M.D. They became active in community agencies and began bringing in federal and state grants to support educational programs, a clinic, a nutritional facility, and program for the elderly.

In 1992, Roberta Hunter, one of the Shinnecock lawyers, became the first non-white ever elected to the Southampton Town Board (Strong 1994: 58–59). Her success highlighted the disenfranchisement of the Shinnecock women. At a tribal meeting early in 1994, the directors of the community programs, most of them women, were praised by the tribe for their impressive accomplishments. Astutely taking advantage of the opportunity, the women again raised the question of the vote and informed the trustees that ethnographic research did not support their claim that the trustee system reflected "traditional values." The men agreed that the time had come for a change and voted to enfranchise the women. The Shinnecock women turned out in large numbers to vote at the annual election that April.

Conclusions

The evidence in the seventeenth and eighteenth-century colonial records clearly indicates that women did hold positions of authority which were equivalent to their male counterparts. Although there is not enough data to determine a clear pattern of matrilineal descent for property or political authority, we do find that, in some instances, women passed political authority down to their children, and there is convincing evidence that women played a prominent role in transactions regarding property. The Appendix which follows, "Legal Transactions Involving Algonquian Women," includes all the documents mentioning women that have been identified including some not specifically discussed in this article.

The example of the Shinnecock women is probably more important as an argument against the unspoken assumptions of male superiority, than all of the academic debates about the "universality of male dominance."

Notes

1. The wampum was valued at six beads per penny. Unfortunately there is no record attesting to the exact number of beads in a foot of wampum. We do know, however, that the town of Southampton paid John Scott £70 sterling for the same tract. The value of the wampum payments to both sunksquaws could not have exceeded £10 sterling.

Appendix

Legal Transactions involving Algonquian Women

Date	Indian Names	English Names	Description	Source
May 3, 1639	Aswaw, wife of Yovawam, sachem of Pommanocc	Lion Gardiner	Sale of Manchonat (Gardiners Island) for 10 coats	Gardiner 1890: 58
March 14, 1649	The wife of Mahahannuck, "an Indian squaw of sachem's blood"	Theophilus Eaton and Stephen Goodyear	Sale of land (Acquebogue)	DSBD, 2: 210-12, 214
June 19, 1657	Wife of Shinnecock sachem (neither identified by name)	John and Richard Howell, Obadiah Rogers, Joseph Raynor, Samuel Clark	Shinnecocks testified about the eastern boundary of their land	RTSH, 1: 114
November 10, 1658	Awena, Ramoth, Nonos, and two "squaws" who are not named	Francis Weeks	Sale of land in Oyster Bay. Seven men also signed the deed	DSBD, 2: 90-91
April 6, 1660	Sunksquaw, widow of Wyandanch	Thomas Talmage and Thomas Chatfield	Confirms deed signed by Wyandanch before his death in 1659	DSBD, 2: 119
May 1660	daughter of Sckemungan		Confirmation of March 14, 1649 sale of land in Southold	DSBD 2: 211-13
August 6, 1660	Sunksquaw of Montaukett (widow of Wyandanch)	Thomas Baker, Robert Bond, Thomas James, Lion Gardiner, John Mulford, John Hand	Sale of Montauk for £100	RTEH, 1: 172-74

February 11, 1661/62	Sunksquaw of Montaukett (widow of Wyandanch)	Thomas Baker, Robert Bond, Thomas James, Lion Gardiner, John Mulford, John Hand	Gift deed to Hither Hills	Smith 1926: 25-29
April 10, 1662	Weany, sunksquaw of the Shinnecock; also identified as Pametsech's squaw	Thomas Topping	Sale of land in Quogue	RTSH, 1: 167-68
April 15, 1662	The old sunksquaw, wife and widow of Wyandanch	John Ogden, Lion Gardiner, Thomas Talmage	Sale of beached whale rights to John Ogden. Indians reserve rights to the fins and tails	DSBD, 2: 156-57; Gardiner 1973: 25
January 14, 1662/63	Wife of Wyandanch, mother of Wyancombone	John Cooper, Lion Gardiner	Boundaries of beach rights confirmed	RTEH, 1: 199-200
January 15, 1662/63	Pametsech's squaw	John Cooper sued Joseph Raynor over rights to beached whales	Boundaries of beach rights confirmed	RTSH, 27-28
November 18, 1663	Assurs (Assurwedd, Asser)	Robert Williams	Sale of land in Hempstead	DSBD, 2: 161; see also DSBD, 2: 165
January 7, 1664	Matinecock woman (accompanied by sachems Tackapousha and Suscaneman)	William Laurens, Robert Terry	Sale of land	NYCD, 14: 540
February 11, 1664	Quashawam	John Howell, Thomas Baker, James Herrick and Joseph Raynor	Quashawam named sunksquaw of the Montaukett and Shinnecock	RTSH, 2: 75
February 11, 1664	Quashawam, sunksquaw of the Montaukett	John Scott, Thomas Baker, Thomas Chatfields	Confirms deed for Crawford (Jamaica)	DSBD, 2: 162

February 25, 1663/64	Quashawam sunksquaw of the Montaukett	John Scott	Confirms deed to land lying westward of Jamaica	DSBD, 2: 159-60
March 12, 1664	Haxxowooke	Edward Jessup and John Richardson	Sale of land in Hempstead	DSBD, 2: 79-80
March 19, 1664	Sawase	Daniel Denton	Sale of land north of Jamaica	DSBD, 2: 235
June 10, 1664	Sunksquaw and wife of Massetewse	John Cooper, Richard Howell	Sale of land in Setauket called "old Manse"	RTBH, Hutchinson: 12-13
December 28, 1664	Assurs, Matinecock woman	Robert Williams	Sale of land	DSBD, 2: 165
June 7, 1665	Sunksquaw, daughter of Wyandanch (not identified by name)	John Ogden, Thomas Halsey	Annual payments from the town of Southampton	RTSH, 1: 171
October 4, 1665	Quashawam	Governor William Nicols and East Hampton town officials	Agreement on the use of land at Montauk and payments to Quashawam	DSBD, 2: 123-27; NYCD, 14: 606
June 22, 1666	Quashawam	Thomas James, John Mulford	Testimony about lands in Huntington	RTSM, 1: 16-17
September 17, 1666	The daughter of Mandush; Goabes, wife and "relic" of Mandush, sachem of the Shinnecock	Thomas Topping	Protests the right of Weany to sell land to Thomas Topping (see April 10, 1662)	RTSH, 1: 169; Strong 1983: 84
February 22, 1666/67	Weany, Goabes' wife, and Cageponas (wife of Mandush's sister)	Thomas Topping	Confirmation of land sale	DSBD, 2: 200-202; Strong 1983: 80
October 17, 1667	Aquabacack and Impeagwam	John Mulford, Richard Howell, and John Laughton	Testimony about boundary between Southampton and Southold	RTSH, 1: 157-60; 3: 110-11; NYCD 14: 600-602

November 3, 1669	Askickotantup, sunksquaw of the Montaukett	John Mulford, Thomas James, Jeremiah Conkling	Montauketts affirm alliance with the governor of New York	NYCD, 14: 627
December 1, 1670	Wuchikitaubit (Askickotantup?), sunksquaw of Montaukett	John Mulford, Thomas James, Jeremiah Conkling	Sale of land to pay fine	Cooper 1993: 167-69
January 17, 1671	Montaukett sunksquaw (Wuchikitaubit?)	Rev. Thomas James	Signs over power of attorney	RTSH, 1: 172
February 19, 1683/84	Jane, the Narragansett Indian wife of Harry Bell	Harry Bell, Thomas Townsend, John Rogers	Gift of land from Suscaneman and Werah	RTOB, 1: 313-14
June 24, 1687	Kasquas, wife of Smonquis	Thomas Dongan	Land on west bank of Hempstead Harbor granted to Tackapousha and his people (Kasquas was named in the grant)	NYCM Endorsed Land Papers, 4: 174
October 6, 1696	Paxqua, wife of John Wamasman and son Mawahtuck	Edward White	Witnessed sale of land by Tackapousha and Wamasaman	RTOB, 2: 283-84
June 2, 1697	Asher (Assur), Ronuse, wife of Wamehas	Edward White, Thomas Townsend, John Williams	Sale of land in Oyster Bay	RTOB, 2: 212-13
September 17, 1697	Massarokan, chief proprietress	William Nicoll	Sale of land west of Blue Point	Bailey 1938: 51-52; Pelletreau 2: 235-36
February 18, 1703	Massarokan squaw and her daughter, Onepape	William Nicoll	Land granted to Massarokan by Nicoll	Bailey 1938: 55
August 16, 1703	Suomo, wife of Pomgumo and sister of Wiangonhut	Stephen Boyar, Arthur Davis, Benjamin Marshall	Sale of land in western portion of the town of Southampton	RTSH, 2: 179-80
April 21, 1707	Wanawcanoes, Chahoes, Nonawanoes, Manero	Thomas Jones, John Townsend	Sale of land in Oyster Bay	RTOB, 3: 255-57

February 2, 1762	Bette Squaw	Trustees of the Town of Huntington	Sale of lands reserved to Indians in 1656	RTH, 2: 450-51
June 12, 1764	Signatures of 29 Shinnecock women	Stephen Rogers and Silas Ludlam	Leasing of Shinnecock lands	SHTA: Indian Papers
November 22, 1793	Sarah, Sarah Titus, Bethiah Jethro, Abigail Solomon, Prudence Cuffee, Elizabeth Manaman, Molly Murrian, Phoebe Ralph, Peg Ruckets, Peg Jordan, and Mary Joe	Uriah Rogers	Lease of Shinnecock land. Women are identified as the "true and lawful heirs to said land"	Papageorge 1983: 145-46
January 7, 1859	Fannie Ashman, Lydia Ward, Harriet Richards, Maria Cuffee, Mary Brewer, Anna C. Kellis, Mary Walker	State Assembly in Albany	Petition signed by 21 Shinnecock protesting the abrogation of the lease to Shinnecock Hills	Strong 1983: 104-5

Sources Cited

Bailey, Rosalie Fellows. 1938. *William Nicoll and the Islip Grange.* Islip, NY.

Bonvillain, Nancy. 1989. "Gender Relations in Native North America." *American Indian Culture and Research Journal* 13 (2): 1-28.

Chilton, Elizabeth. 1994. "In Search of Paleo-Women: Gender Implications of Remains from Paleoindian Sites." *Bulletin of the Massachusetts Archaeological Society* 55 (1): 8-14.

Cohen, Ronald. 1981. "Comment." In *Myths of Male Dominance* by Eleanor Burke Leacock, pp. 162-67, New York: Monthly Review Press.

Cooper, Thomas, ed. 1993. *The Records of the Court of Sessions of Suffolk County in the Province of New York, 1670-1688.* Bowie, MD: Heritage Books.

Devens, Carol. 1992. *Countering Colonization: Native American Women and Great Lakes Missions, 1630-1900.* Berkeley: University of California Press.

DSBD. Department of State Book of Deeds. Unpublished Documents. New York State Archives Series 453, vols. 1-9. Office of the Secretary of State, Albany, NY.

Foster, Martha Harrow. 1993. "Of Baggage and Bondage: Gender and Status Among Hidatsa and Crow Women." *American Indian Culture and Research Journal* 17 (2): 121-52.

Friedl, Ernestine. 1975. *Women and Men: An Anthropologist's View.* New York: Holt, Rinehart and Winston.

Gardiner, Curtis. 1890. *Lion Gardiner and his Descendants.* St. Louis: A. Whipple. (Available in East Hampton Public Library.)

Gardiner, David. 1973. *Chronicles of the Town of East Hampton,* 1871. Reprint, Sag Harbor, NY: Isabel Gardiner Mairs.

Goldberg, Steven. 1973. *The Inevitability of Patriarchy.* New York: William Morrow.

Grumet, Robert Steven. 1980. "Sunksquaws, Shamans, and Tradeswomen: Middle Atlantic Coastal Algonquian Women during the 17th and 18th Centuries." In *Women and Colonization: Anthropological Perspectives,* edited by Mona Etienne and Eleanor Leacock, pp. 43-67. New York: Praeger.

Handsman, Russell. 1992. "Mohegan Women in the last 1,000 Years." Paper presented at the Massachusetts Archaeological Society annual meeting, October 24.

Kehoe, Alice, B. 1976. "Old Woman Had Great Power." *The Western Canadian Journal of Anthropology* 6 (3): 68-76.

Kidwell, Clara Sue. 1992. "Indian Women as Culture Mediators." *Ethnohistory* 39 (2): 97-107.

Kraft, Herbert. 1986. *The Lenape, Archaeology, History and Ethnography.* Newark: New Jersey Historical Society.

Lamb, Trudi. 1981. "Squaw Sachems, Women Who Rule." *Artifacts* 9 (Winter-Spring): 1-3.

Lamb-Richmond, Trudi. 1988. "Native American Women as Leaders in Algonquian Society." *Aritfacts* 16 (3-4): 7-16.

Leacock, Eleanor Burke. 1955. "Matrilocality in a Simple Hunting Economy (Montagnais-Naskapi)." *Southwestern Journal of Anthropology,* 16 (1): 31-47.

———. ed. 1981. *Myths of Male Dominance: Collected Articles on Women Cross-Culturally.* New York: Monthly Review Press.

Menta, John. 1988. "Shaumpishuh, Squaw Sachem of the Quinnipiac Indians." *Artifacts* 16 (3-4): 32-37.

NYCD. 1856-87. *Documents Relative to the Colonial History of the State of New York,* edited by Edmund Bailey O'Callaghan and Berthold Fernow. 15 vols. Albany: Weed, Parsons.

NYCM. New York Colonial Manuscripts, Endorsed Land Papers, vol. 4. State Library Archives, Albany, NY.

Papageorge, Toby. 1983. "Records of the Shinnecock Trustees." In *The Shinnecock Indians: A Tribal History,* edited by Gaynell Stone, pp. 141-225, Stony Brook, NY: Suffolk County Archaeological Association.

Pelletreau, William. 1903. *The History of Long Island.* 2 vols. New York: Lewis Publishing Company.

Rainey, Froelich. 1936. "A Compilation of Historical Data Contributing to the Ethnography of the Connecticut and Southern New England Indians." *Bulletin of the Archaeological Society of Connecticut.* Reprint No. 3.

Reiter, Rayna, ed. 1975. *Toward an Anthropology of Women.* New York: Monthly Review Press.

Rohrlich-Leavitt, Barbara Sykes, and Elizabeth Weatherford. 1975. "Aboriginal Woman: Male and Female Perspectives." In *Toward an Anthropology of Women,* edited by Rayna Reiter, pp. 110-26. New York: Monthly Review Press.

RTBH Book A. 1930. *Records of the Town of Brookhaven 1657-1679,* edited by Osborne Shaw. New York: Derrydale Press.

RTBH Hutchinson. 1888. *Records of the Town of Brookhaven, up to 1800,* edited by Henry P. Hutchinson. Patchogue, NY: Advance.

RTEH. 1887. *Records of the Town of East Hampton,* edited by Joseph Osborne. 5 vols. Sag Harbor, NY: Hunt.

RTH. 1887-89. *Huntington Town Records,* edited by Charles Street. 3 vols. Huntington, NY: Town of Huntington.

RTOB. 1916-40. *Oyster Bay Town Records,* edited by John Cox. 8 vols., New York: Tobias Wright.

RTSH. 1874-77. *Records of the Town of Southampton,* edited by William Pelletreau. 8 vols. Sag Harbor: Hunt.

RTSM. 1898-1931. *Records of the Town of Smithtown,* edited by William Pelletreau. 3 vols. Sag Harbor: Hunt.

Salwen, Bert. 1978. "Indians of the Southern New England and Long Island." In *Handbook of the North American Indian,* vol. 15, *The Northeast,* edited by Bruce Trigger, pp. 160-89. Washington DC: Smithsonian.

Schlegel, Alice, ed. 1977. *Sexual Stratification: A Cross-Cultural View.* New York: Columbia University Press.

Shoemaker, Nancy, ed. 1995. *Negotiators of Change: Historical Perspectives on Native American Women.* New York: Routledge.

SHTA. Southampton Town Archives. Town Hall, Southampton, NY.

Slocum, Sally. 1975. "Woman the Gatherer: Male Bias in Anthropology." In *Toward an Anthropology of Women,* edited by Rayna Reiter, pp. 36-51. New York: Monthly Review Press.

Smith, Raymond, ed. 1926. In *Re Montauk.* East Hampton: Town of East Hampton.

Spencer-Wood, Suzanne, M. 1994. "Feminist Issues Involved in Recognizing Gender in Historical and Archaeological Contexts." *Bulletin of the Massachusetts Archaeological Society* 55 (1): 24-30.

Strong, John A. 1983. "How the Land Was Lost." In *The Shinnecock Indians: a Culture History,* edited by Gaynell Stone, pp. 53-118. Stony Brook, NY: Suffolk County Archaeological Association.

——. 1994. "The Imposition of Colonial Jurisdiction over the Montauk Indians of Long Island." *Ethnohistory* 41(4): 561-89.

——. 1995. "Algonquian Women as Sunksquaws and Caretakers of the Soil: The Documentary Evidence in the 17th-century Records." Paper presented to the American Indian Workshop, Fernando Pessao University, Oporto, Portugal, April.

____. 1997. *The Algonquian Peoples of Long Island From Earliest Times to 1700.* Interlaken, NY: Empire State Books.

Strong, Lara M. and Selcuk Karabag. 1991. "Quashawam: Sunksquaw of the Montauk." *Long Island Historical Journal* 2 (2): 189-204.

Strong, Lisa and Frank Holmberg. 1983. "The Shinnecock Trustee System." In *The Shinnecock Indians, A Culture History,* edited by Gaynell Stone, pp. 226-30. Stony Brook, NY: Suffolk County Archaeological Association.

Tooker, William Wallace. 1962. *The Indian Place-Names on Long Island,* 1911. Reprint; Port Washington, NY: I. J. Friedman.

Ward, Barbara, 1992. "Woman's Property and Family Continuity in Eighteenth-century Connecticut." Paper presented at the Massachusetts Archaeological Society Annual Meeting, October 24.

Williams, Roger. 1973. *A Key to the Languages of America,* 1643. Reprint; Detroit: Wayne State University Press.

Zeisberger, David. 1910. "History of the North American Indians," ed. by A. B. Hulbert and W. N. Schwarze. *Ohio Archaeological and Historical Publications* 19: 1-189.

4. First Women in Aviation

Joanne Lynn Harvey

"If enough of us keep trying, we'll get someplace."[1] This quote from Amelia Earhart, perhaps the best-known woman to fly, suggests that she was not alone in overcoming obstacles to realize her dream. In fact, it was not one woman's efforts, but the persistent accomplishments of many that paved the way for women to earn a place in a world dominated by men in the early 1900s. As women flew and set individual records, they also united together and created a professional pilots organization, the Ninety Nines, that remains strong and active today.

In an era before women's suffrage passed, overcoming barriers of sex, stereotypes, training, finances, and even race were obstacles that did not deter these early flyers. As Long Island provided the environment that gave birth to and nurtured the evolution of aeronautics, it was here also that women challenged the status quo and expanded the boundaries that hindered them. Opinion is divided as to who deserves credit as America's first female pilot, Blanche Stuart Scott or Bessica Faith Raiche.[2]

Blanche Stuart Scott took her first airplane ride in California in 1910 with Charles F. Willard, the first student of pioneer aviator Glenn Curtiss. That summer, she went to Hammondsport, New York, where a reluctant Curtiss taught her how to fly.[3] Many early aviators, such as the Wright brothers, resisted teaching women to fly; this prejudice was also prevalant in aviation schools. Historian Claudia Oakes noted, "Curtiss was not at all enthusiastic about women learning to fly. . . [Scott] was the first and only woman ever taught by Curtiss personally." Curtiss had installed a governor (a block of wood bolted under the throttle peddle) to prevent the plane from flying; yet, a gust of wind picked up the plane approximately twelve feet from the ground on August 18, 1910. Scott claims she then demanded that Curtiss remove the governor which he agreed to do. On September 2, 1910, she reached an altitude of about forty feet, and Curtiss declared her to be America's first aviatrix. In October, Curtiss sent her to an exhibition in Indiana where advertisements billed her as, "The First Woman to Make a Public Flight in an Aeroplane."[4]

Scott's daring exploits gained recognition across the country. Billed as "Tomboy of the Air," she flew inverted twenty feet above ground, beneath bridges, and performed her "Death-Dive," plummeting from 4,000 feet, and leveling out only two hundred feet above ground. In the spring of 1911, she joined Captain Thomas Scott Baldwin who was "sympathetic to the idea of women learning to fly."[5] Scott flew Baldwin Red Devil biplanes in exhibitions at Mineola, New York. She was photographed flying over a Long Island train near the Woodside Railroad Station. She later recalled: "We were all kooks—including myself, and I was probably one of the biggest. We made lots of money—as much as $5,000 a week—but spent it just as fast as we made it. We risked our necks day after day, but the crowds didn't care if you got killed or not, because there was always someone else to follow you and take your place."[6]

Scott was also frustrated because there was no place in aviation for women engineers or mechanics.[7] In 1916, after six years of flying, Blanche Stuart Scott retired from flying at the age of twenty-seven.

Bessica Faith Raiche is also credited as the first woman to fly an airplane in America. Although Raiche's flight took place after Scott's (on September 16, 1910), because it was "intentional," the Aeronautical Society presented her with a gold medal inscribed, "First Woman Aviator of America, Bessica Raiche," on October 13, 1910.

Raiche not only flew planes but built them with her husband, a French airplane designer. They lived in Mineola, New York, attracted by the benefits of living, working, and flying near the innovative pioneers of the day. The plane that Bessica first soloed in (without any prior instruction) was built right in their living room.[8]

The Raiches improved airplane construction; they believed the key to better flying was lighter planes. Their innovative use of silk and bamboo replaced canvas and wood throughout the industry. Bessica Raiche reflected: "We used bamboo struts, China silk wing covering and bicycle wheels because they were the lightest things we could find. Common practice called for the use of stove wire for supporting members but my husband created a sensation by using piano wire, lighter and stronger. I believe we were among the first to use 'flaps' on the wings for control."[9] They formed the French-American Airoplane Company and sold the airplanes they constructed.

After an accident during her fifth flight, Raiche changed from wearing long skirts to riding breeches which did not hinder her movement; it created newspaper headlines.[10] Each woman flyer adapted or designed her own flying costume for comfort or style, often setting fashion statements followed by their contemporaries.

Harriet Quimby was the first woman to receive a pilot's license in the United States on August 1, 1911 in Mineola (license no. 37). Quimby became determined to fly after attending the Belmont Park Aviation Meet, October 22-31, 1910. She asked international aviator John Moisant to teach her, which he agreed to do. Her enthusiasm was not discouraged even after he was killed two months later while performing.

Most pilots had little, if any training. As aviation matured, schools were organized by men for men; women were not accepted in most schools. The Moisant School of Aviation, started by John and Alfred Moisant, opened in April 1911, at Garden City on one thousand acres of the Hempstead Plains. This school was unusual at the time because it encouraged women to enroll in flight school and even included them in advertisments.[11] Their sixteen-page aviation school brochure shows pictures of Matilde Moisant and Harriet Quimby as students.[12] They both supported the women's auxiliary of the Aeronautical Society, which was organized in 1911 to bring attention to the achievements of women in aviation.

The licensing agency for the United States was the Aero Club of America under the authority of the Federation Aeronautique Internationale. Their official field was the Hempstead Plains Aerodrome.[13] The requirement for receiving a pilot's license was landing your plane within 100 feet of where the plane left the ground.

After thirty-three lessons and four months, Harriet Quimby took her first pilot's test which she failed. The following day, August 1, 1911, she landed her plane seven feet from where she took off. She then joined the Moisant International Aviators for exhibitions around the country. The following month she participated in a race at the Second International Aerial Tournament at Nassau Boulevard in Garden City. Quimby beat the celebrated French flyer Helene Dutrieu (who was making her American debut), for which Quimby earned $600.[14] Harriet Quimby and Matilde Moisant were best friends; they studied flying together at her brother's school and flew in his exhibition team. Moisant was the second woman in America to obtain a pilot's license on August 13, 1911 (license no. 44), only two weeks after Quimby. At the Nassau Boulevard Aviation Meet, September 24, 1911, Moisant beat both Quimby and Dutrieu and set a high-altitude record reaching 1,200 feet before 25,000 spectators. That same month, again on Long Island, she broke this record by flying to 2,500 feet.[15]

Pilots were restricted from flying on Sundays due to "blue laws." On October 8, 1911, Moisant not only defied the Nassau County sheriff, but led him and his deputies on a chase as she dodged from one part of the Moisant airfield to another. The judge later refused a warrant for her arrest because he could not see the difference between flying an airplane or driving an automobile on Sunday.[16]

In April 1912, Moisant made her last flight which ended in flames due to a leak from the gas tank. It is believed that the heavy tweed flying suit that she wore saved her. Her close call did not diminish her infatuation with flying: "I cannot watch a machine in the air without being overcome with a desire to fly myself. . . It is an intoxication, and I am afraid I can never be cured. One cannot be worse than killed, and there is only one death, is what I think when I find myself facing a perilous situation."[17]

Why did women risk death to fly? Women flew for many reasons: freedom, setting and breaking records, thrill and excitement, publicity and attention, fame and fortune. Margery Brown, pilot and advocate of women in the 1920s and 1930s said: "Why do I want to fly? Because half-way between the earth and sky, one seems to be closer to God. There is a peace of mind and heart, a satisfaction which walls can not give. . . . It isn't for a fad, or a thrill, or pride. Women are seeking freedom. Freedom in the skies! They are soaring above temperamental tendencies of their sex which have kept them earth-bound. Flying is a symbol of freedom from limitation."[18]

At the time, it was not unusual for newspapers to run articles such as, "Women Should Not Fly," which appeared in the *New York Sun* in July 1912.[19] These articles objected to women in aviation considering it socially inappropriate as well as physically impossible for women to fly. The stereotypes and prejudices women faced in pursuit of flight paralleled the struggles of the women who sought the right to vote. Portia Willis was the first woman to use aviation in the cause of suffrage. In September 1913, the following story appeared:

> Next Saturday on the Hempstead Plains aviation field, at Garden City, Long Island . . . the red hat will be replaced by an aviator's cap. Clad in genuine bird woman's dress and clasping firmly an armful of "votes for women" leaflets, Miss Willis will ascend in a decorated aeroplane, accompanied by the suffrage aviator, Miss Marian Sims. The flight will occur at 2 o'clock precisely, and if during the next twenty minutes the surrounding country is not thoroughly peppered with suffrage literature it won't be Miss Willis's fault. She will attend to the peppering, while Miss Sims runs the ship. This is the first time that suffragists have campaigned by airship, and so anxious are they that nothing shall happen to their craft that a delegation will go to the field Friday, starting from the New York State Suffrage Association headquarters, at No. 180 Madison Avenue, in a big wagon, and they will camp all night in the hangars. . . . Mrs. Herbert Carpenter is organizing a squad of policewomen to keep order on the field. Men are not to be allowed there Saturday, except as spectators. Any mere man who wants to pay his gate money and come humbly to see woman prove her ability to vote by her ability to fly an airship, sleep on the hard ground, cook over a camp fire or arrest a "drunk and disorderly" will be very welcome. To-day Miss Willis will invade Wall street in—no, not an airship, but an automobile, to advertise Saturday's flight. Many of the details for "suffrage aviation day" were thought out by "General" Rosalie Jones, whose idea it was first.[20]

Although women gained the right to vote by 1920, their struggle for a place in aviation was far from over. Women were not permitted to fly in active combat in World War I.[21] Bernetta Miller graduated from the Moisant School, received her license in 1912, and flew in their exhibition team. She was the first woman to demonstrate a monoplane for the United States government.[22] But her request to fly at the front was rejected.

While women were denied the opportunity to fly in combat, early women aviators, such as Marjory Stinson, taught many men pilots who did fly for the United States during the war. Ruth Law was also not allowed to fly in combat; however, she was the first woman authorized to wear a noncommissioned army uniform. She assisted in recruiting tours for the Army and Navy. Law was the sixth woman to receive a license in 1912. In August 1913, she occupied a hangar in the Hempstead Plains between exhibition tours.[23] In November 1913, she became the first woman to fly at night around Staten Island and subsequently made many night flights with flares attached to her aircraft.

Many other women made significant contributions to aviation on Long Island, breaking records almost as soon as they were made, knowing that the risks involved may lead to death. Laura Bromwell was twenty-three when she set two records at Curtiss Field, Mineola, May 15, 1921. "Known the country over as a daring aviatrix,"[24] she set a new speed record for women, flying at 135 miles an hour over a course just under two miles.[25] She then set another world's record for women by looping her plane 199 times in one flight.

> Miss Bromwell . . . mounted to 8,000 feet, where she began the looping in full view of the 10,000 people who attended the exhibition. The wings of the plane flashed time after time in the sun, and she slowly lost altitude until she reached 4,000 feet, then climbed again to 6,000 feet. Once more the plane began turning leisurely, but this time she continued looping until she was 400 feet above the field.
>
> After the last loop she made another tour of the field and landed. The crowd, as the wheels of her plane touched the ground, broke through the lines and poured out on the field cheering. When told that she had missed just one loop from putting her new record at 200 [she] said that she easily could have turned a few more.[26]

Three weeks later, while looping her plane at 1,000 feet above Hazelhurst Field, Bromwell died when her plane plummeted to the ground. An editorial in the *New York Times* stated: "the death of Miss Bromwell is almost sure to raise in many minds at least the question if it would not be well to exclude women from a field of activity in which there [*sic*] presence certainly is unnecessary from any point of view."[27]

Bessie Coleman was denied entry into aviation schools not only because she was a woman, but also because she was African American. No American flying school would enroll African Americans in the early 1900s. Determined to fly, Coleman went to France, where she became the first black person to earn a pilot's license on June 15, 1921. After taking advanced flying lessons and aerobatics near Berlin, she returned to America where she traveled across the country barnstorming. The *Daily Review* reported her local flight in Mineola on September 5, 1922 as follows: "Miss Bessie Coleman, the only colored aviatrix in this country, made three flights from Curtiss Field here Sunday . . . before an admiring crowd of 1,000 people for the most part of her color. This was Miss Coleman's first flight with an American made plane. She was flying in honor of the 115th Infantry, the colored regiment, she said she hoped to create an interest in aviation among her people."[28] It was Bessie Coleman's dream not only to fly, but to open an aviation school for African Americans who wanted to learn to fly.

Viola Gentry learned how to fly at Roosevelt Field in 1925 where she received private pilot's certificate no. 1,822. She established the first official women's endurance record by remaining in the air over Roosevelt Field for eight hours and twenty minutes on December 20, 1928. She hand-pumped fuel while flying between Roosevelt Field and Curtiss Field, approximately a ten mile area. An earlier endurance attempt ended in a plane crash because she was unable to refuel and ran out of fuel in the fog, killing her pilot and seriously injuring herself. Gentry remained active in aviation serving as Vice President of the Women's National Association of Aeronautics and as observer of international world records at Roosevelt and Floyd Bennett Fields.[29]

Elinor Smith from Freeport, was the youngest woman to earn a pilot's license at age sixteen in 1928. Her accomplishments in aviation are unparalleled. She began flying in a potato field in Hicksville at age six. At fifteen she soloed her father's plane at Roosevelt Field two weeks before Lindbergh took off for Paris. Three months later, she set an altitude record of 11,874 feet above the same field, but it was not considered due to her age. Two months later she was the first woman to fly under all four East River bridges between Manhattan and western Long Island.

In 1929, Smith established a new women's solo endurance record at Roosevelt Field at fourteen hours thirty minutes; she then broke her own record flying twenty-six hours and thirty minutes. The same year she set a speed record flying over Long Island at 179.8 mph. A year later Smith set a new woman's altitude record at 27,418 feet at Roosevelt Field. In 1931, she broke this record taking off from Roosevelt Field and flying 32,500 feet over New York City. She was the first woman line test pilot for Fairchild Aviation and Bellanco Corporation. Most of her subsequent speed and altitude records were made at Roosevelt Field. In 1930, she was voted, "Best Woman Pilot" in the United States; Jimmy Doolittle was the best male pilot.[30]

During the Depression, Smith flew with Lindbergh and other pilots to raise money for the unemployed at Curtiss Field, Valley Stream. Exhibition flying afforded a lucrative opportunity to fly. Earnings could range from $5,000-$9,000 per week, and as much as $2,000 per day for stunt flying. Many flyers participated in barnstorming and competitions with the goal of purchasing their own planes or paying for their flying expenses.[31]

Manufacturers also sought endorsements of the aircraft women flew in order to promote the idea that the plane was so safe that even a woman could fly it. Working for aircraft companies often resulted in full-time, paying jobs for women as sales representatives and flight demonstrators. This afforded women the benefit of flying at the company's expense.

Stimulated by the fame of Charles Lindbergh's trans-Atlantic flight, women flew as passengers, not pilots, in their first attempts to cross the Atlantic. Ruth Elder attempted to be the first woman to cross on October 11, 1927, when she took off from Roosevelt Field, just as Lindbergh had done five months earlier. Although the flight was aborted near the Azores, France and New York greeted Elder as they had Lindbergh with a ticker-tape parade. The plane's name, *The American Girl,* became her nickname.[32]

Simultaneously, Frances Grayson, a wealthy real estate broker from Forest Hills insisted on being the first woman to cross the Atlantic in 1927. Fighting against poor weather and the resignation of her first pilot, Grayson planned to take the northern route across the Atlantic, though she was advised it was too late in the year. On December 23, 1927, *The Dawn* took off from Roosevelt Field headed for Newfoundland. The plane never reached its destination, and was lost near Cape Cod.[33]

Mabel Boll left Roosevelt Field on June 12, 1928, also headed for Newfoundland with hopes of being the first woman to cross the Atlantic. To her dismay, she discovered that the pilot she originally contracted to accompany her was flying with another team that included a woman pilot, Amelia Earhart, and that they left Boston Harbor on June 3, 1928, with the same goal, which they accomplished successfully when their plane landed in Wales. Though Amelia Earhart did not pilot the plane, she became the first woman to cross the Atlantic in the air.[34]

These women were criticized for their attempts to cross the Atlantic because of the danger and because the flights made no apparent contribution to aviation. They were considered publicity seekers. Perhaps the severest critics were from their own sex: Eleanor Roosevelt (who considered it "very foolish"); sociologist Dr. Katherine B. Davis ("There is no woman alive today...equipped for such a flight"); and perhaps the most scathing, Winifred Sackville Stone ("If she had wanted to show that a woman was capable of accomplishing what a man had accomplished, that would have been another matter. If she had wanted to show that a woman could fly alone like

Lindbergh, that would have been laudable. But any one can sit in a machine while there is someone to guide it.")[35]

Frances Harrell Marsalis learned to fly in the Casey Jones Flying School at Curtiss Field, Mineola, in the late 1920s. Marsalis followed this school when it was relocated to Valley Stream and frequently flew at Floyd Bennett, Curtiss, and Roosevelt Fields where she was often featured as a woman pilot, which was still rare. She became an acrobatic pilot and flew in many air shows. "Francey" became world-famous when she and Louise Thaden set a Women's World Endurance Record by staying aloft for 196 hours in August 1932, at Valley Stream. The plane was named the *Flying Boudoir* by the press because they requested cold cream and hairpins while aloft.[36] Marsalis sold Waco planes out of Roosevelt Field.

Frances Marsalis was killed in 1934 at the National Women's Air Meet in Ohio when a plane cut in front of hers. Her funeral was held at Roosevelt Field:

> Three Fleet biplanes of the Roosevelt Field Flying School set up the parade. To the sides were a formation of U.S. Army Curtiss Falcons and a formation of U.S. Navy Curtiss Hell Divers. A number of other airplanes . . . fell in line . . . the casket, followed. . . . They flew over Brooklyn, to Floyd Bennett Field to the south, then east over Valley Stream and finally to Roosevelt Field. . . . Frances Harrell Marsalis, just 29, was laid in homage in front of the Waco F-3. The floor was carpeted and heavily banked with flowers. The great and near-great of aviation came to see her and pay their respects. Some stopped to recall incidents, and at times the hangar was choked with people. A few days later, Frances was laid to rest in a nearby cemetery as several airplanes flew overhead dropping roses. It was possibly the greatest unrehearsed send-off in history.[37]

Fay Gillis Wells was the "first woman to save her life by parachuting from a disabled plane." She later reflected:

> It happened when I was learning to be a pilot at Curtiss Field [Valley Stream] in New York. My instructor was Sunny Trunk, a lieutenant in the Air Force. He asked if I'd like to go up while he finished testing an experimental biplane. When he promised to show me some acrobatics, I had to go. Fortunately, I was given a parachute. They required that. They said to count 10 and pull the rip cord. I hadn't thought much about it. There was a great vibration. The tail simply vibrated off. And the motor fell off its mount. The plane simply disintegrated while we were upside down.

Falling from 4,000 feet, Wells pulled the rip cord 400 feet above the ground. Although both were uninjured, this earned her membership in the Caterpillar Club—pilots whose lives have been saved by using silk parachutes.[38]

Ruth Nichols earned her pilot's license in 1924, and was the first woman to receive a seaplane pilot's license.[39] She helped establish Aviation Country Clubs; the first opened in Hicksville in 1928, and in 1929 Nichols embarked on a forty-eight state tour to promote these clubs. Nichols was the only woman to simultaneously hold women's world speed, altitude, and distance records for heavy land planes. In 1930 she set a new transcontinental women's speed record flying from Roosevelt Field to California in sixteen hours, fifty-nine minutes. She returned making a one-stop transcontinental flight in thirteen hours, twenty-one minutes—beating Lindbergh's time. She also broke Elinor Smith's altitude record on March 6, 1931 by 1,325 feet. She set a women's speed record on April 13, 1931, flying 210.7 miles per hour. A champion of women pilots, in 1939 at the outbreak of World War II, she started the first civilian pilot training program that included women. This program was sponsored by the government at Adelphi College in Garden City, although women were still not permitted to fly in combat.[40]

Betty Huyler Gillies earned her pilot's license in 1929. She sold airplanes and flight courses for the Curtiss Wright Flying Service on Long Island, Waco Sales of New York, Country Club Flying Service of Hicksville, and Gillies Aviation Corporation.[41]

In 1932, after only three weeks of instruction, Jackie Cochran received her pilot's license at Roosevelt Field. At the time of her death in 1980, she held more speed, altitude, and distance records than any other pilot, male or female, in aviation history.[42] She also was the first woman pilot to fly faster than the speed of sound.

Cecil W. Kenyon won first prize in the National Women's Championship of the United States Amateur Air Pilots Association held at Roosevelt Field in 1933. She used the $5,000 prize money to purchase her own plane. Taught to fly by her husband, they traveled around the country barnstorming. She also flew more than 3,000 hours as a test pilot for high-performance fighter planes and torpedo bombers.[43]

Many other records were set by women on Long Island. Lillian Gatlin was the first woman to cross the continent by air in 1922, landing in Mineola. Laura Ingalls learned to fly at Roosevelt Field in 1928, and set a transcontinental flight record in 1934.[44]

While these are some of the most notable women who flew on Long Island, and received recognition for their many accomplishments in opening the doors closed to women in aviation, there were countless others who watched, worked, assisted, played a small, humble role in the story of flight. Women such as Alice E. McFaul never set or broke any records, or received a pilot's license, barnstormed, nor earned prize money; yet she worked at Roosevelt Field with aviation pioneers as well as Amelia Earhart. As an employee of Republic Aircraft Corporation, she was required to establish flying skills and did fly several times from Roosevelt Field.[45] How many other countless women played a role in the aviation story? It was the united efforts of not one or two or a dozen women who set records, but the consistent growth in numbers that provided the strength for women to overcome obstacles of sex, stereotypes, training, finances, and to persevere. Their story continues today.

On November 2, 1929, the Ninety-Nines, the first international organization of licensed women pilots was formed at Curtiss Field, Valley Stream. A letter was sent to the 117 licensed women pilots at that time suggesting that they meet and organize; ninety-nine responded to the letter. Amelia Earhart was voted their first president. The charter members included Viola Gentry, Fay Gillis Wells, Frances Harrell Marsalis, Cecil (Teddy) Kenyon, Marjorie G. Stinson, and Louise Thaden. The Ninety-Nines now has over 7,000 women pilots as members world-wide.[46]

In 1929, 117 women held pilot's licenses. By 1933, 599 of 18,457 or 3.25 percent of pilot's licenses were held by women. In 1986, the figure had only risen to 6.1 percent of pilots. According to a Ninety-Nine, the reason for this low figure is, "Women are not encouraged to do it." In 1995, 5.95 percent of licenses belonged to women.[47] Although these figures may be low, they reflect what Amelia Earhart's quote suggests, that joint efforts have gained women a place in aeronautics, and even in space travel. Perhaps the greatest source of encouragement is to read early accounts of the first women in aviation.

Fig. 4.1. Some charter members of the "Ninety-Nines" at Curtiss Field, Valley Stream, 1929. From the left: Mona Holmes, Mary Samson, Elvy Kalep, Ruth Elder, Mrs. John Remey, Amelia Earhart Putnam. Photograph courtesy of the Nassau County Museum Collection, Long Island Studies Institute.

Notes

1. "A Salute to 99s and Women in Aerospace," *The 99 News* 6, no. 9 (November 1979): 15.

2. Claudia M. Oakes, *United States Women in Aviation Through World War I,* (cited hereafter as *Women in Aviation Through WWI*) Smithsonian Studies in Air and Space, no. 2 (Washington, DC: Smithsonian Institution Press, 1978), p. 17.

3. Scott had driven across the country as an advertisement for the Overland automobile to publicize that "driving coast to coast was so simple even a woman could do it." Jerome Fanciulli, the manager of a flying exhibition team organized by Glenn Curtiss, offered Scott flying lessons if she would join their team and travel around the country. When Fanciulli told her of the publicity it would generate, "she was hooked"; she became a member of the Curtiss Exhibition Team. Oakes, *Women in Aviation Through WWI*, pp. 17-18; Edward R. Cowles, "Tomboy of the Sky," *U. A. Beehive,* Summer 1968, pp. 18-22.

4. Oakes, *Women in Aviation Through WWI*, p. 18; Cowles, "Tomboy of the Sky," p. 21. See also personal notarized letter to Blanche Stuart Scott from Curtiss pilot George Milton Dunlap, May 20, 1963, in "Blanche Stuart Scott" file, Cradle of Aviation Museum, Garden City, NY. Other accounts indicate this flight occurred on September 6, 1910; see Cowles, "Tomboy of the Sky," p. 21 and letter from G. M. Dunlap.

5. Matilde Moisant recounts Baldwin asking her brother if there were objections to his giving Scott flying lessons. "There's a young lady here who wants me to teach her to fly. The Wright brothers wouldn't do it. Their sister wouldn't let them teach a girl. I see that you have Miss Quimby and your sister out here, and I thought if you thought it was safe for them it might be all right for her. Alfred Moisant agreed." Sherwood Harris, *The First to Fly, Aviation's Pioneer Days* (New York: Simon and Schuster, 1970), p. 239.

6. Quoted by Cowles, "Tomboy of the Sky," p. 22.

7. Oakes, *Women in Aviation Through WWI*, p. 19. Scott later established a movie production studio on Long Island, then moved to Hollywood where she wrote dialogue for comedies (Cowles, "Tomboy of the Sky," p. 22).

8. Oakes, *Women in Aviation Through WWI*, p. 19.

9. Quoted in Gerald B. Burtnett, "Bessica Raiche, America's First Aviatrix," *Popular Aviation,* July 1931, pp. 44-45.

10. Oakes, *Women in Aviation Through WWI*, p. 19. Burtnett, "Bessia Raiche," p. 44. Raiche eventually moved to California where she became a medical doctor.

11. "Moisant Aviation School" advertisement, *Aircraft,* July 1913, p. 97. Curtiss Flying Schools did not welcome female students. An article advertising the Curtiss Flying School in Valley Stream was tailored to attract men only. See Albert I. Lodwick, "Curtiss-Wright School of Aeronautics, Valley Stream," *Aero Digest,* June 1933, pp. 34-35; and Julie Opell Klym, "America's First Flight Academy," *The AOPA Pilot,* October 1979, pp. 67-69.

12. The Moisant Aviation School brochure, 16 pp, Hempstead Plains file, Cradle of Aviation Museum, Garden City, NY. (See also Doris Rich's forthcoming book on the Moisants. Editor's note.)

13. *Flying,* October 1912, p. 30.

14. Oakes, *Women in Aviation Through WWI*, p. 28. Quimby is internationally known best for being the first woman pilot to cross the English Channel. She was drama

critic for *Leslie's Weekly* and submitted articles on her flying experiences as well, e.g., "How I Won My Aviator's License," *Leslie's Weekly,* August 24, 1911. Her last article, "Ideal Sport for Woman?" appeared in *Good Housekeeping Magazine,* September 1912. She died in a tragic plane accident on July 1, 1912. (See next article in this volume on Quimby by Harry Holden; and Ed Y. Hall, ed. *Harriet Quimby: America's First Lady of the Air* [Spartanburg, SC: Honoribus Press, 1990]. Editor's note.)

15. "Matilde Moisant, Early Flyer, Dies," *New York Times,* February 7, 1964.

16. Harris, *The First to Fly,* pp. 244-47.

17. Quoted in "Matilde Moisant, Early Flyer, Dies," *New York Times* obituary.

18. Claudia M. Oakes, *United States Women in Aviation 1930-1939,* Smithsonian Studies in Air and Space, no. 6 (Washington, DC: Smithsonian Institution Press, 1985), p. 4.

19. "Women Should Not Fly," *New York Sun,* July 1912, clipping in Women in Aviation file, Cradle of Aviation Museum, Garden City, NY.

20. "Portia Willis Up in the Air," September 1913, unidentified newspaper clipping in Women in Aviation file, Cradle of Aviation Museum, Garden City, NY. Unfortunately, the flight did not occur because of inclement weather. (See Natalie A. Naylor, "Harriet Quimby, Aviation and the Suffrage Movement," *Harriet Quimby Research Conference Journal* 2 [1996]: 84-85. Editor's note.)

21. Oakes, *Women in Aviation Through WWI,* p. 21.

22. Miller joined the Women's Overseas Service League attached in the Eighty-second Infantry Division in France, serving first as an accountant, then a canteen worker at the front. She received many citations for her work (ibid.).

23. "On the morning of August 16 . . . Ruth Law and her cortege of managers and mechanics arrived at the Hempstead Plains . . . Instead of shipping her machine by express or freight, which is the usual custom of exhibition flyers, Miss Law has it set upon a truck and pulled behind her automobile from one town to another. In this way she not only saves the railroad fare and express charges, but is always sure to have her machine at the place on time ("Ruth Law," *Aircraft,* September 1913, p. 160). In 1916, Law flew from Chicago to New York setting three records, and in 1917 she set a new women's altitude record of 14,700 feet (Oakes, *Women in Aviation Through WWI,* pp. 39, 41).

24. "Air Heroine Falls to Death Looping Loop," *Nassau Daily Review,* June 6, 1921, p. 1.

25. "She Loops Airplane 199 Times; World's Record for Woman," May 16, 1921, newspaper clippings in Women in Aviation file, Cradle of Aviation Museum, Garden City, NY. Another source reported she had flown 145 miles an hour at Hazelhurst Field (*Nassau Daily Review,* June 6, 1921, p. 1).

26. "She Loops Airplane 199 Times."

27. *New York Times,* June 1921, quoted in Kathleen Brooks-Pazmany, *United States Women in Aviation, 1919-1929,* Smithsonian Studies in Air and Space, no. 5 (Washington, DC: Smithsonian Institution Press, 1983), p. 4.

28. "Bessie Coleman, First Colored Aviatrix," *[Nassau] Daily Review,* September 5, 1922. Bessie Coleman died in a tragic plane crash in 1926. Her courage and dream continues to inspire the Bessie Coleman Aviators, a group of young African American women who are dedicated to acquainting minority women and all races with the world

of aviation and aerospace. See Doris L. Rich, *Queen Bess: Daredevil Aviator* (Washington, DC: Smithsonian Institution Press, 1993).

29. "Still Races Planes Like 60," unidentified newspaper clipping, Viola Gentry File, Cradle of Aviation Museum, Garden City, NY. Also, letter typed from Viola Gentry's handwritten letter to Captain and Mrs. C. V. Dobrescu, Viola Gentry File, Cradle of Aviation Museum, Garden City, NY.

30. Smith became NBC Radio's first woman commentator, and edited and wrote many articles on aviation. Smith's accomplishments in aviation are recounted in her autobiography, *Aviatrix* (New York: Harcourt and Brace, 1981). Although she left flying when she married in the 1930s, she remained an avid spokesperson for the role of women in aviation and worked hard to see an aviation museum established at Mitchel Field.

31. Brooks-Pazmany, *Women in Aviation*, p. 12.

32. Because other women flyers believed Elder to be a publicity seeker, she entered the "Powder Puff Derby," the first women's air race. She finished fifth and won $525 as well as the respect of her colleagues. She eventually went to Hollywood where she appeared in two silent films with Richard Dix and Hoot Gibson. She played a famous aviatrix in Universal's film, *The Winged Horseman*. Brooks-Pazmany, *Women in Aviation*, pp. 21-22; Marcella Harp, "Ruth Elder . . . First Woman over the Atlantic," *FAA Aviation News*, July 1968, pp. 12-13.

33. Brooks-Pazmany, *Women in Aviation*, pp. 22-23.

34. Ibid., pp. 23-26.

35. Ibid., pp. 22, 26.

36. Claudia M. Oakes, "U.S. Women in Aviation: The 1930s," *Air & Space*, Winter 1980, p. 16. Louise Thaden won the 1929 National Women's Air Derby, set speed and distance records, and won the Bendix Trophy Race. Oakes, *Women in Aviation 1930-1939*, p. 9; see also Louise Thaden, *High, Wide and Frightened* (New York: Stackpole Sons, 1938).

37. Bill Rhodes, "Journey to Valhalla," *American Aviation Historical Society Journal*, Summer 1971, pp. 111-12.

38. Lawrence Maddry, "Pilot Led the Life of Fictional Heroine," April 1984 unidentified newspaper clipping in Organization of Ninety-Nines file in Cradle of Aviation Museum, Garden City, NY. Wells assisted famous aviator Wiley Post with his solo flight around the world in 1933 and was the first American woman to fly a Russian plane. She became a White House correspondent, accompanied President Nixon to China, and always remained active in aviation.

39. Nichols lived near Rye, across Long Island Sound, and often accompanied her teacher Harry Rogers to Roosevelt Field, as well as to Miami in 1928. She became the first woman executive of an aircraft company in America (R. M. Valerioti, "Ruth Nichols," *American Aviation Historical Society Journal*, Spring 1984, pp. 27-40).

40. Oakes, *Women in Aviation 1930-1939*, p. 49; Valerioti, "Ruth Nichols," pp. 27-40.

41. Oakes, *Women in Aviation 1930-1939*, pp. 5-6. (On the Hicksville Aviation Country Club, see Carolyn Kelly, "Brief History of Aviation in Hicksville," *Nassau County Historical Society Journal* 51 [1996]: 31-33; and Lynne Matarrese, "Levittown's Aviation Heritage," *Long Island Forum* 59 [Summer 1996]: 18-28. Editor's note.)

42. Cochran, *Flying*, p. 75 and unpaginated summary.

43. Obituaries: "Cecil Kenyon, Test Pilot," *Newsday,* December 16, 1985; "Cecil W. Kenyon Dies; An Early Female Pilot," *New York Times,* December 19, 1985.

44. Brooks-Pazmany, *Women in Aviation 1919-1929,* p. 13. Oakes, Women in Aviation 1930-1939, pp. 47-49; Laura Ingalls biography sheet in Laura Ingalls file, Cradle of Aviation Museum, Garden City, NY.

45. Obituary: "Alice E. McFaul, 75," *Newsday,* November 22, 1985.

46. Joanne Lynn, "Women's Cradle of Aviation: Curtiss Field, Valley Stream," in *Evoking a Sense of Place,* edited by Joann P. Krieg (Interlaken, NY: Heart of the Lakes Publishing), pp. 85-95.

47. "Pilots Show Increase Over Last Year," *Aero Digest,* June 1933, p. 54; Federal Aviation Administration, Statistics and Forecast; in 1986, total pilots were 709,118 and female pilots, 43,080; a 99 member quoted by Diane Ketcham, "Long Island Journal: Aces in the Air," *New York Times,* Long Island Weekly section, March 30, 1986, p. 3; Federal Aviation Administration, Statistics and Forecast, total pilots were 639,184 and female pilots, 38,032 in 1995 (telephone inquiry, February 1996).

Other Sources Consulted

"Aviation's Bloomer Girl." *FAA Aviation News* (April 1970), pp. 12-13.

"Aviator Ruth Elder, 74; Failure Brought Fame." Obituary clipping in Roosevelt Field file in the Cradle of Aviation Museum, Garden City, NY.

"Blanche Stuart Scott, 84, Dies; Made First Solo Flight in 1910." *New York Times,* January 13, 1970.

Burtnett, Gerald B. *Blue Book of Aviation,* 1932, p. 189.

Cadogan, Mary. *Women with Wings: Female Flyers in Fact and Fiction.* Chicago: Academy Chicago Publishers, 1992.

Faries, Belmont. "Aircraft Builder and First Aviatrix." *Boston Globe,* December 7, 1980.

Funk, Virginia. "Grandmother of Aviation [Elinor Smith]." *Modern Maturity,* August-September 1982.

Hodgman, Ann and Rudy Djabbaroff. *Skystars: The History of Women in Aviation.* New York: Atheneum, 1981.

Lomax, Judy. *Women of the Air.* New York: Ivy Books, 1987.

Moolman, Valerie. *Women Aloft.* Alexandria, VA: Time-Life Books, 1983.

"Pilots of the Aero Club of America Licensed Since July 1911." *Aircraft,* October 1911, p. 272.

"Ruth Elder . . . First Woman Over the Atlantic." *FAA Aviation News,* July 1968, pp. 12-13.

Stoff, Joshua. *The Aerospace Heritage of Long Island.* Interlaken, NY: Heart of the Lakes Publishing/Long Island Studies Institute, 1989.

"They Take to the Sky." *Ebony,* May 1977.

5. The Life and Times of Harriet Quimby

Henry M. Holden

Not in her wildest dreams could Harriet Quimby have imagined airplanes flying people from Los Angeles to New York in five hours, or these airliners carrying their human cargo in air-conditioned cabins, pampered with pillows, fax machines, and double martinis. Barely eighty years after her death, these things are a reality. Yet her vision went beyond that of the men in her day. She predicted the day would come when women would earn their livelihood from flying. Her vision was, to most people in Victorian America, a delusion, a fantasy, or for some, a threat.

Harriet Quimby was born a few miles southwest of Coldwater, Michigan, on a farm, on May 11, 1875,[1] but spent her adult life in California and New York. By the age of twenty-six, Quimby was working as a staff writer for the San Francisco *Dramatic Review* and later for the *Call-Bulletin & Chronicle*. In late 1902, Harriet Quimby moved to New York City. Her first freelance article appeared in the January 22, 1903 issue of *Leslie's Illustrated Weekly*. The piece, titled, "Curious Chinese Customs," convinced the editor she had talent. It also reflected her continuing curiosity with America's melting-pot culture and social issues. By 1906, Quimby was *Leslie's Illustrated Weekly*'s drama critic and editor of its "Woman's Page."

Because women were expected to marry and raise families, there were few women in the professions or in business. Harriet Quimby was one of the few women journalists whose voice called for change. She felt strongly about women's rights and individuality. Quimby believed in the emancipation of women from the Victorian lifestyle that followed them into the twentieth century. Whenever possible, her articles were filled with tips about how women could find safe and inexpensive lodging, jobs, and improve themselves.[2]

Quimby wrote on a wide range of subjects, often on the harsh social conditions and public attitudes toward the environment and social equality. An article on prostitution in New York City was so thorough in its report of the facts that the police chief was forced to resign.[3] She wrote on the immigrants and their plight on the Lower East Side of New York, and on other social issues.[4]

Quimby rang the environmental alarm in her article, "How Can We Save Our Birds," in *Leslie's Illustrated Weekly*. Wide hats were in fashion for women in 1911. The hats were platforms piled high with artificial fruit and plunder from the animal kingdom. While the ostrich suffered the embarrassment of missing tail feathers needed to decorate these platforms, actual wrens and thrushes were mounted on hats appearing with wings extended, in frozen death. The star victim of the fashion industry was the egret. This bird was easily caught while it nested on its eggs, and egret feathers became the most popular of the hat ornaments. Quimby wrote,

> I am trying to do my part in sounding a general alarm, and sending messages to about eighty million apathetic and easy-going people before it is too late. For forty years, we have been smarting under the national disgrace of the wicked slaughter of the American Bison. If something is not done, and done quickly, we will be smarting under the disgrace of having looked calmy on while our American Birds are slaughtered and gradually annihilated.[5]

Quimby urged her readers to write to their senators and congressional representatives. The government eventually did hear the pleas of concerned people like Harriet Quimby and passed laws to stop the plunder. By this time, however, it was too late for the American flamingo, passenger pigeon, and great auk, for they had already become extinct.

Harriet Quimby challenged and confronted existing norms of behavior for women and used *Leslie's Illustrated Weekly* with its circulation of 325,000 as a platform to air her opinions. Later, Quimby used the airplane as a platform to encourage woman to break with the traditional behaviors Victorian America expected of them.

In order to appreciate the strong and courageous personality of Harriet Quimby, it is necessary to put her accomplishments into perspective and describe the life women lived in the first decade of the twentieth century. Harriet Quimby was the first woman in America to earn a pilot's license, the first to make a night flight, and the first woman to pilot an airplane across the English Channel.[6]

The Wright brothers had only flown their heavier-than-air flying machine in 1903, just nine years before Harriet Quimby earned her license, and the first public demonstration of an airplane had only taken place in 1906. Harriet Quimby received her pilot's license in 1911, a full decade before Amelia Earhart became a pilot.

National suffrage for woman was a decade away when Quimby began flying. Some women were openly rebelling against the restrictive Victorian values and some were suffering society's consequences. In 1908, Kate Mulcahey was arrested in New York for smoking a cigarette in public. She had violated the Sullivan Smoking Act which prohibited "unlady-like acts in public places." The judge fined Mulcahey five dollars and sent her to jail overnight.[7] An editorial in *Leslie's Illustrated Weekly* hinted at another sign of change. It described an attempt by a major hotel to introduce a "woman's bar," in a small alcove off the main bar. The experiment apparently failed and the newspaper concluded that "women still preferred a cup of afternoon tea to something stronger." The editorial denounced the attempt by saying it was "a barometer of the times. Unfortunately, we have enough modern customs making inroads into the simplicity of life without adding a woman's bar to the list."[8]

Leslie's Illustrated Weekly sent mixed signals to women. An article titled, "Either Business or Home But Not Both," began, "Is a woman naturally unsuited for the business world and does it age her prematurely?" The writer described a doctor who claimed that women who worked on farms were "worn out by thirty-five or forty," although they worked in a healthy outdoor environment. The article concluded, "Some women are naturally suited for some business positions and would find home duties more trying. The important caution is that she should not try to fill a business position and run a home simultaneously. Such double work would be too much for any woman or even a man."[9]

Quimby loved to travel, and from what we can tell from her writing, she may have traveled unescorted. At this period in history, women did not normally travel any distance without an escort (i.e., husband or chaperone). From a trip to Cuba in 1906, Quimby wrote almost a dozen articles.[10] After this trip, Quimby became *Leslie's Illustrated Weekly*'s first travel correspondent.[11] Her job took her to Egypt, South America, Africa, and other countries. She published exotic recipes from her travels, encouraging her women readers to try new things.[12]

In the early twentieth century, the horse and carriage were still the primary method of travel, but the automobile was creating a new social class. In 1906, Harriet Quimby went to an auto race at Belmont Park, in Elmont, Long Island, and managed to convince a race driver to take her around the track in his racing car. This was her first taste of danger associated with speed and Quimby found it intoxicating. From that moment on, automobiles drew Quimby like a magnet. She penned an article from that experience, entitled "A Woman's Exciting Ride in a Motor Car."[13]

In October 1910, Harriet Quimby witnessed John Moisant fly in an air race, from Belmont Park to the Statue of Liberty and back. This was her first experience with an airplane, and Quimby decided she wanted to learn how to fly. She encouraged her friend Matilde Moisant to learn with her. Moisant's brother John was killed in an airplane accident in December 1910, but that did not dissuade either woman from her goal. With the help of Alfred Moisant, another brother who owned and operated the Moisant School of Aviation in Garden City, Long Island, the two women began taking flying lessons in the spring of 1911. Because of the contemporary social pressures, they dressed as men for their lessons. Quimby always took her lessons at sunrise since, at that time, the sessions did not interfere with her work or cause possible criticism or embarrassment for her employer. The air was usually calm and she could keep her activities a secret—or so she thought.[14] When a reporter discovered her charade, the newspapers publicized Quimby as a "willowy brunette" and "The Dresden China Aviatrix," because of her "beauty, daintiness, and haunting blue eyes."[15]

The first official acknowledgement of Quimby's flying lessons came in a May 25, 1911, article in *Leslie's Illustrated Weekly* entitled "How A Woman Learns To Fly." In a follow-up piece on June 22, 1911, titled "Exploring the Air Lanes," her editor added this preface to the article:

> Miss Quimby, the dramatic critic of *Leslie's Weekly* and editor of its Women's Page, is the first woman to manipulate a monoplane. Two years ago she became interested in the flight of buzzards and she wrote an article suggesting that in order for the aeroplane to be successful, it must be devised in imitation of the buzzard's wing and tail. She has been making a careful study of aviation and is giving the results of her interesting experience in the air exclusively in *Leslie's Illustrated Weekly*.[16]

Trousers and a man's shirt were the most practical form of clothing for a woman pilot. For most American women emerging from the Victorian era, however, these were unacceptable or immodest. The few women who had flown as passengers had "hobbled" their skirts by tying them below the knees. This, however, was uncomfortable, awkward, and dangerous. Eventually, a flying outfit would evolve for women pilots, but it would take years to gain public acceptance. The modest costume was a two-piece outfit, a blouse and wide-legged riding pants, with high-top boots, and a soft fabric helmet with goggles.

Until that flying outfit evolved, Harriet Quimby and other women who dared to fly received definite signals from the establishment on what was inappropriate dress. For centuries society severely restricted women's dress and fashions. Skirts dragged the floor and corsets contoured the female form into exaggerated hourglass shapes. Frills, ruffles, and lace also weighed down the costumes. Long flowing skirts had risen slightly in the first decade of the twentieth century, but only a few inches. A Massachusetts school department manual dictated that women, "Must not wear any dress more than two inches above the ankle."[17]

Even *Leslie's Illustrated Weekly,* Quimby's own newspaper, took a position favoring the status quo. In an editorial they commented on a sermon delivered by Bishop Nilan, in Hartford, Connecticut:

> The bishop was particularly critical, and justly so, of the vulgarity of the costumes worn by women today. The "master of fashions," said he, seems to be preparing women to take their place with man by shaping her garments so that they often closely resemble man's attire,

with the result that she disfigures her beauty and deforms her nature. Gone is the old-time womanly expression of sweetness and modesty. . . . Women, without question are exposing their figures as never before in the history of civilization. . . . It has taken advantage of the weakness of woman to accept the style as handed down with too little protest.[18]

Once Quimby began to appear in public, her original flying outfit pieced together from men's clothing was unacceptable to her critics who said she was immodest and corrupting the public's morals by wearing men's clothes. Quimby was not happy with the idea of wearing men's clothes either. Harriet Quimby acquiesced to some feminine mores but was not enslaved by them. She responded to her critics with dignity and a bit of flamboyance. "It may seem remarkable," she said, "but when I began to fly I could not find a regular aviator's suit of any description in the great city of New York. In my perplexity, it occurred to me that the president of the American Tailors' Association, Alexander Green, might be a good advisor; and he was, for it did not take him long to design a suit which no doubt will establish the aviation costume for women in this country, if not the world."[19]

The outfit was extraordinary for 1911. It was a one-piece purple satin outfit with full knickerbockers reaching below the knee, and high laced black kid boots. Her head gear resembled a monk's hood, and Quimby's accessories were flying goggles, elbow-length matching gauntlet-style driving gloves, and a long leather coat for cold weather flying. In colder weather, she wore a full length cape to match the purple outfit. "It was also an ingenious combination," she said. "It can be almost immediately converted into a conventional-appearing walking skirt when not used in the Knicker-bocker form."[20]

Quimby was not intimidated by men and tweaked an exposed nerve:

Men flyers have given the impression that aeroplaning is perilous work, something an ordinary mortal should not dream of attempting, but when I saw how easy men flyers handle their machines I said I could fly. . . . I believe women are more fearless than men, or at least I have more requests for rides from them. Many women write to inquire into the possibilities of aeroplaning as a sport, or as an occupation. It is the present high cost of the machines that prevents many women from flying. I believe that as soon as the price of a machine is within the range of the average person, flying will become a popular pastime for women.[21]

One of Harriet Quimby's greatest attributes was her courage. While on a flying tour in Mexico in 1911, Quimby decided to become the first woman to fly across the English Channel. After traveling to England with her business partner A. Leo Stevens and secretly negotiating a $5,000 fee for her exclusive story with the *London Daily Mirror*, she sailed to France where she obtained, free of charge, a seventy horsepower Bleriot monoplane. This was an airplane similar to the one Quimby had been flying but with greater engine power.

On the day of her Channel flight from Dover, England, to Calais, France, there was fog and mist. Eight decades later it may be difficult to understand the danger in the twenty-two mile flight, so we must put Harriet Quimby's accomplishment in perspective. By all the rules of flying in 1912, Quimby should not have flown. Those rules were simple. One did not fly in the fog, in the rain, or in the clouds, at night, or in more than a five mile-per-hour wind. There were no parachutes in those days, no guidance equipment, radio, or navigating charts. A flight over water, out of sight of land, was perilous. For Quimby, this was her first over-water flight. In addition, the airplane's engine was unpredictable, needing equal amounts of gasoline, prayer, and luck. Her airplane was scarcely more than a winged skeleton with no instruments, and a craft with which she was unfamiliar.

Her successful flight took one hour and six minutes, but Quimby's achievement was lost in other headlines. The night before her flight the *Titanic* had gone down in the Atlantic. Even before Quimby had left England for America, the *New York Times* wrote an editorial commenting on Quimby's feat. The editorial was no doubt influenced by the paper's opposition to the suffrage movement that was in full flower in the spring of 1912. It said,

> Exultation Is Not in Order. Even when so much public attention is on the loss of the Titanic, the fact that a woman alone, depending wholly on her own strength, skill, and courage, has driven an aeroplane across the English Channel, does not pass unnoticed.
>
> Miss Quimby's flight is a considerable achievement. Just a few months ago this same flight was one of the most daring and in every way remarkable deeds accomplished by man. Since then the passage has been repeated by men, and now for them there is little or no glory. The flight is now hardly anything more than proof of ordinary professional competency.

The *Times* warned condescendingly, "The feminists should be somewhat cautious about exulting over Miss Quimby's exploit. They should not call it a great achievement, lest by so doing they invite the dreadful humiliating qualification, great for a woman."[22]

The smell of these sour grapes still lingered when Quimby's steamship docked in New York, on May 12, 1912. She received no hero's welcome, and there was no ticker-tape parade. It was a matter of timing. One week earlier, 15,000 women and 600 men marched up Fifth Avenue in support of women's suffrage.[23] The male leaders of the city had not yet recovered from this demonstration of women's assertiveness, and they were not ready to admit there existed female eagles, let alone honor them.

Quimby never validated her critics, and she was not one to let an anonymous editor have the last word. "I wish I could express my views on this," she wrote. "It's not a fad, and I did not want to be the first American woman to fly just to make myself conspicuous. I just want to be first, that's all, and I am honestly delighted. I have written so much about other people, you can't imagine how I enjoy sitting back and reading about myself for once. I think that's excusable in me."[24]

To fly across the twenty-two mile English Channel in 1912 required extraordinary courage, skill, and self-confidence. Quimby, however, played down her success. "The trip was as easy as sitting at home in an arm chair, and I never had any doubt of my success. Any woman with sufficient self-confidence and a cool head could fly across the Channel as easily as I did. Within months, probably weeks some other woman probably will make the same flight or even achieve some greater undertaking."[25]

On July 1, 1912, Harriet Quimby died in an airplane accident in Boston. Her critics blamed the accident on the fact that she was a woman and unfit to fly. We know today that it was the defective aerodynamic design of her airplane that caused the accident, and not gender or a lack of skill. In 1991, Harriet Quimby was honored by the United States Postal Service on a fifty cent air mail stamp. She was only the third woman aviator to be so honored.

Harriet Quimby's greatest attribute was her vision. She predicted, "The airplane should open a fruitful occupation for women. I see no reason they cannot realize handsome incomes by carrying passengers between adjacent towns, from parcel delivery, taking photographs or conducting schools of flying."[26] Quimby's spirit was no doubt angered by the editorials criticizing her judgement, her "invasion" of the private fraternity of male aviation, and her skill. More than eighty years later, time has vindicated her. Today women fly for the major airlines, work as aerial photographers, and there are thousands of women working as flight instructors. If Quimby were here today, she would smile and point upward to women flying military jets and commercial airliners and say, "See, I told you so!"[27]

Notes

1. *Congressional Record,* June 4, 1987.

2. Harriet Quimby, "Protection and Comfort for American Girl Students in Paris," *Leslie's Illustrated Weekly,* August 15, 1907, p. 150.

3. Harriet Quimby, "How White Slaves Are Shackled," *Leslie's Illustrated Weekly,* June 15, 1911, p. 674.

4. Harriet Quimby, "How Immigrant Girls Are Protected in New York," *Leslie's Illustrated Weekly*, May 24, 1906, p. 508; "Home and the Household—Teaching Self-respect to Children," *Leslie's Illustrated Weekly,* June 29, 1904, p. 616.

5. Harriet Quimby, "How Can We Save Our Birds," *Leslie's Illustrated Weekly,* June 8, 1911, p. 647.

6. Aero Club of America letter dated August 1, 1911; *New York Times,* September 5, 1911. The English Channel trip was on April 16, 1912.

7. *Chronicle of the 20th Century* (Mt. Kisco, NY: Chronicle Publications, 1982), p. 87.

8. Editorial, *Leslie's Illustrated Weekly*, May 25, 1911, p. 617.

9. Minna Ivey, "Call to the Sky," *Leslie's Illustrated Weekly*, October 5, 1911.

10. Harriet Quimby, "First Impressions of Havana—The World's Gayest City," *Leslie's Illustrated Weekly,* May 17, 1906, p. 478.

11. As reported in *Leslie's Illustrated Weekly,* May 17, 1906, p. 488.

12. Harriet Quimby, "No Old Maids, but Plenty of Divorces in Egypt," *Leslie's Illustrated Weekly,* September 5, 1907, p. 222.

13. Harriet Quimby, "A Woman's Exciting Ride in a Motor Car," *Leslie's Illustrated Weekly*, October 4, 1906, p. 328.

14. Harriet Quimby, "How A Woman Learns To Fly," *Leslie's Illustrated Weekly,* May 25, 1911, p. 602.

15. *New York Times,* various issues June-July 1911.

16. Harriet Quimby, "How A Woman Learns to Fly," *Leslie's Illustrated Weekly,* May 25, 1911, p. 602; Harriet Quimby, "Exploring the Air Lanes," *Leslie's Illustrated Weekly*, June 22, 1911, p. 703.

17. Nancy Zerfoss, "Schoolmarm to School Ms." *Changing Education,* Summer 1974, p. 23.

18. Editorial, *Leslie's Illustrated Weekly,* October 5, 1911.

19. Harriet Quimby, "How A Woman Learns to Fly," *Leslie's Illustrated Weekly,* May 25, 1911, p. 602.

20. Ibid.

21. Ibid.

22. *New York Times*, April 18, 1912.

23. *New York Times*, May 5, 1912.

24. George Weston, "Beauty and the Bleriot," *Aviation Quarterly* 6, no. 1, 1980.

25. Ibid.

26. *Good Housekeeping Magazine,* September 1912.

27. Readers seeking additional information on Quimby can consult biographies by Henry M. Holden and Ed Y. Hall, as well as the *Harriet Quimby Research Conference Journal,* 1995-date (P.O. Box 46, Woodland Hills, CA 91365), and www.aircruise.com/aca/quimby. (Editor's note.)

6. "One of Ours": The World of Jeannette Edwards Rattray

Lucinda A. Mayo

East Hampton was settled a long time ago
By some Mulfords and Strattons, a Talmage or so;
A Hand and a Barns and a Rose came here too—
And other names strange now to me and to you.

—Jeannette Edwards Rattray, "Old East Hampton"[1]

It was typical of East Hampton's Jeannette Edwards Rattray (1893-1974) that she would be humble even in occasional verse, but it was unlikely that *any* old East Hampton, Long Island name was "strange" to her. Like other members of Amagansett and East Hampton's founding families, she was closely related to most of the others. Her given name, Jeannette Frances, represents four early East End bloodlines, from her grandmother, Phebe Jeannette Huntting, and great-grandmother, Frances Baker Hedges Osborn.[2] The culmination of one thread of her life as a writer was *East Hampton History* where she polished and documented the work of several generations of amateur historians, and brought together the Town Clerk's Records she had edited with reminiscences and accounts from families all over town and up and down Long Island. It is a notable accomplishment; she simply wrote it to show that the town "is part of our very blood and bones. We have an obligation to it, just the same kind of obligation we owe our parents."[3] Moreover, she quotes Edith Hamilton, "Our word 'idiot' comes from *idiotes,* the name given by the ancient Greeks to those who did not participate in the affairs of the community."[4]

But Jeannette Rattray produced a dozen other books and monographs and she contributed to countless improvements to the town. Even her weekly column, "Looking Them Over," which she missed very rarely during her fifty years on the *East Hampton Star,* was less remarkable to her than they are to us who cannot imagine some of the challenges she faced during those fifty years of dedication. When she wrote the biography of her uncle, Dr. David Edward, she mentioned that his illustrious half-century career was similar to the three East Hampton Presbyterian ministers whose careers evenly divided 150 years of local history.[5]

In her column, she favored stories that were lively.[6] Many were accounts of her fishermen or whaler ancestors.[7]

> The Schellingers, Lopers and Edwardses vowed
> To capture the whales while other men plowed;
> When whaling on vessels the world o'er began
> Each East Hampton Family yielded its man.[8]

Her father, Everett (Ev) Joshua Edwards (1871–1950) relayed the story of her grandfather and uncle capturing the last right whale on the eastern seaboard in 1907. (Everett was on his own boat in the chase, during which Josh and Gabe took the whale whose skeleton is in the American Museum of Natural History.) "Cap'n Ev" said he came ashore in 1930 when the fishing turned poor. Since he still fished "for the table" while pursuing several successful careers on land, the story of *Whale Off!* which Edwards co-authored with his daughter, represented a lifetime's knowledge of the Atlantic.[9]

Her son Everett described her longevity, dedication, fascination with language lore, civic-mindedness, and an attitude that viewed life as an adventure, as "a good way to live a life."[10] She herself thought an autobiography superfluous. "East Hampton people who read our paper know every move I make."[11] In the twenty years since her death and the ten years since her last column was reprinted in the *Star*'s centennial edition, we may need her son David to remind us of some of her most remarkable adventures:

> My mother died in her bed
> one balmy night in May 1974;
> my hair wasn't yet gray.
> At the head of the bed
> was a red-framed print
> of the Summer Palace near Peking
> in salmon pink and tea green
> over a lake with a little steam launch
> and a bridge
> to an island in the foreground.
> She'd been there as a girl
> and for 50 years after
> dreamt of it
> only to awake
> in tears at not returning
> to the summer palace of youth.[12]

While talks with friends of her later years,[13] and a rereading of her work lead us to wonder how many tears she actually shed over lost youth, it would be a shame for East End history not to consider her travel to Peking—and to Constantinople, Connemara, Chianti, and many points in between.

Without her travels, she would never have been a newspaperwoman. Her first *Star* columns were a series of reprinted letters to her parents, and she financed subsequent trips by some resourceful marketing of her writings.

Without her travels, she would not have founded the *Star* dynasty which continues today, for Jeannette Edwards met Arnold Rattray on board the *President Pierce* out of San Francisco bound for the Far East. Without her travels, she would not have discovered what she wanted to "do with her life." To neglect the story of her travels would deprive us of an understanding of the East End's place in a wide social and geographic history.

In 1893, when Jeannette Edwards was born on "the road from the windmill to the ocean" (now Atlantic Avenue)[14] in Amagansett, it was just fifty years since Mercator Cooper had outfitted his whaling ship at Nathaniel Hand's Amagansett store for a voyage that would include a brief, unplanned landing on the "forbidden shores" of Japan, and since Margaret Gardiner and her family had taken the "Grand Tour" of Europe.[15] The long-vigorous whale trade, both deep sea and shore, was winding down; however, many residents still prospered on their shares of shipping, and the hamlet was very much a part of turn-of-the-century America, and of the world.

Amagansett's Frank M. Griffing, a carpenter, had recently mortgaged his house to go to the Columbian exposition in Chicago, and it was not long since Edwards's mother, Florence Huntting Edwards, had been visiting Roman ruins in Europe.[16] The country was in an economic depression, and when the Cherokee Strip opened, one hundred thousand people made a run for land. Gas stoves appeared in the United States; John D. Rockefeller controlled most of the nation's oil; Henry Ford was building his first automobile prototype in his spare time, but Jeremiah Baker, who had been to the California gold fields years before, was still running a stage line from Amagansett to Sag Harbor; Hawaii's Queen Lilluokalani had just been deposed; New Zealand became the first country to give women the vote; Ireland was fighting an active but uphill battle for Home Rule; and the Associated and United Press wire services had just been founded.[17] All of these events would in one way or another be a part of the town's, and "Nettie" Edwards's, future life.

For many of the waves of "city folk" who have visited East Hampton town or to those who have heard of life in the Hamptons from afar, it may seem that the locals spend dull winters or muse that "any place but this / is where love is and where / life will truly begin."[18] That myth of insularity[19] has never been the case, as Carleton Kelsey, emeritus Town Historian, tells anyone who asks. Locals know that love for family and friends, for the seasons of land and sea began here close to four hundred years ago. Many still believe with Jeannette Rattray that:

> it must be terribly hard to be uprooted. From a country—from a town, if you have once put down roots. That's one trouble with the world today, perhaps—there is too much moving about; nothing is permanent. Transients are irresponsible. . . . We must not let East Hampton

change too rapidly. We who have known it always appreciate its
permanence all the more, for occasional absences.[20]

Rattray's travels, though extensive, were sufficiently "occasional" to avoid
that "feeling of loneliness which overtakes country [people] in a city; the
feeling of being unrelated to anything, of not mattering to anybody."[21]

A visiting onlooker could say in 1883: "wonderfully numerous and
varied are the 'characters' of the village; and this adds largely to its aesthetic
value,"[22] but for residents, the value of accepting and being accepted by the
town's "characters" has deeper value. It is no accident that when she began
officially to write a column for the *East Hampton Star* in 1923, Jeannette
Edwards adopted the title of Willa Cather's Pulitzer Prize-winning novel,
One of Ours, as her byline. The novel shows an affection for the foibles of
the community and a respect for its elder members; it celebrates reading and
a love of language and literature shared with women; it reflects a deep love
of countryside. Nature at home is close and evokes distant and wonderful
places; the writing is a mix of homely and sublime. Cather's hero:

> never thought of the sun as coming from distant lands, or as having
> taken part in human life in other ages. To him, the sun rotated about
> the wheatfields. But the moon, somehow, came out of the historic past,
> and made him think of Egypt and the Pharaohs, Babylon and the
> hanging gardens. She seemed particularly to have looked down upon
> the follies and disappointments of men; into the slaves' quarters of old
> times, into prison windows, and into fortresses where captives lan-
> guished.[23]

What Rattray, her mother, and her aunt Minnie Huntting read[24] was not the
"over furnished" parlor literature of the day, but work that dealt with nature
and human detail, "the beauty of the world and its capacity to disappoint,"[25]
and it informed her own writing.

> The wild geese flying over in a V against the moon, and their lonesome
> honking over by Hook Pond in the early spring; the peepers' sleigh-
> bells ringing from the swamp "down Egypt" [part of East Hampton
> village]; the first fragrant arbutus hidden away under the dead leaves
> at Northwest; the salty smell of the ocean and the roar of waves when
> the wind is east—all these mean East Hampton and home. There is the
> special inflection in local expressions, such as "Yes, yes!" and "You
> said it!" There are the old-time nautical terms still in every day use
> here. People say "All clear astern?" when backing out of a parking
> place.[26]

The reviewer Lloyd Becker called her prose "essential events alive in their
own primary language," and compared Jeannette Rattray to Walt Whitman
and to the avant-garde poet Charles Olson.[27] As "One of Ours," Rattray left
herself open to interpretation. Taking her to task as a historian, T. H. Breen

complained recently: "Rattray might have found a way to open up the past, to make it a vital element in shaping the future. She had an opportunity to reinterpret the story—to give it new meanings—and thereby to save local myth from ossification. Instead, Rattray retreated into the safe and familiar world of genealogy."[28]

Rattray would say in the face of such a reading that we must go about our work and develop a thick skin. She didn't "retreat" by any means; while genealogy was a lifelong interest, as it is unavoidably—or irresistably—for most with early East End roots, her *East Hampton History* was ultimately published to finance an addition to the public library. Because her view of her town included global reference points, and her sense that East Hampton had "a special duty to perform—to keep alive an understanding of the foundations on which our America was built,"[29] *East Hampton History* is far from naive, and the mandate is far from ossified.

Her own first "occasional absence" happened thus: "A few days ago a cable message was received by Miss Nettie Edwards, from her brother, Lieut. Clifford Edwards, U.S.N., who has been stationed at Constantinople . . . asking her to join him there, if prepared for a six months' stay. Miss Edwards at once made application for a passport, and will sail for Turkey next Wednesday."[30] Passports were required beginning in 1918 as one of many controls on United States entrances, and exits.[31] Her real preparations for six months away had been much slower. One of seven graduates of East Hampton High School in 1910,[32] she was sent by her mother, who "didn't know what to do with her," to the National Park Seminary near Washington, D.C. where Rattray later wrote she learned absolutely nothing.[33] There she met at least one other future world-traveler, her "house mother" who turned up in Cairo when she was there.[34]

After completing "finishing school," Jeannette Edwards joined her friend Amy Osborn, who was already working as a librarian in Manhattan in a training program which Columbia University ran in conjunction with the New York Public Library.[35] At the end of a year, during which she enjoyed exchanges at the circulation desk and abhorred the behind-the-scenes clerical work, she was told she would never be a "professional." She immediately enrolled in the Pratt Institute of Kindergarten Training in Brooklyn. When she returned to East Hampton with her certificate and two years teaching experience, she founded a private kindergarten. A Mothers Club petition to have it made part of the public school system was successful. It was a measure of the power of women's organizations in the nation at the time and in East Hampton almost always. Edwards taught professionally "just for a year," she later wrote, "but it proved a point."[36]

Next to the announcement of her sailing on the Greek liner *King Alexander* is an advertisement for the local photographer with the motto "We can

Fig. 6.1. Jeannette Edwards in Egypt, 1922. Photograph courtesy of photographic archives, *East Hampton Star.*

live without Photographs. But not so well."[37] It *is* a good thing we have a picture of Nettie Edwards meticulously dressed and wearing a fashionable cloche at the Pyramids (see fig. 6.1). She wrote, "I looked as much at home on that camel as if I had done it all my life, and I felt so; it's a good way to jog along and meditate." She would have expected us to picture her thus in 1922, but reading today, we would expect her to appear a bit more disheveled:

> We have been out in the broiling sun all day, crossed the Nile in a boat then mounted donkeys and rode twelve miles. I have always heard so much about donkeys being sure footed but the one I had certainly belied that statement; twice it fell down with me, flat on its shoulder sending me flying over its head. Once I rolled down a bank, once in the foot deep dust of the road. You can imagine the temper I was in.[38]

An inadvertent irony in the *Star* is the appearance of a wire service article entitled "City of Squalor: Filth and Vice Chief Characteristics of Constantinople," between the local daughter's first and second missives from that very locale.

> A verminous, villanous multitude of every nation under heaven passes continually up and down these streets, squabbling eternally. Women of all nationalities, united only by the common bond of universal vice and universal disease, lurk in their thievish corners.[39]

This is probably *not* why Edwards' excerpted letters fail to discuss Constantinople.[40] She was city-wiser than the wire-service writer, and she travelled with Europeans and Americans from her brother's circle, on compelling—but relatively safe—side trips. She had selected "Byzantium" as a base for adventure, and it whet her travel appetite. In Egypt and Israel with the family of a Standard Oil man, she listened intently to their accounts of travel in China, and determined her next destination. When she and Clifford returned to the States in 1922, we can see wanderlust in her now regular *Star* writings. "Norman Barns skipped out of church with a pretty frisky gait for a Presbyterian trustee, Sunday. Why is he feeling thus? He is going abroad."[41] Interviewing British writer P. G. Wodehouse, she must have mentioned her plan to see China, for he wrote her, "Did I dare to say last week that life held no thrill for me? Did I go round with a world-weary air and assert that nothing short of a trip to China could produce the least bit of a kick?"[42]

Her wish for another "sea change" was nothing strange. Through most of the East End's history, water travel was swifter than passage overland. (A late seventeenth-century traveler "gives us a picture of Long Island with the Sound eliminated, so far as a barrier to travel is concerned.")[43] The local economy made sea travel more usual as well. Local stories contributed an appreciation as well as a healthy respect for the sea as a force in history and upon individual lives. Rattray's grandfather, Joshua Bennett Edwards, was on a whaling ship which narrowly escaped the *Shenandoah,* a Confederate raider, in the Bering Sea. The *Shenandoah* had captured thirty-eight vessels in her career, thirty of them whalers, so the story was not hyperbolic.[44] Rattray would have known, as part of her "blood and bones" grasp of history, that rebel privateers, the sinking of the "stone fleet" in Charleston harbor, the onerous expense of outfitting voyages, and the growing use of kerosene were all reasons for whaling's demise.[45]

She would also know that travel to far-off destinations had become popular with Americans almost as soon as the Civil War ended. England's Thomas Cook made itineraries as dependable as moderately affluent travelers could want, and the distinction was soon made between the purposeful and misguided.

> The genuine traveler will pride himself on not being mistaken for a tourist, will eschew the packaged tour, make an effort to see places off the beaten track, actually attempt to communicate with the natives, or residents, and will refuse to swallow the old bromides developed to characterize every country, city and monument. Instead, the real traveler will seek personal discoveries in every unfamiliar place or custom.[46]

No Pacific "cruise" existed until Hollywood movie stars began taking junkets in 1927, but independent travel on ships such as American Dollar Line's *President* fleet was remarkably popular; even the Depression didn't affect their business.[47] Perhaps such demand was what priced the San Francisco-Shanghai trip at a mere $365. When Edwards decided in the summer of 1924, to accompany her friend Margaret Arnold to join her businessman husband in China, her father told her that the trip was fine as long as she paid for it herself. The trip seemed out of reach; she was making only five dollars a column for the *Star*. Edwards quickly lined up work as an East End "stringer" and social correspondent for six Manhattan and three Brooklyn newspapers, and by November 6, she was sailing for the Orient.[48]

Docking in Honolulu, Edwards was greeted with a flower garland by East Hampton's Catharine Mulford who was working as a public librarian there.[49] The appearance of fellow East Hamptonites all over the world is one of the most remarkable features of her columns. Another time, in a tiny Irish village, she commented on how strange it was that she hadn't seen anyone from "home" that day.[50] After many serendipitous reunions in odd places over the years, it doesn't sound ingenuous.

She was always "at home" on the water. Near Japan, a voice at the rail intoned, "We're six miles from land—straight down! This is the deepest spot in the Pacific, so far as any survey has determined. The Black Hole of Japan, graveyard of all ships! We're going to see some nasty weather before long!" Edwards wrote: "Well, I just laughed."[51]

Adapting to dry land did vex her at times. After "seasoned" Shanghai travelers told her how easy it would be to get around, she snapped, "Oh, quite! Try getting lost. No policeman understands a word you ask him," but she quickly developed a sharp eye and ear. One day she turned a corner and ran into a wedding party:

But that's no new sight any more, . . . you see either a funeral procession or a wedding every time you go out. . . . The only way you can tell them apart is that in a funeral some of the paraders usually wear white, . . . and several people carry food for the departed to eat. And the music is apt to be livelier at the funeral. The Chinese love our brass bands, they use them for all occasions. And at a funeral two of the favorites are "I Wonder Who's Kissing Her Now," and "Over There."[52]

Fig. 6.2. Jeannette Edwards in Manila, 1925. Photograph courtesy of photographic archives, *East Hampton Star*.

After the page one headline, "Miss Edwards is now located at Shanghai, China, where a revolution is in progress," her letter wasn't exactly reassuring: "One American here had to bury five dead Chinese soldiers with his own hands, after appealing vainly to the authorities to take them out of his garden. Mr. B, principal of the American school, was at tea when a bullet whizzed across his tea table. I have been under fire. Yet business goes on as usual, the children go to school, what's the use of worrying?"[53]

While she disparaged her journalistic accomplishments, she covered a variety of news for the *China Press,* and sent columns back to East Hampton, and to the *Brooklyn Daily Eagle.* Later, she moved to Peking, which lies at the same latitude as East Hampton,[54] where she met more hometown friends. In Manila for several months, she wrote for the *Daily Bulletin.* Her *Star* letters were full of sights, sounds, and flavors; some of her contemporaries still remember her evocative worldwide menus which were often signals for her to recall meals and times at home: "she told off on her fingers the many ingredients, but . . . there were things she did not name: the fragrance of old friendships, the glow of early memories, belief in wonder-working rhymes and songs."[55]

When Edwards privately wrote of her intention to marry, her father naturally insisted that she bring Arnold Rattray home for inspection. They arrived in East Hampton in time to wed on Christmas evening, 1925. In its announcement, the *Star* mentioned that the couple planned to settle in the American West, but Montauk, the would-be Miami of the North, was experiencing such prosperity that the publisher hired the couple to start a news agency expressly for the resort. Arnold, warmly accepted by East Hampton, also ran a small travel agency. Jeannette continued to write "Looking Them Over" every week.

In 1935, the couple were able to buy the *Star.* Her husband didn't believe "the boss' wife" should work in the office, so Rattray set up a busy "agency" at home. While they often

Fig. 6.3. Jeannette Edwards Rattray on the dock in Havana, 1940s. Photograph courtesy of photographic archives, *East Hampton Star.*

socialized in New York, and traveled briefly, their life was proscribed by the week in, week out newspaper schedule.[56] By the time son Everett became the *Star*'s editor in 1958, Arnold had died of a chronic heart ailment. Having run the paper singlehandedly for most of four years, Rattray was ready to explore the world again. With her friends Dr. George and Elise Fish, she took rambling trips through Europe that were arranged around international medical conventions. Her letters were lively as ever with East Hampton reminders everywhere, from Welsh graveyards to luxe Florentine ball-rooms.[57]

Musing at home, she was well aware of her own quirks, including fun with the editorial "we ." "We are free to speak our mind, such as it is," she wrote, but also, "we need not say all we know."[58] Along with her own sometimes circumspect look at weekly goings-on, her columns were filled with what *Star* readers wrote of their own travels, with informal interviews, and with distillations of local lectures. She often joked that she got others to do the work of "Looking Them Over." Residents constantly stopped her on the street with news, welcoming her home, or wishing her *bon voyage*.

In the columns of the 1960s and 1970s, she would ruefully predict that she would never go abroad again, so immersed was she in translating her well-reciprocated love of East Hampton into ambitious projects for the Library, for the Ladies' Village Improvement Society, and for Guild Hall, but then there would be a Cardiff or Milan dateline. As she neared eighty, her health declined; however, even from hospital rooms she wrote her worldly column for the Main Street newspaper until "one balmy night in May" 1974, she died at home on Edwards Lane.

Someday, perhaps, there will be an anthology of her travel writing. In the meantime, all of our travels from the East End to actual or vicarious distant climes and to our distinctive past, have been enriched by "One of Ours."

Notes

1. Jeannette Edwards Rattray, "Old East Hampton," sung to the tune of "The Daring Young Man on the Flying Trapeze," manuscript in the Pennypacker Collection of the East Hampton Public Library, and as noted in the *East Hampton Star,* November 1, 1934. She wrote this song for a meeting of the "Ramblers," which is a women's reading and cultural (and "travelogue") group, founded in 1902 by Florence Huntting Edwards, among others. See also, Hugh R. King, "The Ramblers," in the *East Hampton Independent,* August 23, 1995, p. 16.

2. Jeannette Edwards Rattray, *East Hampton History: Including Genealogies of Early Families* (East Hampton: [East Hampton Public Library], 1953), p. 308. This essay uses her maiden name, Edwards, in references before she was married in December 1925, and Rattray after that time.

3. Irene Silverman, "Jeannette Edwards Rattray: A Life of Serenity," *East Hampton Star 100th Anniversary Edition,* December 26, 1985, pp. 4, 17.

4. Jeannette Rattray, "Looking Them Over," *East Hampton Star,* November 16, 1967, sec. 2, p. 3.

5. Jeannette Rattray, "Fifty Years A Doctor: David Edwards," private typescript, probably prepared for the "Ramblers," dated December 16, 1951, p. 1, East Hampton Public Library.

6. Jeannette Rattray, "Looking Them Over," *East Hampton Star,* December 15, 1966, p. 2. For particularly daring seafaring types, she liked the old word, "rank." She was pleased that it and ten or so other local usages were included in research for the *American Heritage Dictionary,* for which her son, David, was an editor.

7. Everett Joshua Edwards and Jeannette Edwards Rattray, *Whale Off* (New York: Frederick Stokes Co., 1932), p. 132. (On the Edwards family, see also "Sand, Surf & Steel," *Newsday,* December 14, 1997, Sec. G, 1, 8-9, 11-12. Editor's note.)

8. J. Rattray, "Old East Hampton," p. 2.

9. Berton Roueche, "Shore Whaler" in the *New Yorker,* September 24, 1949, p. 3; Edwards and Rattray, *Whale Off.*

10. Everett Rattray, "The Fifth Column." *East Hampton Star,* May 25, 1975, sec. 2, p. 1.

11. Jeannette Rattray, "One of Ours," *East Hampton Star,* December 26, 1985, p. 17.

12. David Greig Rattray, "A Red-framed print of the Summer Palace," from *Opening the Eyelid* (Brooklyn: Diwan Press, 1990), p. 4. Poem copyright Carolyn Rattray 1997, and reprinted with her permission.

13. Interviews with Madeline Edwards Potter (October 24, 1995), Mrs. Elise Fish (October 27 and November 10, 1995); telephone conversations with Mrs. Condie Lamb and Enez Whipple (November 10, 1995).

14. Interview with Carleton Kelsey, November 27, 1995.

15. Louise Munsell Field, et al., eds. *Amagansett Lore and Legend* (Amagansett: Amagansett Village Improvement Society, 1948), p. 39; Sarah Tyler Gardiner, *Margaret Gardiner: Leaves from a Young Girl's Diary* (New Haven: Tuttle, Morehouse and Taylor, 1927), p. 6.

16. Interview with Carleton Kelsey, November 10, 1995; Jeannette Rattray, "Looking Them Over," *East Hampton Star,* November 26, 1970, p. II-5.

17. Allan S. Kullen, *The Peopling of America: A Timeline of Events that Helped Shape Our Nation* (Beltsville, MD: Americans All, 1994), pp. 250-60; Judith S. Levey and Agnes Greenhall, eds. *The Concise Columbia Encyclopedia* (New York: Avon Books, 1983), p. 595.

18. Michael Hogan, *Making Our Own Rules* (Greenfield Center, NY: Greenfield Review Press, 1989), p. 38.

19. T. H. Breen, *Imagining the Past* (New York: Addison-Wesley, 1989), p. 63.

20. Jeannette Rattray, "Looking them Over," *East Hampton Star,* November 30, 1967, sec. 2, p. 5.

21. Willa Cather, *One of Ours,* 1922 (Reprint, New York: Random House, 1950), p. 99.

22. Charles Burr Todd, "The American Barbizon," *Lippincott's Magazine,* April 1883, p. 324.

23. Cather, *One of Ours,* p. 170.

24. She grew up surrounded by the complete works of Dickens, Thackeray, Meredith, and other Victorians; by middle life she had also made herself at home with Cervantes, Smollett, Fielding, Richardson, Flaubert, Turgenev, Tolstoy, and Proust, who became a special favorite. Irene Silverman, "Jeannette Edwards Rattray: A Life of Serenity," *East Hampton Star 100th Anniversary Edition,* December 26, 1985, p. 4.

25. Willa Cather, "The Novel Démeublé," in *Willa Cather on Writing* (Lincoln: University of Nebraska Press, 1988), p. 35; Joan Acocella, "Cather and the Academy," *The New Yorker,* November 27, 1995, p. 61.

26. J. Rattray, *East Hampton History,* p. 3.

27. Lloyd Becker, "Two Local Studies," *Street Magazine,* 2, no. 2 (1976): 42.

28. Breen, *Imagining the Past,* p. 56.

29. J. Rattray, *East Hampton History,* p. 5.

30. *East Hampton Star,* September 9, 1921, p. 8.

31. Kullen, *The Peopling of America,* p. 286.

32. East Hampton Board of Education, *Student Manual, 1928-29,* pp. 27-28.

33. Jeannette Rattray, "One of Ours," in *East Hampton Star 100th Anniversary Edition,* December 26, 1985, p. 17. Rattray would also say she "cared for nothing but dancing," but this is the short form of what would be fascinating further research. Reading the *Star* from 1910-1920s side-by-side with Frederick Lewis Allen's *Only Yesterday* (New York: Harper & Row, 1931) and between the lines of the *Star* columns which serve as Jeannette Rattray's informal biography, the direct reflection of social flux and "firsts" after World War I is uncanny. Her world after graduation provided a range of causes and distractions that might have been unsettling to her mother.

34. Jeannette Edwards, "An East Hampton Girl in Egypt," *East Hampton Star,* October 21, 1921, p. 1.

35. Recollection of Mrs. Amy O. Bassford's son from Dorothy King, librarian (Long Island Collection, East Hampton Public Library), November 22, 1995.

36. Jeannette Rattray, "One of Ours." *East Hampton Star,* December 26, 1985, p. 17. She was a daughter of her age; a few years later, a city in Arkansas elected not only a woman mayor but an all-woman city council. Two years later, all resigned, saying they'd proven that women were as capable at government as men (Kullen, *Peopling of America,* p. 287).

37. *East Hampton Star,* September 9, 1921, p. 7.

38. Jeannette Edwards, "East Hampton Girl in Egypt," *East Hampton Star,* October 21, 1921, p. 1.

39. *East Hampton Star,* January 13, 1921, p. 8. She also wrote "Every second shop . . . is a so-called 'Bier-haus'; where the more fortunate sailor is merely drugged, robbed of all he possess and flung out onto the street to be picked up by the patrol. The less fortunate is not flung out and is never heard of again."

40. Constantinople's name would revert to the old Greek for "of the city" *(eis ten polin)* or Istanbul, in 1930, *Encyclopedia Britannica,* 15th ed., 22 (1993): 148.

41. Jeannette Edwards, "Looking Them Over," *East Hampton Star,* October 5, 1923, p. 3.

42. Jeannette Edwards, "Looking Them Over," *East Hampton Star,* July 27, 1923, p. 8.

43. Ettie C. Hedges, "Colonial Travelers on Long Island," in Welby E. Boughton, *Colonial History of Long Island* (East Hampton: The Star Press, 1933), p. 6.

44. Berton Roueché, quoting Capt. Everett Edwards in "Shore Whaler," *The New Yorker,* September 24, 1949, p. 44; Ivan Musicant, *Divided Waters: The Naval History of the Civil War* (New York: Harper Collins Publishers, 1995), pp. 364.

45. Interview, Carleton Kelsey, November 22, 1995.

46. Harold Darling, *Bon Voyage! Souvenirs from the Golden Age of Travel* (New York: Abbeville Press, 1990), p. 2.

47. Charles Owen, *The Grand Days of Travel* (Exeter: Webb & Bower, 1979), pp. 56-69.

48. Jeannette Rattray, "One of Ours," *East Hampton Star,* December 26, 1985, p. 17.

49. "C. Mulford, 91," obituary, *East Hampton Star,* May 31, 1974, sec. 1, p. 2. "Kate" Mulford was brother Clifford's sister-in-law; later, she had a long career as a librarian in Tacoma, Washington. She returned to East Hampton after her retirement.

50. Jeannette Rattray, "Looking Them Over." *East Hampton Star,* June 12, 1969, sec. 2, p. 4.

51. Jeannette Edwards, "Looking Them Over," *East Hampton Star,* January 2, 1925, p. 3. In her January 30 column (p. 5) that year, a "little friend" back in East Hampton is reported as having said as she departed, "I know where you're going. To China, and you're going to get into a war!" Almost fifty years later, "One of Ours" notes that "the *Star*'s editor" (her son, Everett) warned as she left for Europe, "You'll probably wind up in Jordon. Then you'll have something to write about" (October 22, 1970, sec. 2, p. 1). We hear a "Well, I just laughed," between those lines, too.

52. Jeannette Edwards, "Looking Them Over," *East Hampton Star,* January 23, 1925, p. 8.

53. Jeannette Edwards, "Looking Them Over," *East Hampton Star,* January 26, 1925, p. 1.

54. Everett T. Rattray, *The South Fork: The Land and the People of Eastern Long Island.* (New York: Random House, 1979), p. 168.

55. Cather, *One of Ours,* p. 38.

56. Irene Silverman, "Jeannette Edwards Rattray: A Life of Serenity," *East Hampton Star 100th Anniversary Edition,* December 26, 1985, p. 17.

57. She often had assignments from her friend Craig Claiborne to investigate restaurants, so she even had an excuse for the occasional culinary rhapsody. (Interview with Mrs. Elise Fish, October 27, 1995.)

58. *Newsday,* May 23, 1974, p. 92.

7. Women's Lives at the William Floyd Estate and the Poosepatuck Indian Reservation, 1800–Present

Bernice Forrest Guillaume

The William Floyd Estate or plantation and the Poosepatuck (Unkechaug Nation) Indian Reservation form socioeconomic extremes in close proximity to one another in Mastic, New York. Encompassing 631 acres and located on the peninsula known as Mastic Neck on Long Island's southcentral coast, the Floyd domain was carved from traditional Unkechaug territory between the seventeenth and nineteenth centuries. The estate and the reservation personify the exploitative nature of Anglo-American relations with Native Americans in southeastern New England from the colonial age to the twentieth century. A July 1700 deed allotted a total of 225 non-contiguous acres on Mastic Neck to the Unkechaugs, including the village called *Poosepatuck*. By the late nineteenth century, Unkechaug land "shrank" to fifty-two acres and was confined to the reservation.[1]

An essential element in this association is the connection between the women of the Floyd family and those of Poosepatuck.[2] Since Poosepatuck women served as free and unfree laborers on the estate, the link between Native women and their Floyd counterparts ostensibly demonstrates segregation's imbalanced interdependence.[3] However, a closer investigation of Poosepatuck females indicates that they resisted patterns of Euro-American domination. And despite extensive intermarriage with the European and African communities, the Poosepatucks have consistently persisted as a Native people.

Poosepatuck women have played a significant role in maintaining an Indian consciousness. This has been accomplished within three concentric spheres. First, Poosepatuck females function as trustees and transmitters of Algonquian culture. Second, they gravitated toward self-sufficiency within a subsistence economy. Third, Poosepatuck women participate and often lead efforts to retain and upgrade tribal land. Poosepatuck women appear in the capacities they have traditionally occupied through the centuries at Mastic—as *sunksquaws* or female tribal leaders, traders, negotiators of land transfers, agricultural specialists, and so on. In these roles Poosepatuck females parallel other eastern seaboard Algonquian social structures and force conscientious observers to acknowledge that skin color or biological inheritance is not tantamount to culture.[4]

A Woman's World at the William Floyd Estate: An Overview

From its inception the estate housed females of Floyd descent.[5] As guardians of the patrician status quo, Floyd women adhered to acceptable spheres of female activity such as childbearing and household management, local missionary work with the Poosepatucks, and aesthetics such as painting, poetry, short stories, and novels. There is also an extensive family correspondence.[6] Their records detail the role of Floyd women as overseers of Poosepatuck household workers and highlight the prevailing negative sentiment toward the reservation and its residents.[7] Moreover, the documents of Floyd women illuminate the religious and moral justifications for ethnocentrism projected by Euro-Americans toward people of color.[8]

An example of the dominant views toward the Poosepatucks is reflected in the works of Rosalie Delafield Floyd (1877–1943). Rosalie was the daughter of John Geltson Floyd, Jr. (1841–1903) and Julia Floyd DuBois (1844–1893), and the great-great-granddaughter of William Floyd. She never married, spending the balance of her life on or near the Floyd estate and retaining her own land at Mastic.[9]

Through her writings, Rosalie expressed a jocular disdain for the socioeconomic conditions of Poosepatuck women. Her manuscript called "The Backwoods Book," contains a parody titled "The Reservation; A Song of Fiahwatah" (firewater) modeled on Longfellow's *Hiawatha*.[10] "The Reservation" mocked the "June Meeting," a Christian adaptation of the ancient Algonquian gathering known as the Feast of the Dead.[11] Rosalie's poem exposes the majority community's preoccupations with Native American stereotypes and its unfamiliarity with the nature of southern New England's Algonquian cultures in the post-colonial era. For example, Rosalie unveiled assumptions about what has been termed "a recognizable Indian phenotype" in southern New England:[12]

> Mathah, of the broad high cheek bone
> And the scalplock straight as Sebra's —
> (Royal chieftain's Redskin daughter
> Who was Mathah's mother's mother —)
> Tells the fortune in the tea leaves.[13]

Other Poosepatuck women are portrayed as an immoral rainbow coalition:

> Here are Tilly with her dozen;
> Blanche, of anthracite complexion,
> With her Amy — Amy Nothing —
> Fathers are more scarce than mothers;
> And Viohla, likewise burdened,
> Bearing burdens annually —
> Native lullabys a-crooning:
> "Gotosleepyoupickaninny."[14]

Rosalie offers limited insight into the lives of Poosepatuck women, but provides much information about her own cultural horizon and those of other Floyds. Their understanding of humanity is limited by the self-imposed assumptions of superiority inherent in Euro-American civilization. Central to this mind-set is the "oppositional dualism" of Western culture which posits the good/corrupt, civilized/evil, "Princess/Squaw" stereotype.[15] Similarly, the poem shows the influence of the postbellum Cavalier school of literature, which patronizingly romanticizes people of color in order to justify maintaining one's distance from them.[16]

But there is an even more compelling disclosure in the last two lines quoted above: how can the word *pickaninny* be justified in the context of *Native lullabys*? The use of these terms signifies three complex and problematic responses interwoven throughout the Floyd's association with the Poosepatucks. The Floyds acknowledged the retention of what they regarded as Indian culture among the Poosepatucks; within this construct the Floyds distinguished between the "Indian nature" of selected Poosepatucks and what they believed to be the more "Negro nature" of others. Regardless of the perceived amount of "Indianness," by the mid-eighteenth century, the Floyds categorized *all* people of color in Mastic as morally, mentally, and physically inferior.

The works of Katharine Floyd Dana (1835–1886), who published a number of books, supply further illustration of this perspective.[17] Her 1889 novel, *Our Phil and Other Stories,* reflects a growing insistence on classifying the Poosepatucks as "colored," as in *Negro,* rather than "colored," as in *Indian.*[18]

Our Phil is a thinly-disguised satire of Poosepatuck life that casts Native women in the predictably stereotypical roles of the faithful retainer/mammy, the blissfully ignorant free spirit, and so on. All characters of color sport dialects worthy of Joel Chandler Harris's "Uncle Remus" stories; indeed, the novel constitutes a literary parallel to blackface minstrelsy.[19]

Furthermore, between 1850 and 1860 Katharine composed a sketchbook of Mastic encompassing the estate and the reservation.[20] She traversed this terrain well because she and her sister, Sarah Kirkland Floyd Turner (1837–1923) accompanied their mother on proselytizing expeditions among the Poosepatucks.[21] In compositions with titles such as "Guss 'lazing sound,' under the bushes at Poospatuck—Dick carrying 'Bunkers'" (1855), "Poospatuck Foot Bridge. . ." (1855), and "Sketch of a house on Poospatuck Creek" (c. 1852), Katharine augmented the perception of n'er-do-well "Negro Indians." By promoting these images of the Poosepatucks, Katharine contributed to the continued misconceptions surrounding Algonquian culture in the Northeast and to the institutionalization of segregation based on physical appearance.

Katharine's sister Sarah used more forceful language to summarize her opinion of the local natives. In her manuscript titled "Sunny Memories of Mastic," Sarah mused in Social Dawinist fashion on their "condition": "In the youthful days of Sady and Kitty, Poosepatuck had degenerated into a settlement of miserable little cabins, where Blacks and Indians together raised their mongrel breed of children and corn. . . .The Indians and darkeys had married and intermarried till they had sunk into a mixed race weak in body and mind."[22]

Sarah's notions of Poosepatuck life occasionally took a neo-Romantic turn. Writing to Katharine in July 1880, she expressed her own longing for "a little of the *darky 'idleways'* and take-it-easy kind of atmosphere about it all" that she imagined Katharine enjoyed at the estate. While noting Poosepatuck Hannah Ben Edward's loss of her daughter Phoebe, Sarah added: "poor old Aunt Hannah—she is a good old soul and faithful & true to her duty, quite above the Poospattuck standard of darkyism."[23]

Further evidence abounds in the papers of Cornelia Du Bois Floyd Nichols (1882–1977), sister of Rosalie Delafield Floyd and sister-in-law of Sarah Kirkland Floyd Turner.[24] Cornelia was an avid collector of family and local history, but papers also disclose the Floyds' tight-fisted magnanimity toward Poosepatucks. In a post-Christmas letter to Katharine Floyd Dana, Cornelia reported:

> I promised to let you know how I disbursed your money to the darkies, on the tree. . . . Owing to many delays, the Christmas tree was given on the 12th of January! I hope I have not overthrown the religious faith of the community by this disregard of times [illegible]. They were not at all shocked apparently, and came trooping along one and all, those that were asked and those that were not. . . . The presents were varied—the cheapest being five cents, the dearest twenty-five. And you would be surprised if you knew what really pretty things I got for that money! Soldier caps, & guns, & tin trumpets, & red carts, & horses, & all manner of "bric a brac." As all my purchases were made after Christmas, I made wonderful bargains.[25]

Through the eyes of the Floyd women one plumbs the depths of Anglo-American responses toward the Poosepatucks and other people of color.

An Alternative View of Unkechaug

References to Unkechaug (Poosepatuck) females are found in the earliest documents of the Floyd estate. In the early eighteenth century, a time of rapid expansion by the Floyds, Unkechaug women appear as the chief signers in land acquisitions by the Floyds. An Unkechaug woman named "Hannah" is one of the signers in a 1730 land exchange with William Floyd's father, Nicoll Floyd (1705–1755), which transferred one hundred acres of

Unkechaug territory.[26] "Doll, Betty, Sarah . . . and Sarah Ben-Carson" are among seven signers in a 1789 re-affirmation with William Floyd of the 1730 deed. The reaffirmation also gave fifteen more Unkechaug acres to the Floyds.[27]

Moreover, Unkechaug women played pivotal roles in the Anglo-American thrust to exclude dealing with the tribe as communal users of land. This was in order to make, as Ellice Gonzalez notes, "negotiations . . . with separate individuals for specific plots of land":

> This indenture made [October 30, 1791] between Sarah Solomon of the one part and William Floyd of Brookhaven of the other part witnesseth that the said Sarah Solomon Indian squaw hath given granted bargained and sold and by those [present] doth freely fully and absolutely give grant bargain and sell . . . unto the said William Floyd and to his heirs and assigns forever all my right title interest property claim and demand in and to a certain neck or tract of land called Pospattuck Neck for and in consideration of the sum of one pound sixteen shills.[28]

The exchange or "trade" of land by Unkechaug women was no anomaly brought on by the absence of men. It was consistent with the original pattern of Amerindian-European commerce throughout the Atlantic coast.[29]

Even with the forced and wage labor systems established by the Floyds and their counterparts, the Unkechaugs at Poosepatuck retained traditions of power within gender which differed from their white neighbors. For instance, the Algonquian custom of a female co-chief or *sachem*, councilor or wise woman *(sunksquaw)*, survived. In 1851, "Caroline [Hannibal], Queen of the Poosepatucks," implored the Floyds to hire her husband as a wood cutter.[30] Another Poosepatuck female, "Julia Squawssucks" (sunksquaw), served as a nurse for Floyd children in 1854. Julia's last name and function indicates that she probably combined tribal leadership *(sunksquaw)* with traditional healing *(pow-wow* or *pniese)* authority.[31] There are also Long Island newspaper articles on the deaths of *sunksquaws* Elizabeth Job and Martha Hill in 1830 and 1895, respectively.[32] Thus prior to the Native American revitalization movements germinating in the late nineteenth century, Poosepatuck women continued to share decision-making roles.

A Poosepatuck female appearing in several nineteenth-century Floyd documents was Hannah Ben Edwards (1808–?). In the 1880 federal census for Mastic she is listed as a 72–year-old "Black" who "kept house," i.e. was a homemaker in the household of Benjamin Edwards.[33] Hannah Ben was reputedly the daughter-in-law of "'old' Aunt Hannah," another Poosepatuck.[34] In her younger days, Hannah Ben was a laundress for the Floyds and Delafields. In this manner she continued the link between

Poosepatuck and Floyd women as providers and recipients of domestic labor with all the socioeconomic ramifications of that arrangement.[35]

We know remarkably little else about Hannah Ben's early life. It is possible (if not probable) that she, like many New Englanders of color, was "bound-out" or indentured in her youth.[36] Hannah Ben also appears as a recipient of Floyd charity, receiving used clothing and household goods as well as an occasional allowance.[37] Sarah Kirkland Floyd Turner featured a photograph of her in "Sunny Memories," and added a caption noting that although Hannah Ben was holding a book, she "could not read a word." Sarah's praise for Hannah Ben was directed toward her household skills, her subsistence expertise in field and stream, and her general assimilation of the Christian work ethic. It is not known how fellow Poosepatuckers regarded this model of propriety, but from the Floyd perspective, Hannah Ben is viewed as a stable force in Poosepatuck life. Turner offered this idyllic if not pastoral image of the "loyal retainer" at the conclusion of the "Sunny Memories" chapter titled, "Hannah Ben's":

> Conscientious according to her light and knowledge, kind and well principaled, faithful to her children and attached to our family, she is spending her latter days in the cabin that has held all that was dear to her. . . . All Mastic will miss Aunt Hannah when her cabin door is closed and the morning-glories droop outside her wall.[38]

Notations on another Poosepatuck woman, Martha Mayne (or Maines; 1835–1933), are available not only in the Floyd documents but in sources throughout Long Island. This notoriety was due to Mayne reportedly being what non-Natives considered the "'last' full-blooded Indian" at Poosepatuck. In 1990 and 1992 interviews, Martha Mayne's granddaughter, Mary Emma Maynes Brackett Green-Dees (1899–1993), known as Mrs. Brackett, stated that she knew her grandmother well and that Martha was "one of the last Shinnecock fullbloods" who "married a Cuffee of Poosepatuck."[39] The belief in Mayne's Shinnecock origins was echoed by William Floyd Nichols (1922–1989).[40] This contrasts with Ellice Gonzalez's 1984 work on the Poosepatucks listing Mayne as the "last known full-blooded Poospatuck," and with similar comments in Poosepatuck Juanita Langhorn Mayo's sketch, "History of Poosepatuck Reservation" (1958).[41] However, the determination of whether Mayne hailed from Shinnecock or Poosepatuck may be secondary to the *cultural reality* of eastern Long Island Amerindian culture, i.e., the Island's "tribes" were actually autonomous groups linked by kinship.[42] Furthermore, Brackett, Nichols, and Mayo agree on one point: a photograph of Martha Mayne is located in the Heye Center, National Museum of the American Indian, New York City.

Mayne is also mentioned by Cornelia Du Bois Floyd Nichols who wrote, "Martha was given her freedom in the early 1850s . . . and had been 'bound' to the Floyds in her youth. An employer gave $50.00 to the parents of the bound child, whose services ended at the age of 18."[43]

Moreover, Mayne reportedly played a prominent role in the "June Meeting" at Poosepatuck Reservation, which was also the first site of Presbyterian missionary work in North America.[44] Her leadership activities at this most important of all spiritual occasions for New England's Algonquian populations indicates Mayne was regarded at least as an honorary Poosepatuck wise woman or *sunksquaw*.

Martha Mayne's death was widely noted on Long Island. Cornelia made this personal entry: "July 9th—funeral of Martha Maines, aged 98, at Poospatuck. A fairly large crowd, black and white, and many of them sight-seers."[45]

Furthermore, judging from the pronounced Native American consciousness and traditional practices of descendants like Brackett, one perceives Mayne fully embraced her Native self and passed on the necessity of self-preservation to her progeny. It is to Brackett that we now turn to witness a fulfillment of numerous Poosepatuck and Algonquian cultural traits.

From World War I until her death, Brackett figured as one of the most influential Poosepatuck women. She is listed in the 1925 New York State census as the twenty-six-year-old "Black" homemaker and wife of Richard Brackett.[46] But the most significant data identifies Brackett as a Poosepatuck woman and stems from her own words, newspaper articles, and New York State judicial and legislative documents.

For example, in addition to the 1990 and 1992 interviews with this author, Brackett granted an interview to researcher James W. Farr in 1978. With Farr, she cited her employment with the Floyd family since the age of five, her family lineage and those of several others, including the Wards and Edwardses. The Farr interview also chronicles the ethnobotany inherent in the hunting, gathering, and agricultural basis of life at Poosepatuck that extended into the twentieth century:

> The men fished and fed themselves. They raised animals such as chickens, ducks, cows and horses. They fished for eels and sea turtles in Poospatuck Creek. . . .
>
> The Indians collected wild plants such as lamb quarters, dandelion greens, wild turnip, coffee bean, May pink leaves, princess pine and wild cherry. They made rootbeer from sassafras mixed with wild cherry, wintergreen, princess pine, molasses and sugar . . . grandfather Smith used to always make it.[47]
>
> It used to be all woods. Huckleberry and deer were all over the place. . . . When Emma was growing up, she lived on huckle-berries, blackberries, cherries, apples, and wild animals. . . . Everything was home made.[48]

The late Donald Treadwell (Chief Lone Otter) of the Poosepatucks recalled Brackett's corn and potato fields on the reservation. With some chagrin he recounted being commandeered to labor in it by Brackett when she worked as a school bus driver and stopped the bus at the fields instead of his home.[49]

In addition to reiterating some of the information given to Farr, in 1990 Brackett disclosed traditional Indian beliefs to this author. She asserted that the Unkechaugs belonged to the Deer clan, and that the typical regalia was tan in color.[50] The clan totem was the turtle, which she named as the chief ancestor or spirit figure. She declared that "the eagle is our strength," and said that when she sees "him" flying overhead she greeted and paid homage to him—she gave me a demonstration of this. Brackett also asserted that the Unkechaugs worshipped the stars and the moon, and that she heard Native ancestors on the reservation singing and dancing. This, she said, occurred primarily at night, near the reservation's burial grounds and near the water (the Forge River and Poosepatuck Creek merge on the reservation). Brackett also vocalized the "whoop" sound she had heard the ancestors make, and provided me with the "correct" pronunciation for wampum: *waam-puum.*[51]

Brackett expressed other traditional beliefs in witches, spirit guides, and in what may be the most characteristic example of Algonquian cultures, the belief that dreams are, in her words, the "messages of the spirit-guides." She also asserted that as a child she had spent one week on the Mohawk Reservation in upstate New York and had "seen them [Mohawk ancestors] on hills" in Albany. Even accounting for European and African-influences—in her words, "the Indians were mixed with slaves"[52]—Brackett's world-view is a testimonial to the continuity of Native culture at Poosepatuck. Her spirituality, augmented by a devout Christianity, conforms to the Amerindian world-views explored in other works.[53]

Moreover, I was informed by Donald Treadwell that Brackett once provided several researchers with Unkechaug words, but that they never credited her as the source. I asked Brackett if she spoke the language. She gave me a vague response, and I did not press the matter. I then said that scholars claim that the Indian language, i.e., the eastern Long Island "r" dialect of Algonquian, was dead. She paused momentarily and then very assertively declared that "there were at least two men at Shinnecock [Reservation] who spoke the Indian language." She did not provide their names; I chose not to ask. Incidentally, researchers presume that Thomas Jefferson's ethnological excursion to Poosepatuck in the summer of 1791 coincided with the extinction of spoken Unkechaug. This may be the wrong assumption.[54]

In the public record, Brackett emerges as a defender of Poosepatuck land rights. The first instance was the attempted nullification in 1935 of the July 1700 deed by an adopted Floyd heir, William Shepherd Dana.[55] The rift between Dana and the Poosepatucks stemmed from the former's claim that the reservation had never been formally classified in Albany as such, and that his payment of taxes on the land meant he possessed title to Poosepatuck. Brackett led the Poosepatucks and countered that several factors gave reservation status to Poosepatuck. These included the July 1700 deed, the establishment of the first Presbyterian mission-school in North America at Poosepatuck in the 1740s by the Reverend Azariah Horton, and the state's maintenance of the school from the 1870s to the time of the Dana claim.[56]

With the assistance of Brackett the Poosepatucks gained important allies, including the Reverend Earnest E. Eells (pastor of the First Presbyterian Church at East Hampton), the Brookhaven Town attorney, and the Attorney General of New York State.[57] After an initial year's closing of the reservation school and its reopening, Dana's claim was defeated in the Suffolk County Civil Courts. In *William Shepherd Dana v. Luther Maynes, Frances Maynes, Edward Gales and Elaine Gales* (1936), the state cited the validity of the July 1700 deed as well as the continuity of occupation at Poosepatuck by the Unkechaug descendants.[58] In leading the Poosepatuck contingency, Brackett functioned as a *sunksquaw*, for the Poosepatucks simultaneously had a chief (Horace Ward) and a traditional healer (Obediah Ward) at the time of the Dana suit.[59]

The second example of Brackett's leadership came in 1943 when New York State held hearings on the socioeconomic condition of the Poosepatucks.[60] The responses of the six sworn Poosepatuck witnesses reflected the reluctance to share tribal beliefs and practices to outsiders. But when asked if she had any additional comments to make, Brackett pointedly noted her understanding of the July 1700 deed and the erosion of tribal acreage:

> This [Unkechaug] land is 52 or 53 acres, and it is supposed to be 225 acres that belongs to us. It is not all in one place. We would like for all that to be settled. There isn't enough land here to farm on, and if any of them [the Poosepatucks] wanted to make a living farming, they couldn't.[61]

Near the conclusion of the hearing, Brackett revealed that she and another Poosepatuck possessed documents relating to the tribe.[62]

Red Corn Woman and Contemporary Unkechaug Culture

In Karla Arita Miller (Red Corn Woman, *Squayo Wewauchumnai*, 1945–), the determination and spirituality of the Unkechaugs find contemporary expression.[63] Miller is of Unkechaug, Montauk, and Shinnecock lineage and was born "at the time of the waning cold moon" in Brooklyn. Raised in Flushing and Hunts Point, she attended public schools in the Bronx and Manhattan and graduated from the High School of Music and Art in

1964. Her esthetic sensitivity and expertise were enhanced by a two-year scholarship to Pratt Institute. After employment in publishing and public relations firms, Miller relocated to Arizona and worked in Native American organizations until 1980. She returned to New York in 1980 and was employed with a national fellowship program and an investment banking firm.

Red Corn Woman credits her teachers and instructors for her entree into formal art, but the major spiritual influence came at the age of sixteen from a relative. During a family gathering in honor of Chief John Standing Waters, his daughter, Heather Flower, took Red Corn Woman aside and presented her with an Indian regalia dress which Red Corn Woman borrowed to "attend every pow-wow on Long Island." Heather Flower also taught Red Corn Woman the Fish, Round, and Rabbit dances, introduced her to American Indian activism, and encouraged her to research her genealogy. This immersion in the Indian self strengthened her artistic expression in the form of what Red Corn Woman refers to as "'traditional' Indian art and symbolism with impressionism." An essential part of this spirituality is Red Corn Woman's sacred shield. Its images were seen in a dream by a Cherokee friend who conveyed the vision to Red Corn Woman. The shield consists of symbolic designs painted on canvas and is surrounded by eagle and hawk feathers, a beaver claw, and a bear paw.[64] Concurrently, Red Corn Woman was a Poosepatuck Tribe Land Trustee during the late 1980s and was influential in getting the reservation connected to the Suffolk County public water system.[65]

Red Corn Woman is an outspoken advocate for the survival of Poosepatuck and Unkechaug culture:

> The historical relationship between the Floyd estate and the Poospatuck Reservation was clearly one of plantation owner to indentured servants and slaves. They [Floyds] had a ready-made cheap workforce. However, had the Unkechaugs not been under the aegis of the Floyd family, they might have been murdered by other white settlers eyeing their lands as many other small bands and tribes that disappeared on Long Island.
>
> It is the same with any Indian Reservation where whites have built up their communities smack-up against reservation boundaries. They wish we would go away, they think we should be paying property taxes, we should forget that we are Indians.[66]

She decries "a pervasive criminal element" on the reservation and equally deplores a "black intrusion" with children who "sport dreadlocks, afros, corn-rows, buzz-cuts, and talk blackese." She contrasts the "traditional" (tribal) memberships that

Fig. 7.1. Red Corn Woman (Karla A. Miller) on right, with mother (*left*) and aunt (*center*) at the Poosepatuck Reservation, June 1991. Photograph courtesy of Bernice Forrest Guillaume.

have maintained their ceremonies and cultural identity and with the help of our current Chief and his wife, those children who are interested are learning dance, singing and drumming as well as the Unkechaug language, our customs, and history. Even with these efforts, Indians are a minority on their own reservation.[67]

Red Corn Woman's comments echo the centuries of female guardianship of Poosepatuck, "I see little hope for the survival of the Unkechaug people unless legal action is taken once and for all to remove the squatters from the reservation and efforts [are made] to regain our land base. We must also look at viable tribal business enterprises to fund our own programs."[68]

Conclusion

The weight of gender and race-biased data on eastern seaboard American Indians has suppressed public knowledge of Poosepatuck/Unkechaug cultural continuity. Moreover, historical obstruction hides cogent links between the women in this scenario: those of the reservation and those who functioned as overseers of the Floyd manor. The customary feminist canon offers scant illumination on race and class-based exploitation within the female paradigm of American culture and may lead to the continued stereotyping of American Indian women as *squaw-drudges*.

Despite the burdens of more than three hundred years, Poosepatuck women persevere as females functioning within an Algonquian-based cultural context. They have proved flexible in accommodating to non-Indian socioeconomic pressures and continue the tradition of council-based, non-sexist tribal leadership among Northeastern Native Americans. Poosepatuck women sustain the Unkechaug Nation now, as they always have, on Mastic Neck.

Notes

1. The estate is named after William Floyd (1734-1821), the Long Island signer of the Declaration of Independence. Floyd held various political and military posts in the early republic. Data on the Floyds, their relations with the Unkechaugs (Poosepatucks), and the administration of the estate are contained in the Department of the Interior, National Park Service, Archives of the Fire Island National Seashore, William Floyd Estate, Collections (hereafter referred to as WFEC), 1-14, Catalog nos. 9664-9681 (1991), Floyd Estate, Mastic, NY.

2. The terms *Poosepatuck* and *Unkechaug* have endured various spellings. The Poosepatucks are recognized as the Unkechaug Nation by the State of New York. The Unkechaug village called *Poosepatuck* and its inhabitants became synonymous as a result of the July 2, 1700 deed from Colonel William "Tangier" Smith, Proprietor of the Manor of St. George (Mastic, NY) to the Unkechaugs. The deed transformed Poosepatuck into a "reservation" and its inhabitants became lessees on their own land. The Floyds acquired the Smith land patent between the late seventeenth and early eighteenth centuries. Consult: William Wallace Tooker, *The Indian Place-Names on Long Island and Islands Adjacent, With Their Probable Significations* (New York: Putnam's Sons, 1911), pp. 193, 265-67; *Records of the Town of Brookhaven, Suffolk County, New York, Up to 1800; As Compiled by the Town Clerk* (Patchogue: Advance Press, 1880), pp. 91-92, passim; Donald Treadwell (Chief Lone Otter), *My People the Unkechaug: The Story of a Long Island Indian Tribe* (Amsterdam: De Kiva, 1992); "Poospatuck Indian Nation: Tribal Rules, Customs and Regulations," (1957), in Ellice B. Gonzalez, "From Unkechaug to Poospatuck," TS (typescript), Ellice Gonzalez File H3019, "Study of Poospatuck Indians," 1984, William Floyd Estate Archives (hereafter referred to as WFEA), Floyd Estate; Bert Salwen, "Indians of Southern New England and Long Island: Early Period," in vol. 15 of *Handbook of North American Indians*, William C. Sturtevant, general editor (Washington, DC: Smithsonian Institution, 1978), 15: 160-76; Laura E. Conkey, Ethel Boissevain, and Ives Goddard, "Indians of Southern New England and Long Island: Late Period," in *Handbook,* ed. Sturtevant, 15:177-86; Department of Commerce, *Federal and State Indian Reservation and Trust Areas* (Washington, DC: Government Printing Office, 1974), pp. 409-10; U.S. American Indian Policy Review Commission, *Task Force Ten: Report on Terminated and Nonfederally Recognized Indians: Final Report* (Washington, DC: Government Printing Office, 1976), pp. 97-100; John A. Strong, *"We Are Still Here!": The Algonquian Peoples of Long Island Today* (Interlaken, NY: Empire State Books, Long Island Studies Institute, 1996); and John A. Strong, *The Algonquian Peoples of Long Island from Earliest Times to 1700* (Interlaken, NY: Empire State Books, Long Island Studies Institute, 1997).

3. In addition to transactions involving slaves and indentured servants in WFEC and in town records throughout Long Island, consult: Cornelia Floyd Nichols, "Old Mastic House" (1949), in *Addresses Delivered on the Occasion of a Visit to the General William Floyd House at Mastic, Long Island* (Setauket, NY: Society for the Preservation of Long Island Antiquities, 1950), not paginated (copy in Long Island Collection, East Hampton Public Library); Cornelia Floyd Nichols, "As Told by the Attic Letters of Cornelia Floyd Nichols," TS (1952), pt. 1, p. 4, Suffolk County Historical Society, Riverhead, NY (hereafter referred to as SCHS); and Almon Wheeler Lauber, *Indian*

Slavery in Colonial Times Within the Present Limits of the United States (New York: Columbia University, 1913), pp. 114, 200-202, 209, 232, 280-82.

4. The expanding literature on the complexity of gender roles and the visibility of women in Algonquian and other Native American societies includes: Kathleen M. Brown, "The Anglo-Algonquian Gender Frontier," in *Negotiators of Change: Historical Perspectives on Native American Women*, edited by Nancy Shoemaker (New York: Routledge, 1995), pp. 26-48, and Shoemaker's "Introduction," pp. 1-25; Robert Steven Grumet, "Sunksquaws, Shamans, and Tradeswomen: Middle Atlantic Coastal Algonquian Women During the 17th and 18th Centuries," in *Women and Colonization: Anthropological Perspectives*, edited by Mona Etienne and Eleanor Leacock (New York: Praeger, 1980), pp. 43-62; Lara M. Strong and Selcuk Karabag, "Quashawam: Sunksquaw of the Montauk," *Long Island Historical Journal* 3, no. 2 (1991): 189-204; and in Laurie Weinstein, ed., *Enduring Traditions: The Native People of New England* (Westport: Bergen and Garvey, 1994), passim. See also John A. Strong's essay in this volume, "The Role of Algonquian Women in Land Transactions on Eastern Long Island, 1639-1859."

5. Tabitha Floyd *née* Smith married Nicoll Floyd (1705-1755); they were the first inhabitants of the estate house. See Early Floyd Family Papers, 1666-1833, WFEC.

6. One Floyd woman expressed frustration at her husband's scarce funding of Poosepatuck missionary work; see Sarah Bachus Kirkland Floyd to John Geltson Floyd, Jr. (son), October 12, 1860, John Geltson Floyd, Jr. and Family Papers, WFEC. Consult also "The Cult of Domesticity," chap. 5 in *Major Problems in American Women's History*, edited by Mary Beth Norton (Lexington: D. C. Heath and Co., 1989), pp. 112-45.

7. The issue of intermarriage among the Unkechaugs and other Atlantic coast Amerindian cultures is a continuing source of debate. Negative responses include: Nicholl Floyd III to Jason H. Guthrie, November 8, 1883, Bicentennial Misc. File, SCHS; William A. Ritchie, *Indian History of New York State, Pt. 3: The Algonkian Tribes*, New York State Museum and Science Service, Educational Leaflet no. 8 (Albany: New York State Museum, 1953), p. 24; New York Legislature, *Report of the Special Committee to Investigate the Indian Problem of the State of New York, Appointed by the Assembly of 1888* (Albany, 1889), pp. 53-55; Alexander F. Chamberlain, "Negro and Indian," in *Handbook of American Indians North of Mexico*, Smithsonian Institution, Bureau of American Ethnology, *Bulletin* 30, edited by Frederick W. Hodge (Washington, DC: Smithsonian, 1912), pp. 51-53; Peter Ross, *A History of Long Island, From Its Earliest Settlement to the Present Time* (New York: The Lewis Publishing Co., 1902), pp. 38-39; and A. R. Dunlap and C. A. Weslager, "Trends in the Naming of Tri-Racial Mixed-Blood Groups in the Eastern United States," *American Speech* 32, no. 2 (April 1947): 81-87. See also a discussion on the "taint of African blood" in George Washington Cable to Nicoll Floyd, December 24, 1881, Nicoll Floyd and Family Papers, WFEC. More balanced views are in Ellice B. Gonzalez, "Tri-Racial Isolates in a Bi-Racial Society: Poospatuck Ambiguity and Conflict," in *Strategies for Survival: American Indians in the Eastern United States*, edited by Frank W. Porter III (New York: Greenwood, 1986), pp. 113-37; Ann McMullen, "What's Wrong With this Picture? Context, Coversion, Survival, and the Development of Regional Native Cultures and Pan-Indianism in Southeastern New England," in *Enduring Traditions* edited by Laurie Weinstein, pp. 123-50; Bernice F. Guillaume, "Character Names in 'Indian Trails' by

Olivia Ward Bush (Banks): A Clue to Afro Assimilation into Long Island's Native American Culture" (1986), reprinted in *The History and Archaeology of the Montauk*, edited by Gaynell Stone, 2d ed. (Stony Brook, NY: Suffolk County Archaeological Association [hereafter SCAA], 1993), pp. 357-62; William S. Simmons, *Spirit of the New England Tribes: Indian History and Folklore, 1620-1984* (Hanover: University Press of New England, 1986), p. 269; A. Irving Hallowell, "American Indians, Black and White: The Phenomenon of Transculturalization," in *Contributions to Anthropology: Selected Papers of A. Irving Hallowell* (Chicago: University of Chicago Press, 1976), pp. 498-529; Peter B. Hammond, "Afro-American Indians and Afro-Asians: Cultural Contacts Between Africa and the Peoples of Asia and Aboriginal America," in *Expanding Horizons in African Studies*, edited by Gwen W. Cater and Ann Paden (Evanston: Northwestern University Press, 1969), pp. 275-90; and Kenneth Porter, *Relations Between Negroes and Indians Within the Present Limits of the United States* (Washington, DC: The Association for the Study of Negro Life and History, 1937).

8. On the development of cultural categories based on color along the eastern seaboard, see McMullen, "What's Wrong With This Picture?" p. 146 n. 7. Also Jack D. Forbes, *Africans and Native Americans: The Language of Race and the Evolution of Red-Black Peoples*, 2d ed. (Urbana: University of Illinois Press, 1993); Alden T. Vaughan, *Roots of American Racism: Essays on the Colonial Experience* (New York: Oxford University Press, 1995); and *Nonrecognized American Indian Tribes: An Historical and Legal Perspective,* edited by Frank W. Porter III, Occasional Papers Series, no. 7 (Chicago: The Newberry Library, 1983).

9. Rosalie Delafield Floyd Papers, WFEC.

10. Rosalie Delafield Floyd, "The Reservation: A Song of Fiawatah," in "The Backwoods Book," c. 1915, TS, WFEC, pp. 61-68.

11. Bernice Forrest Guillaume, "The June Meeting as an Evidence of Cultural Survival Among the Poosepatuck of Long Island" (paper presented at the 48th International Congress of Americanists, Stockholm and Uppsala, Sweden, July 1994).

12. McMullen, "What's Wrong With This Picture?" p. 124.

13. R. D. Floyd, *"The Reservation . . ."* p. 64. *Mathah* is Martha Mayne (1835-1933), reputedly the last known full-blooded Poosepatuck who is discussed later in this essay. *Sebra* may be Sabra Waters (1804-?), cited by Gonzalez, in "From Unkechaug to Poospatuck" as Martha's mother, not grandmother. This essay will not probe the issues surrounding Poosepatuck blood rights.

14. Ibid., p. 66.

15. Rebecca Tsosie, "Changing Women: The Crosscurrents of American Indian Feminine Identity," in *Unequal Sisters: A Multicultural Reader in U.S. Women's History*, edited by Vicki L. Ruiz and Ellen Carol DuBois, 2d ed. (New York: Routledge, 1994), pp. 508-30.

16. On the confluence of science, religion, and literature in attitudes toward Native Americans, see: Forrest G. Wood, *The Arrogance of Faith: Christianity and Race in America from the Colonial Era to the Twentieth Century* (Boston: Northeastern University Press, 1991); Thomas F. Gossett, *Race: The History of an Idea in America* (New York: Schocken Books, 1965), and Robert E. Bieder, *Science Encounters the Indian, 1820-1880: The Early Years of American Ethnology* (Norman: University of Oklahoma Press, 1986).

17. Katharine Floyd was the daughter of John Geltson Floyd, Sr. (1806-1881), a New York Congressman, state senator, and county judge, and Sarah Bachus Kirkland Floyd (1810-1872), who hailed from a well-known Utica, New York political clan. Katharine resided at the Floyd estate from 1843-1855, then married William Buck Dana (1829-1910). She frequently used the pen name Olive A. Wadsworth ("Only A Woman") while writing stories for her husband's papers, the *Commerical and Financial Chronicle* (precursor to the *Wall Street Journal*), the *Bulletin*, and *The Merchants' Magazine*. Her other works include: *Kit, Fan, Tot & the Rest of Them* (Boston, 1872); *Heavenward Bound; or, Words of Help for Young Christians* (Philadelphia, 1871); *Bill Riggs Jr.—A Story of a City Boy* (n.d.); and, under the psuedonym, Neil Forrest, *Fiddling Freddie* (1871). See Katharine Floyd Dana and Family Papers, WFEC.

18. See note 7 above.

19. Consult Gossett, *Race: History of an Idea*, pp. 198-286; and Eric Lott, *Love and Theft: Blackface Minstrelsy and the American Working Class* (New York: Oxford University Press, 1993).

20. United States Department of the Interior, National Park Service, Fire Island National Seashore, *The Silent Dawn: Views of Nineteenth Century Mastic; a Collection of Sketches by Katharine Floyd Dana*, William Floyd Estate, June 1991.

21. See the sketch titled "Meetin'," in Turner, "Sunny Memories of Mastic," TS, not paginated, John Geltson Floyd Sr. and Family Papers, WFEC.

22. Turner, "Sunny Memories of Mastic."

23. Sarah Floyd Turner to Katharine Floyd Dana, July 30, 1880, Katharine Floyd Dana Papers, WFEC.

24. See note 3 above on Cornelia's personal writings. Also consult manuscripts such as "Letters to my Great-great Granddaughter," Cornelia Du Bois Floyd Nichols Papers, WFEC.

25. Cornelia Du Bois Floyd Nichols to Katharine Floyd Dana, January 16, 1881, Katharine Floyd Dana Papers, WFEC.

26. Nicoll Floyd Papers, WFEC. Gonzalez, in "From Unkechaug to Poospatuck" (3:9) gives this transaction as Account 10, deed 125, but this would place the deed in folder 27 (1745). Gonzalez's research was conducted before the Floyd collections were cataloged. See WFEC 1, p. 7.

27. Gonzalez ("From Unkechaug to Poospatuck," 3:8) cites this as Account 10, deed 102; see William Floyd Papers, WFEC, box 2, folder 34.

28. Ibid.

29. Grumet, "Sunksquaws, Shamans, and Tradeswomen"; Sara M. Evans, "The First American Women," chap. 1, *Born for Liberty: A History of Women in America* (New York: Free Press, 1989), pp. 7-19.

30. Sarah Bachus Kirkland Floyd to John Geltson Floyd, Sr., December 18, 1851, John Geltson Floyd Sr. and Family Papers, WFEC.

31. John Geltson Floyd, Sr. to Sarah Bachus Kirkland Floyd, September 8, 1854, ibid. Likewise, the (documented) continuity of Poosepatuck male political leaders *(sachems)* and traditional healers has been overlooked in conjunction with the scholarly disdain for field work at the reservation.

32. For Elizabeth Job, see *Handbook of American Indians North of Mexico*, p. 281. Consult also Thomas R. Bayles, "The Poosepatuck Indians," an undated clipping from

the *Long Island Advance*, in Long Island Collection, Patchogue-Medford Library, Patchogue, NY.

33. U.S. Bureau of the Census, State of New York, Suffolk County, Brookhaven Township, Supt. Dist. No. 2, Enumeration Dist. No. 314, pp. 2-4. The inconsistency of state and federal census compilations for the Poosepatucks and other Long Island Amerindians was coupled with the ethnic bias of census takers. Consequently, throughout the nineteenth century at least forty-five "non-white" Long Island families were arbitrarily and contradictorily enumerated by federal census takers solely on the basis of their physical features, without regard to cultural affiliations. See "Indian/Black Families, 1810-1880, Long Island File," Archaeology-Kinship File Box for the [Federal] Census, Anthropological Library, Nassau County Museum, Sands Point Preserve, Port Washington, NY.

34. See the chapter on "Old Aunt Hannah," in Turner, "Sunny Memories of Master," WFEC.

35. Chapter "Hannah Ben's," in Turner, "Sunny Memories of Master," WFEC.

36. The custom of placing people of color in "bound-out" or indentured servitude survived the 1827 ending of slavery in New York. Gonzalez gives 1843 as the date the Floyds ended the practice ("From Unkechaug to Poospatuck"). Town records indicate Anglo-Americans violated their own tradition of citing maternal lineage for determining "race," for mixed-blood children of Indian maternity were frequently not treated as Native Americans, but as "colored." See the indentures of the children of Sary Arch and Rachel Ceasar in *Records of the Town of Brookhaven, Suffolk County, New York* (Port Jefferson: Times Steam Job Print, 1888), pp. 12, 30, 94, 432.

37. Turner, "Sunny Memories of Mastic." Also Augustus Floyd to Nicoll Floyd: May 27, 1881; February 9, 1891; November 10, 1891; May 3 1893; and August 26, 1893 in Nicoll Floyd and Family Papers, WFEC.

38. Turner, "Sunny Memories of Mastic."

39. Mary Emma Maynes Brackett Green-Dees, interviews by author, Poosepatuck Indian Reservation, Mastic, NY, June 1990 and May 29, 1992.

40. William Floyd Nichols, personal communication with Steven Kesselman, Superintendent of Floyd Estate, 1978, WFEA.

41. Gonzalez, "From Unkechaug to Poosepatuck," Appendix 2: Main/Mayne[s] Family Genealogy." Gonzalez also cites the Langhorns as Maynes descendants. Mayo, "History of Poosepatuck Reservation," TS in Center Moriches Public Library, Center Moriches, NY.

42. The Shinnecocks and the Poosepatucks have shared overwhelmingly similiar cultural traits. This is denoted in the wealth of scholarship on coastal Algonquian peoples as well as the tradition of the "June Meeting" (see note 11).

43. Cornelia DuBois Floyd Nichols, "Letters to my Great-great Granddaughter," ms., p. 95, Cornelia DuBois Floyd Nichols and Family Papers, WFEC.

44. See "Martha Mayne, of Poosepatuck Tribe, Dies at 98; Sole Pure-Blood Survivor of Long Island Indian Tribe Succumbs to Illness . . .," *New York Herald Tribune*, July 7, 1933; and discussions of Native and non-Native Christian missionaries in *The History and Archaeology of the Montauk*, edited by Gaynell Stone (Stony Brook: SCAA, 1993), pp. 147-283.

45. Cornelia DuBois Floyd Nichols, entry in guestbook, 1933, Cornelia Du Bois Floyd Nichols and Family Papers, WFEC. See the obituaries for Mayne in the Ader E.

Martin [Squires] Indian Scrapbooks, compiled by Harry B. Squires, indexes by A. W. Kappenberg, 1933-1938, SCHS.

46. New York State Census, 1925: Suffolk County, Town of Brookhaven, Assembly Dist. no. 1, p. 10.

47. Emma Brackett, interview by James W. Farr, 1978, pt. 1, WFEA. Brackett's data is consistent with ethnobotanical practices throughout the Amerindian Northeast. Long Island Amerindians still cultivate and gather plants for botanical purposes (Peggy Carter Cause and Michael Cause, interview by author, Shinnecock Indian Reservation, Southampton, NY, June 11, 1991). In response to my remarks about a certain plant growing next to his house, the late Donald Treadwell (Chief Lone Otter) declared that it was *mullain,* also called "rabbit's tobacco" by the Poosepatucks. He recalled that his mother used to mix it with goose grease for use as an astringent and antiseptic, and with wintergreen leaf as an analgesic. The use of mullain is documented among other Algonquians, notably the Anishinabe (Chippewa or Ojibway) people by ethnologist Frances Densmore in the early twentieth century. Treadwell interview by author, Poosepatuck Indian Reservation, June 12, 1990. Consult also Aisba Tupahache, "June Meeting," *The Spirit of January Monthly*, no. 13 (June 1991), p. 1; and Barrie Kavasch, "Native Foods of New England," in Weinstein, *Enduring Traditions,* pp. 5-30.

48. Brackett interview by Farr, part 2.

49. Donald Treadwell (Chief Lone Otter) interview by author, Poosepatuck Indian Reservation, June 10, 1990.

50. Treadwell confirmed that the Unkechaug believe "a White Deer was the first to dig a hole in the group with a hoof, for the Earth Mother [who fell from on the back of the turtle when she came from the sky? (cf. Iroquois tradition)] so that the Unkechaugs could plant corn and survive." The author and Treadwell concurred that the deer was a symbol of the quiet, solitary, and placid nature of the Unkechaugs, who could nevertheless be roused to blind fury in the face of repeated hurt. Treadwell added that Unkechaug men's traditional dress was "a tan tunic, with a soldier strap; leggings underneath; and symbols painted on the tunic." Treadwell interview by author, June 7, 1990.

51. Brackett interview by author, June 13, 1990.

52. Ibid.; and Brackett interview by Farr, Part 1.

53. See Ruth Benedict Fulton, *The Concept of the Guardian Spirit in North America: Memoirs of the American Anthropological Association,* no. 29 (Menasha, WI: The Collegiate Press, 1923); William S. Simmons, *Spirit of the New England Tribes* (Hanover: University Press of New England, 1986); and Gaynell Stone Levine and Nancy Bonvillain eds., *Languages and Lore of the Long Island Indians* (Stony Brook: Suffolk County Archaeological Association, 1980).

54. Treadwell interview, June 7, 1990; Brackett interview by author, June 13, 1990. See also "Vocabulary of Unquachog or Puspatuck collected by Thomas Jefferson at Brookhaven, Long Island, on June 13, 1791," and "Unkachog words contained in 'A Manuscript Comparative Vocabulary of Several Indian Languages' by Thomas Jefferson, 1817," in *Languages and Lore of the Long Island Indians,* edited by Gaynell Stone Levine and Nancy Bonvillain, (Stony Brook, NY: Suffolk County Archaeological Association, 1980), pp. 17-20.

55. As an adoptee, there are no dates available for Dana. Katharine Floyd Dana and Family Papers, WFEC, Catalog no. FIIS 9661, p. 2.

56. John Strong, "Azariah Horton's Mission to the Montauks," in *History and Archaeology of the Montauk,* ed. Stone, pp. 191-94; "The Diary of Azariah Horton in *The Christian Monthly,*" reprinted in *History and Archaeology of the Montauk,* ed. Stone, pp. 195-220; State of New York, "Consolidated School Laws: Indian Schools," ch. 556, Title 15, article 13:34-37, in the *Forty-Seventh Annual Report of the Superintendent of Public Instruction, 1895-1896* (Albany, 1901), Appendix 1: 110, 162-66; New York Department of Public Instruction, "Report of the Superintendent of the Shinnecock and Poosepatuck Reservations," *Twenty-Sixth Annual Report of the Superintendent . . .* (Albany: New York State Library, 1880), pp. 86-87; and Bernice Forrest Guillaume, "Dual Dilemma: Ethnology, Politics and the Abolition of the New York State Poosepatuck (Unkechaug Nation) Indian Reservation School, 1875-1944" (paper presented at the Organization of American Historians, April 1991, Louisville, KY).

57. "The Poosepatucks Appeal to Town for Legal Fight," "Eells Urges Town to Help Indians," *Patchogue Advance,* June 14, 1935; "Mastic Indians Ask School Aid," clipping in Martin Scrapbooks, SCHS; "Indian School is Doomed," *Suffolk Daily Island News,* April 4, 1935; "Indians Face Eviction Threat on Long Island," *Herald Tribune,* October 5, 1935; "Rev. Eells Warns Mastic Indians," *Suffolk Daily Island News,* May 29, 1935.

58. Copy of summary proceedings in Gonzalez "From Unkechaug to Poosepatuck." The county reported that "we cannot locate the file" (no. 3561, vol. 28, p. 179, microfilm reel 1150), Suffolk County Clerk to author, November 2, 1995.

59. "Mastic Indians Hail New Lease on School Life," *New York Herald Tribune,* September 1, 1935; "Indian Plea Made by Medicine Man," *Patchogue Advance,* October 11, 1935.

60. New York Legislature, Joint Committee on Indian Affairs, "Public Hearing Had in School House, Poospatuck Reservation, Mastic, Long Island, New York, October 14, 1943." TS., New York State Library, Albany.

61. Ibid., p. 29.

62. Ibid., p. 31.

63. Karla Arita Miller, letter to author, November 30, 1995.

64. Miller, interview with author, June 8, 1991. See also Delinda Passas and Anabela Marques, "The Use of Feathers in Native New England," Weinstein, *Enduring Traditions,* pp. 169-83; Joan Lester, "Art for Sale: Cultural and Economic Survival," in ibid. pp. 151-67; and Sam D. Gill, *Native American Traditions: Sources and Interpretations* (Belmont, CA: Wadsworth, 1983), pp. 8-16, 60-76.

65. Linda Saslow, "Indian Reservation to Get Clean Water," *New York Times,* Long Island Weekly section, March 1, 1988, p. 1 ff.

66. Miller letter to author, November 30, 1995.

67. Ibid.

68. Ibid.

8. "To Blush Unseen"
A View of Nineteenth-Century Women

Kathryn Curran

It is in the common place and in daily occurrences that a society is built. The traditions and cultural activities that become part of everyday endeavors, chores, and events set the standards and values for a specific place and time. As keepers of the home and tenders of the family, the average, and largely anonymous, Long Island women of the nineteenth century defined, in large part, the social history of this period.

Today when the media reminds us of equality and political correctness, it might be difficult to fathom the social and moral expectations placed on Long Island women of the nineteenth century. The written record of letters, diaries, autograph albums, and journals gives an intimate insight into patterns of their lives. Women took time to jot down their activities, to keep in touch with family and friends, or merely to reflect. In their own words and in the words of others who observed them, Long Island women appear to be remarkably similar in attitudes and demeanor to our own neighbors, sisters, mothers, and friends.

The significance of the obscure women of Long Island was noted by no less a personage than Timothy Dwight, the president of Yale College. In his *Travels in New England and New York,* he chronicled his journeys along the American eastern seaboard. Passing through Long Island, he stopped in Smithtown in May 1804. Dwight records the evening:

> Here we dined. . . . In this humble mansion, however, we found a young lady about eighteen, of a fine form and complexion, a beautiful countenance, with brilliant eyes animated by intelligence, possessing manners which were a charming mixture of simplicity and grace, and conversing in language which would not have discredited a drawing room or a court. Her own declarations compelled us to believe, against every preconception, that she was a child of this very humble, uneducated family; but nothing which we saw in the house could account for the appearance of her person, mind, or manners. I was ready, as I believe all my companions were, when we left the spot, to believe that some
>
> Flowers were born to blush unseen,
> And waste their sweetness on the desert air.[1]

Timothy Dwight recorded this testimonial after an evening spent in the company of Phoebe McCoon (1786–1868); see fig. 8.1. Phoebe McCoon

Fig. 8.1. The silhouette of Phoebe McCoon, c. 1820 is a hollow cut with detail added in ink. Silhouettes were the least expensive form of portraiture, making them both obtainable and popular. Though not attributed to a specific artist, the very distinctive rendering of Phoebe McCoon's mutton style sleeve and tiny hand, lead to similar examples of this unknown artist's silhouette work that can be found in the collections of the Museum of American Folk Art in New York City and the Abby Aldridge Rockefeller Collection in Williamsburg. The silhouette is in the Smithtown Historical Society Collection. Copy courtesy of the Smithtown Historical Society.

might have had an insight into the effect of her own comeliness and charm. Her selection of sampler verse stresses the power of youth and attractiveness over age as the monarch to be worshipped:

> When I was young and in my prime
> I did set down and mark these lines
> Now I am old I must forbear
> For old age creeps on me like a snare
> Welcome beauty, banish fear
> You are queen and mistress here
> Your wishes speak your will
> And swift obedience meets me still.[2]

Phoebe McCoon's sampler is rather homely in appearance. The sampler would be overlooked for detail, or style, or competency of the artist's hand by many art historians. It is a sampler that could be one of the hundreds found locally. But this piece of young woman's art is different. It is the text, the written word, the first-person observation of Phoebe McCoon, by Dwight, given after a single meeting that moves the sampler from obscurity to a unique piece of Long Island history.

Similarly, a mammy's bench from the Haven's House on Shelter Island is a beautifully crafted piece of Long Island furniture. The discussion of it as evidence of local craftsmanship might include ingenuity in design, wood, derivation of style, condition, provenance. But when this same object is viewed after reading the plain and heart-breaking account of the loss of a child in the bereaved mother's own words, the bench takes on new meaning.

It becomes a symbol of a mother's love and loss; it becomes a reminder of loneliness and grief.

When the words of the women of Long Island, or the words of their contemporaries, are involved in the viewing of their everyday objects (objects that were used and needed in their lives), their comments change our perceptions of what we are seeing. The pot or jug or blanket is no longer just a tool, an object; it becomes an extension of the author herself. Its daily use is placed in the context of the user's life. The objects are transformed; a context of immediacy is created. As we read the documents of the past, and see the artifacts of daily endeavor, we are brought to a new understanding of lives of Long Island women in the nineteenth century.

The importance of demeanor, deportment, and disposition in the nineteenth-century woman constituted the ideal that Dwight described as including "a gentle and affectionate temper, ornamented with sprightliness and gilded with serenity."[3] The appearance of propriety was part of a burgeoning cultural force on Long Island which was caught up in an attitude of moral improvement at the time.[4] Temperance organizations and tract societies brought social decorum into the domain of the wife and mother. As popular life changed, as perspectives changed, a woman's role was to incorporate those changes into the fabric of daily life.

Motherhood took on a new dimension at the beginning of the nineteenth century. After the American Revolution and under the influence of the Age of Enlightenment, attitudes changed giving a new appreciation of childhood. Ralph Waldo Emerson, quoting a contemporary said, "It was a misfortune to have been born in an age when children were nothing and to have spent mature life in an age when children were everything."[5]

The Puritan philosophy of the child as a little adult condemned at birth and in search of redemption was changed with the teachings of John Locke. His theory of *tabula rasa,* that the child was a clean slate, "to be filled in by observation and reasoning," altered the parental role from soul saver to sole savior. Parents became the guardians of the precious gift of a child. This idea was reinforced in contemporary periodicals published for both parents and children: "Childhood is like a mirror, catching and reflecting images. One impious or profane thought uttered by a parent's lip may operate upon the young heart like a careless spray of water thrown upon polished steel, staining it with rust which no after scouring can erase."[6]

Beyond the ideal of the child as a valued present from heaven and childhood as golden moments, Adele Sherill noted the reality of the demands and strain of motherhood in her journal written in East Hampton. On March 17, 1871, she described her sister having to contend with six sick children, "It strikes me that it makes a perfect slave of a woman to have so many children, and I do not think it right."[7]

Adele Sherill followed her remark about the bondage of tending a large family with a heartfelt notation. The incidence of childhood death was all too common. Children of the nineteenth century were still regarded as temporary visitors whose lifespans were determined by a Higher Power. This privation was endured and even accepted, but it was never forgotten. Four years later, on February 7, 1875, Adele Sherill wrote: "One year ago today my baby was born—it does not seem possible when I think of it—such a large fat baby as he was—weighed 11 lbs. and seemed perfectly healthy precious baby—I do so long to have him, but I know he is better off—but sometimes it is hard to feel so."[8]

By the nineteenth century, education moved from the auspices of the church to the town. In January 1850, Helen Rogers described a Cold Spring Harbor district meeting where the length of the school year was debated:

> "If you vote for school through out the year, you will beggar yourself, your property will be ruinated," shouted the opposition in one ear.

> "If you vote for four months your daughters will grow up to be ignoramuses and live to curse the day their father was so penurious," cried the other deputy in the other ear.[9]

It is possible to trace the private schools that dotted the Long Island landscape from town to town through their newspaper advertisements. Each one stresses a different accomplishment offered to young ladies:

Clinton Academy

> Miss Mary Dayton has been employed to take the charge of the female department in this Academy, a Lady in whose ability we have great confidence. The course of instruction, in this department, comprises the various branches of Literature necessary to an entire system of female education. The French language, drawing and Painting, and embroidery, will be taught if required—Special attention will be given to the manners and morals of the pupils.[10]

Needlework, drawing, and dancing were all part of the genteel disciplines offered well-to-do girls in the day schools, academies, and seminaries. The primary skill stressed was needlework. The assortment of samplers is a road map of the regional wealth and position of their makers. The 1831 alphabet cross-stitched sampler of ten-year-old Mary Ann Carll of Babylon displays this child's skill with a needle and thread. There is a hearty, wholesome girl in the stitched letters and church and willow of Mary Ann Carll. On the other hand, Esther Ann Whipple's 1826 sampler, which features the verse "Virtue" and baskets, bowers, and urns embroidered in the finest silk threads, demonstrated the control and quality of this child's art.[11]

Theorem painting was also a popular pastime for young ladies of the nineteenth century. These were the creations of still life compositions of fruits and flowers painted with stencils in water color on velvet or paper.

As the nineteenth century progressed, the idea of childhood was altered to an ideal of childhood. The halcyon youthful days on Long Island are best described by Annie Cooper of Sag Harbor, who recorded in her diary in August 1880: "I have spent my summer mostly in rowing, boating, sailing, crabbing, fishing, minoing [*sic*], riding horseback, sewing buttons on shoes, mending stockings, gloves, and trimming boat hats, tanning my arms and wrists brown as a pancake, helping Mama in a few places when I could, and not helping her in a thousand ways when I could."[12]

The concern for the well-being of a child was tempered by the need for feminine restraint and moderation. A woman's placid demeanor was crucial to maintain a calm and well-ordered home environment. "There is nothing that has a more abiding influence on the happiness of a family than the preservation of equable and cheerful temper and tones of the housekeeper."[13]

A woman's duty was to create a happy home environment, to be the support and silent strength behind her spouse. Juliet Hand copied into her journal of 1867 a poem from Samuel Rogers' *Human Life.*

The Wife

> His house she enters there to be a light
> Shining within, when all without is night
> A guardian angel ore his life presiding
> Doubling his pleasures and his cares dividing;
> Winning him back when mingling in the throng
> From a vain world we love alas too long,
> To fireside happiness and hours of ease,
> Blest with that charm, the certainty to please
> How oft her eyes read his! his gentle mind
> To all his wishes all his thoughts inclined,
> Still subject-ever on the watch to borrow
> Mirth of his mirth, and sorrow of these sorrows.[14]

Here is a poetic example of the compliant, dutiful, and inspiring spouse of the mid-nineteenth century. In the selection of this verse to be included in her journal, Juliet Hand appears to have accepted this idealized view of the role of the wife.

Cornelia Huntington had marriage on her mind when she wrote to Deborah Blydenburg on October 5, 1828, about the rumor that Blydenburg was married.

> I commence by asking bluntly and plainly if you are married—for I
> have heard so often that you were on the brink of the matrimonial

precipice that I am by no means certain that you have not taken the leap—I will take it for granted that such is not the case since I have not heard so, and continue to regard you as a fellow sufferer in the cause of celibacy until I am informed that the case is otherwise.[15]

The obligation to maintain the household was the responsibility of the wife, or in the case of Cornelia Huntington, the daughter. In her journal of 1826 she wrote: "I have been busily employed in various domestic duties—such as making sausages, candles, and mince pie, etc., etc. and now having plenty of beef, pork, lard and tallow laid up for many days I intend to 'eat, drink and be merry' that is as far as I can do and not sin."[16]

The diaries and journals from the nineteenth century consistently note the factors that affected the daily routines of their writers: the weather, religion, chores, and celebrations. Meetings, whether social, religious, or organized for a greater cause, were focal points in their lives.

Entertaining ranged from short overnight stays by friends and family to large extravagant celebrations. Visitors to a household would be noted whether they came for an afternoon or for an extended call. Mobility in the 1800s for a Long Island woman meant traveling to a church service, to friends, to parties, to town, or to care for other family members. Women were responsible for the preparation and for the entertainment at social functions. Long Island hostesses often included comments about their guests in their records of occasions from weddings to funerals.

The indomitable Cornelia Huntington wrote in her journal from East Hampton in December 1826: "I have had a party this week, and heaven deliver me from being doomed to living through another such a miserable evening. I had rather reap an acre of barley then to be condemned to be 'Lady Hostess' to people who will neither afford or receive entertainment."[17]

Celebration came to nineteenth-century Long Island in all forms. On December 30, 1870, Laura Sophia Davis and Daniel Woodhull Davis sent out invitations to the then traditional "Tin Wedding," for their tenth anniversary gathering in Mount Sinai. Guests brought oversized tin gifts to celebrate the event. Emma Davis, writing to her sister Estelle, described the preparations, menu, and gifts of the evening:

> There were about 150 there. . . . Mother made fruit cake, pound cake, coconut cake, and doughnuts. We made nearly 300 of them besides the other cakes.
>
> There were 6 turkeys roasted, 4 batches of bread and over 300 biscuits.
>
> At the same time Laura and I were sewing. We made Woodhull a whole suit throughout, Lesther a black velveteen suit and Lena a little blue sack trimmed with white and pinked. . . .

> I suppose you want to know a few of the presents . . . a set of tin jewelry, a shaker bonnet, a tin hat, a pair of slippers, a watch . . . a large Bible.[18]

For yet another tenth wedding anniversary party, Janie Bayles of Port Jefferson decided on a costume theme. Among the invited friends and guests was the "Port Jefferson Literary Society." On January 12, 1875, a newspaper reported: "Mrs. J. E. B. presented a living picture of *Harper's Weekly;* and was one of the most unique costumes worn, as every part of her dress, even her shoes and gloves and handkerchief were covered with the illustrations from the paper. The Elephant and Boss Tweed being the most conspicuous; her hat was the Goddess of Liberty and a plume of different colored tissue paper."[19]

On a more intimate scale, some gatherings were for the enjoyment of feminine company. Women joined in creating a commemorative gift with friends or a gift to celebrate a coming event. "Made out to go to Mary Miller's to quilting. I had a nice time."[20]

In Wading River, Angeline M. Woodhull started an album quilt in 1843. The squares of the quilt are signed and dated by friends and family from Manhasset, Woodville (west of Wading River), and Baiting Hollow. Completed in 1850, this quilt is a *tour de force* of design and craftsmanship. The two center blocks (see fig. 8.2) are believed to have been inspired by popular art prints sold and circulated during this time period.[21]

Images that filled the daily world of local ladies were incorporated into their handiwork. Involved and aware of the political consciousness of the 1800s, Long Island women created objects that reflected the emblems of the New Republic. As always, needlework constituted the majority of their creative expression. A white-work bed cover signed S. Carse depicts the popular symbol of an eagle. Worked into a banner is emblazoned the pledge, "Unity and Health" 1816.[22] In another example of young ladies' art, the visit of Lafayette was commemorated in a sampler done by ten-year-old Esther Ann Whipple, who was later to become Mrs. Luther Skidmore of Riverhead. Dated 1827, young Esther's sampler (see fig. 8.3) included the eagle image, along with a laurel wreath, Lafayette, and the already deceased George Washington.[23]

Patriotism became a part of women's lives during the Civil War. Long Island women joined relief associations to aid the troops. These women knitted mittens, crocheted socks, and raised money to support the northern armies. Dr. Elizabeth Blackwell, the first woman in America to receive a medical degree, organized the Women's Central Association for Relief, or the Women's Sanitary Commission, in 1861.[24] Women volunteered to raise money to fill the Union Army's need for bandages, blankets, medicine, and food. In Southampton in 1861, the Ladies Relief Union heeded Blackwell's

Fig. 8.2. Center panels from a friendship quilt started in 1843, by Angeline M. Woodhull of Wading River, and completed by A. Agnes Brunderhoff of Manhasset (1842-1930). Photographs courtesy of the Suffolk County Historical Society.

Fig. 8.3. Sampler wrought by Esther Ann Whipple. The 1825 sentimental return of Marquis de Layfayette gave young America another hero to idealize. The nation was in a celebratory mood. Esther Ann Whipple, a young girl, was as caught up in commemorating the General's nostalgic return as were professional artists of the day. Photograph courtesy of the Suffolk County Historical Society.

call. In the notebook of the Southampton Ladies Relief Union, there is an invoice of their contributions:

> Sent to James H. Post of the 44th Regiment: Mittens, gloves, socks, scarves, blankets January 7, 1962–September 18, 1861.

> 19 members, dues 25 cents. Collected $82.26, the festival $68.62. Sent $125 to the New York Ladies Relief Union.[25]

Religion influenced the daily lives of Long Island's nineteenth-century women. The anticipation of salvation, the duty to belief, and the appeal to God for answers were aspects that entered into all of their endeavors. In her June 1835 letter to her son aboard a whaling ship, Sarah Horton wrote from Shelter Island: "We have news that you have experienced religion, I pray that there may not be any mistake about it . . . the affliction which I allude to . . . was nothing less then the death of your father . . . you may imagine my situation, left with 6 children and the prospects of a dreary winter."[26]

In the nineteenth century, a woman's role in response to a death in the family was to become the visual embodiment of mourning. She was obliged to maintain an appearance of mourning in her clothing. She created symbols of remembrance in her handiwork. Lorana Whitman Smith's mourning picture, recorded the death of her son Alexander in 1806 in silk on linen. In this rendering, the mourners weep unconsolably before the classic motifs: a weeping willow and urn, incorporated into the needlework design.[27]

A myriad of emotions and expectations can be found in the written expression and in the art and artifacts representing Long Island's nineteenth-century women. Though their lives were full, harried, and often times turbulent, society expected these women to appear with constant composure and equanimity. As wife, mother, daughter, and sister, feelings and emotions were to be concealed for the benefit of others. The words of these women become more intimate when they are placed in the context of the life of Long Island, a life that was both enjoyed and endured.

Notes

To Blush Unseen: 19th-Century Long Island Woman was an exhibition in the David Filderman Gallery of the Hofstra Museum, February 1–March 24, 1996, curated by Kathryn Curran. This essay is drawn from the exhibit catalog; most of the artifacts and documents cited were part of the exhibit. (Editor's note.)

1. Timothy Dwight, *Travels in New England and New York,* 1821-1822, edited by Barbara Miller Solomon (Reprint, Cambridge: Belknap Press of Harvard University Press, 1969), 3: 200, 399n.5. Dwight ends his commentary with a quote from a popular poetic piece by Thomas Gray (1716-1771), "Elegy Written in a Country Churchyard." The title of the exhibit and this essay is taken from lines 55-56.

2. Phoebe McCoon, sampler in Smithtown Historical Society collection, Smithtown, NY.

3. Dwight, *Travels in New England and New York,* 4: 334.

4. P. G. Buckley, "Truly We Live in a Dying World, Mourning on Long Island," in *A Time to Mourn, Expressions of Grief in Nineteenth Century America,* edited by Martha V. Pike and Janice Gray Armstrong (Stony Brook, NY: The Museums at Stony Brook, 1980), p. 109.

5. Quoted by Arthur W. Calhoun in *A Social History of the American Family from Colonial Times to the Present* (Cleveland, OH: Arthur H. Clark, 1917), 2: 67.

6. *Forrester's Boys' and Girls' Magazine and Fireside Companion* 9 (January to June 1853): 58.

7. Adele Parsons Sherill, Diary, in the Pennypacker Long Island Collection, East Hampton Public Library.

8. Ibid.

9. Harriet G. Valentine, *The Window to the Street: A Mid-Nineteenth-Century View of Cold Spring Harbor, New York, Based on the Diary of Helen Rogers* (Smithtown: Exposition Press, 1981), p. 45. Helen Roger's Diary is in the collections of the Whaling Museum in Cold Spring Harbor which reprinted Valentine's book in 1991.

10. *Sag Harbor Record,* April 13, 1839.

11. The samplers wrought by Mary Ann Carll and Esther Ann Whipple are in the Suffolk County Historical Society Collections, Riverhead, NY.

12. Anne Cooper, Diary in the Pennypacker Long Island Collection, East Hampton Public Library.

13. Harriet Beecher Stowe and Catherine Stowe, *The American Woman's Home,* 1869 (Reprint, Hartford, 1875), p. 212.

14. Juliet Hand, Amagansett, Diary, in the Pennypacker Long Island Collection, East Hampton Public Library.

Samuel Rogers (1763-1857) first published *Human Life* in 1819. It is included in his *Poems* (London: Edward Moxon, 1842), pp. 61-116. The lines Juliet Hand copied (pp. 77-78) are part of a longer section; the version included in the copy of the 1842 edition does not have any subheads in the entire poem. The subject is certainly "the wife," but Juliet Hand may have provided the title for these lines rather than Samuel Rogers. (Editor's note.)

15. Letter in Smithtown Historical Society Collection, Smithtown, NY.

16. Cornelia Huntington, East Hampton, Diary, in the Pennypacker Long Island Collection, East Hampton Public Library.

17. Ibid.

18. Emma Davis to Estelle, December 30, 1870, in the collections of the Historical Society of Greater Port Jefferson, Port Jefferson, NY. The society's tin wedding objects in its collection were in the Hofstra exhibition.

See also Kate W. Strong, "Tin Wedding of 1870," *Long Island Forum* 9 (May 1946): 95; reprinted, 51 (spring 1988): 82 (Editor's note).

19. Clipping, unnamed newspaper, January 12, 1875 in collection of the Historical Society of Greater Port Jefferson, Port Jefferson, NY.

20. Julia Hand, Diary, 1870.

21. Quilt in collection of the Suffolk County Historical Society, Riverhead, NY.

22. White work bedspread in the Shelter Island Historical Society collection.

23. Esther Ann Whipple, sampler in Suffolk County Historical Society collection, Riverhead, NY; see Barbara E. Austen, "Lafayette's Visit to Newark, New Jersey Sampled," *The Magazine Antiques,* April 1994, p. 512.

24. Jacqueline M. Atkins, *New York Beauties: Quilts From the Empire State* (New York: Dutton Studio Books, 1992), p. 26.

25. Records of the Southampton Ladies Relief Union, founded August 1, 1861, Southampton Colonial Society collections, Southampton Historical Society, Southampton, NY.

26. Sarah Horton, June 1835 letter, in the Pennypacker Long Island Collection, East Hampton Public Library.

27. Mourning picture by Loran Whitman Smith, 1806, in the Smithtown Historical Society collection, Smithtown, NY.

9. Long Island Women and Benevolence: Changing Images of Women's Place, 1880–1920

Alice Ross

Service to the community has always been one of the primary responsibilities of American women. Following colonial New England custom, women's charge included service to neighbors and congregations, as it did to their extended families. During the course of nineteenth and early twentieth-century urbanization, men shifted their focus away from the corporate family farm and religious community to the urban marketplace; women throughout the nation filled the void by assuming increasingly powerful roles in benevolence and related local reform. Their major task was fundraising, despite the apparent contradiction between its business nature and the idealized married woman's role that insulated them from the public workplace. This blurring of women's roles worked because their fundraising fulfilled their traditional pattern of service and depended on the domestic skills and products (food and handicrafts) that had always been their domain.

Following this national pattern, Long Island women involved themselves increasingly in community philanthropy. According to a local directory (probably incomplete), the women's charitable organizations of Suffolk County grew from one in 1850 to fifty-two by 1920.[1] The spread of organized small town benevolence was facilitated by the Long Island Rail Road's improved transportation, new telephone lines, and the growing complexity of the male-dominated business community. During the course of socializing, shopping, or attending meetings and lectures, local women were increasingly inspired by Brooklyn's philanthropic networks. Moreover, urban influences permeated local villages through summer visitors (friends, family, business associates, church dignitaries, and vacationers) and relocated New York City charities. For example, Suffolk County hosted the St. Johnland Home (King's Park, 1865), the New York City Agricultural and Industrial Society Orphanage (Kings Park, 1904), the summer residences of Locustdale, the Brooklyn Home for Children (Hauppauge, 1907), and the Howard Colored Orphanage and Industrial School (St. James, 1906).[2]

Local women involved themselves in national trends by opening chapters of national organizations and embarking on such projects as the Suffolk County chapter of the Women's Christian Temperance Union (W.C.T.U., 1888), the County Home for Convalescent Babies in Sea Cliff (1894), the East Hampton Ladies' Village Improvement Society (1895), the Village Welfare Society in Port Washington (1906), the Society for Lending Comforts to the Sick in Smithtown (1910), and the Mineola chapter of the American Red Cross (1917).[3] Outnumbering these secular groups were the proliferation of church-affiliated ladies' aid societies, sewing circles, and missionary societies which had functioned in numerous Long Island churches throughout the century. Secular as well as religious groups reflected the strongly Christian influence of both national and Long Island culture; the obvious example is the W.C.T.U.[4] However, even newly-formed, secular libraries retained the Christian identification, a connection reflected in a 1901 Greenport newspaper announcement that "The King's Daughters of East Hampton . . . have sent some seventy-five books to Springs to aid in establishing a public library there. No more truly Christian service could be rendered."[5]

Women of Suffolk and present-day Nassau Counties undertook similar kinds of local charitable work. Situated nearer to New York City, Nassau County showed surprisingly fewer benevolent organizations than did Suffolk. This rather minor but interesting point opens some speculation. Did Suffolk County feel more need for local organizations because of its distance from New York City? Perhaps its relatively modest, semi-rural communities were accustomed to functioning as autonomous entities whose limited economic resources required more effort. Perhaps Nassau women channeled more of their energies and resources into New York City organizations. In any case, as a whole, Long Island women put substantial efforts to financing community welfare.

Strategies

The most obvious means of raising funds was through donations of cash, whether gift or subscription. During times of crisis, both individuals and communities contributed time and effort. For example, during the Civil War, Long Island women raised sums of money to support the work of the Brooklyn Sanitary Commission.[6] This kind of strategy was documented in local diaries; Ella and Phebe Smith of Smithtown noted their own periodic efforts (and those of others) to remind members to send in Women's Society dues in the early 1900s.[7]

Few Long Island causes, however, could depend entirely on contributions; most of the work involved marketing the products of women's household skills. Throughout the nineteenth century, church women organized cooperative "donation parties," social gatherings intended to raise a local minister's salary. Held regularly at the home of a prominent congregant, such fundraisers depended on the women's voluntary contributions of good home-style food and entertainments intended to increase conviviality and loosen purse strings. Participants were generally members of the congregation, and, on some occasions, included supportive outsiders. Mrs. Amelia

Brush of Cold Spring Harbor, wrote in 1863 that she helped by "soliciting for a donation in this place for Mr. Sterns," and attended many other such events, among them the "tea party at Mr. Gathard's to raise funds to pay the Preacher at Coldspring" in 1864. Likewise, Mrs. Handley in Hauppauge in 1867 received an "invitation to Mr Sinclars donation party" and was enlisted "to make some cake and some biscit [biscuit] for the donation party for Mr. Stansberry" the following year.[8] The scope of donation parties was clearly in line with the domestic character of women's roles.

Some of their financial success may be attributed to the social nature of these events, which provided an important source of community diversion in a time before the growth of modest public restaurants and entertainments. Their value to the community was suggested not only in the diary notations above, but also in newspaper articles. The *Long Island (Port Jefferson) Leader,* reporting on a Southampton event in 1877, noted that "Donation Parties are in order at this season."[9]

Even before 1880, donation parties began to evolve into larger, more public affairs. The Brooklyn Sanitary Commission Fairs had set a standard for large-scale charitable sales; indeed, local women had submitted items for sale, and were found "in attendance at the Long Island tables."[10] After 1880, with the commercial growth of Long Island's villages, the enlarged facilities of churches and civic centers included social halls with institutional kitchens. Larger events were possible; church and civic suppers, festivals, fairs, and entertainments attracted participants from other congregations and communities. They came to mingle and to be entertained, as well as to support a cause. They chose their purchases from a variety of donated items, still prepared in small quantities at home, which represented traditional domestic culinary and decorative skills.

The expanding scope of these projects required stricter organization and coordination, a public role that had otherwise been denied women. Such women as Ella Mathilda Smith, who chaired women's society fund-raising committees of the First Presbyterian Church of Smithtown (1894–1920), developed business skills otherwise delegated to men. In the course of her philanthropic duties, Ella learned to estimate what would sell, to solicit items to be sold, to coordinate volunteers, to arrange for the hall and its furnishings, to see to the transportation of large items, to oversee the cleaning and serving, to arrange for printed handbills and newspaper notices, to secure financial credit when necessary, and to prepare the final accounting.[11] She had moved beyond the confines of domesticity.

The further development of convention dinners required a larger step into the public world of business. The annual conventions of a number of associations required sites at which large numbers of people could attend sessions and be served meals. The Suffolk County Temperance Conventions

(Northville, 1876), the 127th Regiment Reunion in Greenport (1904), the Christian Endeavor Convention (Orient, 1901), and the annual Suffolk County Teachers' Conferences were among the many organizations whose meetings fed the coffers of local women's societies.[12]

A number of groups raised funds by hosting such conventions and serving mammoth dinners. No longer the simple buffet meal comprised of coordinated donations prepared in congregants' homes, convention dinners were generally mass meals prepared, *in situ*, by semi-professional volunteers in the institutional kitchens installed in large public and church halls. For example, the Sound Avenue Grange and two cooperating Protestant churches in Smithtown drew repeats on Sunday School Teachers' gatherings and Presbyterian conferences. Efficient menus, close planning, bulk buying, and the special skills of quantity cookery were essential for the desired profit; sometimes bank loans were necessary to cover the initial investment in supplies. In addition to financial considerations (among them the initial investment in the physical plant), it became necessary to work out efficient service required by conferences' strict schedules.[13]

Women learned these business techniques from each other. Ella Smith's note to Mrs. Fan Latham, who had chaired the Presbyterian convention in Orient the year before, asked advice on the most popular dishes and the quantities needed for two hundred people. Mrs. Latham's response included appropriate figures, as well as a comment suggesting both the challenges of originality and cooperation:

> We think it quite a complement that you, who have had the care of getting up dinners so many times, should ask about ours for this was a sort of experiment with us and we are delighted to think it was a success, before we have taken as many cakes & such things as people gave but this time when we had over sixteen cakes we told them they would have to give something else, and I think it was the right way.[14]

One of the most ambitious of the charitable undertakings was the compiling and publishing of fund–raising cookbooks. It brought middle-class women into direct contact with the public business community. The preparation of manuscripts required extensive canvassing of the women's community, selecting recipes, editing, preparing the text and layout, distributing, and promoting its cookbook. In addition, the most innovative and socially-challenging task involved selling advertising to meet the costs of publication. A woman walking into downtown shops and asking merchants to buy space in cookbooks apparently provoked social and emotional obstacles to both genders. The editors of the Northville Congregational Church's *Practical Cook Book* (1886) described the ordeal humorously:

> Here come some Ladies with a roll
> But now I'm beggar-wise

And if they're working for a fair
I will not advertise
He looked so cross and frowned so hard
We did not dare to ask;
so bought some pins
And left the store,
To find an easier task.

Another man so gracious was,
And looked so sweet and wise,
When someone said "We've come to see
If you would advertise;"
That we all thought "We'll get one here,"
But no! for answered he,
If you don't till your papers
Come back again at 3!"

He smiled us out and said "Goodbye"
Who nevermore we'd see
For if we ever called again,
He "not at home" would be.
One man looked so benevolent,
And took great interest
In what we told him of our work
And said it would be blessed.

He advertised right willingly,
And cheered us on our way
With kind regards and good advice
"How nice he was," said they.
"Yes, so he was," another sighed,
"But really, so polite,
He would have given twice the sum
If we had worked it right."

Oh! mercenary charity,
Benevolence and greed;
Oh! human nature students, please
Pass on and do not read.

—Selected.[15]

Ella Smith who completed a church cookbook manuscript, failed to publish it; her work stalled just at the point of selling advertising, suggesting that such encounters with the business community were an insurmountable obstacle for some of her generation.[16]

As the following generation of women continued to penetrate the masculine sphere, the early discomfort of both sexes about women's organizations slowly eased. It gradually became clearer that female philanthropy benefitted both the community and businessmen who began to see the value of advertising and good will. Local community cookbooks published before 1920 contained increasing numbers of pages of advertising and the editors' admonitions to patronize cooperative establishments.[17] This deviation from the idealized married, middle-class female role (that had promoted domestic isolation) was actually one facet of nationwide redirection toward women's social independence. "Modern women" found new expressions in athletics, travel, the women's clubs, a more public style of socializing, and, of course, the business of charity work.

Completing the gender transition, a new institution—Women's Exchanges—helped to soften gender lines. Like earlier forms of philanthropy, they encouraged women in need of support to sell their own high-quality domestic products for their own profit. The Exchanges, women's own retail shops, sold such products for a small commission. Generally situated in business district store fronts, they competed directly with neighboring merchants. Women's success with Exchanges depended on both the quality of merchandise and the business skills of their all-female boards of directors who determined standards, evaluated contributions, and supervised the running, promoting, and financing of the shops. Suffolk County's Exchanges followed these advances as philanthropic women took an unaccustomed public place alongside men in such establishments as the Patchogue Woman's Exchange and Tea Room and the Port Jefferson Women's Exchange (1911). Some communities, not large enough to maintain a permanent location, supported part-time efforts; for example, in the years just before 1920, Ella Smith ran a modest Saturday Exchange in her home.[18]

The Women Most Involved With Change

The backbone of women's philanthropic activity came from the general population of middle-class homemakers who contributed available time and skills. Their small scale, domestic efforts were oriented to traditional home activities. However, small groups of more privileged women had the means, leisure, authority, and desire for leadership. They marshalled their resources for the gender networks in which they had high standing, and they developed appropriate economic and organizational skills. Each community was served by a small coterie of established leaders whose efforts merged, particularly through the strong religious orientation that structured so much of Long Island society. Thus local churches, particularly the predominating Protestant denominations, provided a basic avenue of service.

Fig. 9.1. Ella Smith, c.1866. Photograph courtesy of the Smithtown Historical Society, which owns the portrait.

Mrs. Ella Smith (Smithtown, 1849–1922) exemplified the women dedicated to such work. Like other local female leaders in benevolence, she came from a well-established local family, the descendants of Patentee Richard Smythe, Smithtown's founder. In a pattern typical of her family, she was deeply committed to the First Presbyterian Church of Smithtown, and she was well aware of the social precepts of the noted Calvinist revivalist reformer Lyman Beecher (an old family friend) and his famous daughters Catharine Beecher and Harriet Beecher Stowe.[19] Ella's enterprising husband Theodore Willis Smith took an active role in community fairs as a successful businessman, Superintendent of the County Farm, and President of the Riverhead Agricultural Association. For Ella, authority and leadership were natural roles.[20]

Ella possessed the means and the inspiration with which to dedicate her life to good works. With relatively few demands on her time and her next-door sister Phebe to help when needed, Ella focused on charitable works. Despite numerous accomplishments, she followed the social mores and expectations of her day, embracing the self-effacing role of cheerful example, selflessness, and anonymity, rejecting personal, financial, or other reward. The diaries of Ella and her unmarried sister Phebe Smith, as well as the minutes of various women's associations, documented Ella's strong commitment to this social model through church work. Repeated references to her activities included weekly meetings and chores for the First Presbyterian Church Ladies' Aid Society, the Woman's Missionary Society, Christian Endeavor, and Cheerful Workers; in addition, she worked for the local lecture series, the library and fire house projects, and campaigns to help Fresh Air Children and European famine victims. In this great variety of good works her name appeared perpetually as an office holder.

In addition she served as Honorary Vice-President of the Nassau Presbytery Branch of the Missionary Society (Jamaica), as a board member of the Smithtown Library, and periodically as a delegate to regional religious conferences.[21] Her reputation, widely known and honored, was preserved in an unprecedented eulogy written into the minutes of the Woman's Missionary Society, which noted, "No one can measure the good she has done not alone in her own home village but reaching far out in places we little know of. Only those closely associated with her have any idea of her many deeds of charity and they did not know one half."[22]

Ella's pattern of means, leisure, and dutiful leadership was typical of the women who assumed the most responsibility for local philanthropy. Although they tended to dedicate themselves primarily to a favored cause, they also contributed their skills and experience to other local projects. Among Ella's peers at church, Mrs. W. F. Darling also organized Smithtown's Society for Lending Comforts to the Sick. In East Hampton, Mrs. Dayton served her church and founded the East Hampton Ladies' Village Improvement Society.

It is not surprising that unmarried women with more leisure often found their vocations in benevolence; for example, Miss Helen Blydenburgh, a colleague of Ella's with similar credentials, followed her lead in church and civic projects and established the Society for Lending Comforts to the Sick (April 1906). Like other village societies, its roster of officers included the same small coterie of authoritative "aristocracy" who represented interrelated and relatively prosperous families—Mrs. Buel T. Williams and Mrs. Emma A. Tyler, who served similarly in the Presbyterian Church. Mrs. Tyler was also closely associated with the local chapter of the W.C.T.U., and served as its chair for many years.[23] Indeed, Long Island charities were directed by the same established, often interrelated families again and again; among them we find Smith, Darling, and Blydenburgh (Smithtown), Townshend (Quogue), Handley (Hauppauge), Wells (Northville), Tooker and Young (Riverhead), and Dayton (East Hampton).

Fortified by the network of its leadership, social and charitable organizations connected throughout the Island, and benefitted from large bases of mutual support. Although Long Island's women's societies tended to be fairly homogeneous within themselves according to ethnicity and religious denomination, most Protestants patronized each others' events. Thus Ella and Phebe Smith attended the public suppers and entertainments by the African American A.M.E. Bethel Church in Smithtown and Northport, as well as local Methodist, Episcopal, or Congregationalist affairs in town.[24] There is no data suggesting that the strong anti-Catholic sentiment of the early twentieth century greatly affected Protestant attendance at Catholic charitable food events, despite religious and social differences. Judging by their great financial successes, it is likely that Catholic festivals drew some degree of general community support. The matter of comparable Jewish fund-raising events with food brings up a deeper mystery, as there is no documentation that such affairs evolved. Perhaps the non-Christian nature of Jewishness distanced the Protestant establishment which could, after all, sponsor local minority Protestant Blacks. Suffolk County black women were tied to Protestant families through local "missionary" efforts (personal, economic, and religious); and there was a relatively close connection between the many black women who cooked in white households and shared their cuisine. The scarcity of Jewish community fund-raising affairs with food may be related to more distanced social involvements and to the non-kosher food at Protestant charitable events which, far from binding, presented a barrier.[25]

The great success of women's fund-raising projects and their general importance within communities lie in their substantial earnings and their key role in community development. Annual reports show that they often supplied a major share of a group's yearly income, and enabled critical improvements.[26] For example, they expanded, maintained, and furnished churches, the essential social center of most communities. In one fair, the Catholic ladies of Central Islip raised $1,500 for stained glass windows (1909). In small villages the money was sometimes raised more gradually. The Ladies' Aid Society of Smithtown's First Presbyterian Church furnished their new wing with an institututional kitchen and dining room equipment through a series of modest affairs: Mrs. Handley's buffet supper at Smithtown's Presbyterian Church chapel in 1912, earned $115 ("a success" for the small village), and a Presbyterian Church turkey supper brought in $125 in 1900.[27] In the words of Joella Vreeland, historian of the Universalist Unitarian Church of Southold, "The men built the church and the women kept it going."[28]

Other groups undertook signal community beautification, and expanded their communities' social and educational resources. The annual fairs of East Hampton's Ladies' Village Improvement Society earned $500 in one day (1907) by selling their members' homemade products and cookbooks, and used the money to preserve the handsome historic lagoon and park area, to plant trees, and to install street signs. Their enhancement of attractive local features helped to launch the vacation and tourism industry that thrives to this day. Similarly, the Ladies' Committee of the Quogue Village Improvement Society raised $933.87 at their 1910 country fair, and $1,131.80 the succeeding year, and applied it to town beautification with the same results. Even a small group like the Society for Lending Comforts to the Sick earned three-fourths of its income in 1908 through cake sales (the rest came from membership dues or donations), with which they purchased and supplied equipment and nursing care for homebound invalids.[29]

With growing experience, women became proficient in many aspects of business administration. Their ability to undertake otherwise unorthodox activities in the course of their philanthropic endeavors was probably due, in part, to their secure social positions and relative imperviousness to local disapproval. Their blurring of gender work divisions must have been further facilitated by their consistant use of domestic articles in fundraisers and their traditional role of community service. While there is little evidence that these women used their new skills for careers or personal gain in the public sphere, their pioneering experiences opened further doors for the middle class women of their daughters' generations. As a case in point, Ella Smith's daughter Faith chose not to marry, embarked instead on the running of a Smithtown insurance agency and developed the reputation of being Smithtown's first career woman.[30] Faith Smith's advancement beyond her mother's accomplishments is a reminder that these steps were gradual, and often generational.

In summary, the women who met their societal responsibilities by fundraising for important community causes found themselves in a complex, sometimes conflicted role. The work of benevolence offered a means to the fulfillment of their prescribed female-specific roles, and led them, at first, to undertake proscribed "un-feminine" acts. If Ella's failure to publish her cookbook was indeed related to the restrictive rootedness of the nineteenth-century gendered society, by the end of her life (1922) she had nevertheless progressed substantially from the limited ideals of domesticity.

Notes

1. Henry J. Lee, ed., *Long Island Almanac and Year Book, Nassau and Suffolk Counties, 1930* (Brooklyn: Eagle Library Publications, 1930), pp. 132-82.

2. Carleton Kelsey (former Town Historian and current Librarian of the Archives of the Amagansett Historical Society), interview with author, May 17, 1995. For New York charities on Long Island, see in the Long Island Collection, Smithtown Library: *Harper Review,* April 1866; "Annual Report, 1912-13, Howard Orphanage and Industrial School"; Joan Elizabeth Harris, "The Progressive Era in Smithtown, New York: A Study of Five Charitable Institutions," unpublished report for the Smithtown Historical Society (November 28, 1981), pp. 3, 6, 25, 38-41.

3. Lee, *Long Island Almanac,* pp. 122, 131, 140, 169, 175; Annual Report Minutes, Society for Lending Comforts to the Sick, Smithtown Historical Society. (See also the articles below, "The Ladies' Village Improvement Society: A Century of Force in East Hampton" by Eunice Junkett Meeker, and "Civic-Minded Women: The Sayville Village Improvement Society," by Norma White. Editor's Note.)

4. "Minutes," W.C.T.U., Riverhead Chapter, November 1916 and passim, at the Library of the Suffolk County Historical Society, Riverhead; *Riverhead News,* March 21, 1891, p. 3.

5. *Republican (Greenport) Watchman,* October 26, 1901, p. 1.

6. "Executive Committee," *History of the Brooklyn and Long Island Fair, February 22, 1864* (Brooklyn: n.p. 1864), pp. 149, 184-45.

7. Phebe Smith, Diaries: end page list of accounts, 1900, 1906; January 28, 1908, June 23, 1908, November 16, 1908, December 17, 1908, November 1, 1910, October 3, 1911, June 2, 1913, July 9, 1913, October 2, 1913, October 13, 1913. Ella Smith, Diaries: intermittently through March 1898 and 1900, May 2, 1901, February 8, 1904, October 3, 1918, November 25, 1918, Smith Family Papers Collection, Smithtown Historical Society, Smithtown, NY.

8. Mrs. Amelia Brush, MS Diaries, Cold Spring Harbor, March 24, 1863, November 11, 1864, original in Huntington Historical Society Library, Huntington, NY; Mrs. Mary Handley, MS Diary, Hauppauge, March 18, 1867, March 1, 1868, original in Richard Handley Papers, Long Island Collection, Smithtown Library.

9. *The Long Island (Port Jefferson) Leader,* December 22, 1877, p. 4; *Babylon South Side Signal,* August 31, 1884, p. 3; Eliza Jane (Fisk) Glover diary (L.V.I.S. reference), July 27, 1907, Pennypacker Collection, East Hampton Library, East Hampton, NY; Phebe Smith Diary, May 28, 1912; Ella Smith Diary, December 12, 1900.

10. "Executive Committee," *History of the Brooklyn and Long Island Fair, 1864,* pp. 149, 184-85; Kelsey, interview.

11. Minutes, Woman's Missionary Society, First Presbyterian Church of Smithtown, Smithtown, NY, Church Archives, passim; Ella Smith, Diary, January 9, 1904.

12. *Greenport Republican Watchman* 50 no. 33 (February 19, 1876): 2; 79 no. 13 (September 3, 1904): 2; Ella Smith, Diary, October 25, 1920.

13. Laura Downs (1901-), interview, Sound Avenue, Riverhead; October 17, 1994; Phebe Smith, Diaries, November 12, 1901, October 27, 1902, October 28, 1904, June 12, 1907, May 4, 1912, October 28, 1912; Ella Smith, Diary, October 25, 1920.

14. Ella Smith to Fan Latham, Orient, November 17, 1901; Fan Latham to Ella Smith, n.d. Smith Family Papers Collection, Smithtown Historical Society.

15. Mutual Benefit Society, "Introduction," *The Practical Cook Book* (Northville: Northville Congregational Church, 1890), p. 2.

16. Ella Smith, manuscript cookbook (c. 1905), collection of the author.

17. Alice Ross, "Domesticity, Work, and the Food of Married, Middle-Class Women, Suffolk County, N.Y., 1880-1920" (Ph.D. diss., SUNY at Stony Brook, 1996).

18. Charles L. "Pie" Dufour and Samuel Wilson, *Women Who Cared: The 100 Years of the Christian Woman's Exchange* (New Orleans: by the author, 1908); Margaret F. Buck, *One Hundred Years of The Woman's Exchange* (West Hartford, CT: by the author, 1988); P. G. Hubert, Jr., "Occupations For Women," in *The Woman's Book* (New York: Charles Scribner's Sons, 1894), pp. 29-39; *Montauk Business Directory of Long Island . . .* (Brooklyn: Montauk Directory Company, 1911), pp. 122, 133; Inez Hubbs, Smithtown resident, interview with author, April 27, 1995; Helen Thompson Jones (1913-), Smithtown resident, interview by author, April 3, 1995, July 25, 1993; Phebe Smith, Diaries, January 18, 1900, February 13, 1900, July 26, 1906 expenditure listed in her year-end accounts; Phebe Smith to Ella Smith, January 21, 1900, described an Exchange she visited while on vacation, giving details of stock and prices. (See also article below by Martha Kreisel, "Candace Thurber Wheeler and the New York Exchange for Woman's Work." Editor's Note).

19. Ella Smith, Scrapbooks, Smith Family Papers Collection, Smithtown Historical Society, Smithtown, NY.

20. Charlotte Adams Ganz, *Colonel Rockwell's Scrapbook* (Smithtown: Smithtown Historical Society, 1968), pp. 127, 164-65; Smith Family Papers Collection.

21. Ella Smith, Diaries, passim; "Minutes," Ladies' Aid Society, and "Minutes," Presbyterian Church's Woman's Missionary Society, Auxiliary to the Woman's Home and Foreign Missionary Society of the Presbytery of Nassau, undated [1922], Archives, First Presbyterian Church of Smithtown; Ella Smith Diaries, January 14, 1904, February 5, 1905, October 5, 1918, October 1-2, 1908, January 13-15, 1921.

22. Minutes, Woman's Missionary Society of Smithtown, undated [1922].

23. *Society for Lending Comforts to the Sick, Smithtown Branch, L. I., Second Annual Report, 1907-8,* Long Island Collection, Smithtown Library; Jones interview; *Smithtown Presbyterian Church Yearbook, 1906* (Smithtown: First Presbyterian Church of Smithtown, 1906), p. 8; and ibid., 1907, p. 8.

24. Phebe Smith, Diary, February 22, 1909; Ella Smith, Diary, May 11-14, 1920.

25. The sources used for this paper revealed no Jewish women's philanthropic organizations, despite their existence in larger communities of Brooklyn. It seems possible that local Jewish communities were too small or too insular to support such work, although men's Hebrew organizations of a different nature did exist.

26. Annual Report, Society for Lending Comforts to the Sick, 1904, Archives, Smithtown Historical Society Collections, Smithtown, NY.

27. *The Long Island Leader (Port Jefferson),* December 22, 1877, p. 4; *(Babylon) South Side Signal,* August 31, 1884, p. 3; Glover diary, L.V.I.S., July 27, 1907, Pennypacker Collection, East Hampton Library, East Hampton, NY; Phebe Smith, Diary, May 28, 1912; Ella Smith Diary, December 12, 1900.

28. Joella Vreeland, author of *This Is The Church* (Mattituck: Amereon House, 1988), interview with author, Southold, October 17, 1994.

29. "Annual Reports," Society for Lending Comforts to the Sick, Smithtown Branch, L.I., 1907-1909, Smithtown Historical Society.

30. Helen Jones interview; Clifford Crafts, of Crafts, Smith, Nowick and Goodwin Insurance Agency (partner of Faith Smith), interview by author, Smithtown, November 19, 1984.

10. The Forebears Were Women
Three Smith Sisters

Norma A. Cohen

While seemingly contradictory, the terms "ordinary" and "exemplary" are appropriate to the lives of three Long Island women, Josephine Elsworth Smith (1884–1969), Frances Mildred Smith (1886–1972), and Dorothy Miller Smith (1890–1970), who spent many of their days in the house where I have worked for ten years. Although they found themselves embroiled in both national and, during wartime, international issues, the sensibilities of these women were shaped by the mores of the home and the community that nurtured them. This was a world peopled, prodded, and propelled by the Smiths of Smithtown; a world where the commingled concept of progeny and land predominated; a world where civic service was a noble and vital concern; and generally a world that did not turn unless a man told it to. By examining this world, one is treated to a glimpse of Long Island's past, as if looking at one of the antique picturebooks in the attic of the Smith family home, the Mills Pond House (c.1838), which now hosts the Smithtown Township Arts Council. I dedicate this essay to the spirits of the women whose presence I have keenly felt in the home I have shared with them.

To understand the sisters' sense of family, place, and country, one must examine the historical ties that bound them to the land on which they lived and to the town that bears their name. This was a family where male lineage was singularly important for the inheritance of property and for personal prestige. The forebears listed in all obituaries were exclusively male. By the time Josephine and Mildred Smith became the owners of the Mills Pond House, it had passed through several generations of Mills and Smiths beginning in 1692. The homestead came to the Smiths when E. DuBois Smith, father of Josephine, Mildred, and Dorothy, inherited the property in 1888. In addition to running the farm, DuBois Smith became a realtor with an office in New York City, speculated in Long Island real estate, and continued with extensive stock breeding. These were all activities that would have direct bearing on the interests and occupations of the three Smith sisters.

Josephine, Mildred, and Dorothy were the beneficiaries of the Mills and Smith legacy, which included a love of the family land, a desire to serve their community, and a keen respect for their ancestry. These qualities motivated these rather conventional women to lead rather unusual lives.

The Smith sisters were raised with their brothers Malcolm Elsworth and Edmund Thomas in St. James, a small village within the Town of Smithtown.

At the turn of the century, the Mills Pond House was a producing farm with barns, wash house, cider mill, apple orchards, planted fields, crops, animals, farm hands, and servants. The sisters' playmates and social set were chiefly family and close family friends. Their social status determined their upbringing, which was provincial, upper class Victorian, influenced by business and social contacts in Manhattan and Garden City. It was a family in which gender had a great deal to do with roles and responsibilities.

During the school year the family moved to Garden City, where the children were educated. A planned suburban community, Garden City was founded by A.T. Stewart, a self-made multimillionaire and a cousin by marriage to the Smiths. His wife Cornelia Clinch Stewart was Bessie Smith White's "Auntie," and when the childless Stewarts passed away, their twelve million dollar fortune was divided between Bessie and her sisters. Each built a magnificent home, designed by Stanford White, in Head of the Harbor on Long Island Sound.

Josephine and Mildred went on to the Veltin School for Girls in Manhattan where they studied literature, history, art history, and Latin. As young women they were exposed to the vibrant cultural life in Manhattan, were escorted to society dances, and were introduced to only the "right people." Although they were condescendingly called "Country Smiths" by their "City Smith" cousins, the "Mills Pond girls" were not simple farmers. By the turn of the century, St. James and Head of the Harbor attracted the rich and the famous. Mayor Gaynor of New York City lived down the road at Deepwells from 1913 to 1917. Stanford White's Box Hill was a country seat for the Who's Who of New York society. William J. Ryan, publisher of the prestigious *Literary Digest,* hosted some of the leading lights of literature at fetes and soirees on his estate in Head of the Harbor. New York actors and actresses rented summer homes and performed in local theaters. For the Smiths these were times of simple pleasures: croquet, swimming, boating, country walks, carriage rides, berry picking, playing with chicks and goats, sewing, debates around the dining room table, parlor games, church services and socials, and entertainments such as lotto, whist, and making paper roses.

Nevertheless, big changes were taking place in the country. The 1890s ushered in the era of Standard Oil and the Beef Trust, a time when millions of men and women earned their living in sweat shops. It was an era defined by the machine age and machine politics, rackets and organized vice, by the melting pot, universal suffrage, women's rights, and charity balls. Electricity, the telephone, automobiles, cinemas, subways, and ocean travel were coming into general use. With Irish and Italian immigrants moving to St. James, the older, wealthier landowners attempted, with new zoning laws, to control what they considered an encroachment by the masses.

Fig. 10.1. The three Smith sisters (*left to right*), Josephine, Mildred, and Dorothy. Photographs courtesy of the Smithtown Township Arts Council.

When the Smith sisters emerged into young womanhood, they had not been part of America's work force. In 1907, twenty-three year old Josephine and twenty-one year old Mildred took a five-month Grand Tour of Egypt, Italy, Switzerland, France, and England, an unusual undertaking for the average Long Island woman, but not for women of the moneyed class. Given that travel on the Nile and in the desert was rather primitive, that all baggage transfers were personal responsibilities, and that there were countless hotel connections and travel details to negotiate, such a trip for the sheltered sisters was an adventure. Traveling with a chaperone, Aunt M, and carrying introductions to the right people in European capitals, the Smiths dressed in long skirts, petticoats, corsets, and flowered and feathered hats whether touring the pyramids and the sphinx on camel or having tea with the Prince and Princess Delletori at the Hotel du Vesuve in Naples. They shopped for jewelry, dresses, hats, and lace wherever they could. Following their interest in art and architecture, Josephine and Mildred explored every important museum, cathedral, and castle. Their daily journal was sent home in letters.

Ten years later, in 1917, when America made its entrance into the Great War, it was a time of national action. Women joined, and in some instances formed, organizations such as the Red Cross, the YWCA, and the United War Campaign. This was a time when ordinary people with all their peculiarities and human frailties accomplished the extraordinary. "Reacting to instincts of righteousness and humanity," the Smithtown chapter of the Red Cross filled their various quotas: 12,130 hospital and refugee garments; 91,620 surgical dressings; 2,925 knitted articles and 51 comfort kits.[1] One of Mildred's kits prompted a letter from Edward H. Hug, headed "Longitude 14 degrees West, At Sea, Aboard U.S.S. *Buck,* Nov. 6, 1918":

> Having found your name and address on a slip of paper in my Red
> Cross kit, I took it as an indication that you might like to hear from the
> recipient of said kit. . . . Really I do not see how we fellows in the
> service can thank you women of the Red Cross half enough. Wherever
> we go we see evidences of your thoughtfulness and unselfish devotion.
> May we be worthy of this attention which we get from the greatest
> Mother in the world (next to a man's own mother), the Red Cross.[2]

The United War Work Campaign was instrumental in raising funds for
Liberty Loans. Dorothy Smith, with unequaled diligence and perseverance,
successfully solicited donations from friends and family, while Mildred, then
an interior designer, turned her business contacts toward the war. The Bank
of Smithtown served as a conduit for Liberty Loans. Chaired by Edward
Smith, Dorothy's cousin and future husband, the chapter raised more than
three times its previous quota.

Mildred and her sisters also became canteen workers at Camp Upton. On
more than 10,000 acres of swampy, mosquito-ridden land that is now the
Brookhaven National Laboratory, 15,000 skilled workers and laborers struggled through the hot, wet summer of 1917 to build barracks for 37,000
soldiers, mostly draftees. The Seventy-seventh Infantry, predominantly
Long Islanders and New Yorkers, were trained here and sailed to France to
fight in the critical Battle of the Argonne Forest.

Mildred Smith also found herself in the Argonne in 1919. She was
thirty-three years old, single, and bursting with patriotic pride. She had
volunteered to go to France as a canteen worker for the National War Council
of the YMCA, a civilian arm of the American Expeditionary Force in Europe.
Of the three sisters, Mildred had the most forceful personality. Highly
opinionated, she had a sometimes unpleasant nature. This disposition would,
in later years, lead to several nicknames that included Aunt Moo and Mildew.
She was also intelligent, creative, and extremely goal-oriented. From February 1919 through June 1919, she was stationed in Verdun, Romagne, and
Sampigny, setting up new canteens; cooking and serving doughnuts, cakes,
coffee, hot chocolate, and fried eggs; arranging evening entertainment; and
providing conversation for the soldiers. Mildred's letters to her family reflect
her enormous pride and satisfaction in her work, particularly in the canteen
called the "Kozy Korner," which she had helped to organize. "I love to watch
the boys come in," she wrote.[3] "They say, 'Gee that's some Y, some class to
this [place]. . . . Look at the curtains!' If I must say so it was my idea. They
do not need food so much, but a place to call home."[4] She was also sensitive
to criticism regarding the importance of Y work and to speculation about the
character of the "Y Girls." "Our work is interesting and lots of it, as girls are
scarce and greatly in demand. We adore working with the boys and in spite
of Elizabeth's evil-minded criticism, the boys would have a very much more

unhappy lot had none of us come over. Time after another, I hate to have the boys leave, when they start for home. The one cry seems to be for decent girls, and the girls sent over are a decent lot."[5]

It is difficult not to feel that Mildred had a good time during the war. She and the other Y girls traveled around France. They spent time in Paris. They attended dances and plays and officers' dinner parties, and they were besieged with flowers by German prisoners. Mildred wrote: "So you see how we stand in the eyes of the world . . . they all look up to us."[6] This positive outlook is based, in part, on the fact that peace talks were underway by the time Mildred arrived, but it is also obvious that she did not want her family to worry about her. Her work was formally recognized on May 7, 1919, in a Letter of Commendation from the Officers Salvage Service, First and Second Army Battle Areas. "Miss Shaw and Miss Smith entered upon their YMCA work with the troops and worked and lived under the most adverse conditions. Their cheerfulness and enthusiasm was a comfort to all and their presence gave a touch of home-life and refinement to the camp that endeared them to both officers and men."[7]

Like many Americans, especially those of her social station, Mildred was chauvinistic and even discriminatory when it came to nationality. Although she quietly suffered primitive living conditions in bombed-out towns, she complained of having to share a third class train compartment with "people of all nationalities."[8] In later years, Mildred would refer to most first, second, and third generation European-Americans as "foreigners." She thought American soldiers were better looking in uniform than French soldiers, and she disapproved of American "boys" pairing with French "girls."[9]

An avid horticulturist and a lifetime member of the North Shore Garden Club, Josephine Smith had the strongest feelings about the land and its use. During the war she directed a group called the Farmerettes to help the food rationing program. William Wickham Mills, first president of the Long Island Agricultural Society, had a keen interest in decorative and exotic plantings, and Josephine carried on the custom in which neighbors challenged each other and traded the most exotic and beautiful shrubs, flowers, and trees. She also shared with Mills his deep concern for the principles of the St. James Episcopal Church. Like Mills, Josephine was interested in the Oxford Movement, which sought to incorporate more Catholic tradition into the Episcopal service.

In the early 1930s, Smith money was less plentiful. By 1939, Josephine and Mildred were living together in the Mills Pond House, and out of necessity they developed additional sources of income. Josephine opened the Orchard Tea Room in Coram in 1940, and in 1950 the J. E. S. Tea Room in a small pre-Revolutionary War building in St. James. She ran a catering business until the early 1960s from the kitchens of the house. At a time when it was unusual for women to start businesses, Josephine had become an entrepreneur. Perhaps women's active participation during World War I had set the stage for this, for by 1930, Mildred was working with her brother in the family real estate business. By 1933, Dorothy was a widow earning a living for herself and her three young sons. She sold home-baked goods and firewood to local shops, and she also sold land owned by her late husband. Continuing in the Smith tradition of public service, Dorothy served as Nissequogue Village Clerk for twenty years, a position comparable to that of Timothy Mills, the original Mills Pond owner, who provided Smithtown with its first Book of Records in 1715 and was appointed Town Assessor in 1719.

During the Second World War, when women represented thirty percent of the production force, service to their country was once again a powerful motivation for the Smiths. In 1940, Mildred collected money for the British Ambulance Corps; Josephine grew a Victory garden, canned food, and worked with the Red Cross. In this war there was much "man's work" to be done without sufficient men to do it, so Josephine worked at Dade Aircraft making gliders and Mildred worked at Grumman Aviation as a riveter. If, as the popular song promised, "Berlin will hear about / Moscow will cheer about / Rosie the Riveter," then Mildred Smith was internationally appreciated.

If Josephine was passionate about the beautification of land, Mildred was equally passionate about the history of Smithtown. Until this time, family records were held informally by the various Smiths, and the original Smith homesteads were in need of restoration. In 1957, Mildred helped spearhead the formation of the Smithtown Historical Society. For seventeen years she was its first president.

As Mildred and Josephine were both working artists, and shared a studio in one of the house's out-buildings, it is fitting that their bedrooms now are studios for artists-in-residence. The Long Island painter William Sidney Mount, who lived nearby on Stony Brook Road, was a descendant of the family and a frequent visitor to the Mills Pond House. His portraits of William Wickham, Eliza Mills, and other family members hung in the house for many years. What the Smiths could not know is that for fundraising purposes, the Arts Council now rents the house for catered private parties. Josephine would be pleased!

In the sisters' obituaries, particular attention was paid to their forebears: Matthias Nicoll, first English secretary of the province of New York, Mayor of New York, and Justice of the Supreme Court of the province; William Nicoll, patentee of the Town of Islip; the Reverend Nathaniel Brewster, Setauket's first minister; and Roger Ludlow, eminent colonial statesman and the founder of Fairfield, Connecticut. One hopes that the present generation of Smiths will realize that forebears need not necessarily be founders of townships, and need not necessarily be male. They could be like the ordinary Smith women, Josephine, Mildred, and Dorothy, who quietly but irrevocably stretched out the boundaries that defined women's roles in their communities. Undriven and unhindered by ambitions of acquisition or self-aggrandizement, they succeeded in leading interesting and exemplary lives.

Notes

1. Henry Isham Hazelton, *The Boroughs of Brooklyn and Queens, Counties of Nassau and Suffolk, Long Island, N. Y.* (New York: Lewis Historical Publishing Company, 1925), 2: 588.

2. Smith family papers. Private collection held by Edward H. L. Smith. All subsequent citations are from this source.

3. April 21, 1919.

4. May 25, 1919.

5. March 23, 1919.

6. May 25, 1919.

7. May 7, 1919.

8. April 16, 1919

Other Sources

Bailey, Paul, ed. *Long Island: A History of Two Great Counties, Nassau and Suffolk.* New York: Lewis Historical Publishing Company, 1949.

Bookbinder, Bernie. *Long Island: People and Places Past and Present.* New York: Harry Abrams, 1982.

Flick, Alexander C., ed. *History of the State of New York.* New York: Columbia University Press, 1933.

Howell, Nathaniel Robinson. *Know Suffolk: The Sunrise County Then and Now.* Islip: Buys Brothers, 1952.

Manley, Seon. *Long Island Discovery, An Adventure into History, Manners and Mores of America's Front Porch.* Garden City: Doubleday and Company, 1966.

Overton, Jacqueline, and Bernice Marshall. *Long Island's Story and Sequel, The Rest of the Story 1929-1961.* 2d ed. Port Washington: Ira J. Friedman, 1963.

Smith, J. Lawrence. *The History of Smithtown.* Smithtown: Smithtown Historical Society, 1961.

Studenroth, Zachary N. "Mills Pond House, Smithtown Arts Center, Adaptive Re-use Report." Historic Structure Report. Typescript. Town of Smithtown, 1977.

White, Claire Nicholas. "The Land of the Smiths: A Collection of Personal Memoirs." Unpublished typescript, 1976.

11. Mother de Chantal Keating, CSJ
A "Notable, Noble American"

Sister Edna McKeever, CSJ

When she died, the *New York Freeman's Journal* eulogized her this way:

> She first set foot on American soil, July 4, 1852. Grand Army men are still proud to say: "She was one of us." Today, the Stars and Stripes float half mast over her home—for she lies dead. Who is this notable, noble American? She is the mother of 1000 orphans, or rather of thousands of orphaned boys because for thirty-four years, Mother Mary de Chantal has gathered under its sheltering wings and guarded and guided back into the world's arena all who could be crowded into St. John's spacious Home for Orphan Boys. She had a wonderful memory, a cheerful, even disposition, a great openness and charity of mind, and a keen sense of humor and a certain "approachableness" that made her the interested confidante of everyone she met, from the wounded soldier lad of her war days to the youngest baby in the home she governed so well.[1]

Born on September 30, 1833 at Kedra Mill, County Tipperary, Ireland, Jane Keating was the fourth of eight children of William Keating and Anne Fitzpatrick. Their thatched roofed house was next to the mill which was about a city block from the road and reached by a tree-bordered drive with a fish pond on one side. They had a large kitchen, large living room, and several bedrooms. A small fence of pointed logs enclosed a garden of lilies and roses. The family trade was raising and selling wheat which, in that region, required much processing to dry. After the repeal of the Corn Laws, American wheat, which did not need this treatment, began to replace Irish wheat and the Keating mill began to lose revenue. Therefore, several of the Keatings decided to head for other parts of the world.[2]

Jane and her sister Elizabeth came to New York in 1852. At first they were both employed in Ridley's, a department store in New York City. Soon they moved to Westbury where Jane was asked to help in the library in her spare time. According to her niece, Mary Woodlock, the town fathers asked Jane to leave her job because "she didn't seem to be able to keep track of the books. She did not think it necessary to report that the book shortage was caused by her decision to burn all the anti-Catholic volumes."[3] At the same time, Jane served as postmistress at Westbury where she wrote letters for the farmers who could not read or write.[4]

When Jane expressed her desire to become a Sister of Charity, Bishop Loughlin suggested that she join the newly founded community of the Sisters of St. Joseph who had come to Brooklyn on September 1, 1856. On March 1, 1857, at age twenty-four, Jane entered the fledgling group at St. Mary's in Williamsburg. On June 17, 1857, along with three other young women, Jane was given the habit in a public reception in the parish church where she received the name Sister Frances de Chantal. Shortly after, the "Frances" was dropped and she was simply called "de Chantal." She pronounced her vows in 1859. From 1862 to 1864, Sister de Chantal served in the newly founded Mother House in Flushing both as a teacher in St. Joseph's Academy and as the Directress of Novices.

At that time in Wheeling, West Virginia, another group of Sisters of St. Joseph was struggling. Sisters from Carondolet, Missouri, had responded to the request of Bishop Richard Whelan to establish the community there in 1853. Several Sisters were sent, and then slowly women from the local environs began to enter. When it was decided that the Sisters of Wheeling would become independent of Carondolet, those Sisters who wished were free to return to their origins. Sister Mary Stanislaus Matthews, a native Virginian, was named the first Mother Superior. Within a year she became seriously ill and died, leaving a newly professed Sister and two novices to carry on the work of the newly founded community.

It was this exigency which prompted Bishop Whalen to request help from the Sisters of St. Joseph of Brooklyn, today known as St. Joseph of Brentwood. He requested that the Sisters send a person to train the new group. Sister de Chantal was dispatched until such time that she would no longer be needed by the Wheeling Sisters. Three days after her arrival in West Virginia, on February 18, 1864, Bishop Whelan invested her as the Reverend Mother.[5] At that time the Sisters were in charge of one hospital which had a wing for orphaned children and two schools.

West Virginia had just recently undergone severe trauma. Delegates at the Convention of June 1861, had declared their independence from Confederate Virginia, and in 1863, West Virginia was made the thirty-fifth state by Abraham Lincoln.

During the early years of the Civil War, the Sisters of Wheeling visited prisoners of war in order to supply them with food and reading material. When asked whether the Sisters would take care of military patients, Mother de Chantal made arrangements for forty-seven patients to be transferred to the Sisters' hospital in March 1864. In April, the federal government, finding that the Sisters' hospital was the best in the area, requested the use of the south wing for wounded soldiers. Mother de Chantal agreed to rent the wing. She and the other Sisters were soon conscripted and given the status of Army nurses with Dr. John Kirker in charge. An entry in the *Annals,* presumably written by Mother de Chantal, states: "At 7:30 p.m. Ewald Over came to the hospital and ordered the entire house taken possession of as some two hundred invalids had arrived very unexpectedly; accordingly they were sent up as fast as ambulances could be procured for them. We laid them on the floor on rows of blankets, supplied them with immediate requirements and left them to repose as they might after a toilsome journey."[6]

She did not write, however, that she had to send the orphans under the charge of three Sisters to an old house on the property. The remaining Sisters willingly gave up their beds and moved to the Chapel, sleeping on the floor and undergoing many other hardships such as lack of food and rest, in order to provide physical and spiritual help to these poor young men.

Mother de Chantal did not allow any discrimination to be made between Union or Confederate soldiers, and each received equal attention and care. If one soldier requested a sandwich, then every soldier in the ward received a sandwich. Naturally, many of the southerners, not having previous knowledge of religious women, were somewhat skeptical about them. One soldier's mother when visiting inquired, "Be they injuns?" Their good reputation spread; nevertheless, there were those who were not completely sure of their loyalties. Often soldiers from both sides were, at different times, given shelter and reprieve by the Sisters. One time, a very young Sister died from smallpox and despite the sadness of the situation, Mother de Chantal decided not to report her death, not wanting to subject the house to inspection while she was protecting several Confederate soldiers. In the middle of the night, she and another Sister wrapped the Sister in her habit and buried her in the back yard with all the religious ceremony possible under the circumstances.

Mother de Chantal was in charge of the hospital and was alert to every need. There was not a pharmacist available, so she searched the troops that came in until she found a seriously wounded pharmacist. She had his bed moved into her office, and under his guidance, she gave out all the medications. Her kindness and interest in the welfare of the men under her care has been documented by the many who kept up correspondence with her over the years.

Mother de Chantal was a very kind, trusting woman, but she was not naive. She wrote in her diary on February 6, 1865: "Having much trouble regarding the rent of the hospital and despairing of justice without a personal application, I will leave Wheeling today for Washington City accompanied by one of our orphan girls, an insane soldier and his guard, my transportation being paid by the Government."[7] She would see General Grant. She described him as being rude to the point of boorishness, but he recognized her and took means to facilitate payment.[8]

When the war was over, Mother de Chantal gave all her energies to enlarging and strengthening the Community. Her voluminous correspondence reveals that she sought help from many priests and friends to be alert especially for immigrant young women who might express an interest in religious life. By 1872, the Community had grown to fifty-seven Sisters. In Wheeling, there were five schools, one hospital, and one orphan asylum. There were also schools in Grafton (100 miles away), Clarksburgh (120 miles away), and Charleston, comprising 1,150 children in all.

Mother de Chantal's life was seldom an easy one. Besides the exigencies of war, there was much illness and death among her Sisters. Her hard work in establishing schools was recognized far and wide and thus she received many requests for "educated women" to make foundations in other dioceses. Around 1873, she too became ill and was near death. This trial seems to have continued until the time of her extreme difficulties with the new Bishop, John J. Kain, who was appointed in 1875. There is not much documentation about what those concerns were; however, her correspondence reveals that she was very distraught and sought guidance from several of her dearest friends. One friend counseled that she be more acquiescent and respect the authority of the clergy who were the spokesmen for God. She was told that more good would be achieved by handing out honey than vinegar. On the other hand, another correspondent told her:

> In America, and indeed in other countries too, Bishops are endowed with very extensive powers; but not content with this, they occasionally appropriate to themselves authority which they do not derive from the Canon Law, and which has not the sanction of common sense . . . so I am not quite surprised that this youthful dignitary of yours should think himself in a position to lend you some of his superfluous wisdom to aid you in the management of your community—a matter which I conceive to be exclusively your own . . . I cannot but approve your resolution to bid him farewell. I have read that it is a slave that makes the tyrant, and the more tamely you submit, the more frequent you will find his abuses to be.[9]

In 1876, Mother de Chantal left Wheeling. There were many ceremonies of recognition by the local people expressing their gratitude for all that she had done and their sorrow in losing her.

On her return to Brooklyn, Mother de Chantal was appointed Superior of St. Malachy's Home in East New York. Here she continued to labor for the orphans trying to make their lives as satisfactory and healthy as possible. In 1883, on the death of Mother Baptista, Mother de Chantal was asked to take over St. John's Home, in Brooklyn. Her arrival there was not a particularly happy one for the boys whose loyalty and love were for Mother Baptista. No one could take her place! On the evening of Mother de Chantal's arrival, a celebration was planned and the boys were to sing a lovely welcome song. One boy refused to sing and pouted all through the ceremony. When the song

Fig. 11.1. A widower consigning his motherless children to the care of the Sisters of St. John's Home Brooklyn. Mother de Chantal, the Superintendent of St. John's Orphan Asylum, is standing in the doorway. Photograph courtesy of the Archives of St. Joseph's Convent, Brentwood.

was finished, Mother de Chantal went up to the stage. She put her hand lovingly on the boy's shoulder and said, "Would you like to sing this beautiful song to me again?" Confused, he did so, and when his beautiful voice reached the audience, he immediately became a hero and a star. He was won over!

As head of St. John's Home, Mother de Chantal made sure that the boys had more than adequate provisions. She made sure she knew each boy by name. Without the assistance of modern machinery and with the helpful hands of the loving and faithful Sisters who labored there, a thousand boys were provided with home-made clothing, clean laundry, three meals a day, and an excellent schooling up to grade seven. Because eye disease was a common problem of the day, each boy received a clean towel daily.

About 1888, Bernard Earle, a Hicksville resident, offered 125 acres of his land to the Sisters of St. Joseph to be used as a quiet place to train the young sisters. This was not deemed plausible by Reverend Mother Mary Teresa Mullen. When Mother de Chantal Keating heard of the situation, she immediately prevailed upon Mr. Earle to donate the land to the Society for St. John's Home. She felt it would provide a healthier environment and allow for more activities for the sickly boys from the "city." St. John's Protectory for sick and underdeveloped boys was established in 1890 and lasted until 1935.[10]

When she asked the Commandant of the Navy Yard to recommend a Drill Master for the Home boys, he replied discourteously that he did not consider that part of his duty. Mother de Chantal sent the letter to Theodore Roosevelt, then the Assistant Secretary of the Navy, who replied that the matter would be taken care of. It was. In 1898, when Colonel Theodore Roosevelt was setting out for the Spanish-American war, she sent him a letter containing a medal, to which he promptly replied:

> Your letter gave me the greatest pleasure and touched me deeply. All I am sorry for is that I was able to do so little for you, but it was a great pleasure to do even that little. Indeed it will give me the greatest pleasure to keep the little medal you enclosed always with me. I cannot very well wear it around my neck, but I will carry it with two or three things I most value and never leave away from me. Again cordially thanking you and with the best of good wishes, believe me faithfully yours, Theodore Roosevelt.[11]

He apparently typed this letter himself and it bears his own signature.

Her time at the Home was not without its difficulties, too. One of the greatest hardships was the fire of December 18, 1884, when Sister Mary Josephine Brady and twenty-two boys died. One can only wonder how her motherly heart could bear it.

In 1904, the Grand Army of the Republic decided to recognize all those religious women who served so well during the Civil War. They gave Mother de Chantal a bronze medal inscribed "Comrade to Nurses," a most highly prized honor. She was so proud of it that every Decoration Day she wore the medal openly on her big flowing sleeve with the original red ribbon attached to it. In 1896 she had been granted a pension from the Army and at her death she received a military burial. Her grave in Mount St. Mary's Cemetery in Flushing has two tombstones: a community headstone and one given by the government of the United States. Her profile appears in *Nuns of the Battlefield* by Ellen Ryan Jolly.[12] A monument to these "Nuns of the Battlefield" can be found at the intersection of Rhode Island and Connecticut Avenues in Washington D.C.

Mother de Chantal's fame spread far and wide. When she died on June 4, 1917, many expressed their sorrow at such a great loss. The editor of the *Fortnightly Review* wrote, "We became acquainted with this rare nun some twenty years ago through the kind offices of a Bishop in far-off India who told us that according to a certain prelate in very high standing, 'there are only two men in America—Archbishop Fabre of Montreal and Mother Mary de Chantal.'"[13] The *New York Freeman's Journal* said of her: "The man of public affairs found her a well-read, widely informed woman, with well digested opinions upon the questions of the day. The businessman gathered hints from her wide grasp of affairs and keen insight. The little crying boy passing his first lonely day in St. John's Home was comforted by her motherly arms."[14]

In the Convent of St. Joseph, Brentwood, there is a beautiful stained glass window on the main staircase. It is a memorial to Mother de Chantal Keating given with love by her boys from the Home. Not only does it remind the Sisters of St. Joseph of this woman who was one of them, but it speaks to all women, and most especially to women of Long Island, about the many talents and abilities of womankind who, when unhampered, are capable of great achievements for all of humankind.

Notes

1. *New York Freeman's Journal,* Saturday, June 9, 1917.

2. Mary Woodlock, unpublished manuscript life of her aunt, Mother de Chantal Keating, at the Archives of St. Joseph's Convent, Brentwood, NY (hereafter ASJCB).

3. Ibid.

4. Notes of conversation with Mother Jane Francis Dowling, good friend and co-worker of Keating, by Sister Mary Ignatius Meany, ASJCB.

5. *Annals,* February 18, 1864, Archives of the Sisters of St. Joseph, Wheeling, WV.

6. *Annals,* July 26, 1864, Archives of the Sisters of St. Joseph, Wheeling, WV.

7. Handwritten notes of Mother de Chantal Keating, ASJCB.

8. Woodlock manuscript.

9. John Scanlon to Mother de Chantal Keating, November 8, 1875, ASJCB.

10. St. John's Protectory was located not far from the railroad depot on Jericho Avenue within St. Ignatius parish. The boys were each given their own private garden to cultivate, and competition among them ran high. They were given courses in agriculture as well as the usual academic subjects. The major farming, which provided milk, butter, and vegetables for the larger institutions of St. John's, was done by laymen.

11. Correspondence of Mother de Chantal Keating, May 21, 1898, ASJCB.

12. Ellen Ryan Jolly, *Nuns of the Battlefield* (Providence, RI: Providence Visitor Press, 1927), pp. 170-80.

13. Arthur Preuss, *The Fortnightly Review* (St. Louis, Missouri), 24, no. 13 (July 1, 1917): 203.

14. *New York Freeman's Journal,* June 9, 1917.

12. Gender and Race Consciousness: Verina Morton-Jones Inspires a Settlement House in Suburbia

Floris Barnett Cash

The study of women, including black women, must be incorporated into every aspect of history teaching and research. It is the responsibility of serious scholars of African American history and women's history to assume the task of researching and interpreting the historical contributions of black women. African American women have been invisible, not only in United States history, but in African American history and gender studies as well. Not until the mid-1970s did scholars begin to notice the omission of black women in historical studies. The "sound of silence," says historian Evelyn Brooks Higginbotham, "reflects the failure to recognize black women's history as not only an identifiable field of inquiry in its own right, but as an integral part of Afro-American and women's history."[1] We must take control of our own destiny, says historian Rosalyn Terborg-Penn.[2] We need to tell our own story and write our own history.

Black women activists played major roles in building community organizations. Research on the female leadership of a vital institution and its contribution to the survival of a community challenges scholars to write black women into history. An examination of the Harriet Tubman Community House in Hempstead and the role of Verina Morton-Jones in founding that institution is an attempt to broaden our perspective of African Americans in local history. It sheds light on both a prominent black woman activist and a significant community institution on Long Island. This is not a history of the Harriet Tubman House, but an attempt to show the powerful role that black women played in the social, economic, and political survival of African Americans in a specific black community.

Emphasizing women and community work is one way of presenting the unique culture and history of black women. Cheryl Townsend Gilkes has asserted that African American women and their community work are vital to the creative process of social change. Other scholars, such as Jacqueline Rouse in *Lugenia Burns Hope: Black Southern Reformer,* have chronicled the experiences of black women activists who shaped change through their community work.[3]

Working for racial progress began during slavery and escalated during the late nineteenth century. Middle class black women engaged in efforts of racial advancement were referred to as "race women." A race woman was assertive, an advocate of racial pride and racial consciousness. As community activists, race women were concerned with social, political, and economic issues and their impact on African Americans. A race woman derived prestige and personal satisfaction from advancing the race.[4] Therefore, leading black women in local communities were engaged in church work, club work, day care nurseries for working mothers, homes for orphans and the elderly, settlement houses, and other voluntary efforts.

Verina Harris Morton-Jones's awareness of community issues and broader concerns shaped her social consciousness as an advocate of civil rights and women's rights. A founding member of the Brooklyn Equal Suffrage League, she succeeded Sarah Garnet as president of that women's organization. She was active in the National Association for the Advancement of Colored People (NAACP), the National Urban League, and a founder of the local Brooklyn chapters of those organizations. A Brooklyn physician, Dr. Morton-Jones was the primary organizer and superintendent of the Lincoln Settlement House in 1908.[5] Twenty years later, she was a founder of a social settlement in Hempstead, Long Island.

Born in Columbus, Ohio, in 1857, Verina Harris Morton-Jones was the daughter of free Blacks who had migrated to the North prior to the Civil War. She attended Benedict College in Columbia, South Carolina, and taught school there for two years. In 1888, Verina Harris graduated from the Medical College of Pennsylvania and became the physician at Rust College in Mississippi. Two years later, she married a Brooklyn physician, Walter A. Morton. Following the death of both an infant daughter and her husband in 1895, Dr. Morton, with her young son, sought relief temporarily in the college environment of Rust College as its doctor in residence. Within a few years, she re-opened her medical office in Brooklyn and married Emory Jones in 1901.[6]

African Americans were in Hempstead long before the twentieth century. Founded in 1644, Hempstead was the first European settlement in present-day Nassau County. Only twenty-one miles from New York City, it was linked to the city by stage coaches and the railroad. Hempstead was incorporated as a village in 1853. The Town of Hempstead was included in the new County of Nassau in 1899.[7] Blacks, transplanted from Africa, were among the first inhabitants of colonial Hempstead. Black men and women working beside the white settlers, provided much of the labor that helped to develop the land and maintain the households. By 1799, a system of gradual emancipation was begun, and in 1827, a final decree freed all 10,000 slaves in New York State.

Blacks on Long Island developed their own organizations and churches prior to the Civil War, namely, the Bethel African Methodist Episcopal

(A.M.E.) Church in Amityville founded in 1815, the St. David's A.M.E. Zion Church in the Eastville community of Sag Harbor in 1840, and Huntington's Bethel A.M.E. Church in 1844. The earliest recorded deed for the Setauket Bethel A.M.E. Church is 1848, although a burying ground, the Laurel Hill Cemetery, was set apart for Blacks in 1815. Many of these churches were founded by former slaves and Native Americans. Although small in number, African Americans on Long Island worked and participated in the general activities of their local communities.

Numerous black families migrated from New York City to Nassau and Suffolk counties in the 1920s to provide a better environment for their children. This included the homesteaders who founded the community of Gordon Heights near Coram and Yaphank in Suffolk County in 1927. "They sought the serenity and quality of life which the rural area offered. They wanted a peaceful place to live and raise their families."[8] The community, with families from Brooklyn, Harlem, and the Bronx, was named for the original owner of most of the property in the area, "Pop Gordon." It was promoted by Louis Fife, the president and founder of the Gordon Heights Development and Building Corporation. The homesteaders, having roots in the South and the West Indies, shared a dream of land ownership.[9]

When Verina Morton-Jones moved to Hempstead in the 1920s to be near her in-laws, the Jones family, she found a community that needed her professional services. At the age of seventy, Dr. Morton-Jones resumed her medical practice which she had suspended as responsibilities associated with her settlement work in Brooklyn increased. At such an advanced age, it was unusual for a community to warmly welcome any woman, black or white, into its inner circles; yet, she was the first black woman physician in Hempstead and her role as caregiver to African Americans was essential. Known for her practice in obstetrics and pediatrics, she delivered many babies in the local Long Island community.[10]

African American women frequently focused on club work and practical activities such as kindergartens, child care centers, clinics, hospitals, orphanages, homes for the elderly, libraries, playgrounds, and settlement activities.[11] Verina Morton-Jones's work in women's clubs, especially the National Association of Colored Women, the Empire State Federation, and the Northeastern Federation of Women's Clubs, brought years of experience and community service to the Long Island community. She exerted leadership in a strong network of black women. As a catalyst for the establishment of the Harriet Tubman Community Club and the Harriet Tubman Community Center, she was "interwoven into the fabric of the club."[12]

Visionary community leaders crossed class boundaries in providing assistance and social services for working women and mothers. Thus, a small group of women, including Verina Morton-Jones, organized the Harriet

Tubman Community Club as a community social club on April 26, 1928, in the home of Maggie Broglin of Hempstead. Among the charter members of the community organization were Della Ballard, Cornelia Brewster, Annie Noble, Julia Pinckney, and Rose Harvey. The community club, which met regularly for business meetings, held monthly literary programs and invited both black and white speakers to public meetings and forums.[13] It was incorporated in 1931 under the name Harriet Tubman to commemorate the freedom fighter and "conductor" in the nineteenth-century Underground Railroad for runaway slaves. Tubman, who also worked after the Civil War for the advancement of the African American community, converted her Auburn, New York, house into a home for the aged. In 1903, she deeded her property to the Thompson Memorial African Methodist Episcopal Church. It assumed the mortgage and gave her a small pension until her death in 1913.[14]

Verina Morton-Jones was a pioneer in self-help and volunteer activities. In 1933, after the Harriet Tubman Community Club rented a two-story building at Mill Road and Grove Street for club and community activities and lodging for women, she moved to that residence. As the director of the Tubman settlement house, she took care of its business and directed its activities. The community house provided a homelike environment and wholesome recreational activities for working girls and those temporarily unemployed.

Dr. Morton-Jones, as she was known in Hempstead, had an outgoing assertive personality. Her profession, her social position, and her community leadership enabled the settlement to attract people of diversified talents and backgrounds to the house. Among the speakers were: Oscar De Priest of Chicago, the first black Congressman since Reconstruction; Jessie Fauset, a Harlem Renaissance writer and literary editor of the NAACP journal, *The Crisis;* and Matthew Henson, the Harlem resident and Arctic explorer who accompanied Robert Peary in the discovery of the North Pole in 1909.[15]

The Harriet Tubman Community Center was called a settlement house because its programs and services closely resembled those provided by settlements for European immigrants, such as Hull House in Chicago and the Henry Street Settlement House in New York City. Unlike Jane Addams' Hull House, however, the director, Dr. Morton-Jones, was the only resident at the Harriet Tubman House. The women's club provided the community of women that managed the settlement house. Therefore, the Harriet Tubman House was modeled after the settlement houses established by black club women such as the White Rose Home and the Lincoln Settlement House in New York City.[16]

Many of the black women who migrated to the North found domestic service work the only employment open to them. Although the local club women initially planned to provide child care and other social services to the community, it soon became interested in the plight of black women working in domestic service. Some were sleeping in damp basements; others had lost their positions and were in need of temporary housing. There was no place for black women to go for recreation on Thursday, their day off. Thus, the Harriet Tubman Community House developed a twofold purpose: to provide settlement activities and programs for the local community and to provide housing for black women who migrated from the South seeking employment and better opportunities. One of the most important functions of the Hempstead settlement house was to provide lodging for "girls in the [domestic] service" who migrated from the South to Long Island. Initially, there were twelve boarders. They were employed primarily in domestic service in the surrounding affluent villages and cities.[17]

The great migration of Blacks to the North during the early twentieth century represents both immigration and freedom, asserts the historian Nell Painter.[18] The decade of increasing migration, 1910 to 1920, was a period of international crisis and domestic social change. Generally, the conditions producing the migration were economic and social. The outbreak of World War I opened up new economic opportunities for black workers. Northern industries sent recruiting agents to the South seeking black workers to help meet the labor shortages created by a decrease in European immigration. The migration of the African Americans from the South reached a peak in 1916. Of the migrants who went to New York, historian Herbert Gutman states, "Nearly three in ten women aged fifteen or older were lodgers or lived alone." Large numbers of single women, who left their families and migrated to the North, were attracted to the potential job opportunities in domestic service.[19]

Simultaneous with the migration, World War I attracted black men to service from across the country. Of the 750,000 men in the regular army and the National Guard at the beginning of the war, 10,000 were in the black units of the regular army and 10,000 were in the units of the National Guard. During World War I, two military air installations, Hazelhurst, which became Roosevelt Field, and Mitchel Field were laid out on the Hempstead Plains. The site was also the home of Camp Mills. During World War I, 30,000 American men were encamped at Camp Mills.[20] Black soldiers were stationed farther east, also, at Camp Upton in Yaphank, Long Island, now the site of Brookhaven Laboratory. Cooperation and mutual volunteerism existed among organizations, such as the settlement houses, in providing social services and assisting the black troops at Camp Upton.[21] After the war, many black men and women remained in the North.

Historian Darlene Clark Hine links the National Association of Black Women's Clubs to the migration of black women from the South to the Midwest. She considers the significant role played by the club women in

creating and sustaining new social, religious, political, and economic institutions. Hine writes, "These clubs were as important as the National Urban
League and the NAACP in transforming black peasants into the urban
proletariat."[22] Hine emphasizes the non-economic motives for black female
migration such as the desire for personal autonomy and to escape from sexual
abuse.

Harsh agricultural labor and field work were contributing factors in
motivating black women to leave the South. A Hempstead resident stated
that she left Batesburg, South Carolina, in 1928, at the age of seventeen, and
came to New York as a "sleep in" domestic in East Williston, Long Island.
Recommended by a friend rather than recruited by an agency, she migrated
to the North to find a better life. Hattie Bell Johnson was disappointed with
the isolated suburban environment, but "at least she was not in the fields all
day." She earned $40 a month and she was off every Thursday and every
other Sunday. Hattie Johnson married Pope Williams the next year, joined
the Union Baptist Church, and left her domestic position.[23] Not all migrants
were so fortunate.

Upon arriving in the North, black women were employed predominantly
as domestics. Numerous migrants, including women, found it difficult to find
employment and housing. Some, who were taken advantage of, lost their
money, or were drawn into vice, crime, and even prostitution. Young women,
in particular, were often victimized by procurers disguised as legitimate labor
agents.

In response to these problems, women's organizations in many urban
areas set up special programs to protect newly arrived single and widowed
women. Chief among these were settlement houses with boarding facilities,
travelers' aid services, and the League for the Protection of Colored Women,
whose primary functions were travelers' aid and job placement. The White
Rose Mission, founded in Manhattan in 1897, was one of the earliest
settlement houses providing lodging for black migrant women. Later called
the White Rose Home for Working Girls, it established a travelers' aid
service in 1905 to direct women to the Home. Not all black settlement houses
provided lodging for women. Both the White Rose Home in New York City
and the Harriet Tubman Community House on Long Island provided shelter
to black women migrating to metropolitan New York City. Black churches
in the New York City area cooperated with these institutions in offering
spiritual and economic assistance. The women who volunteered their time
and efforts were members of the community churches and organizations.

In 1935, the local club women were able to expand their social services
upon acquiring their own building. The new home housed eleven girls who
each paid a modest fee of two dollars a week. The fund-raising activities of
the Harriet Tubman Club included dinners, rummage sales, card parties, and

teas to pay off the mortgage on the building. Churches and civic groups contributed linens, bedding, curtains, and other items to the Community House. Some programs, such as the annual open house teas, were open to the public. An interracial advisory committee organized to provide a sustaining fund for the club's welfare work.[24]

The Harriet Tubman Community Club, the backbone of the settlement house, became an important social service agency in the local community. Contributions from friends, fundraising of the club members, and donations from the local churches provided support for the Harriet Tubman Community House. Members of the community club, who attended churches of different denominations, led the churches in fund-raising efforts. Therefore, several black churches were indirectly associated with the settlement house, namely, the Jackson Memorial African Methodist Episcopal Zion (A.M.E.Z.) Church, St. John's Episcopal Church, Union Baptist Church, and the Antioch Baptist Church.[25]

Interracial cooperation linked the Harriet Tubman Home to other social service and educational organizations such as the Red Cross and the Parent Teacher Association (PTA). These organizations brought health care and vocational education to the black community. One of the most valuable services of the settlement house was a Red Cross course in home nursing and care of the sick, which was provided by the Nassau County Chapter of the Red Cross. The Hempstead PTA sponsored classes in cooking and sewing.

Lobbying, petitions, voting, and personal contacts were used by settlement house workers and club women to achieve community improvements. As part of their tactics for survival, they sought political as well as social goals. With the opening of the new Harriet Tubman Community House in 1935, the mayor of Hempstead, George M. Estabrook, and other village officials joined the residents of the community in a formal ceremony. The trend of political activism escalated in more recent years with mayors George Milhim and James Garner, the first black mayor of Hempstead.[26]

The Harriet Tubman Community House received support from the federal government during the administration of Franklin D. Roosevelt. The president appointed Mary McLeod Bethune to head the office of minority affairs of the National Youth Administration (N.Y.A.), a New Deal program of youth employment. Bethune, the founder of Bethune-Cookman College and the National Council of Negro Women, joined several black leaders in seeking employment and other opportunities for African Americans. The social uplift work and social services offered by the Harriet Tubman Community House attracted the attention of the federal government and led it to place a youth project in Nassau County. Through the W.P.A. program, a social worker was employed and a full schedule of activities incorporated. Children under seven years old were cared for in the day nursery, and more than sixty children in the Village of Hempstead were innoculated for diphtheria.[27]

The Harriet Tubman Community Center became one of the participating agencies of the Hempstead Community Chest. Like Lugenia Hope's Neighborhood House in Atlanta, Georgia, it was more fortunate than most of the black settlement houses. Many black institutions and organizations simply could not meet the requirements for assistance from local, state, or national agencies. With increased funding and additional resources, the Harriet Tubman Community Center was able to broaden the scope of its activities and programs. Various clubs and classes were organized for the youth of the community, such as the Girl Scouts, Boy Scouts, Brownies, children's arts and crafts, 4–H clubs, and a play school for pre-school children.[28] The Hempstead Public Library provided books for the community house library.

Upon becoming affiliated with the Community Chest, the community house could guarantee a director's salary and employ a small staff. Unfortunately, it was too late for Verina Morton-Jones and other pioneer black women community leaders who had volunteered their time and service. Dr. Morton-Jones retired from public work in October 1939 and returned to Brooklyn. She remained with her family until her death in 1943 at the age of eighty-six.

The Harriet Tubman Community House played a primary role in race relations. Although the focus of this article is on Verina Morton-Jones and the origins of the Harriet Tubman settlement house and not the history of the settlement house, there are several recent trends and developments that have had an impact on the local community and deserve mention. In 1948-1949, several community organizations, including the Harriet Tubman Community House, the League of Women Voters, the Young Women's Christian Association (YWCA), and the Hempstead Woman's Club, formed a housing study group to make the public aware of the need for low-income housing. The project, which became the Parkside Gardens Housing Development, held its ground-breaking ceremonies in the fall of 1949.[29]

During the period 1930 to 1950, the small black population of Hempstead sustained the Harriet Tubman Community House. The settlement house developed in suburbia not only because of the ideology of self-help and institution building, but race was a key factor. De facto segregation in the North demanded that Blacks form their own institutions and organizations. As one resident recalls, "You had your Girl Scouts, Boy Scouts, and Four-H club meetings there. It was the only place where young people could socialize. We had the Harriet Tubman Community Center and the church, and you couldn't dance in the church."[30] Black and white youth attended separate proms until the early fifties, with black teenagers holding their parties and socials in the Harriet Tubman Community Center.

The Harriet Tubman Community House is located in New York State's first predominantly black suburban district. Hempstead Village is a community of nearly 40,000 people in the center of Hempstead Town, just south of Garden City. It is the oldest settlement in the town, and among the most populous in the county.[31] By 1920, 6,382 persons lived in Hempstead Village due to its central location on the island and a growing business district supported by the railroad. The total racial make-up of the population of the village of Hempstead changed between 1930 and 1970. In the decades preceding World War II, the black population of the village grew slightly from 6 percent to 9 percent of the total population. The trend toward a growing black population in Hempstead escalated with the post-World War II migration to the village.

Between 1950 and 1960, the black population increased from 2,600 persons or 9 percent of the total to 7,754 or 22 percent. The black population of the village nearly doubled between 1960 and 1970. According to the demographics of the village of Hempstead, "the number of black residents in Hempstead increased substantially from 7,754 persons or 22 percent of the population in 1960 to 14,506 or 36 percent of the population in 1970."[32] By 1980 the black population had increased to 23,033 or 57 percent of the total population. While the total population changed slightly, the number of black families increased as the white families decreased in the village.[33]

Changes in the racial and ethnic composition of Hempstead Village did not revitalize its community institutions. Instead, it brought many social concerns, including the feminization of poverty which is shared by black and white women. Poor families are likely to be single female-headed; women's households with children make up a large percentage of the poor. Influenced by gender, race, and class, the "feminization of poverty" is compounded by race because racial discrimination further limits access to housing, education, jobs, and good salaries.[34] Poverty, however, is not limited to women.

In some black communities today, poverty, homelessness, drug abuse, AIDS, and domestic violence are among the salient issues. As a preventive measure, a high level of community organizational networks are generally associated with a low level of abuse and victimization.[35] Similar local concerns led to inquiries regarding the use of the Harriet Tubman Community Center as a shelter for battered women. Not only has this matter not been considered because the personnel is limited to one elderly matron at the home, but housing battered women was not in the social mission of the founders.

The Harriet Tubman Community Center of Hempstead has a legacy of strength and survival against the odds. It has survived because of the continuous guidance of black club women and the generous support of friends. The community house now serves a myriad of functions, which help to provide for its maintenance and expenses, as a temporary home for a local church congregation, a meeting hall for several community civic, social, and fraternal organizations, emergency and temporary housing for women, and as a training site for home health aides under Health Forces, Inc. Among the activities are cultural and recreational programs for children and senior citizens.[36] The Harriet Tubman Community Center has provided social services with a caring hand for nearly seventy years in the Hempstead community.

Verina Morton-Jones, and black community activists on a local and national level, established settlement houses by organizing grassroots support.[37] They utilized women's networks in churches, women's clubs, and community organizations. They strongly believed in social organization, education, the family, and community involvement. African American women served as brokers between the settlement houses, the black community, and the local politicians. Recognizing discriminatory practices and racial prejudice, community women protested and demanded justice and equality. Self-help and institution building were the fabric of the social mission of black women.

To what extent, if any, did these women exercise social control in the black community? Despite their emphasis on morality, respectable behavior, good character, and other family values, the leaders shared a close kinship with the residents of the communities they served. Yet, this is not enough to explain their actions. I contend that Verina Morton Jones, and other women leaders, raised the level of consciousness with regard to race and gender and, in the process, infused community relations with a democratic perspective for the common good.

Notes

1. Evelyn Brooks Higginbotham, "Beyond the Sound of Silence: Afro-American Women in History," *Gender and History* 1, no. 1 (Spring 1989): 175-91.

2. Quoted in Judith P. Zinsser, *History and Feminism: A Glass Half Full* (New York: Twayne Publications, 1993), pp. 81-82.

3. Cheryl Townsend Gilkes, "'If It Wasn't for the Women': African American Women, Community Work, and Social Change," in *Women of Color in U. S. Society,* edited by Maxine Baca Zinn and Bonnie Thorton Dill (Philadelphia: Temple University Press, 1994), pp. 229-46; Jacqueline Rouse, *Lugenia Burns Hope: Black Southern Reformer* (Athens: University of Georgia Press, 1989).

4. St. Clair Drake and Horace Clayton, *Black Metropolis: A Study of Negro Life in a Northern City,* 1945 (Reprint, Chicago: University of Chicago Press, 1993), p. 394.

5. The Lincoln Settlement worked closely with the Brooklyn Urban League after 1913 when it opened a local branch at 185 Duffield Street; see Guichard Parris and Lester Brooks, *Blacks in the City: A History of the National Urban League* (New York: Little, Brown, 1971), p. 60. For an additional reference to black women and institution

building, see Floris Barnett Cash, "Radicals or Realists: African American Women and the Settlement Spirit in New York City," *Afro-Americans in New York Life and History* 15, no. 1 (January 1991): 7-17. Although Professor Clarence Taylor does not focus exclusively on the activities of black women, he presents the religious, social, and political activism of Blacks in *The Black Churches of Brooklyn* (New York: Columbia University Press, 1994). The volume explores the history and culture of a large urban community. See review by Floris Cash in *The Long Island Historical Journal* 8, no. 1 (Fall 1995): 129-31.

6. Judge Franklin W. Morton, grandson of Verina Morton-Jones and his wife Mrs. Gwendolyn Morton, telephone interview by author, August 1985.

7. Natalie A. Naylor, ed. *The Roots and Heritage of Hempstead Town* (Interlaken, NY: Heart of the Lakes Publishing, 1994), p. 7.

8. *Gordon Heights Golden Anniversary, 1927-1977,* Gordon Heights Progressive Civic Association, Inc., 1977.

9. The Gordon Heights community survived the depression and surged forward. With the organization of the Gordon Heights Progressive Civic Association in 1945, the historical black community reached a pinnacle of self sufficiency and progress. For a discussion of another Long Island African American community, see historian Marquita James's article, "Blacks in Roosevelt, Long Island," in *Ethnicity in Suburbia: The Long Island Experience,* edited by Salvatore La Gumina (Garden City, NY: Nassau Community College Foundation, 1980), pp. 91-103.

10. Mrs. Fay C. Latimer, interview by author, Hempstead, NY, September 1995. Dr. Morton-Jones delivered Mrs. Latimer's youngest brother more than sixty years ago.

11. Anne Firor Scott, "Most Invisible of All: Black Women's Voluntary Associations," *Journal of Southern History* 56 (February 1992): 3-22. (See also Scott's *Natural Allies: Women's Associations in American History* [Urbana: University of Illinois Press, 1991]. Editor's note.)

12. "Brief History of the Harriet Tubman Community Club, Inc. of Hempstead," one page unpublished typescript, Mrs. Fay Latimer.

13. Ibid.

14. Al Cohn, "Money Woes Revisit an Ex-Slave's Church," *Newsday,* October 13, 1983. For a recent secondary source, see Darlene Clark Hine, "Harriet Ross Tubman," in *Black Women in America: An Historical Encyclopedia,* edited by Darlene Clark Hine, Elsa Barkley Brown, and Rosalyn Terborg-Penn, 2 vols. (Brooklyn, NY: Carlson Publishing, Inc., 1993), pp. 1,176-80.

15. Reda Ezell (Mrs. Frederick) Williams, interview by author, November 1995. Raised in Harlem, Reda Williams recalls that her family and the Hensons attended the same church, Abyssinian Baptist. Lucy Henson and Williams' grandmother, Margaret Banks, were friends and both women sang in the church choir. As a youth, Williams was unaware of Henson's historical contributions, since black history was not emphasized in the school curriculum.

16. See Mary Lynn Bryan and Allen F. Davis, eds., *100 Years at Hull-House,* 1969 (Reprint; Bloomington: Indiana University Press, 1990).

17. "Brief History of the Harriet Tubman Community Club."

18. Nell Painter, "Foreword," in *The Great Migration in Historical Perspective, New Dimensions of Race Class, and Gender,* edited by Joe William Trotter (Bloomington: Indiana University Press, 1991).

19. Herbert Gutman, in *The Black Family in Slavery and Freedom, 1750-1925* (New York: Vintage Books, 1976), p. 453; George E. Haynes, "Negro Migration," *Opportunity,* October 1924, p. 273; Charles S. Johnson, "The Black Workers in the City," *Survey,* March 1925, pp. 641-43.

20. "Historic Hempstead," *Long Island Press,* June 29, 1975.

21. Similarly, the Setauket Neighborhood House, with a predominantly white clientele, added a ballroom as a place to entertain injured World War I soldiers from Camp Upton; see, "The Three Villages of Historical Interest," *The Three Village Times,* October 1996; and Floris Barnett Cash, "Radicals or Realists."

22. Darlene Clark Hine, "Black Migration to the Urban Midwest: The Gender Dimension, 1915-1945," in *The Great Migration In Historical Perspective,* edited by Joe William Trotter.

23. Inez, Frederick, and their older sister, Helen (died, c. 1992) were raised by their parents, Pope and Hattie Williams in Hempstead. They attended meetings and activities in the Harriet Tubman Community Center. (Interview by author, November 1995, of Hattie Williams, assisted by her daughter, Inez Williams.) Hattie Williams died in June 1997.

24. The Harriet Tubman Community Club of Hempstead, *Biennial Dinner and Debutante Cotillion Program,* 1994.

25. As African Americans increasingly settled in the area, they established their own institutions. Only one church, the Jackson Memorial African Methodist Episcopal Zion (A.M.E.Z.), was established prior to the Civil War and, thus, compares to other historical black churches on Long Island. The founding dates of churches associated with the Harriet Tubman Community House are: Jackson Memorial A.M.E.Z., 1827; St. John's Episcopal Church, 1904; Union Baptist Church, 1922; and Antioch Baptist Church, 1929.

Shirley Small used the Tubman Community Center's library for homework assignments. The Small family lived next door to Dr. Verina Morton-Jones when she first came to Hempstead. In 1921 the Union Baptist Church began with prayer meetings in the home of McDonald and Rosetta Small. Natives of Barbados, they moved from the Bronx to Long Island and helped establish a Baptist church for the increasing number of persons migrating from the South who were of that denomination. (Interview by author, April 1997, of Mrs. Shirley Small White.)

Mrs. Fay C. Latimer is the daughter of the Reverend S.M.B. Usry. Under his pastorate, the Union Baptist Church was built and he founded Antioch Baptist Church. He came to Hempstead prior to 1925 from Atlanta, Georgia.

26. Harriet Tubman Community Club, *Biennial Dinner Program,* 1994.

27. "Brief History of the Harriet Tubman Community Club."

28. The Girl Scout Troop 44, organized at the Harriet Tubman Center in 1936, was the first black troop on Long Island.

29. "Harriet Tubman Community," in *Hempstead Then and Now* (Hempstead: League of Women Voters, 1959, 1968).

30. Inez Marie Williams graduated from high school in Hempstead in 1948. A black youth growing up in the 1940s looked forward to the programs and activities provided by the Harriet Tubman Community Center. Williams believes that it was a vital community organization. Interview by author, November 1995, of Inez Williams.

31. James Baron, "New Plea for a Troubled Village," *New York Times*, February 20, 1983; "Brave New Whirl for Nassau's Hub," *Newsday*, April 25, 1972. A persistence of race consciousness in Hempstead goes back to slavery days, despite the fact that some persons associate it with the racial change that occurred in Hempstead in the 1960s.

32. See *Population Trends in the Village of Hempstead, New York* (Community Housing and Planning Associates, Inc., HUD Project, 1972).

33. Sandra Schoenberg Kling and Patricia Wang, *The Demographic Profile of Hempstead Village: 1960-1985* (Hempstead, NY: Hofstra University, Center for Community Studies, 1985). For a broader perspective of Long Island, see Barbara Kelly, ed., *Suburbia Re-examined* (Westport, CT: Greenwood Press, 1989).

34. For an assessment of the loss of jobs and an increase in the underprivileged, see William Julius Wilson, *The Truly Disadvantaged: The Inner City, The Underclass and Public Policy* (Chicago: University of Chicago Press, 1987). Wilson explores how the loss of blue-collar jobs has affected American society in his most recent book, *When Work Disappears: The World of the New Urban Poor* (New York: Knopf, 1996).

35. See N. H. Cazenave and M. A. Straus, "Race, Class, Network Embeddedness and Family Violence: A Search for Potent Support Systems," *The Journal of Comparative Family Studies* 10 (1979) 281-300; "Battered Women: The Transformation of a Social Problem," *Social Work* 32, no. 4 (1987): 306-11.

36. "Brief History of the Harriet Tubman Community Club."

37. For examples of service to the black community in the urban North and the South, see Adienne Lash Jones, *Jane Edna Hunter: A Case Study of Black Leadership, 1910-1950* (New York: Carlson Publishing, Inc., 1990); Rouse, *Lugenia Burns Hope.*

13. Women of Faith: The Spiritual Legacy of the Founders of St. Francis Hospital

Sister Lois Van Delft, F.M.M.

The "spirit" of St. Francis Hospital is a dynamic, authentic energy that is all-pervasive and inclusive; it is the fruit of love, self-sacrifice, compassion, caring, and vision that has had its roots in its poor beginning and is bequeathed as a "legacy" to all who have worked and seen St. Francis evolve over the years.

From the earliest days of their work, the founders of St. Francis Hospital were women of great faith who were hard-working and deeply committed to the children entrusted to their care. The example set by these early religious women has come down to us as a legacy of caring. Their tradition is something to be treasured. I would like to tell you their story.

I began working at St. Francis in April 1986, and my first months were spent meeting people, getting oriented, and learning my job responsibilities. I had come from a position of chaplain in a community hospital to supervise the St. Francis Pastoral Care Department. As I met and talked with employees and volunteers with years of service, I began to hear many similarities in their stories. They spoke often of the "old days," as they called them, telling me of happy times where they were "like one big family, sharing joys and sorrows." They often went on to say that things were starting to feel different now. The hospital was growing; it was getting bigger and more impersonal, and they were fearful of losing the "family spirit." Time and again, I heard stories of how everyone had worked together, helping each other, caring for the children in the earlier days of the sanatorium to provide an extended, loving family for the first patients at St. Francis.

I heard their concern; yet, as I became more accustomed to my own position, I began to sense that indeed, even now, there is still something quite special in the hospital environment, an intangible quality, but real none-the-less. To me it quickly became a friendly place where people were genuinely nice to each other, helped one another, and gave wonderful care and attention to the patients. Often I heard the nurses say that the hospital allowed them to give good bedside care to patients because the hospital provided an excellent nurse-patient ratio. But apparently, even this feeling was being threatened by an increasing patient census.

More and more, I began to appreciate that there was indeed a special feeling about the place and turned to reading and reflecting on the beginnings of our St. Francis Hospital history and how it was possible to create the wonderful sense of family and caring that was still so obvious.

I went back to the little collection of stories about Mr. and Mrs. Carlos Munson, a wealthy couple who lived in Roslyn in the early 1900s. Carlos Munson, a Quaker, was the owner of the Munson Steamship Line that sailed up and down the eastern seaboard. Munson, a businessman and a generous man, owned considerable property on Long Island and had recently acquired a property adjacent to his own land called Elmsfour. This particular parcel of fifteen acres was later to become the site of the present St. Francis.[1] The land included the original home, stables, and small farm storage buildings.

In 1920, two Sisters of the Franciscan Missionaries of Mary (F.M.M.) came to Long Island, as they had done many times before, to sell handmade linens to the wealthy families of the North Shore. Mrs. Munson was always happy to see the Sisters and often purchased various linens for her home. The Sisters usually stayed for tea, and the conversation more than likely got around to stories about the children they cared for at their convent in New York City.

These Sisters were called "Commissioners," because their work was to sell the fine handmade linens door-to-door to make money for the support of the works of the Congregation. From the earliest days, the Franciscan Missionaries of Mary were reminded of the words of Mother Mary of Passion, our foundress, to follow the inspiration of the Holy Family when she wrote: "We must live by the work of our hands."[2]

Our foundress of the Institute of the Franciscan Missionaries of Mary, a woman of great vision and self-sacrifice, was Helen de Chappotin who would one day be known as Mother Mary of the Passion. She was born in Nantes, France, of the noble household of the de Chappotin de Neuville who had united with the Galbaud du Fort at the time of the French Revolution. She was the youngest in a large family, a child of exuberant disposition, keen intellect, and a marked, upright character who always clung tenaciously to the truth. Her loyalty to the political interests of the royalists, her determination to adhere only to the truth in all matters, and her disregard for human respect were healthy strengths that were soon channeled into a deep loyalty which was to absorb her whole life.

Years passed. Helen entered first the Poor Clares only to have ill health force her to leave. She regained her strength, and she sought once more the contemplative life, this time with the Congregation of Marie Reparatrice. While still a novice, her virtue and ability were so sound that she was deemed ready to leave for the missions of India.

At the age of twenty-nine, she became Provincial of the Congregation's three houses in India where her programs for raising the status of Indian women by teaching them to work picking, cleaning, spinning, and weaving cotton in their work rooms became very successful. However, her desire to extend her work beyond India to all nations remained, and she left the Congregation of Marie Reparatrice with three companions.[3]

She sought the direction of the Holy Father and received his blessing to found a new order on January 6, 1877. It was called the Institute of Missionaries of Mary, and Mary of the Passion was appointed its first Mother General by the Holy Father. In 1882, the order adopted the Franciscan Rule and became known as the Franciscan Missionaries of Mary.[4] Mary of the Passion died in 1904, leaving three thousand sisters and eighty-six convents in Europe and the missions to carry on the work she had begun.

Just about that same time in 1904, the Franciscan Missionaries of Mary came to the United States and, at the request of the Bishop of the Diocese of Providence, Rhode Island, began to care for orphaned children in Woonsocket, Rhode Island. In 1906, the Sisters came to New York City and opened a day nursery and a workroom where young girls were taught cooking, sewing, and general home economics. It must be stated that in the view of Mary of the Passion, "wherever missionaries go, they proclaim forcibly the dignity of the human individual."[5] Workrooms were set up so that women and young girls might be educated to a means of livelihood, to an increase of self-respect, and to gain a certain amount of independence as the custom of the locale would permit. It was from this same community in New York City that the two Sisters came to Roslyn and met Mr. and Mrs. Munson. The Munsons were childless, and the stories of the children cared for in the Divine Providence Day Nursery obviously touched their hearts. In 1920, the Munsons gave the fifteen acres of their Elmsfour property to the Franciscan Missionaries of Mary with the understanding that it be used for the care of poor children.[6]

The Elmsfour land had been used during the first World War by groups of girls from Washington, college graduates who cultivated fruits and vegetables for the Army.[7] The small community of Religious farmed the same acres for many years, providing food for themselves, for the children who were to come, and for the poor families they met along the way.

On May 17, 1921, St. Francis Camp was opened. Mother Amata and five Sisters undertook the difficult task of running it. The first children from the day nursery in New York City came to enjoy the fresh air of the country during the summer months. The camp was unique in that it provided the vacations for pre-school and nursery school age children as well as for children with disabilities, notably a group of forty deaf children who came to the vacation camp every summer for two weeks.[8]

It was never an easy task; yet, even at this early date, we find that women from the surrounding towns offered their help. Nothing was too menial for these first volunteers. They helped with laundering the children's clothes and entertained them with handmade dolls and animals, and their help was gratefully received.[9] Every generous gesture was rewarded with recognition of their work.

In 1936, an incident occurred that began the transition from summer camp to sanatorium. Mrs. James Slattery, then President of Immaculate Conception Day Nursery in Brooklyn and a member of the Auxiliary of Kings County Hospital, sent a group of sixteen children to St. Francis for their two weeks' summer vacation, as had been her custom for several years. In this group was a little Spanish girl, a frail and quiet child. It was only a matter of a few days before she became very ill and developed pneumonia. Seeing the seriousness of the situation, the Superior at the camp made every effort to contact the parents of the child to obtain their permission to hospitalize her. Unable to reach them in any way, she took upon herself the responsibility of sending the child to the hospital. After the crucial period was over and the child was on her way to recovery, she returned to the camp for convalescence where she regained her health and new strength. Mrs. Slattery herself followed the day-by-day progress of the child, and it was during this time of continuous contact with the St. Francis community, that she learned to appreciate the solicitude for the lives of others, both spiritual and physical, which animated the Sisters.[10]

At about this same time, Mrs. Slattery became aware of the complete lack of and urgent need for physical facilities for the care of the rheumatic and cardiac children of Kings County. Dr. Leo M. Taran, Chief of the Children's Cardiac Clinic of Kings County Hospital had appealed for such an institution.[11] Mrs. Slattery spoke of this need to the Superior of the camp who immediately agreed to meet with Dr. Taran, and the planning began.

On February 8, 1937, the first twelve cardiac children were admitted for convalescent care. The Sisters converted a stable on the property into a small sanatorium until more permanent and appropriate buildings could be provided. The Superior of the convent, Mother Kevelaer, was faced with almost insurmountable problems. Medical opinions differed regarding the treatment of rheumatic fever. They needed a continuous oxygen supply. No endowments were forthcoming to help defray expenses. During the early years of the Great Depression, funding from the City of New York was practically non-existent. The families of the rheumatic heart patients were themselves mostly poor, ill fed, jobless, and living in cold water flats. Caring for children was a struggle. The Sisters made do with whatever they could raise themselves or beg from the surrounding farms.

From 1937 to 1940, the number of patients increased from twelve to fifty. The policy governing admissions had to adjust to the better understanding of rheumatic fever. By 1940, most of the patients admitted had active rheumatic fever. Since the concept of rheumatic activity was changing, the policy regarding length of stay geared itself to the program and allowed for longer periods of treatment.[12]

In 1941, at the request of Mother Kevelaer, thirteen women from the surrounding neighborhoods came together to form a women's auxiliary, a permanent organization to aid the work in whatever way possible, and the St. Francis Cardiac Guild was born.[13] The Guild's first endeavor was to raise funds for oxygen for the children. No effort was spared. These early Guild members ran sales, bridge parties, luncheons, Sunday fairs, and raffles of all sorts to help raise money for the needs of the hospital.[14]

As admissions increased, the Sisters sought the means to build another unit to house twenty-five additional patients. The Superior wrote to various charitable people for help to no avail. Finally, she contacted the Martha Hall Foundation. The President, Mr. James Jay Morgan, responded by providing funding for not one, but three brick pavilions, each housing twenty-five children, and upon their completion, the Hall Foundation donated money for another three buildings for an additional seventy-five patients for a total of one hundred and fifty.[15] In November 1949, another fifty-patient wing for acute cases was completed, bringing the total capacity to two hundred.

There was more than physical expansion happening at St. Francis. The policies, methods, and standards of patient care were evolving, so that by 1942, when the buildings were completed, the sanatorial method of care for acute rheumatic cases replaced the convalescent care method and the establishment became known as St. Francis Sanatorium for Cardiac Children. The aim of operating under a sanatorial plan was first to provide the diagnostic and therapeutic facilities of an acute hospital and second to retain the home atmosphere by creating a small family group in each unit.[16]

Sanatorial care was the approved type of care most conducive to restoring physical and emotional health to children with rheumatic fever and rheumatic heart disease; however, there were, in the early years, sociologists who warned that prolonged institutional care might produce a state of invalidism. They identified three factors inherent in institutionalization that can easily disorganize the personality: separation of the child from home and parents; creation of dependency and problems such as the lessening of incentive, of healthy rivalry, or initiative; and impersonalization and the merging of a child's personality into the group. At the same time, sociologists agreed that an efficient, scientific, institutional or convalescent hospital designed to create a home atmosphere and to provide a school program could offer the best result for acute rheumatic patients in spite of the above factors. If managed with an eye to the overcoming of its psychological shortcomings, an institution can function in a de-institutionalized capacity. It is this goal that St. Francis attained in its first fourteen years of existence.[17]

In 1949, with the completion of St. Elizabeth's Building, the first lay personnel were hired. A new operating room suite and a research laboratory were built and the hospital's services were extended to include adult patients suffering from heart disease in 1954.[18]

In 1961, a new surgical suite and adult patient unit were completed with the opening of Maria Assunta Unit, and admissions were expanded to patients suffering from other than cardiac problems. The hospital was then considered to be a general hospital with a cardio-vascular specialty.[19]

The 1970s saw the greatest period of growth in the history of St. Francis with the completion of the Heart Center. With this new facility, services were again expanded; sophisticated equipment was installed, the number of admissions increased, and the number of cardiac surgical procedures likewise increased.

Today St. Francis stands as New York's premier cardiac specialty hospital. Today we also pay tribute to the dedication and leadership of the men and women who so skillfully led St. Francis into the 1970s, 1980s, and 1990s, with the same spirit of dedication and caring that began in the very earliest days of the work.

Founded by a group of Catholic nuns on property provided by the Munsons, a Quaker family, inspired by a lay woman's intuition, and directed by Leo M. Taran, a Jewish physician, the effort from the start was unbiased and a perfect environment for poor children desperately in need of care and nurturing. The children were welcomed on the basis of their need and were provided with a loving atmosphere, healthy food for recuperative strength, and the ability to continue their schooling while undergoing supervised treatment and rest for their illness.

The sanatorium's home-like atmosphere, the grouping of children according to their ages and degree of activity allowed, provided playmates and competitors. Talents were developed through the educational programs and celebrations and parties abounded. The staff often served as the appreciative audience for the children's plays and recitals that were an encouragement to the youngsters to reach beyond their illness to new possibilities.

The staff gave of themselves tirelessly for the children and rejoiced at the progress made. These are the years when the feelings of being "one big family" undoubtedly originated. The feelings were nurtured during the following years by an in-house publication, *The Francardial,* a monthly news sheet that reported the happenings: births, deaths, weddings, and news of all kinds that was of particular interest to the growing numbers of staff and volunteers. It gave them a sense of being part of something greater than themselves, something truly worthy of their efforts.

The first open-heart surgery performed in 1957 became national and international news through the Franciscan Order and certainly swelled a

Fig. 13.1. Nuns and children at St. Francis Sanatorium, c. 1943. Sister Monica is in the back, facing the camera. Photograph courtesy of St. Francis Hospital.

sense of pride among the members of the growing hospital family.[20] In the years following, new technology and progressive improvements in introducing new cardiac methods and treatments have continued to build the reputation of the hospital. Most significant is the compassionate, skilled, and attentive care given to each patient. This is testified to daily by the numerous letters of appreciation that patients and families send back to the hospital after discharge.

This intangible something that continues to permeate the hospital environment and to live on in all of us is our legacy—a legacy of spirit that demands our attention—contained now in the words of our mission statement. In keeping with its central beliefs, the St. Francis Heart Center articulates the following values as operating principles for all involved in carrying out its mission:

- Respect for the dignity of each individual as a person with individual needs, beliefs, and characteristics. This respect requires an emphasis on the whole person—their physical, spiritual, and emotional needs.
- A commitment to serve—which entails a commitment to the people we serve as well as a commitment to our purpose.
- An unending striving for excellence as demanded by our belief in human dignity and our commitment to service.
- An emphasis on compassion as the hallmark of treatment at St. Francis.

- An insistence on integrity to our mission, in practice, in dealing with others, and to ourselves.[21]

Notes

1. Maude R. Kimball, "St. Francis' First Volunteer," 1975. St. Francis Hospital files. All references cited are located in the St. Francis Hospital files.

2. Rev. Thomas F. Cullen, *The Very Reverend Mother Mary of the Passion and Her Institute* (Providence, RI: Franciscan Missionaries of Mary, 1929), p. 6.

3. Sr. Mary of Blessed Claude De La Colombiere (Dufault), F.M.M., "An Historical Survey of the St. Francis Sanatorium for Cardiac Children, Roslyn, L. I., 1937-1951, with Emphasis on the Social Service Department" (M.S.S. diss. Fordham University, 1951), p. 22.

4. Ibid., p. 23.

5. Ibid., p. 24.

6. Sr. Mary Petrosky, F.M.M., "How an International Institute Treats Particular Cultural Problems," 1955, The Franciscan Missionaries of Mary files, The Provincial House, Bronx, NY.

7. Cullen, "Mother Mary," p. 36.

8. Dufault, "Historical Survey," p. 52.

9. Ibid., p. 53.

10. Ibid., p. 54.

11. Petrosky, "International Institute," p. 19.

12. Dufault, "Historical Survey," p. 55.

13. Ann Mikkelsen, "An Historical Story of the Guild of St. Francis Hospital," 1956, typescript, p. 2, St. Francis Hospital files, 1956.

14. Ibid., p. 7.

15. Mary Hall, "Sixty Years . . . A Retrospective Review," St. Francis Hospital Staff *News,* vol. 2, no. 1, February 1980.

16. Dufault, "Historical Survey," p. 56.

17. Ibid., p. 65.

18. Kimball, "St. Francis' First Volunteer."

19. Marie Foscato, Historian, "Annual Guild Meeting Report," June 3, 1974, St. Francis Hospital.

20. "Far Away Missions," 1956, Franciscan Missionaries of Mary, Providence, RI.

21. The Mission Statement, "Strategic Long-Range Plan for St. Francis Hospital the Heart Center, 1993," pp. 51 and 52.

14. Homeless in Huntington:
Struggling Mothers and Their Care Givers

Cynthia J. Bogard

There's a woman who lives on the main street of Huntington village, a woman named Carrie. Carrie is a large black woman perhaps in her fifties. She can often be found with her grocery cart laden with plastic bags shouting obscenities at passersby from her regular bench on a downtown corner. Sometimes she'll have a pleasant morning conversation with the many business owners and workers that after all these years, have come to almost expect an interaction with Carrie as part of their morning routine. Sometimes she just yells at them to get out of her face. No matter how lucid Carrie may seem on any particular morning though, no matter how cold or rainy the weather, Carrie is clear on one subject: she refuses all offers of shelter, all attempts to get her to leave the street where she's become part of the local scene for the past twelve years. Carrie is Huntington's mascot bag lady—and she knows it.[1]

In the public mind, it has been Carrie and women like her, who constitute the typical homeless woman. For a while, during the late 1970s, this image of the typical homeless woman had some validity.[2] Today, about twenty years after the media first focused on the problem of the homeless, women like Carrie constitute only a tiny, though highly visible, minority of homeless women. The typical homeless woman of the mid-1990s is a woman in her late twenties, a mother trying to raise her two or three young children, a woman disproportionately likely to be African American.[3] Her problem is not mental health; it's poverty.

She is not often visible to the casual observer. She does not beg for money or yell at strangers or live on a cardboard-covered subway grate. Instead, today's homeless woman lives in a public or private shelter with her children, a shelter that she has come to after a long period of doubling up in substandard housing with whatever relatives or friends that would take her and her children in.[4] The subject of this essay is the public response to this kind of homeless woman whose homelessness is overwhelmingly derived from untenable economic conditions and whose housing crisis is privately-experienced and quietly-resolved. I will concentrate on one township on Long Island, the Town of Huntington, a town that has been successful at relieving the homelessness of local women.

The Town of Huntington, Long Island, the site of some of my most recent research on homelessness, is a largely suburban township of 200,000 people divided among nineteen separate communities. The wealthy and liberal community of Huntington Village is the cultural hub of the township. The adjacent community, Huntington Station, is relatively impoverished. According to the 1990 U.S. Census, the average family income in the town is $65,800—putting Huntington in the top ten percent of the nation's communities. Overall poverty rates in the Town are quite low. Only 3.2 percent of residents, about 6,000 people, fall below the poverty line. Over two-thirds of these are children. In 1990, there were 550 single-mother families living below the poverty line in the Town; a third of these had children under five years of age only.[5] These 550 single-mother families include the vast majority of the women in the Town vulnerable to homelessness, and it is the story of these women, and the women who are concerned about them, that I now address.

In 1994, my colleagues at the Institute for Social Analysis at SUNY-Stony Brook and I were commissioned to do an investigation of homelessness in the Town of Huntington. The funding for this study itself speaks volumes about the Town's commitment to its impoverished citizens and about the way funding for charities is handled by committed community members. A group called the Huntington Coalition for the Homeless, which has been in existence for thirteen years, commissioned the study. The funding for the comprehensive study of homelessness done by our research team in the Town was raised in a single evening by a black-tie dinner and awards event organized by a wealthy woman patron of the organization and held in a large mansion used by members of the Town for such charitable purposes. Activities included an auction, a drawing for a $10,000 prize which, it was assumed, the winner would sign over to the Coalition, a sale of various items such as "house pins," ceramic pins made by the homeless. In addition, a souvenir program of the event was printed that featured advertisements bought by sponsors of the event. There was a photo exhibit of homeless women and children and an award given in absentia, to a previously homeless woman who had once been housed in the Coalition-funded homeless shelter but now held a good-paying job and rents her own home. There were no homeless women at the event. Caviar and champagne flowed freely; there was a formal sit-down dinner provided by an upscale catering service; a classical music quartet played background music. The patron's appreciable community cachet ensured that local politicians, business leaders, and the top tier of wealthy people in the community attended.

This single annual event raises a significant amount of the private funding used for programs sponsored by the Coalition for the Homeless, an organization which, to date, has focused largely on homeless mothers. The Coalition operates a short-term homeless shelter for seven to eight families and ten longer-term houses known as "transitional housing" for families just getting back on their feet. A portion of these houses are set aside for families with members who have AIDS. In addition, the Coalition serves as an informal coordinating agency and clearinghouse for local information and referral concerning homelessness, and it participates in ancillary projects such as collecting and distributing holiday meals for impoverished local families. The Coalition is the only organization in the Town dedicated to serving homeless families. There are many other organizations, however, that play important roles in containing the extent of homelessness in the Town.

Given the local commitment, very few women vulnerable to homelessness actually become homeless in Huntington Town. Part of our mission in conducting a study of homelessness in Huntington was to take the census of homeless men, women, and children in the Town. We found seventy-two adults and no children living on the streets of the Town in the fall of 1994; only four, including Carrie, were women. Huntington has five homeless shelters, including the two that are operated by the Coalition. We counted the number of residents in each shelter at two different points in time and found an average of fifty adults, forty-two of whom were women. Thus, at first glance, it would appear that slightly less than one in ten, or forty-two of the 550 known poor, single-mother families residing in the Town becomes homeless.

Further investigation of shelter dwellers, however, revealed that few mothers were actually residents of the Town. Indeed, at both enumeration points in our study, only nine families had originated from the Town. The others had been placed in Huntington shelters by the Department of Public Assistance, but had come from other towns in the county. A check with the Director of Emergency Housing Services in Suffolk County confirmed that all homeless mothers from the Town of Huntington were placed in shelters in the Town because the County Department of Social Services attempts to place homeless families in shelters as near as possible to their last addresses. The county administrator reported that there are only nine or ten families from Huntington Township among the nearly 500 families that the county provided emergency housing for each month.

As far as we could determine, a maximum of thirteen women, four single women and nine mothers, from the Town of Huntington actually could be classified as homeless. The rate of female homelessness in the Town of Huntington is substantially below that of any other measured rate in the country.[6] While fewer women than men become literally homeless (usually only one-third of the homeless adults in a given area are women), women's homelessness is especially rare in Huntington where only fifteen percent of homeless adults are women. This is because in Huntington, the homelessness of women is almost totally *prevented*, and it is prevented largely through the efforts of other women. Let me explain how this process works and why it is successful.

Unlike most studies of homelessness which focus largely or exclusively on the homeless themselves, our study took an ecological approach to studying homelessness in the Town.[7] Beyond counting and interviewing homeless men and women in the Town, we investigated community resources, how they operated, and how various community members intervened in the lives of homeless or nearly homeless residents of the Town.

We found a concentrated, devoted, and largely successful effort to prevent family homelessness among a large number of charitable organizations. We have come to call what we observed a "gendered" ecology of homelessness because both providers and recipients of the Town's services were so distinctively divided by gender.[8] The types of care severely impoverished women received, the types of services available to them, and the amount of attention paid to the problem of poor women far surpassed the time and resources spent on men.[9] Moreover, it was women, for the most part, working in charitable organizations in the Town, who had ensured that care was provided for the impoverished women of the Town. Care providers and care recipients traded on the common bond of motherhood as a means to access or to organize the delivery of services.

It has long been known that homelessness is structured by gender, and even more critically, by child-rearing responsibilities. Indeed, the homelessness experienced by women with children is so markedly different from that experienced by men that applying the same term, homelessness, to both groups seems almost inappropriate as the experiences of the two groups have so little in common.[10] Taking an ecological approach to investigating homelessness reveals why this is so.

In Huntington, services can be divided into three somewhat overlapping groups: secular service organizations, religious organizations, and coordinating organizations. The first, secular service organizations, includes large public bureaucracies like the Department of Social Services and many smaller groups, some of which utilize volunteers. These groups are primarily characterized by a solid funding base from state, county, or federal sources or from other charity organizations such as United Way. Groups like the Housing Rights Project, the Nassau-Suffolk Legal Services, and the Long Island AIDS Action Council provide information, advocacy, and intervention around specific issues; others, like Power, Inc., Stepping Stones, or Town of Huntington Youth Bureau provide a variety of services to specific populations: ex-offenders, mentally-ill adults, or teens, respectively.

The second type of provider, religious organizations, are primarily volunteer organizations funded by local members. They provide a variety of services and often fill in the service gaps of the secular organizations. Many

provide emergency services such as food pantries, grocery vouchers, clothing, and cash for utilities, rents, and mortgages subsidies. These last-minute,
ad hoc services often are instrumental in forestalling the onset of literal
homelessness for their clients. Most of these groups, such as Helping Hands
Mission, St. Anthony of Padua, St. John's Episcopal, Temple Beth David,
Trocaire House at St. Pat's, and St. Hugh of Lincoln focus on delivering
services to families. The seven major religious groups in the Town serve
1,030 families every month and spend over $9,000 a month on emergency
cash transfers. Through a complicated set of calculations, our research group
estimated that the combined emergency services provided by the religious
organizations alone directly prevented 104 families from becoming homeless
each month on average.[11]

Finally, there are also several coordinating organizations such as Long
Island Cares, which is a food pantry distribution organization, Huntington
Community Food Council, Northport-East Northport Ecumenical Lay Council, the Jewish Nutrition Network, which is another food pantry coordination
organization, and Catholic Charities, an organization that aids individual
parishes in their efforts to provide services. Family Services League provides
both coordination and direct services for the poor. Finally, there is the
Huntington Coalition for the Homeless, the only organization whose sole
mission revolves around aiding the homeless. These groups ensure that the
Town's resources are adequately and efficiently distributed to those in need.
Again, most of these groups focus on aiding families.

By combining the 104 families who did not become homeless in the
Town with the nine who did, we estimate that there are 113 families who are
directly at risk of homelessness each month in the Town. Since only nine
families do become homeless, the Town's efforts prevent ninety-two percent
of those families at risk from actually becoming homeless. This is a prevention rate unparalleled in the nation.[12]

Although the top administration of both secular and religious organizations are oftentimes men, almost all of the middle management and hands-on
service delivery personnel in these organizations are women. Women, then,
make many of the policy decisions of these organizations and are responsible
for assisting and keeping track of impoverished individuals served by the
organization. Overwhelmingly, these women charity workers in Huntington
have decided to help other women.

When we interviewed service providers, whether volunteer or paid
professionals, making sure that children were provided with the necessities
of life ranked as their highest priority. Since having an adequate caregiver
for poor children was defined as a necessity, providing for care giving
mothers also became a priority for many organizations. These groups saw
their mandate then, as providing food, clothing, and cash transfers to poor

mothers, so that the meager financial resources available to the mothers through work and/or public assistance could be used to pay the rent. It is well known that Long Island has some of the highest rents in the nation. Families pay an average of $700 per month for a two-bedroom apartment. These rents are almost double the amount of the New York State $360 maximum rent allowance from Aid for Dependent Children (AFDC). A mother and two children receive about $575 per month in public assistance which leaves $235 a month, after the rent, to cover utilities, food, and personal items not covered by food stamps, clothing, and all incidental expenses including transportation.[13]

Because it is next to impossible to survive on AFDC alone, poor mothers have increasingly turned to charitable organizations for aid. The typical poor mother in the Town of Huntington visits several of these charitable organizations each month. Food is the most common service provided; in addition, a poor mother might receive clothing, money for incidentals, and an occasional cash transfer to help with a utility bill or another necessary expense. Mothers also use free day care services and employment aids such as job training, job boards, employment counseling, and free transportation.

The impoverished mothers we interviewed often had an encyclopedic knowledge of what charitable organizations provided which services and how often. Caregivers too could string together a list of referrals so that a mother in need could get a grocery voucher from one organization, a utility voucher from a second, a trip to the food pantry one week a month from a third, and free clothing from a fourth organization. Almost all organizations presume that their service recipients live in a private home with cooking facilities. The Town had no soup kitchen, and most food pantry foods required cooking.

Both recipients and providers were united in their conviction that the services in Huntington were just barely enough to meet the needs of the relatively small group of impoverished citizens and then only through the sometime superhuman efforts and overwhelming generosity on the part of providers. Both groups also were united in condemning the publicly provided services of the Department of Social Services (DSS) as both inadequate and punitive. We heard numerous stories of religious organizations that felt a need to provide rent money and food to an AFDC-eligible family simply because of DSS paperwork that caused delayed or absent payments.

Providers complained that their resources are constantly strained to the limit. Recipients of services noted that accessing the resources their families need to survive from the thirty-one different provider organizations is itself a full-time job. Still, both mothers of poor children and the largely female staff members of voluntary and paid organizations were united in feeling that somehow the children and their primary caregivers must and would be taken care of by the Town's largess. Both groups were correct in feeling that somehow the Town did manage to support its relatively small proportion of impoverished families in a manner that prevented the most obvious consequence of severe impoverishment—homelessness.

In preventing severe impoverishment in Huntington, both the group of middle-class women volunteers and agency workers and the impoverished mothers rely on a construction of womanhood that is focused on private, family-centered mothering and its public manifestation—charity work. Providers constructed poor women as persons worthy of charity only insofar as they were responsible for caring for their children. Impoverished women also highlighted their need for goods and services in order that they might better fulfill their role as mothers. Charity workers, both paid and unpaid, work in order to "help others." Although some men are involved in both volunteer and paid charity work, and some poor fathers make use of these services, by and large, women take care of women for the sake of the children in the Town of Huntington. To the extent that poor women and their middle class sisters have a common goal—the care of poor youngsters—they also share a workable system for the redistribution of wealth in the Town that is remarkably successful in preventing family homelessness.

Notes

Funding for the study cited in this work was provided by the Huntington Coalition for the Homeless, Huntington, New York. All views expressed in this work are those of the author.

1. For a complete report on homelessness in Huntington, Long Island, New York, see Cynthia J. Bogard and J. Jeff McConnell, "Homeless in Huntington: A Study of Homelessness in a Resource-Rich Community," report presented to the Huntington Coalition for the Homeless, February 15, 1995.

2. Stephanie Golden, *The Woman Outside: Meanings and Myths of Homelessness* (Berkeley: University of California Press, 1992).

3. Martha Burt, *Over the Edge: The Growth of Homelessness in the 1980's* (New York: Russell Sage Foundation, 1992); Leland J. Axelson and Paula W. Dail, "The Changing Character of Homelessness in the United States," *Family Relations* 37 (1988): 463-69.

The vast majority of homeless women in the 1990s are mothers living with children. The small minority of single homeless women differ both from homeless women living with their children and from homeless men in that they have significantly higher rates of drug and alcohol addiction and higher rates of serious mental illness.

4. Empirical support for this description can be found in Kay Young McChesney, "A Review of the Empirical Literature on Urban Homeless Families Since 1980," presented at the American Sociological Society Annual Meeting, Los Angeles, CA, 1994; also Joel Blau, *The Visible Poor: Homelessness in the United States* (New York: Oxford University Press, 1992).

5 United States Bureau of the Census, *Census of the Population 1990* (Washington, DC: United States Government Printing Office, 1992).

6. Burt, *Over the Edge.*

7. Paul A. Toro, Edison J. Trickett, David D. Wall, and Deborah A. Salem, "Homelessness in the United States: An Ecological Perspective," *American Psychological Association* 46, no. 11 (1991): 1-11.

8. For a more detailed explanation, see Cynthia J. Bogard, "Revealing the 'Gendered Ecology' of Homelessness: A Multi-Method Study of Community and Connection," paper presented at the Eastern Sociological Society Meeting, Boston, March 1996.

9. For a recent example, note policy changes made to Philadelphia's homeless shelter system; when the budget fell short of meeting the demand for shelter, single men were barred from using the shelter system (Michael Janofsky, "Welfare Cuts Raise Fears for Mayors," *New York Times*, July 30, 1996).

10. For a discussion of changing meanings of homelessness, see Peter H. Rossi, *Down and Out in America: The Origins of Homelessness* (Chicago: University of Chicago Press, 1989).

11. For a description of the calculations, see Bogard and McConnell, "Homeless in Huntington."

12. Homelessness prevention rates are difficult to come by, however. See Martha Burt and Barbara Cohen, *America's Homeless: Numbers, Characteristics, and the Programs That Service Them* (Washington, DC: Urban Institute Press, 1989), for an initial look at this problem.

13. Figures approximate mid-1990s New York State allowances.

15. The Ladies' Village Improvement Society A Century of Force in East Hampton

Eunice Juckett Meeker

When a handful of East Hampton housewives decided to get together in 1895 to find solutions for improving the unsightly appearance of their community, they weren't primarily focused on what might happen a hundred years down the road. The basis for the organization they formed at that November meeting and called the Ladies' Village Improvement Society grew in stature and public acclaim. Today the hundred-year-old LVIS, as it is widely known, is a model for other communities to study. Their emissaries come. They see; they ask questions; they take photographs; and they return home determined to try the LVIS approach to civic beauty.

They think they have solved the LVIS mystique, but the real reason why the LVIS formula works is not that simple. It is a combination of people, ideas, work ethic, and careful attention to tradition. It is also the result of innovative leadership and willing workers. From its beginning the new East Hampton group courageously undertook major civic projects. Its activities ranged from simple beautification to conservation, restoration, preservation, and education.

Membership has grown from twenty-one to more than four hundred. Activities have moved from greens, ponds, and trees to parking, zoning, and preserving local landmarks. Its history-based 1995 Centennial was marked by praise on local, state, and national levels including accolades from the White House. The LVIS lives up to its name.

These projects did not develop overnight, but the seeds of community awareness were well planted. Becoming a working force in the community took years of nurturing. The LVIS keeps itself alive and active as daughters replaced mothers on the membership roster. Heritage mandated the leadership role the LVIS had set for itself. With an ideal setting—a long expanse of wide sandy ocean beach, good fishing with bays and additional waterfront, fertile soil made even more productive with heavy dews—East Hampton had not only room to expand, but well developed residential and business areas to support its growing population. It is interesting to note that the men in the community didn't get around to incorporating the village until nearly a quarter century after the ladies had made them aware of their civic responsibilities. Cooperating with the village, the LVIS helped develop a planned growth formula with zoning regulations, Building and Remodeling Codes, and government Planning and Ethics Boards.

The cooperation continues today; a recent project shared by the LVIS and the Village Board added a third shingled windmill, the 1804 Gardiner windmill, to its Landmark Roster. East Hampton cherishes its windmills which were built primarily during the early nineteenth century. Commercially obsolete, but historically priceless, these relics of earlier days are a unique village heritage. East Hampton has more early windmills than any other community in America. Three of the town's six surviving windmills are now village-owned and located on Main Street, two in their original locations.

Through the years, the ladies suggested, the men listened. In their early days the ladies saw that dusty, unpaved Main Street was watered (and eventually paved), that weeds disappeared from the picket fences enclosing the North and South End cemeteries, and that a beautification program was carried out at the new LIRR station. The LVIS work there continues as does their supervision of "Heart-of-the-Village" trees, greens, and Town Pond (a seventeenth-century goose wallow, and now a lovely tree-graced oasis).

Bicycle paths were built; the principal streets were not only paved but lighted, and unsightly signs disappeared. East Hampton's much-envied arboreal street beauty emerged as more trees were planted. The LVIS now cares for more than 7,000 trees. Greens are maintained and historic Main Street structures supervised. Town Pond's unique setting makes a striking entrance to the village's mile-long main thoroughfare.

History lives on Main Street. An LVIS Landmarks Luncheon was held in December 1995. At that time, the LVIS honored Village Board members for their work in preserving landmarks such as the Lyman Beecher house, the Old Barn, and the Gardiner Mill. They purchased the Beecher house for the new Village Office, kept the Old Barn under close watch to see that no drastic changes were made, and purchased the Gardiner Mill, stabilizing and restoring it with private subscription in 1996–1997. It is slated to become a museum. Mayor Paul Rickenback envisions it as part of an annual Windmill Celebration. The first is tentatively set for fall 1998 when it will be part of the year-long 350th anniversary celebration.

Six surviving members of the original LVIS Landmarks Committee, who in 1974, worked for recognition of the Heart-of-the-Village Historic District by the National Register of Historic Places, were honored at the first Landmarks Luncheon at the Maidstone Club in 1994. Preservation is an active ongoing project. The third Landmark's affair honored a couple who painstakingly restored one of Main Street's oldest farmhouses, the 1658 Miller-Hedges homestead.

The big test of the LVIS's ability to respond to the community came as a result of the 1938 hurricane, the unexpected storm that brought very high winds and pelting rain to the village that was unprepared on that early fall afternoon. Age-old elms were toppled like matchsticks. In three hours, Main Street became an impassable jungle of downed branches and huge trunks. About a third of the older elms were uprooted.

Surveying the damage, the village and the LVIS had to make important decisions: which trees were irretrievable, which were worth righting and guy-wiring, which, with judicious pruning, could once again be worthy of their places in the Heart-of-the-Village. This was the beginning of that much-admired LVIS street tree program. Annually, it purchases and plants selected replacement trees. These trees not only have to withstand the challenge of automobile emissions, but they have to have growth patterns that carry leafy bowers high above the streets. All new trees must also respond well to watering, feeding, and pruning. Trees other than elms are gingerly tried out for beauty and for their resistance to disease.

Contributed memorial trees are a real boon in meeting the extra expense of the vast tree program. Memorial/anniversary trees, currently more than 320, are an important part of LVIS's current annual tree budget which is slightly less than $50,000. Today the LVIS Tree committee numbers forty hard-working volunteers who "baby sit" assigned areas of the village. They check for downed branches, and they monitor trees that are "in trouble" and not responding to treatment. The women, in their uniforms identifying them as LVIS workers, also snip off unwanted sprouts and scrub the memorial plaques. Each tree is discussed and a decision is made by women, working with tree specialists, who have become experts about trees and their growth patterns. A few elderly elms are still being lovingly cared for, including the David Gardiner Elm, the giant tree in front of the LVIS headquarters which is the grand-daddy of East Hampton street trees. Its trunk, now twenty-two feet in circumference, has a divided lateral branch arching seventy feet over Main Street.

Another long-established committee oversees the area's five greens. The principal green, still called Village Green, joins the Town Pond on the main Montauk Highway. Another green, at the other end of Main Street, provides the setting for the Hook Windmill. Still another green, Sheep Pound, lies in front of the post office. Two other greens, one on the Montauk Highway that is named for former mayor Judson Bannister, and Egypt Green, a large tract near the popular Nature Trail Preserve, provide additional "open space." Each green is seeded, fed, watered, and mowed regularly.

Colorful mini flower beds are also part of the village beautification program. Planted urns at the post office and library, and the fence roses at the station are supervised cooperatively with the Village and the local garden clubs. Christmas trees, including a lighted tree set up in the middle of Town Pond, lights outlining the arms of the Hook Mill, and lights on trees on the Main Street turn East Hampton into a December fairyland of lights.

As the village grew, the local economy changed. So did the LVIS, but the basics of their organization remained in place. By the 1960s, while the LVIS still raised funds for the library, churches, hospital, and museums, and cared for their cherished greens and trees, they became more aware of other community concerns. In fact, a few years ago they established an important new committee, Community Concerns.

Slowly and carefully, the ladies enlarged their overall purpose. They maintained their original "keep East Hampton beautiful" concept, but now they also worked toward inner beauty. They stressed a caring philosophy; the "finer things"—environment, conservation, recycling— became important. This broader mandate includes the appreciation of East Hampton's rich heritage and the development of programs preserving East Hampton's unique lifestyle for generations to come. No mish-mash of neon glitz and quick fix building are acceptable for East Hampton.

This program takes considerable long-range planning, organization, and hard work, not only to devise financially sound and ethically acceptable fundraising activities, but to spend the proceeds wisely. Requests for aid are many and funds limited.

Basically the LVIS is determined that this one-time farming and fishing village forever remain a beautiful place. Ugliness will be banished; factories will not belch smoke; litter will disappear in the early morning hours; order will be maintained discreetly but efficiently, and the precious environment nurtured.

That East Hampton would also become a top-rated country seaside resort was almost, but not quite, secondary. Controlled and focused zoning ordinances appeared in 1925. Then came the Planning and Design Review Boards and the monitoring of village meetings by the LVIS.

Going back to the early 1900s, perhaps the most significant early-on change facing the community was the arrival of large numbers of "city folk." The first wave of visitors in the closing quarter of the nineteenth century, were those who had heard about eastern Long Island's cool summer breezes and the relaxed atmosphere of the small rural community "by the seaside." Adapting quickly to the potential for renting rooms, and even homes, when residents moved to even cooler simple harbor-side "cottages," twentieth-century Main Street families brought about the Boarding House Era. Among the notables who arrived in this fashion, and later settled into their own dune homes, were Pan American's Juan Trippe. His wife, Betty Trippe, eventually became an LVIS president.

Many visitors were undoubtedly influenced by the paintings of Manhattan's Tile Club. These outstanding artists captured on canvas the wind-carved dunes, the ever-changing sea, the quaint harbors, and the well-weathered shingled homes sitting demurely behind the attractive picket fences which lined Main Street. The artists' paintings, including those of Childe Hassam and William M. Chase, are still much sought after. Thomas Moran, whose paintings were largely responsible for establishing national parks like Yellowstone and Grand Canyon, was another early painter who popularized the area as a summer haven.

As the country moved well into the twentieth century, travel to the eastern tip of Long Island "for the season" became a habit. While they were contemplating building the beginnings of what became "THE summer colony," the city visitors, who also came from further afield like Cincinnati, Washington, and even Texas, took careful note of what the LVIS was doing.

There is no written record, but it's not hard to imagine a Wall Street financier, a Madison Avenue tycoon, or even a moneyed member of the city's Four Hundred saying to his spouse, "Why don't you look into what the local ladies are doing? It might be interesting for you to participate." The women complied. At first the summer visitors made modest contributions of money, vegetables, and flowers from their gardens for the LVIS Fair. Eventually they volunteered to assist at the booths. "It wasn't easy to get to know the local women," Mrs. Trippe once confided. "They were pretty clannish and we had to earn our spurs before we were accepted."

As the final quarter of this century approached, still another kind of LVIS member appeared—professional women who come to East Hampton for the weekends. Many are skilled in art and theatre, communications and retailing, advertising, and production. They have money, but generally little time; yet, they eagerly joined the LVIS which by now had well-defined membership qualifications. (Two years of serious work on one or more committees and recommendations by at least two established members.) Other welcome professional, talented, and energetic workers are faculty members from the local schools.

Martha Stewart joined the LVIS early in 1995; she serves on the Tree Committee. Jacqueline Bouvier Kennedy never joined (she couldn't meet the residence requirement), but she contributed recipes to LVIS cookbooks. Others whose names appear regularly in metropolitan dailies, as well as in the local *East Hampton Star,* also contribute.

LVIS projects cost money. In the first decade of the LVIS, the ladies found that, if they wanted things done, they had to do the work themselves, or raise funds to pay professionals. Through the years their prime fundraisers have been a summertime Fair, and cookbooks featuring local dishes that are published every ten years or so. Occasionally, fundraising is supplemented by sponsoring a theatre benefit, a horse show, or a house tour. Bequests from wills also help the LVIS treasury.

Their first fund-raising effort was a bazaar—patterned after what the ladies had previously done for their churches. It was held inside what was then called Clinton Hall, the birthplace of the LVIS. Here the LVIS ladies heaped hand-made quilts and sweaters, pot holders and aprons, baby clothing and tea sets on sale counters. Other areas of the bazaar featured their famous cakes, pies, jellies, and jams. Soups and pastas as well as appetizers and salads are recent additions to local culinary offerings.

Today's colorful July lawn fair was developed gradually. The weatherman usually cooperated. Mrs. Louise James, who chaired a mid-fifties Fair, is rumored to have stood on the lawn of nearby St. Luke's and, looking skyward, to have said, "Lord, you simply cannot rain on MY fair." He didn't.

Early fairs were staged at The Creeks, the Herter's Georgica Pond estate; on the Herrick Playground, and on the Village Green. Unfortunately it took a few years for the LVIS to realize its Village Green Fair was counterproductive. They were spending too much time and money to repair the traffic of far too many fair-day feet. Miraculously an alternative site was proposed and quickly commandeered.

Civic leaders in two weeks in 1946 raised $48,000 to purchase a James Lane saltbox property known as the Mulford Farm which overlooks the Green. One room had been slated to be carted off to the Brooklyn Museum. Local concerned citizens couldn't tolerate this and they opened their purses. The LVIS was involved and eventually the property was turned over to the East Hampton Historical Society. The LVIS yearly paid a token $5,000 rental for its use for Fair Day.

Thus, in 1949, the summer fair moved. Its booths now had ample room to spread out on land that had remained in the Mulford family since the village was settled in 1648. Playland, occupying the rear pasture, featured kiddie rides on fire trucks and haywagons. Booths sold knick-knacks, souvenirs, second-hand books and clothing, farm and garden produce, mystery packages, and contributed new gift items.

A "no cost" booth took in hundreds of dollars selling votes for "Cutest Baby," "Best Dressed Matron," "Worst Golfer," and other such titles. The Maidstone Club crowd moved en masse to the Mulford Farm. Some husbands even became adept barkers. The crowds loved them, and the take zoomed skyward. Rotogravure society photographers clicked away. East Hampton's fame spread. Each year's Fair Chairman was expected to produce a full slate of profit-making booths and events, and she usually did. Today's one-day fair now brings in more than $50,000. The popular cake booth still sells out soon after the 10 a.m. opening.

Meanwhile the Mulford Farm gained new status as a landmark. The well-weathered saltbox, basically the twin of John Howard Payne's saltbox cottage museum next door, became a museum showing early building techniques in East Hampton. Rachel's Garden, where early LVIS fashion shows were held with debutantes as mannequins, now has an authentic colonial period dooryard garden.

For many years the LVIS Fair Fashion Show was a proven money maker. It was held outdoors in the farm's dooryard garden. The young girls who modeled upheld the LVIS honor. They managed to look cool and comfortable even when the fall outfit they were showing, perhaps with a mink, silver fox or sable stole draped over one shoulder, was better adapted to winter temperatures. One year the Fair volunteer models, using the St. Luke's Rectory as a backdrop, even modeled original bridal gowns of previous years loaned by LVIS members. The show was a big hit.

Today's fairs are no longer held at the Mulford Farm. The Historical Society now uses the former farm for historic encampments and demonstrations, and for antique shows. Since 1990, the LVIS has staged its summer fair on its own grounds further east along Main Street. Tree-shaded and creating less traffic, the new site has worked well. The house, once the home of the Gardiner family, was built in 1748. It was occupied by British officers during the Revolutionary War. It is said that the plot to take West Point was hatched here while the owner's son, an officer in George Washington's Army, was hidden in the mansion's "secret room."

The long-neglected Main Street house and its overgrown sunken garden, was purchased in 1987 for over a million dollars and completely renovated. It houses not only the two LVIS year-round shops, Bargain Books and Bargain Box, but its office, archives, and board room. A barn holds Fair equipment. Generous gifts of plantings have enhanced the setting which lends itself well to the LVIS Fair. A Restoration ball in 1989 and a matching fund gift from Dudley Roberts wiped out the mortgage.

Each Fair evening sees a growing interest in the traditional BBQ supper in the sunken garden, followed by country music, dancing, and the announcement of the day's lucky winners. Big interest is always shown in the lovingly hand-crafted dollhouse whose "shares" earn thousands of dollars year after year. Colorful creative posters are also a revenue source. They soon become collectors' items. A variety of tote bags and T-shirts, distinctly LVIS-related, are also big sellers. New, too, are creative chapeaux. *East Hampton Heritage,* an architectural, historical overview of outstanding area homes, was reprinted in 1996.

The Fair makes a regular appearance on metropolitan summer listings, attesting to its growing importance. In return for doing the evening Fair cooking, the LVIS invites the Lions Club to stage its own earlier barbecue on LVIS grounds, another example of the LVIS working with other organizations in town.

Probably of all its activities, except for the summer fair, the LVIS is proudest of what it has accomplished with its thirteen cookbooks. Starting in 1896 with the first of its editorial efforts, the LVIS has consistently put out "best sellers" built around local housewives' creativity. These early, and now priceless well-thumbed books, sold for $1 and with their quota of advertising, made good money for the parent organization.

The recipes in the LVIS cookbook are known for their creative use of Long Island fruits, vegetables, and seafood. Treasured family recipes are a mainstay. Clams, oysters, scallops, lobster, and swordfish, done "Bonac Style" (after Acabonac Harbor in Springs) keep the local term alive. Other local recipes are based on blueberries and blackberries, wild beachplums, and grapes (free for the picking), as well as on potatoes, cauliflower, and cabbage, all home-grown or available at farm stands.

Samp, clam chowder, duffs, and puddings, clam bakes, and church supper-style casseroles appeared in early editions, along with pithy sayings and well-tested household hints. Gradually, though, offerings became more sophisticated, and in recent years, it became popular to ask national figures, as well as noted local chefs, to contribute unusual recipes "to flesh out" old time Bonac favorites.

Each new cookbook (published in 1896, 1898, 1908, 1911, 1916, 1924, 1939, 1948, 1955, 1965, 1975, 1995, and 1996) enhanced the LVIS' reputation in the culinary world. Both local and national food writers have given definite "thumbs up." Their reviews once tended to use "quaint," "original," and "country," but now "sophisticated" and "imaginative" creep into descriptions.

Today the LVIS cookbooks still reflect the Down East feeling of the area, a tribute to the early cooks and their mastery of local cuisine. But these books also reflect changing times. No longer are recipes done in paragraph form, but in more standard cookbook style, listing ingredients in order of use. Recipes now include categories for appetizers, cold soups, exotic fruits, and vegetables. Desserts have become more complicated. But old favorites are frequently repeated—by popular request.

Older books, except for the 1995 Centennial 300-page hardcover, were long out-of-print and unavailable except at high prices, and then only rarely. In 1996, a new and different LVIS cookbook appeared. Originally conceived as a reprint of the initial 1896 cookbook, put out when the society was still in its infancy, the 100th anniversary book, the society's thirteenth, is called *A Full Century of Tip of the Island Cooking Wisdom, 1896–1996.*

Cooking Wisdom, as it is now known, has an unusual format. The original cream-colored one hundred pages of the 1896 book, from its cover through its recipes and household hints, to its advertisements, have been wrapped around with fifty new white pages. The new cover, a drawing of the 1804 Gardiner Windmill on James Lane, the village's latest landmark, reflects the forward look of the new book which also casts a retrospective and reflective look at the first hundred years of publishing cookbooks to fund LVIS civic projects.

The new wrap-around section gives glimpses of group dining—at boarding houses, and at such local get-togethers as church suppers, strawberry festivals, and pot luck dinners. It also contains a memoir of four generations of cooking for "hands" at the area's historic 1798 Fulling Mill Farm. It also features the work of the noted national home economist and early cookbook editor, Catharine Beecher, who was born in East Hampton in 1800. (Beecher's famous younger sister, Harriet Beecher Stowe, author of *Uncle Tom's Cabin,* was born later in Connecticut.) Catharine was born in the Beecher home on Main Street in the house now home to East Hampton village offices.

Cooking Wisdom's history is done in year-by-year style featuring major accomplishments from 1896–1996, by current archivist and former treasurer, Virginia Smith Schenck, the book's co-chairman. The 1996 cookbook also contains two and three page selections from the ten cookbooks between 1896 and 1995. Each was prepared by a pair of related old-family LVIS members and is introduced by a small print of the original cover flanked with a different clam chowder recipe.

Cooking Wisdom was designed to be "a good read" as well as a retrospective survey of "the way we cook in East Hampton." It thus follows the tradition of the older books that combine typical recipes using local bounty of land and sea, with insights into the culinary history of Long Island's South Fork.

As part of the publicity for the Centennial 1995 cookbook, the LVIS staged a contest to find the owner of the largest LVIS Cookbook collection. Seven turned out to be the magic number, with two top "winners," each receiving a special copy of the newest edition. Five of the winning circle collectors were part of the staff of the 1996 reprinted edition, *Cooking Wisdom.* It is rumored that the LVIS cookbooks are so well treasured that a local girl, undecided which suitor to choose, will select the one whose family has a cookbook collection. Pure rumor, of course, but indicative of the value placed on early LVIS books.

Full collections of LVIS cookbooks at the East Hampton Public Library and in the LVIS Archives are available, with careful handling, for research, and are frequently used. A Radcliffe Master's candidate chose the LVIS cookbooks and their influence on local cooking as a thesis in 1992.

Today East Hampton attracts visitors almost year round. An expert at adapting to the needs of year-round visitation, the LVIS has lighted Town Pond for wintertime skating. Come December, the LVIS and the Village turn the community into a beautifully-decorated, multi-wreathed village. Special events, like house tours, caroling, historically oriented lectures, craft shows, and concerts are scheduled.

Weekends through the winter and into spring bring many visitors, thanks to the oil burner which enables second home owners to keep their places open year round. Some even have put in indoor pools. Bargain Books and Bargain Box remain open weekends from January 1 to April 1. Thus, with warm weather sales, they earn more than $45,000 a year for Bargain Books and more than twice that for Bargain Box.

"The Village is almost as crowded on holiday winter weekends, as it is in summer when we have to compete with the beach," commented a longtime cashier at Bargain Books, which recently took in more than $650 on an "iffy" sunny-cloudy August Tuesday. "Books are priced under a dollar—mostly for children's, and $1 to $5 dollars for adult fare. First editions and recent best sellers are slightly higher. Art books are especially popular. Local history are snapped up as quickly as they are shelved. Some days we receive almost as many donations as we sell, with popular 'summer reading' turned over two and three times a season."

The casher is one of fifty volunteers who sort, price, shelve, cull, and sell contributed books and records. They also give newcomers information about "things to see and do in the area" as a measure of hospitality. The LVIS Sunken Garden is number one on the list.

Through the archway another thirty-five volunteers use "Closed Mondays" to price donated gifts of clothing, bric-a-brac, china, linens, lamps, and furniture. (The Bargain Box began in 1951 and Bargain Books in 1964.)

Hard-working members chair the twenty-two active committees that carry on the work of LVIS. Many volunteer for more than one committee. The Fair itself requires between thirty-five and fifty chairmen and co-chairmen, and hordes of green-striped apron assistants. Recruited teenagers are active in helping on Fair Day (and learning about LVIS activities in so doing). Other members set up the Fair, "man" the gates (donations, not an entrance fee), run the accounting, and oversee the evening BBQ.

Obviously the LVIS is already looking to the future, and more specifically the LVIS's role in the twenty-first century. Currently on the agenda is the restoration of the deteriorated historic picket fence that once separated the Gardiner Brown LVIS home from Main Street. The fence contains 420 pickets, but only 262 belong to the LVIS. "It would be great if eventually we could control the full length of fencing. Outsiders assume we own it all—but so far, we don't," explained former LVIS president, Andrea Cooper.

East Hampton's newest Historic Hook Mill District was created in 1996 at the north end of Main Street. This contains not only the 1806 Hook Mill and the adjacent green, but also the North End Cemetery and the Sheep Pound (green) and many historic homes. National Register status for this historic district is anticipated soon.

Other civic projects for future LVIS attention: additional landscaping for new parking areas; changing meeting days and hours to make it possible for more of our new working members to attend; creating greater interest in LVIS work by our young people, and (older members may protest) inviting men to become working dues-paying associate members. Back in 1896, a few men enjoyed this privilege, at $3 each.

"The current changed profile of the typical LVIS member is also making it harder each year for us to staff the Bargain Books and Bargain Box shops with volunteers. Many members now have full-time positions," a current officer explained. "They're an integral part of a two-income family. Once their children are in school, they rejoin the work force. When they retire, between ages fifty-five and maybe sixty-five, they can give the LVIS at best fifteen prime years as volunteers. We need to supplement our member volunteers with teenagers, and part-time workers—perhaps internships.

She continued, "We also need to find other ways to finance LVIS work in beautification, education, conservation, preservation, and community service. We could perhaps suggest heftier contributions, and more anniversary as well as memorial tree money. Maybe a program to ask members to remember the LVIS in their wills, the way colleges are now doing."

With many similar-size communities not only "Up Island" but in other parts of the country looking to the LVIS to learn how it now functions, and why it has been so successful, the ladies are understandably careful about moving in new directions. "It's like living in a glass house," said a longtime Board member. "We are duty bound to 'do the right thing.' It's expected of us. After all, we ARE the Ladies Village Improvement Society."

Sources

Books, clippings, photos, graphs, and memorabilia including LVIS cookbooks, as well as other pertinent records at the LVIS Archives, LVIS Headquarters, 95 Main Street, East Hampton.

East Hampton Library's historical material on microfilm, including issues of the weekly, *East Hampton Star,* and the Pennypacker Collection of Long Island historical material in the East Hampton Free Library, 159 Main Street. (The *East Hampton Star* was founded in 1885 and was an early champion of the LVIS. It is located at 153 Main Street, East Hampton; back issues are a prime source for researchers.)

Interviews with LVIS officers and other long-time members and the author's own personal involvement with the LVIS since 1946.

16. Civic-Minded Women: The Sayville Village Improvement Society

Norma White

In *Natural Allies: Women's Associations in American History,* Anne Firor Scott charts the course of women's organizations from their beginnings. "During the Revolution some women . . . banded together to raise money, provide amenities to the soldiers, and support the movement for independence. These groups dissolved when the war was over, but the memory of their accomplishments lingered." In the early decades of the nineteenth century, voluntary organizations of all kinds sprang up to "supplement the old institutional structures of family, church, and local government." These first "female societies" were in coastal cities, but within two decades, women in smaller communities throughout the country followed suit. Scott notes that these organizations were usually "led by wives and daughters of the most visible and respected families." By the early decades of the twentieth century, women's sphere of influence had expanded beyond the four walls of home to include the neighborhood, the village, and the town or city, and the efforts to improve community life had achieved increasing momentum. Women became "municipal housekeepers" and turned their attention to civic improvements in public health, public safety, education, beautification, and recreation.[1]

In Sayville, women joined the civic action movement in March 1914. Mrs. Francis Hoag, a woman of vision who was wife of the editor of the *Suffolk County News,* called a meeting at the *News* office with the object of forming a civic association for Sayville women to address these concerns. She was inspired by the efforts of the Ladies' Village Improvement Society of East Hampton. To her amazement, the office overflowed with women eager to work for the betterment of Sayville. By the end of the first few weeks they had formed the Women's Village Improvement Society, elected officers (Hoag was president), and adopted a constitution and by-laws. Dues of $1.00 were approved and $50.00 was collected. One of the members provided two rooms above a store on Main Street for a meeting place. The rooms were fitted and wired for electricity, thanks to the generosity of another member. Some gave or loaned furniture, including a stove, and the Society bought chairs at forty cents each. The president invited all members to her home for a "Suggestion Tea" on March 21, 1914. Each person was to bring a suggestion as to how the village could be improved and each suggestion was to include a ten cent donation. Unfortunately, we do not have a record of the suggestions but we know that $10.60 was added to the treasury.[2]

Garbage disposal was a major concern. A dozen rubbish baskets were donated and more were available. The baskets were painted and stenciled by the members and placed around town. Household garbage was either buried in backyards, thrown in empty lots or wooded areas, or put in the Mill Pond. The women contacted the Board of Health about this situation. The town responded that it would be glad to cooperate by setting aside some town property for a garbage dump and by forbidding all dumping in the Mill Pond. The Town of Islip designated the meadows from Terry Street to the Oyster Houses near the bay as a garbage dump. This area today provides parking for those using the ferries to Fire Island.

A committee checked on the most unsightly places in the village where rubbish had been dumped. This was carted away to the new public dumping ground. A man hired for a day and a half at $7.50 cleaned up three streets, Greeley Avenue, Main Street, and Foster Avenue. Later the Society hired a man with a horse and wagon to pick up trash in the spring and fall at a charge of ten cents a barrel. This continued for about ten years until town garbage collection started.

The Society's efforts to beautify the village included the placing of signs at the three entrances. The grounds of the railroad station were beautified with flowers and the Long Island Rail Road Company was asked to provide additional seats. One group contacted the motion picture men concerning the proper distribution of dodgers or handbills. Thereafter the boys who were hired for this purpose improved in their method of delivery and further action was not taken. But the women kept a watchful eye in case the problem resumed. When some streets were paved, a group set about to preserve the trees in the area.

The Society had to raise funds for its various projects. A very successful "parada" or show using local talent was held at the Opera House. The souvenir program was generously patronized by the village merchants. Tickets were sold at thirty-five cents, fifty cents, and seventy-five cents. Four performances were given on Wednesday, Thursday, Friday, and Saturday, in March 1914. This netted $242.44.

The Society grew: more members, more dues, more chairs. Smaller entertainments were put on and citizens made donations toward various projects. At the May 25, 1914 meeting, the treasurer reported a balance of $292.54 after the payment of all bills.

Some members worked on public safety which involved muzzling dogs, filling in a mudhole in front of the Post Office, stopping speeding, muffling auto noise, and prohibiting motorcycles and bicycles from riding on the sidewalks. A traffic policeman was hired for $50 to be at the corner of Main

Street and Candee Avenue during the summer on Saturdays, Sundays, and afternoons during the week.

A committee was appointed to look into the possibility of having a light at the end of the stone pile at the entrance to Brown's River from the Great South Bay. A letter was forwarded to the Lighthouse Department in Washington. The Acting Commissioner of the Bureau of Lighthouses sent a reply. It stated that when funds became available, measures would be taken to establish a light in the submerged end of the west Breakwater at the entrance to Brown's River. It was believed this would meet the needs of navigation in that locality.

At the May 25, 1914 meeting, a letter was read from Dr. W. E. Gordon of Patchogue to the Northport Society describing how Mr. Carnegie had helped Patchogue get its library. The secretary was instructed to write to Andrew Carnegie to find out what had to be done to get an appropriation from him for a library. When help was not forthcoming from the Carnegie Foundation, a group of five members was appointed to look into the matter of starting a library. The following week they reported having written to eight publishers for catalogues, price lists, and lists of approved books. They also wrote to Albany to see what aid the state would provide.

The committee had a promise of forty-one books and decided to start a library in one of the Society's rooms. One member promised to give a tea to raise money for a library fund. The group recommended that a Utility Sale also be held to raise funds. Its name was later changed to a Library Bazaar, and it was held at the Opera House on August 12 and 13, 1914. Fifty dollars was given by the Society to the Library Fund. At the July meeting, the Library Committee gave an extensive report with the recommendation that a Library Association be formed. This was accepted and a fifteen minute recess was declared for the purpose of enrolling members in the Library Association. Thirty-eight women signed up at $1.00 each. At the August 3, 1914 meeting, an intermission of fifteen minutes was declared so that members could sign the Constitution of the Library Association.

They learned from Albany that $1,500 in operational funds was needed to apply for a charter. The charter would authorize the Library Association to transact business to hold property and to draw an annual appropriation from the State for the purchase of books.[3] The Library Bazaar was held and netted $503.47. The Society turned the money over to the Treasurer of the Library Association. No time was lost in raising the $1,500. The bazaar proceeds, a private donation of $500, and many smaller donations provided the needed amount. The necessary papers were sent to Albany where the officials were surprised that the funds were raised in less than two months.

Sayville residents donated books including reference books. Louise Forslund, a local author, gave copies of her books. Lumber was donated for a sign as well as the labor to build it. Various fund raisers were held and the Board of Education agreed to give an appropriation of $200 a year to help meet expenses. The Library was thus assured of a yearly income.[4]

The Society remained involved with the library for many years, financially at times and with various other gifts. All members of the Library Board of Trustees were Society members until 1952 when it changed from a Library Association to a School District Library. Its assets were $85,000 when the library was turned over to the school district, a far cry from the $50 originally donated to it by the Society.[5]

All of these improvements happened in the space of about six months. The Society was interested in a still wider variety of improvements. There was a Junior Women's Village Improvement Society, which had ten charter members who were interested in starting a tennis club. A local woman offered the use of her tennis court. The junior members, with the help of some seniors, submitted plans for membership and for rules. They elected their own officers, raised their own funds, and put the donated tennis court into shape. The tennis club continued for several years.

The women were interested in the safety of school children. They requested that signs be placed at the entrance to School Street with a warning to automobile drivers and motorcyclists. They wanted to promote industry in Sayville and consulted with the Board of Trade regarding how to stimulate the chicken industry. They wrote to the Islip Town Supervisor protesting advertising signs hung across Main Street. The Society felt that it was unfair to businessmen who did not advertise in this manner, that it would obstruct light from the arc lights soon to be installed, and that it tended to cheapen the appearance of the village. They asked for present signs to be removed and that in future they be prohibited from disfiguring the beautiful streets.

The Society endorsed the proposal to extend Foster Avenue to North Main Street. The women wished for a public parking field by the railroad station as well as for a parking field in the village. They proposed that a flag be flown daily on the newly installed flag pole at Sparrow Park, and they originated the idea of a community Christmas tree in Sparrow Park and the singing of carols around it. The traffic officer who had been hired for the summer was later replaced by a "silent policeman." They paid for someone to clean the glass and light the lantern each night.

An Auxiliary Branch of the Red Cross was established and most of the Society's work was devoted to wartime activities during World War I. An Honor Roll listing the names of those in service was placed on the lawn of the library which, by then, was in its own building on South Main Street and Collins Avenue. Later, a bronze plaque was placed inside the library in honor of the men and women of Sayville and West Sayville who served in World Wars I and II.

As early as 1915, the Society had a committee to investigate the possible purchase of property by the Town for a shore front public park. At that time a piece of land was available for $15,000. The women were advised that a petition should be signed by twenty-five voters or taxpayers and presented to the Town Board. Although twenty-five signatures were obtained, the women were told that this was an inauspicious time to petition the Town for such an appropriation as several others were to be brought up at the meeting. The proposition was turned down when put to a vote. But the women were not to be denied. In 1924, the Blue Points Company agreed to sell some of its shore front property to the Society for about $5,000. The Society planned to buy the land and turn it over to the Town of Islip to be maintained at Town expense. The women raised $3,700 through door to door solicitations and subscriptions. The Blue Points Company promised the deed if the Society could arrange financing for the balance. Oystermen's Bank in Sayville loaned the additional money needed. The officers of the Society signed the note which was paid off after many money-making affairs. The land was given to the Town of Islip in 1925 to be developed as a public beach. The women petitioned the Town for twenty-five bath houses. The Town appropriated $1,000 for construction and to provide a caretaker for two months. The beach was opened to the public on July 1, 1925, and a plaque commemorates the Society's role in its acquisition.

Unlike most of the Society's activities, the purchase of a village clock took many years. In fact, in 1920 one donor asked for his $25 back since the clock had not been purchased. His money plus interest was promptly refunded. Finally, in 1937, when a new fire house with a tower was built, the Society purchased a four-faced Seth Thomas clock and had it installed.

The Gillette House, a large Victorian home with extensive property, was donated to the Town of Islip. The Society suggested that town officials allow local groups to hold their meetings there. This was approved and each organization now pays a nominal fee to the Town for meeting space. The Society, which started in two rooms on Main Street, has met, over the years, in members' homes, in Columbia Hall, and in the Fire House, now meets monthly at the Gillette House.

The Society, in conjunction with the Town, was recently involved in redecorating the meeting rooms. The large windows are now framed by burgundy drapes and the walls have been painted an antique white. A beautiful Victorian style burgundy wallpaper border complements the drapes. An additional cabinet was installed in the kitchen.

Each May, the Society arranges for half barrels filled with flowers to be placed throughout the main shopping areas in the village. In 1995, there were thirty-five barrels beautifying the streets. These flowers are watered and maintained from May to October by members. The last two years the flowers were removed in November, and pine trees were planted in the barrels. The Society tied red and gold bows on the trees which were further decorated by Scout troops and other youth groups.

In recent years the Society led in having the railroad underpass repaired and landscaped. In 1983, a Sundial was placed at the Islip Town Restoration Village in Sayville to commemorate the Town's Tri-Centennial. It has been instrumental in having the Town require litter to be cleaned up in shopping areas, in removing unauthorized signs, and in removing derelict boats from Brown's River.

The Society is involved in working with the special needs of groups and individuals within the Sayville community. Among these are veterans and the Sayville Project which provides support services and counseling. Members also donate to the Sayville Food Pantry. The Society donated $1,000 to the Fire Relief Fund when Sayville had the terrible fires in 1992 that raged in the business district. A scholarship of $1,000 based on academic achievement is awarded annually to a senior at the Sayville High School.

A program of tree maintenance has been one of the Society's projects through the years. The lovely elms that once graced Sayville's main streets fell victim to Dutch elm disease. A beautification committee sponsored by local merchants was responsible for donating money to the Society to plant honey locust trees on the main streets. Seventy-eight were planted by the Society. In recent years, a local business woman started a drive to bring the elm trees back to Sayville. Disease resistant trees known as the American Liberty Elms were purchased, planted, and nurtured for a few years in what was called the tree nursery next to the Chamber of Commerce building. They had to be cared for and grown to a sufficient size before being replanted. Donation cans were placed around town in local shops to help defray the initial expenses. Local citizens then purchased the trees, which the Society planted in Sayville at locations of their choice. The first tree was planted at the home of the originator of the idea and was nicknamed "Elmer." Others were placed on private property, along streets, in church yards, at the library, on school grounds, at the Historical Society and in parks. A metal plaque went with each tree. The purchaser could have a brief inscription on it which the Society would have placed on the ground next to the tree. Some people used the plaque as a memorial.

In the mid-1990s, a grant was given to the Baymen's Soccer Club for the purchase of shrubs and evergreens to be placed at the entrance to the soccer field. The Society supported the Chamber of Commerce in opposing the relocation of the Long Island Maritime Museum from its beautiful location in West Sayville to Patchogue. It also joined with merchants and residents who requested that foot patrolmen be restored to the streets.

Just as the women in bygone years had to fundraise constantly with sales, paradas, bazaars, entertainments, solicitations, and card parties, so today money has to be raised. Poinsettia sales, Antique and Collectible Fairs, geranium sales, and raffle tickets with prizes donated by local merchants have been some recent fundraisers. Drawings of the raffle tickets are held at the annual Christmas party which is also a fundraiser.

The year 1994 marked the 80th Anniversary of the founding of the Society. (In 1931, when it was incorporated, the Society had changed its name from the Women's Village Improvement Society to the Sayville Village Improvement Society. Despite its name change, the members have always been women.) A Victorian Tea was held at the Gillette House. As part of the celebration, twelve beige pebble stone receptacles were given to the Village to replace the open metal rubbish containers along Main Street. Surely the women of 1914 would have appreciated the appropriateness of the donation.

Perhaps the two highlights of the Society's work over the years were the formation of the library and the providing of a public bathing beach for residents before all waterfront property was sold to private owners. But the smaller achievements count no less in improving the quality of life in the community. In a speech given at the 25th Anniversary of the Society, Mrs. Bertha Huntoon, a charter member and former president said: "Civic pride is just a form of patriotism, the kind of pride that makes a person just as anxious to clean up his backyard as to head a parade." The Society began its eighty-second year in 1996. The Sayville Village Improvement Society is an outstanding example of the power of women working unselfishly together to make their community a desirable village in which to live.

Notes

1. Anne Firor Scott, *Natural Allies: Women's Associations in American History* (Urbana: University of Illinois Press, 1991), pp. 12, 13, 141, 150.

2. Information on the Sayville Village Improvement Society is based on the Record Books of the Secretary's Minutes and other papers of the Society. Elinor Huntoon Haff (1903-1990) did the original research on the Society's history. Haff taught school in Bay Shore for ten years before becoming Sayville's librarian in 1937, a position she held for more than thirty years. Norma White (1922-1996) revised the history in 1991 and 1996 for Hofstra's conference. Unfortunately, White unexpectedly died shortly after submitting her essay; it was presented at the conference by Suzanne Robilotta, vice-president of the Sayville Village Improvement Society.

3. Lila Lukosk, "A History of the Sayville (New York) Library from 1914-1967," (M.S. report, C. W. Post Library School, 1968), p. 10.

4. Ibid., p. 16.

5. Ibid., p. 44.

17. Abigail Eliza Leonard: Quiet Innovator

Dorothy B. Ruettgers

By the turn of the last century, many women were becoming known in leadership roles, especially in those areas which pertained mostly to "women's spheres" of activity. On Long Island, however, many of these were women of wealth or position who spent their summers on the Island and their winters in New York City. They gave of their money and their time, but they were not necessarily an integral part of the communities. The names of women like Alva Belmont, Katherine Mackay, and Harriot Stanton Blatch are the ones we read about in the books about women's suffrage parades and money-raising events, and certainly their work was important. There are others, however, who worked long and tirelessly in their own communities to bring about changes and improvements, whose names are forgotten or at least barely recognized today even in the towns and villages where their work was done. One of these virtual unknowns did not do all of the work single-handedly, but without her driving force, it probably would have taken far longer for the improvements she suggested to have been accepted and undertaken in Farmingdale.

Abigail Eliza Leonard, born in rural Woodstock, Vermont, in 1852, was one of several children of a farmer and his wife. Abigail attended the local one-room school and later went on to get teaching certification at Randolph State Normal School in Randolph, Vermont. She began her teaching career in Vermont in another one-room school. Not much is known about this phase of her career, but she must have been successful with her students, as she soon became a teacher of teachers at Castleton Normal School in Vermont. How long Miss Leonard taught in Vermont, whether in a small schoolhouse or in a normal school, the records do not show. However, we do know that she came to Brooklyn and taught at Girls' High School for several years. At that time, she was about twenty-four or twenty-five years old. Reports vary as to whether her subject was mathematics or Latin. My guess is that she probably taught both.[1]

From 1897 until her retirement in 1911, Miss Leonard taught English at Erasmus Hall High School in Brooklyn.[2] Her students in the class of 1901 were the first to be graduated from Erasmus Hall under the greater New York school system. Miss Leonard was very proud of these students, many of whom became prominent in their fields. Lewis Pink became state superintendent of insurance; Charles Skinner was Dean of Tufts College; Charles Cords, Clarence Bachrach, and Sydney Roffman became well-known lawyers; Donald Gorden was a well-known New York physician; and Lawrence Sperry, a pioneer aviator and inventor, and son of the founder of Sperry Aviation. For more than three decades, members of the class of 1901 and others of her students took Miss Leonard to dinner every year on her birthday. This continued even after her retirement, until she became ill at the age of ninety.[3]

What makes this Miss Leonard so different from thousands of other teachers of her time whose students thought they were wonderful? How does she fit into a book about activists and innovators? What did she do outside of a classroom? What Abigail Leonard did in her adopted community of Farmingdale to try to improve it is still evident.

In 1912, Miss Leonard moved to Farmingdale, a village of less than two thousand people on the Nassau-Suffolk county line. She built a large house on Hallock Street which she called "Aftermath." She became acquainted with the wives of some of the prominent men in that small village, and together they formed the Women's Club of Farmingdale. Although some say she founded the club, the records show that she was one of a group and served as the club's first secretary. She did become the Women's Club president in 1915 and served in that office for ten years until 1925. There is no question but that Miss Leonard was influential and perhaps the most forward looking of the women.[4]

The major issue at some of the earliest meetings of the Women's Club was that of votes for women. Miss Leonard's minutes of the meetings are, unfortunately, a bit terse, but there are a number of entries of occasions on which she urged the other women to join suffragist marches in Port Washington, Garden City, or Hicksville supporting votes for women. She does not seem to have had a great deal of success in getting others to participate, but that did not stop her from trying. In 1917, she did successfully organize a committee of one hundred to support women's suffrage.[5]

A major achievement of the Women's Club during Miss Leonard's presidency was the formation of the Farmingdale Free Public Library. At the turn of the century there had been a small circulating library, but it was of the type where the borrower had to pay a subscription in order to use the books. This first library had gone out of existence, and no library of any sort had taken its place. The Women's Club worked long and hard to get the library. They persuaded the Board of Education to let them have a room in the old Kolkebeck house which the Board owned on Main Street next to the school. They had to raise the money for books, and to this end they held bake sales and fancywork sales; they put on dinners, and did everything they could think of to raise the necessary money.

When they applied to the state government, they were told that they could have the certificate they needed to become a free, public library for only one

Fig. 17.1. The Women's Club started Farmingdale's first public library in this house in 1924. Women founded many of the libraries on Long Island. Postcard courtesy of Gary R. Hammond; photograph by Irene McQuillan.

year. After that they would need to apply again and be inspected by the state. Nothing daunted Miss Leonard and her ladies, and they forged ahead. They cleaned and painted the room, put up their shelves, asked the local citizens to give them an assortment of books in good condition, borrowed a desk and some chairs, and prepared to open the Farmingdale Free Library. The local paper, the *Farmingdale Post,* in its issue of January 11, 1924, had as its front page headline, "Farmingdale Free Library to open next Saturday at seven p.m. Over 700 selections. Everyone invited to borrow a book."

On another page, a small notice told that Miss A. E. Leonard and Jesse Merritt, editor of the *Post,* visited Doubleday, Page and Company to select books for the new library. For several years Miss Leonard served as the one person committee for the selection of books. On January 18, 1924, the front page of the paper was full of details about the opening of the new library. "The Library is located in a sunny, cheerful room in the old residence north of the high school. Farmingdale again has a library which it has lacked for nearly 25 years, the original one being dissolved to the disgrace of the village."

No one remembered to publicly thank Abigail Leonard. The Farmingdale Public Library presently is situated in a new, spacious building, erected in 1994. It outgrew its first home, its second in the high school building, its third in a former bank building, its fourth in two separate buildings in two different parts of town. The plaque on the front credits the Women's Club as the founders. I don't suppose Miss Leonard really minds that she is not mentioned at all.

Abigail Leonard's interest in learning of all kinds extended far beyond her influence in the Farmingdale Free Library. During her presidency of the Women's Club, a local Parent-Teachers Association (P.T.A.) was established in the Farmingdale school twenty-eight years after the founding of the national organization. The P.T.A. and the Women's Club worked together to obtain a school nurse five days a week and to offer business courses at the high school level. In 1920, the Woman's Club established a scholarship in the name of Miss Abigail E. Leonard. Recipients are chosen for academic excellence, club participation, and community service. The scholarship is still presented yearly at the Farmingdale High School graduation. Abigail Leonard was the first woman in Farmingdale to serve on the Board of Education. She was appointed to fill a vacancy in 1918, and then she was elected for a full term in her own right from 1919 to 1922.[6]

Farmingdale was growing, but it was difficult to find your way around because there were no street signs in the village. Advertisements simply read "south of Conklin Street" or "three buildings south of the railroad tracks on the east side of Main Street." The Women's Club, with Miss Leonard as president, raised money through contributions and benefit movies, and by March of 1918, it was able to raise $147.20 with which to order twenty-three signposts for the village streets.[7]

Some of the work done by the women under Miss Leonard's leadership may not seem very important now, but at the time it meant a lot to this small community. The women encouraged the Village Board to get streets paved, to get home delivery of the mail, and to begin garbage collection. From 1916 to 1929, the Women's Club decorated a community Christmas tree each year on the front lawn of the school and presented a program featuring carol singing and candy for the children.

Miss Leonard was a tall, well built woman, with a rather masculine way of walking. She had a dominant, no nonsense personality, and her friends and acquaintances (and I imagine her pupils, too) realized that she was used to getting her own way, and that it would be difficult to put anything over on her. She may not have been easy to live with, but she also had a strong sense of humor. When she had a goal in mind, she worked long and hard to achieve it. She enjoyed people and being active in community affairs.[8]

When women got the right to vote, Miss Leonard called her neighbor Philip Denton to drive her to the polling place every time there was an election of any kind, as long as she was able to leave her home.[9] For most meetings she would walk to the village, about three quarters of a mile away. However, in the 1930s, when she was in her middle-to-late eighties, she resigned from her organizations and committees, citing the deterioration of her eyesight and hearing, and her inability to walk to town to attend meetings. For the last three years of her life, Miss Leonard was a semi-invalid. Her sister, and later one of her nieces, came to live with her. She died at her home in early August of 1945, at the age of ninety-three.[10]

Abigail Leonard was known only in her own community; yet, in her own way, she affected many lives in positive ways. Her work for women's right to vote, for improvements in education, for improved living conditions on her local level, and her pride and continuing interest in her students—are all evidence of what one woman accomplished in the area in which she lived. She never raised large amounts of money, or participated in marches in cities to promote the causes in which she had an interest. Most of this work was done after she retired. Her work in education was never recorded in journals; she just was the kind of teacher who made her students remember her fondly enough to entertain her yearly for nearly forty years. A flourishing public library exists where there had not been an active one before she came. Abigail Eliza Leonard—she did not work to be known or to be thanked. She worked for the good of her community, and for that she deserves to be remembered.

Notes

1. Obituary, *The Farmingdale Post,* August 8, 1945.
2. List of faculty members, *The Erasmian* 11 (February 1909): 153.
3. Telephone conversation with son of Louis Pink, '01, August 1996.
4. Minutes, The Women's Club of Farmingdale, original book, March 7, 1913. Not paginated. Information not otherwise cited is from these minutes. (The minutes were later copied, but that set is not always accurate or complete.)
5. Minutes, April 25, 1913, May 23, 1913, May 8, 1914.
6. Minutes.
7. Minutes.
8. Telephone conversation with Emily Denton Jordan, daughter of neighbor Philip Denton, September 1996.
9. Ibid.
10. Obituary, *The Farmingdale Post.*

18. Kate Mason Hofstra and Alicia Patterson
Founding and Building Hofstra University

Geri E. Solomon

Hofstra University opened its doors in 1935. Its beginnings, however, were contingent upon several fortuitous circumstances and the money and devotion of two women from different eras. Although neither Kate Mason Hofstra nor Alicia Patterson were born on Long Island, each made Long Island their home for more than thirty years. There are other similarities in their lives as well, including more than one marriage, the fact that neither had children, and that both had considerable wealth. But it was neither similarities nor differences in lifestyle that make them significant in Hofstra University's history. Rather, it was their commitment to creating something permanent on the Long Island landscape—something that would last after they were gone.

Kate Hofstra did not stipulate that an educational institution be established with her fortune, but she did envision something humanitarian and research oriented. Alicia Patterson had not been extremely interested in her own education, but she proved herself to be a champion of education by using her power and money to further Hofstra's cause. If either woman had not contributed in precisely the way that they did, it is certain that Hofstra University would not exist at all.

Kate Mason: Founding a College

Although Kate Mason Hofstra was born in Boston and married in New Orleans, she spent over thirty years of her life as a Long Islander. And, although she was a wealthy woman who was able to afford an opulent home, servants, and fine furnishings, she left almost all of her wealth to establish an institution for "charitable or public good."[1] The story of Kate's life has not been fully explored and may never be known completely, but many lives have been affected by her, nonetheless. In establishing Hofstra University, the landscape of Long Island has been considerably affected.

It was in 1903 that William and Kate Hofstra bought land in Hempstead to build their home. They resided in the Gulden home in Garden City and the Garden City Hotel while the house was being completed. Howard Brower, William's business partner and a family friend, called the potential homesite a "hayfield with a small house."[2] A year earlier, William had purchased the J. K. Van Wranken estate for twelve thousand dollars to run the Nassau Lumber Company. It was a move that Brower likened to "having a toy."[3] By this time, William Hofstra had considerable money from his investments in lumber and pulp paper mills. He had been in the lumber business for more than twenty years and had owned mills in Michigan, Canada, New Orleans, Florida, and New York. This venture on Long Island allowed the couple to travel extensively in and out of New York for business and pleasure.

The Hofstra home, completed in 1904, was designed by H. Craig Severance and it is possible that this was Severance's first residential design. He later went on to design the Bank of Manhattan, the Hotel Taft, and Nelson Tower, all in New York City.[4] The Hofstra mansion, referred to as "The Netherlands" for William Hofstra's ties to his Dutch ancestry, was set back from the road and included all of the latest amenities.

With large hand-split shingles and a slanted roof, the Hofstra residence was considered to be an elegant and gracious country home. It included a breakfast room, a butler's pantry, a servant's sitting room, a small reception room, a large living room with windows that opened to a rose garden, as well as a drawing room, a sun parlor, and a sleeping porch. The stables and garage were set at a suitable distance from the house.[5]

The grounds, which encompassed approximately fifteen acres, had been planted with many specimen trees: there was a curved drive and formal gardens. In addition to the main house, there was a barn, a greenhouse, a caretaker's cottage, and a small steam-heated structure which was built for Kate's cats. Not only did she have angoras and prize-winning felines, but, according to Mr. Brower, she picked up plain old alley cats.[6]

Both of the Hofstras were active in a variety of community activities and were noted for being generous and charitable. Kate Hofstra was Vice President of the Bide-a-wee Home Association in New York City from 1903 until her death in 1933. She was also President of the Atlantic Cat Club and offered the Hofstra Challenge Cup at Madison Square Garden cat shows. The silver trophy, valued at one hundred twenty-five dollars in 1904, was awarded for the best cat in show. Her fondness for animals prompted her to leave ten thousand dollars to Bide-a-wee in her will. In addition, she left enough money to care for those pets that survived her which included twenty-five cats, four dogs, and three parrots.[7]

Kate Mason married William Hofstra late in life and the couple did not have any children. She was seven years older than he and it was a second marriage for both. Kate's first husband died; William was divorced with two children from his first marriage, Laura and Margaret. Both girls lived with their mother Anna Laura Morton, who re-married and moved with her daughters to Chicago.

Kate and William lived a comfortable lifestyle with four or five house servants, a chauffeur, and groundsmen. The Hofstras entertained in New

Fig. 18.1. Kate Mason Hofstra in her wisteria arbor, c. 1928. Photograph courtesy of the Hofstra University Archives.

York City and had a room at the Plaza or the Sherry-Netherlands Hotel for this purpose. They attended the Metropolitan Opera on Monday nights and often stayed in the city for several days. By the mid-1920s, William's business concerns made him a millionaire several times over. He was the largest shareholder of Price Brothers stock outside of the Price family itself. Price Brothers, a Canadian firm, manufactured and sold wood pulp and newsprint. It was estimated that the company owned more than forty-five million cords of pulpwood sufficient to produce thirty-one million tons of newsprint paper. William Hofstra was a director of the company.[8]

William died on May 11, 1932, leaving the bulk of his estate to his wife. Bankers Trust Company was the administrator of the estate. William also left approximately a quarter of a million dollars to his surviving daughter, Margaret Hofstra Angelin, and her two sons. When he died, however, the stock market was close to bottoming out. In spite of this, Bankers Trust persuaded Mrs. Hofstra to sell off stocks and securities to meet the amount for Margaret and her sons, William C. Billinghurst and Lennart Angelin. Because of the market's condition, the dollar value of the estate was considerably depreciated. By waiting to sell many of the same stocks, Mr. Brower recounted that he made a considerable sum more than the Hofstras did. Kate Hofstra did not like the way Bankers Trust handled the estate and wrote a new will in April of 1933 naming Howard Brower and James Barnard trustees and cutting out Bankers Trust.[9] She never told Brower of her intentions, although she talked to him numerous times about her dissatisfaction with the way her husband's estate had been handled.

On September 15, 1933, after being served her morning coffee by her housekeeper, Mrs. Hofstra died at 8:30 a.m. of coronary thrombosis. She left a lengthy will with specific gifts including those to Bide-a-wee, to St. George's Church of Hempstead, and to several friends and relatives. The remaining estate and property were left to create a memorial to her husband. She wished that her trustees set up the estate for, "the furtherance and development of such public, charitable, benevolent . . . or research purposes as they shall in their absolute discretion determine to be in the public interest."[10]

In the fall of 1934, Truesdel Peck Calkins, superintendent of public schools in the village of Hempstead and director of the Bureau of Appointments for New York University, took a seat next to Howard Brower on the Long Island Railroad and during their ride from New York City to Hempstead, and they discussed the future of the Hofstra estate. Dr. Calkins suggested that New York University, which was already offering some courses at Hempstead High School, might be willing to offer extension courses on Long Island. A few days later Calkins invited Brower to dinner at the Hempstead Country Club and discussed the possibility of using the Hofstra estate as a facility for higher education. Brower shared Calkin's enthusiasm and initiated the action that led to the creation of Hofstra University.

Two years after Kate's death, New York University's Nassau College-Hofstra Memorial opened its doors. On September 23, 1935, the college admitted its first class of 159 day students and 621 evening students. All of the classes met in the Netherlands, once Kate and William's opulent home, now renamed Hofstra Hall. Oil paintings of Kate and William hung in the living room and the furniture was much the same as when it was a residence.[11] The dining room became the Board Room for the Trustees; the living room became the student lounge. Other out-buildings became the bookstore and athletic locker rooms. The estate began to resemble a campus.

Alicia Patterson: Building Hofstra University

When Alicia Patterson was asked to be on the Board of Trustees of Hofstra College on December 16, 1943, the young school was in desperate need, not only of leadership, but also of a larger student body and a more developed physical plant. World War II had hit the campus hard and acting President Howard Brower was close to shutting the doors. With the placement of key Long Islanders on the Board, however, they hoped that great strides could be made. When Hofstra's first Board of Trustees was configured, the men were from the local community. Two were principals from Long Island schools, one was a superintendent, most were businessmen and bankers. Robert Moses, President of Long Island's State Park Commission, and Augustus Weller, President of the Meadow Brook National Bank were appointed to the Board in 1943, and in 1944, LeRoy J. Weed, the New York Director of Ginn and Company. These men brought strength and political skills to Hofstra. The appointment of Alicia Patterson, the founder and editor of *Newsday,* was also invaluable to an institution that was trying to make a name for itself.

Alicia was born on October 15, 1906, and grew up in Chicago in a family of newspapermen. Her great great-grandfather, Judge James Patrick, started the second Whig newspaper in eastern Ohio in 1819. In addition, her grandfather, her father, and her aunt were all in the newspaper business. Alicia was the middle child of three daughters to Joseph Medill Patterson and his wife Katharine. She was educated at a variety of institutions including the University School for Girls, Saint Timothy's in Maryland, and a Swiss boarding school. Mostly, it was her rebellious spirit and disobedience that prompted the change of schools. After touring Europe with her mother and sister, she went to work at her father's newspaper, *The Daily News,* in 1926.[12]

When her father fired her after she incorrectly identified a name in a divorce proceeding that caused the paper to be involved in a libel suit, Patterson went back to Chicago and married there in 1927. The marriage lasted only one year. She learned to fly, went hunting in foreign countries, and wrote a series of journalistic pieces that were published. In 1931, she married Joseph W. Brooks, a family friend. Her father furnished a house for her at Sands Point. She also went back to work at *The Daily News.* This marriage also ended in divorce.

Patterson married for the third time in 1939. Her new husband, Captain Harry F. Guggenheim, also a Sands Point resident, managed his family's fortune. Patterson and Guggenheim started *Newsday* in 1940, the first paper hit the streets on September 3rd. By 1943, the paper had a circulation of 35,696.[13] As her family had done before her, Alicia Patterson became the voice of the local community. Although Guggenheim had a controlling interest in the enterprise, *Newsday* was really Patterson's. She was known to remark, "Harry go on upstairs to the money. You're not supposed to meddle in editorial."[14] Although she was not born on Long Island, she soon became protective of it, sure that she knew what was important for Long Islanders to know, confident that she could figure out what was best for her "home turf."

When the war was over, Patterson joined the Post-War Planning Committee on Hofstra's Board of Trustees and was involved in acquiring new pieces of residential property as they became available for the college. In 1935, the estate encompassed approximately fifteen acres; by 1946, the campus was twenty-six acres, and by 1955, the campus had grown to seventy-five acres. She gave generously for the advancement of the college, not only for the physical plant, but for individual departments, for faculty salaries, for the library, and for scholarships.[15]

When John Cranford Adams, a Shakespearean scholar, became president of the college in 1944, she was impressed by his popularity within the educational community and often gave his speeches and accomplishments coverage in the paper. In the 1953 "Back to School" magazine section, she invited Adams to write an article on *"The Future of American Education."* In a letter to Adams she remarked, "I hate to burden your busy life but I feel that it is important for Long Islanders to have your views on this subject."[16] Adams admired Patterson and in a letter exclaimed, "The only growth more extraordinary than Hofstra's these last ten years that I have known Long Island has been *Newsday's*."[17]

Patterson's interest in Long Islanders' education soon became of paramount importance for Hofstra. In 1961, the Air Force Base at Mitchel Field was officially closed. There were those who wished to see the old airstrip become a private air field, among them, the head of the Federal Aviation Administration, Najeeb Halaby. Through *Newsday,* however, Patterson argued against such a move and the community was convinced that it would be a nuisance. Patterson went to see President Kennedy, whom she had supported during the election, to convince him that the airfield should be closed. Kennedy questioned Halaby as to whether or not he could relax his stand. Halaby later commented, "I mentally consigned this fine lady to whatever purgatory is re-

Fig. 18.2. Alicia Patterson (on right) at Hofstra Commencement, c. 1960. From Alicia Patterson Photograph Albums Collection, Hofstra University Archives.

served for those who forget in how many instances airports were there before real-estate developers moved in, thus creating noise problems that never would have arisen if proper zoning had been applied. But I wasn't about to challenge John Kennedy over the issue of keeping a small airport open—especially since it was clearly a losing battle in the community."[18]

When the base was officially closed, Hofstra's president went to the Government Services Administration and petitioned for 125 acres of land directly to the north of the college campus. Architect Aymar Embury, who had designed the first permanent structures on the campus, sketched a proposed plan for the "campus-to-be." By the time the negotiations took place and the deal was closed, the allotment became almost 150 acres, but Embury had retired. And before the campus could be built, Patterson died suddenly at the age of fifty-six.

Adams, a staunch admirer, was shocked. "Like all who knew Alicia Patterson," he wrote, "I am stunned and grieved at this news of her untimely death. She was undoubtedly one of the colorful, courageous and imaginative leaders in America. . . . She was in her nineteenth year as Trustee of Hofstra University. . . . Always a wise and farsighted counselor, she was deeply concerned with the growth and welfare of the University, performing services beyond count as well as contributing generously to its programs and needs."[19] Nearly 1,000 people attended Patterson's funeral service.

In an address given at a Communication Arts Symposium in 1953, Patterson had remarked that "Much that I learned I learned from my father. . . . Nothing was too insignificant for him to notice. . . . This trait helped him to understand why people do as they do. . . . He was geared with invisible antennae that alerted him to the shifting moods of the times."[20] Patterson, too, had this gift. She "felt" what Hofstra needed and often, as if by magic, it appeared. As Hofstra's first woman trustee, her generosity allowed the institution to explore ways in which it could accommodate the needs of its students.

Alicia Patterson's interest and voice on Hofstra's behalf allowed the University to grow to almost ten times its size during her nineteen years as trustee. The North Campus remains the largest single acquisition of land in the history of the University, and it was made possible, in great part, through her lobbying efforts. This acreage now houses not only six high-rise dormitories, a student center (leading into a pedestrian overpass, known as the Unispan, which terminates at the lobby of the library), but physical recreational facilities, an infirmary, and a variety of additional student residences, as well.

Hofstra continued to grow both physically and in terms of its educational spirit after Patterson's death. In 1963, it officially changed its name to Hofstra University. Then in 1964, the division of Education became the School of

Education; by 1965, the School of Business was established, and in 1970, a Law School. In 1995, Hofstra celebrated its sixtieth anniversary. Most recently, a School of Communication was added in 1995, and surely Alicia Patterson would have appreciated that!

The University's development often amazes both Long Islanders and those beyond our shores; our acreage now totals 238 and there were 112 buildings at last count. There are still some who remember the days when Hofstra Hall housed every classroom and was home to the student lounge, cafeteria, and drama society practice session. That initial campus changed dramatically as the buildings and ideas that make a place a "University" took hold. Yet even Hofstra's recent alumni can tell you about the warm school spirit and family feeling the campus exudes. And although Kate Mason Hofstra and Alicia Patterson probably never knew each other, it was through their combined efforts that Hofstra University has taken its present life.[21]

Notes

1. Will of Kate Mason Hofstra, dated April 6, 1933, in Hofstra History Collection, box 4, folder 20, Hofstra University Archives, West Campus.

2. Howard Brower, Cassette Tape no. 460, Audiotape collection, Hofstra University Archives.

3. Howard Brower, Cassette Tape no. 461, Audiotape collection, Hofstra University Archives.

4. For additional Manhattan structures designed by Severance and for information about his business partners, see *New York Times* obituary, September 3, 1941, p. 23.

5. See Information file, Hofstra estate—interiors, Hofstra University Archives.

6. See Howard Brower, Cassette Tape no. 460, Audiotape collection, Hofstra University Archives; and Wilburt Schultz, Cassette Tape no. 111, reminiscing about the Hofstra campus, Audiotape collection, Hofstra University Archives.

7. See Howard Brower, Cassette Tape no. 460, Audiotape collection, Hofstra University Archives; and *Hempstead Sentinel,* December 31, 1903, p. 8, and January 7, 1904, p. 8.

8. Howard Brower, Cassette Tape no. 461, Audiotape collection, Hofstra University Archives; and also see *International Directory of Company Histories,* edited by Adele Hast, vol. 4 (Chicago St. James Press, 1991), pp. 245-47, as well as the *Moody's Manual of Investments,* (New York: Moody's Investors' Service, 1933), pp. 3,157-58, for information about Price Brothers & Co., Ltd.

9. Howard Brower, Cassette Tape no. 459, Audiotape collection, Hofstra University Archives.

10. Will of Kate Mason Hofstra, April 6, 1933.

11. Mrs. Joe Horan, wife of first night watchman, Cassette Tape no. 109, Audiotape collection, Hofstra University Archives.

12. See Robert F. Keeler, "Alicia Patterson," in *American Newspaper Publishers, 1950-1990,* edited by Perry J. Ashley, vol. 127, *Dictionary of Literary Biography* (Detroit: Gale Research, 1993), pp. 225-35. (See also article by Robert F. Keeler, "Alicia Patterson and the Shape of Long Island," Chapter 26 below. Editor's note.)

13. *"Newsday's* Boss (. . . and Hofstra trustee)," *Alumni Magazine,* November 1951, p. 9. (Copy in Hofstra University Archives.)

14. Special section, *Inside Newsday,* April 22, 1975, p. 9, in Alicia Patterson biographical vertical file, Nassau County Museum Collection, Long Island Studies Institute, Hofstra University.

15. Annual financial reports for Hofstra University, 1943-1963, Hofstra University Archives.

16. Alicia Patterson to John Cranford Adams, July 17, 1953, Board of Trustee Correspondence, box 15, folder 10, Hofstra University Archives.

17. John Cranford Adams to Alicia Patterson, September 21, 1954, Board of Trustee Correspondence, box 15, folder 11, Hofstra University Archives.

18. Najeeb E. Halaby, *Cross-Winds: An Airman's Memoir* (New York: Doubleday & Co., 1978), pp. 156-57.

19. Correspondence—Alicia Patterson, box 15, folder 12, draft dated July 3, 1963 for a Memorial Statement, Board of Trustees Collection, Hofstra University Archives. Also see final printed copy in the *Hofstra Newsletter,* vol. 8, no. 38, July 16, 1963, Hofstra University Archives.

20. "The Trials and Tribulations of a Publisher," speech given by Alicia Patterson at the July 15, 1953 Communication Arts Symposium at Fordham University. Text in Info-file, Alicia Patterson, Hofstra University Archives.

21. On the history of Hofstra, see also Edward J. Smits, "The Founding of Hofstra College," *Nassau County Historical Society Journal* 40 (1985): 1-16; David Christman, "Architecture as History on the Hofstra Campus," in *Long Island Architecture,* edited by Joann P. Krieg (Interlaken, NY: Heart of the Lakes Publishing, 1991), pp. 139-53; and brief histories available from the Hofstra University Archives which, of course, also has Hofstra publications and manuscripts. The Archives are located in the Library Services Center on Hofstra University's West Campus, 619 Fulton Avenue, Hempstead, NY 11549; 516-463-6407. (Editor's note.)

19. Energizer and Actualizer—the Nassau County League of Women Voters

Arlene B. Soifer

The League of Women Voters (LWV) was created by suffrage leaders in 1920 after the Nineteenth Amendment was ratified granting women the vote throughout the United States. Since the national, state, and Nassau County League of Women Voters each celebrated a seventy-fifth anniversary in 1995, it seems plain that local women rapidly made the transition from suffragist to League member. Bolstered by a meticulous archive of its executive board minutes, 1920 to 1932,[1] this paper, in its first part, will survey what the County League targeted for attention and what it accomplished. Through these early years, League members were active. They always studied local and national issues; they often were speakers; and the record shows their strong proactive positions. In the second part, this paper will name and outline the innovative paths that have been both a process and a culmination of career paths for a significant number of recent and current Nassau Leaguers.

Sketches of League women's lives in Nassau County can be extrapolated from these minutes. At the outset, note must be made of their caliber and the resources they commanded. Who were the first members? Predictably, they reflected the upper-stratum educated group that formed the suffragist base of the League. Primarily in western Nassau, members lived in Garden City, Rockville Centre, Hempstead, East Rockaway, Woodmere, Glen Cove, Lynbrook, Floral Park, and West Hempstead. Executive Board meetings were usually held at the president's home; Mrs. George Pratt, of Glen Cove, hosted the first convention in her home.

By the late 1920s, League women were scheduling executive board sessions, ten months a year, around the county. At least once a year, a certain board member invited the group to a meeting at her home in Manhattan. Did they drive? Were they chauffeured? Did they ride the train? We have no clue, except for one terse comment, in 1923, when a convention was in the planning, "as the road to Long Beach was in such bad condition . . . arrangements were made with the Garden City Hotel." That great old hotel did not get a contract; the Blossom Heath Inn in Lynbrook won out. Its three-course luncheon was $1.25. After hours, the Inn was the notorious Texas ("hello, sucker") Guinan's speakeasy.[2] Otto Kahn, proud of his new home, Oheka, offered it as a convention site; it was declined. There was a convention in Garden City in 1925 and in subsequent years. The 1931 convention was the last entry in this source. The League directors box-lunched it in the Presbyterian church hall in Glen Cove. The convention recorder noted that a motion was carried, "the Nassau LWV favors reduction of county salaries, except those in the lower brackets," and it remanded a study of same to its resolutions committee.[3]

What were the parameters of their concerns? Looking at the standing committees gives a perspective on the broad areas under which studies took place: Child Welfare, Education, Efficiency in Government, Finance, International Cooperation, Legal Status of Women, Legislation, New Voters, Radio, Women in Industry.[4] Radio is no longer a committee, but Public Relations is. Today, Women and Women's Work are combined. Environmental Issues, appearing first as Water Resources studies, expanded the League's scope. Voters' Service, the League's hallmark, merited mention each year, but we have no details except to note that in 1929, Permanent Personal Registration was a meeting topic. Undoubtedly, the League focused on registration of new female voters. In fact, among Nassau's earliest members, Mrs. Jennie Meinz, of Roslyn Heights, is recorded as having cast the first ballot in November 1920.[5]

Prominent speakers from the county government appeared frequently (some were spouses of League members). There were discussions and studies of the proposed county charter from 1922 to 1938 (a sixteen-year endeavor for the League, the first time around), on the county's road and highway system, on hospitals, and on our school systems, which even back in the 1920s, faced demands for consolidation. The League petitioned the county to place a woman on the board of directors of Meadowbrook Hospital, and to appoint one as Overseer of the Poor. In this, our Nassau League kept pace with the State League, which in 1920 petitioned Albany to select a woman to sit on the Board of Regents.[6] The local League advocated establishment of a county health department and urged county supervision of children placed in "homes."

On the international front, the League studied the World Court; nationally, they investigated child labor. Knowing of League members' expertise, other groups invited League board members to lecture, which meant traveling to New York City, to Westchester, and around the county. In 1923, Mrs. Moulton of the Federation of Jewish Clubs asked the League for a speaker. The board approved and the minutes record the League's counter-suggestion that Mrs. Moulton's organization be invited to have a representative sit on the League board.

The Nassau League worked for legislation to restrict child marriage, then on the Albany docket, and recorded approval when New York State raised the legal marriage age to fourteen for girls and sixteen for boys. The League surveyed the effect of the so-called forty-eight hour law for women workers and recorded that two bakeries in Rockville Centre employed girls who worked fifty-four hours a week in 1930.

That the League is a grassroots, mentoring organization shows up in its recorded manners and mores. Members were listed by their husbands' names, Mrs. John Jones. First names did not appear until the late 1930s in the archives examined, except for the intrepid first voter, Mrs. Jennie Meinz. When Prohibition was the law, the Nassau League invited a "wet" speaker to address it; the minutes stipulated that no question period be allowed afterwards. And, as recently as 1969, the State League reminded members to "plan your outfit for a speaking engagement—if you are going to be on a raised platform, dress accordingly."[7]

Along with the mentoring and networking, the League provided friendship. The first two terms are anachronistic for the 1920s; the last seems almost to have faded from the feminist lexicon. A recent "glass ceiling" article in the *New York Times* listed the University of Wisconsin as having the strongest representation total amongst women leaders in business.[8] The Port Washington League, one of Nassau's first, was founded by three 1916 graduates of Wisconsin. One recalled that two days after she moved to Port, a college chum, now neighbor, said, "Bring $2 for membership and come along, you'll like the people."[9]

Eleanor Roosevelt, a State League vice-president in the 1920s, when speaking to a League group in the mid-1930s, said the League, "fits you to make up your mind about what the [parties] stand for; it makes it possible for you to study impartially measures that come up before the electorate." Mrs. Roosevelt opened this speech by recalling her chagrin as a younger woman, when her host asked for an explanation of the difference between our states' governments and the federal government, and she didn't know.[10] Eleanor Roosevelt remained a Nassau League member and a significant resource person for the League.

Among the County League's earliest concerns was crime in movies. In 1931, the minutes state that the executive board joined with the American Legion and the Board of Censors of the State in a resolution deploring "the number of motion pictures of gangsters and racketeer types that are on the [movie] screen today." Further, they urged that "this type of pictures [*sic*] be abolished or . . . features removed."[11] The Legion figures again in League history twenty-five years later. From 1945 on, while Nassau experienced exponential changes in demographics, the League clarified its role "to promote political responsibility through informed and active participation of citizens in government."[12]

Knowledge about government was a need that spoke to Nassau residents. Shortly after Nassau's forward-looking County Charter took effect in 1938, the New York State League commented, "This League is in an area of complicated governmental setup which makes action [on] a local level difficult."[13] Nassau County's "complications" have generated study and action, but they have been constraining as well. League governance coped with this mix of astonishing growth and complexity by periodically expanding and/or regrouping the units within the county. As a counterpoint to consolidations in the 1938 County Charter, local Leagues reorganized by community: Port Washington, Great Neck, Baldwin, Farmingdale, Woodmere, and Garden City.

The years 1936–1944 were a quiet time for most Leagues. Economic depression, wartime and patriotic concerns, limits on meetings caused by gasoline rationing, and Nassau's lack of public transportation put this League into a somewhat quiescent state. Nevertheless, child welfare, a civil service system, and jury service for women were on local League agendas. Mention of members' careers appear, but information is scant. In 1938, Mrs. Collatt, chairman of the Five Towns' child welfare committee, took a paid position with the Milk Consumers Protective Committee. Career attorneys are mentioned, among them Mary Louise Nickerson and Helen Hansel. Both later became judges. Dr. Maude H. Seabury, of Hempstead, elected president of the County League in 1941, was the first woman public health surgeon. She was in charge of housing for the 1939 World's Fair. By the late 1940s, members were teachers, or wives of teachers and of professional men.[14]

The United Nations entered the League's immediate postwar agenda with two Nassau Leaguers then rising to prominence in the field of international cooperation. Port Washington's Frances Thomas was a delegate to San Francisco when the United Nations Charter was drafted; she subsequently became Director of Education for the American Association for the United Nations. Ellen Crawley became an official United Nations observer for the national League. Locally, large numbers of women were trained to run discussion groups to help citizens understand the United Nations Charter.[15]

Back to the American Legion. Encouraged by McCarthyism and the House Un-American Activities Committee in the 1950s, the Legion blisteringly attacked the League. Its particular target was the "Freedom Agenda," a series of League–written and distributed pamphlets that had received substantial financial support from the Fund for the Republic through the Ford Foundation. Eloise Ostrander, Nassau County Council Chairman, described the booklets as "dedicated to the better understanding by the American people of the role that individual rights play in our system of constitutional democracy." The League was not alone. Other groups who were targeted included the Girl Scouts, the National Education Association, the Foreign Policy Association, and interfaith organizations.[16] In Port Washington, League husbands received telephone calls informing them that their wives were communists; one husband won a lawsuit because he had publicly been called a communist.[17] Oceanside got into a struggle with the local Legion commander, the superintendent of schools, and the board of education, all of whom opposed the distribution of the "Freedom Agenda" in the classroom; the Five Towns League reported that the local paper had been "friendly until we ran into trouble with the school district."

Nine Leagues in New York State had difficulty with the Legion; the State and National Leagues aided all of the local leagues. Long Island was a "hot spot." Most Leagues did not flinch. Invited by Charlotte Shapiro, 1956 president of the Levittown League, Eleanor Roosevelt came to discuss the "Freedom Agenda" at the high school. A thousand people turned out. What was in the "Freedom Agenda"? One point of contention was a short paragraph on loyalty which mixed Biblical and secular references.

Beginning in the 1950s, the League provided public roles for women denied access to the usual sources of power, and the League made these roles available at the local level where women could more easily be politically involved without necessitating drastic changes in family arrangements.[18] In localities with special districts, League members were often the first elected or appointed commissioners of housing, sanitation, water, and urban renewal. Agendas of Nassau Leagues included schools, sandpits, low income housing, noise pollution, water, and First Amendment issues.[19] Twenty years later, John Gardner called the League "the greatest school of political science in the world."[20]

Nassau County was the first county League in New York to institute Permanent Personal Registration. While it is completely taken for granted now, it took eighteen years of League work to make the ballot more accessible to voters. When it was finally made law by Governor Harriman's signature in 1956, the *New Yorker,* in a twenty-seven page article, described the League's Legislative Conference in Albany. Kinkead, the reporter, relates that the legislators referred to us as "girls."[21]

The League is probably best known for its non-partisan election activities. Voters' Service sets up questionnaires for every candidate on the ballot, publishes their answers, along with basic details about the position they seek. The annual "Voters Guide" has many distribution channels, primarily the result of legwork by League members. LWV raises the money to publish the guides. Candidates meetings are held, with the League as impartial moderator, and strict participation rules. In 1995, in addition to dozens of community meetings, Cablevision News 12 aired a large number of half-hour debates, moderated by League members, that featured the new legislative districts, one by one. Each year after the elections, the League issues, "They Represent You," a pamphlet listing elected officials. Abby Kenigsberg, head of the Long Island Coalition for Fair Broadcasting, stated that "the League's credibility is never questioned. They provide service to citizens that the media ought to do, but does not."[22]

A survey of Nassau League leaders who rose in the LWV and distinguished themselves in government, in non-profit fields, in the professions, and business reveals that these women praised the long-term, vigorous, and rewarding friendships forged in the League. The League also nurtured leaders, activists, and innovators.

Thirty-two individuals were interviewed in October and November 1995. Only one felt the League had nothing to do with her subsequent development, even though a peer thought it did. The information that follows is based on these interviews. One very well-known Nassau activist faulted the League in strong terms. "They only want to study, they didn't take stands, I take action." She attends League functions, however, and continues to be interested enough in the League to have returned my telephone call.[23] Others were overwhelmingly positive in their assessment of the League and its effect on their lives and careers.

League members understood government. The Levittown League especially coped with the combined absence of any immediately responsible government, and layers of overlapping tax–supported districts. There are still 3,300 possible combinations of homeowner tax bills, county-wide. Levittown was, to Charlotte Shapiro, "a community without elders, one that developed leaders overnight." She moved through an innovative teaching career marked by a model peace studies course to retirement, when she then worked as a lobbyist for the Coalition Against Domestic Violence. Her 1982 study of women's employment with Leaguer Lillian McCormick became "Women on the Job," a unique grassroots agency helping women become aware of their rights in the workplace. More recently, Shapiro was County League president, tirelessly advocating for the successful referendum that established the Nassau Legislature in 1995. Now she is chairing the League's statewide study of educational finance.[24]

In government, Carol Berman, three–time winner of a state Assembly seat and presently member of the State Board of Elections, said, "I'm still a member, Five Towns; it's been nonstop." She had been campaign manager for County Executive Eugene Nickerson and for Representative Herbert Tenzer. "The League is inspirational and informative, and I thought so even when it badgered me and other legislators." She feels the League earns full credit for the National Motor Voter Act.

Voters' Service resonated differently for Ann Plummer, a past Port Washington president. By teaching residents of a low-income housing unit how to vote, she found her interests moving toward human services and went on to a seminary. "I had no working world experience. League training was in basic competence; it provided me with the groundwork to operate in many areas of public life, which is the life of a minister." Now Associate Rector of Christ Church (Episcopal), in Oyster Bay, she recalls that her first League speech was to the Lions Club. Other League members who have held prominent positions include: Judge Beatrice Burstein; Rosalyn Udow, Chairman of the Board of Nassau Community College; Carolyn Willson appointed Deputy Mayor of Glen Cove, 1976; and Rosalie Rosenberger, founder of the Nassau County Women's Bar Association.

Virginia Blakeslee recalls how the 1952 League kept her mind vigorous. At the same time, the League merged with her family life. Meetings were held in homes, while members' children were cared for in an adjoining house. Chairman of the first Charter revision study, Blakeslee was later active at state and national levels. Lilo Leeds, co-chair of CMP Publishers and forty-year plus League member, founded the Great Neck/Manhasset Child Care Partnership, and the Institute for Community Development, a special program for at-risk high school girls. Leeds also instituted on-site day care in CMP. Two years ago, she donated office space in one of CMP's buildings to the League.

League work pulled Phoebe Goodman into studying revenue sharing in the 1970s. That experience led her to co-found and later to direct the Nassau Citizens Budget Committee (NCBC). NCBC has completed a two-year study of the need to reassess Nassau's homes. (They have not been reassessed since 1938.) Goodman is both board member and committee chair of United Way, and sits on the Long Island Association's tax policy committee. Of the bygone years of her presidency of the Roslyn League she recalled, "I met these people who seemed to know everything in the world. It shaped me up. I learned objectivity, learned to suspend judgment, and learned to do my homework."

Nassau League threads sometimes start or end in New York City. A school internship involving Permanent Personal Registration led Sandy Mintz into a Brooklyn Heights League. In Nassau, she became Hempstead East president, then County president. When a paid career beckoned, on her resume she equalized League years with paid employment. "In League, I had learned to study matters to excess." First with Planned Parenthood, Sandy is now a development executive with United Jewish Appeal. Her League participation continues.

Frances Himelfarb, once active in Baldwin's League, was 1960 candidate for Town Clerk in the Town of Hempstead. She became special assistant to County Executive Nickerson, and recently retired as Associate Director of Meetings for the prestigious Council on Foreign Relations. Now she is active with the Brooklyn Botanic Gardens and an East End garden group.

Claire Stern states her knowledge of government, learned in Levittown, led her to form the Long Island Environmental Council, which united many small advocacy groups into an effective lobbying coalition. Understanding government, she then set up her own corporation which assisted cable television franchisers in obtaining local government approval throughout the United States. In her business, she set up flextime for employees with childcare needs.

While the League examines governments and instructs women about government, plans for our future Voters' Service should include Nassau's immigrant community in order to lead them to citizenship and to the voting machine. With the new Legislature, women have an opportunity to enter and to improve public finance and government organization. (Women were elected to four of the nineteen seats in the new legislature in 1995.) For the energized, active, innovative, and ultimately actualized Nassau women who learn and work under its mantle, the League will continue to be a tool and resource for problem solving.

Appendix

Research for this article elicited additional information on individuals active in League which is presented here. These women and those mentioned earlier are a sampling of the hundreds of women active in Nassau Leagues and the various paths they have followed. Quotations are from telephone and personal interviews conducted by the author.

Eleanor Berger of Great Neck built her reputation on the effective way she trained Leaguers to be discussion leaders. This is pivotal to the whole Voters' Service process.

Ruth Bornn, who rose within the New York State League, wrote *This is New York State* in 1954. This became the prototype for all subsequent League publications on localities. Our Leagues, and Leagues throughout the state, issue "Know Your [village, town, county]" booklets, at least once a decade.

Ella Isaak, a corporate personnel officer, had a strong interest in social welfare. As a vice–chair of the Citizens Union, the NAACP, and similar committees in the Women's City Club of New York, Isaak found that "by learning about legislation, one could learn new areas very well. My activities put me in frequent contact with New York City League members; when I moved to Nassau, I joined." She became chair for Women's Issues.

Roslyn Lea, led activities in the Five Towns League. She became the only Nassau president of the New York State League in 1957.

Ora Meyer has been a multi-term president of the Great Neck League, Voters' Service chair for many years, up to and including the present, and a multi-term president of the County League. She is guardian of the first book of County minutes that figure in the early history explicated here.

Lesley Pollak in more than forty years of membership has met the administrative challenges of the League in many board positions. Her awareness "has always been challenged from Eleanor Roosevelt to the late Ada Goldberg's expertise in health and human resources." She further noted, "My most interesting and stimulating friends are League members."

Corinne Coe is a forty-year member and Voters' Service chair in Great Neck and the County. She became a multi-term mayor of the Village of Thomaston and its library was built during her term. She reported, "The League was my education and source of my friends."

Judith Schmertz became interested in government when she took a group of Girl Scouts to Hempstead Town Hall in 1967. Learning about government through Voters' Service ultimately led her to be one of five individuals who petitioned through the courts to overturn the County charter in the 1970s. Other petitioners—all LWV members—were Ann Borner, City of Glen Cove; Adele Fox, Town of North Hempstead; Carol Carlton, City of Long Beach; and Barbara Josepher, Town of Oyster Bay. Schmertz also came through the Levittown crucible. She speaks frequently to other groups, and often moderates debates.

Anne Stokvis, stimulated by articles about the League and Port Washington's sandpits, served for years on Voters' Service and chaired the New York State League's Voters' Service. She reports that she finds "stimulation in the women of all ages empowered by the League. As a member of the mid-generation, this is my way to be part of the new feminism. I learned skills; I go to meetings on complex affairs, and know that I know the things being discussed." Stokvis was President of the Nassau County League in 1995–1996.

Georgette Zwerlin conducted candidates' meetings and registration campaigns. She became vice-president of the Community Chest in her community. "Fulfilling and meaningful" is how she evaluates the League.

There are people for whom the League was a touchstone, but who, although no longer members, still express warm feelings towards it.

Judge Abbey Boklan was an attorney when she joined the League and other civic groups in Roslyn in the 1970s. Her good feelings for the League stem partly because women's groups supported her first appointed candidacy.

Winifred Pasternack, an attorney, remembers the League as an outlet for loneliness. She chaired its speaker's bureau for many years and served on judiciary and election law committees. Interviewing judges and chief clerks led her to law school. Pasternack's law partner is that first League friend's husband.

Notes

1. Record of Minutes, Nassau County League of Women Voters, June 1920–July 1932, *passim* (hereafter cited as LWV Minutes). This book is held by Ora Meyer of Grat Neck, current County President. Other Nassau LWV Archives are in the Library at SUNY, Stony Brook. Local League archives need to be compiled.

2. Village of Lynbrook, *50th Anniversary Journal* (Lynbrook, NY, 1960) p. 19.

3. LWV Minutes, pp. 163-64.

4. Ibid., passim.

5. New York State League of Women Voters Archives, box 3, p. 7, Rare Book and Manuscript Collection, Columbia University Library, New York City (hereafter cited as NYS-LWV Archives). Special thanks go to New York State League historian Hilda Watrous of Albany, whose enthusiasm and information about the location of the New York State archives effectively started my research.

6. Ibid., box 15, Minutes.

7. Ibid., box 12, Election File. Mini skirts were in fashion at that time.

8. Judith H. Dobrzynski, *The New York Times,* October 29, 1995, Money & Business Section, p.1.

9. "50th Anniversary, A Brief History," Port Washington-Manhasset League, April 1987, p. 6.

10. NYS-LWV Archives, box 17, biographical files, speech no. 53.

11. Minutes, p. 161.

12. Nancy M. Neuman, *The League of Women Voters in Perspective: 1920–1995* (Washington, DC: LWVUS, 1994), p. 24.

13. NYS LWV Archives, box 3, p. 7.

14. Port/Manhasset, p. 6; Five Towns League, folder.

15. Ibid., passim.

16. NYS-LWV Archives, box 15, American Legion file.

17. Neuman, *The League of Women Voters in Perspective,* p. 11.

18. NYS-LWV Archives, box 15.

19. Neuman, *The League of Women Voters in Perspective,* p. 34.

20. New York State LWV Archives, box 15.

21. Katharine T. Kinkead, "A Reporter at Large," *New Yorker,* May 5, 1956, pp. 118-45.

22. Interview with Abby Kenigsberg. The League's reputation as a resource has a long history. In 1949, the Village of Cedarhurst issued a "no handbills" ruling. In opposing this as a First Amendment violation, the League supplied the village mayor with a brief on the United States Supreme Court rulings on the illegality of such local ordinances. This was assembled with the help of the State League. That ended the situation. Marian Mayer, historian, Five Towns League folder.

23. This and other quotations in the balance of the essay are from personal or telephone interviews with individuals by the author.

24. See Charlotte Shapiro's article, "Women on the Job, Long Island's Grassroots Action for Pay Equity," Chapter 32 in this book. (Editor's note.)

20. Candace Thurber Wheeler and the New York Exchange for Woman's Work

Martha Kreisel

Candace Thurber Wheeler, mother, needlework artist, textile designer, interior decorating partner of Louis Comfort Tiffany, teacher at Cooper Union, and author and director of the exhibit of women's work in the Applied Arts Building at the Chicago World's Columbian Exposition of 1893, was also a founder of the New York Exchange for Woman's Work. It was, perhaps, one of her most enduring legacies to women.

Born on March 24, 1827, in the small town of Delhi, New York, Candace Wheeler was the second daughter and the third of eight children born to Abner Gilman Thurber, dairy farmer, fur dealer, deacon in the local Presbyterian Church, and ardent abolitionist. The Thurber home was a stop on the underground railroad during the Civil War. Candace's mother, Lucy Dunham Thurber, renowned for handspun linens and highly skilled in the "household arts," taught her how to spin, knit, sew, and weave, skills which would be important to her throughout her life. As she put it: "Mother manifested all the human practical virtues, and Father supplied the heavenly fire which sanctified them."[1]

At seventeen, Candace married Thomas Wheeler, ten years her senior and a bookkeeper for a mercantile firm in New York City. The Wheelers moved to Brooklyn where they had their first two children. Wheeler reveals her thoughts on living in Brooklyn in her autobiography: "The early years of our married life were spent in Brooklyn, which was then so merely a convenience to working and growing New York as to have received from that haughty metropolis the name of 'The Bedroom.' Yet like many another gibe, it held within it a consoling truth, for it was not only the resting-place of tired workers, but a refuge and refreshment to many who were doing great work for the world."[2]

For Wheeler, Brooklyn was a wonderful place to live and bring up children: "In those early days Brooklyn was a village with green fields lying against its narrow length, with all of pastoral and farming Long Island spread behind, and the great barrier of water between it and New York. The ferry-boats were not too crowded, and people went over to New York for pleasure as well as for business."[3]

In 1854, they built their country home, "Nestledown," in Jamaica, Queens. Nestledown was to become a gathering place for some of the great literary and artistic figures of the time. Wheeler later recalled, "When I began to count my years into the twenties we left our Brooklyn days and Brooklyn home behind us and built a new abiding-place, one quite to our minds, twelve miles out on Long Island. . . . We built our family shelter and made our home on the flats of Long Island, among the descendants of the old Dutch farmers, who recognized us for forty years only as 'those new people.'"[4]

While raising her growing family, Wheeler had the opportunity to continue as an amateur painter, taking inspiration and advice from such luminaries as William Cullen Bryant, Frederick E. Church, Albert Bierstadt, Sanford Gifford, and Eastman Johnson. These were the years when some of the greatest influences in her life surrounded her. This was when the poets and the painters of the Hudson River School gathered in her home, where they spoke of beauty and color, and she remembered.

To understand the importance of Candace Wheeler, and her work with the New York Society for Decorative Art and with the Woman's Exchange Movement, the historical and social situation women were experiencing at the time must be understood. The intolerable working conditions for women in the second half of the nineteenth century were a combination of several social and political conditions. Between 1845 and 1855, thousands of women arrived as immigrants from Europe. Most settled in the larger cities, swelling the ranks of the labor force. Factory towns sprang up around the major cities. The girls and women of the mills labored long hours, under the poorest conditions for the basic necessities of life. They worked for an average weekly wage of $3.75.[5]

In addition, after the Civil War, thousands of Southern women came north in hopes of finding work in the factories. Family breadwinners in both the North and the South had been killed in the war, and the system of slave labor was shattered. Away from their homes, Southern women hoped they could hide the fact of their economic plight. What they would find were hardships and thousands of other women in similar situations.[6]

With the Civil War came the invention of the sewing machine. What was to be a labor-saving device with the potential of lightening the burden of workers proved to be a "curse." "Brought into competition with machines that could do more and better work in one day than was possible for six women, working twenty hours apiece, to accomplish, these [women] had either to starve, or force their way into some other wage-earning industry."[7] It is calculated that in 1862, some 73,000 women were displaced by machines in order for employers to gain large savings [in] wages and time in the manufacturing industries.[8] Wheeler writes in her history of the development of embroidery in America: "The sewing machine took upon itself the toil of the seamstress, but it left the seamstress idle and hungry. This was a new and even darker situation than the last, but Englishwomen came to the rescue with a resuscitated form of needlework, and embroidery tiptoed upon the empty stage, new garments covering her ancient form, and was welcomed with universal acclaim."[9]

Alice Rhine, in an 1891 essay, "Women in Industry," concurs, stating that thousands of wage-earning women in New York City were in a "constant fight with starvation and pauperism."[10] It was obvious that the old ways of helping the needy would no longer work on such a large scale. The philan-thropic efforts of women would come into their own.

Candace Wheeler's belief in the need for charity towards others came from her parents and their Puritan values. "The principles in which their children [Candace and siblings] were reared had the Puritan narrowness belonging to Puritan thought, and, as they were practically applied, they made our lives quite different from those of the rest of the community. The inevitable censure called out by this habit of life was modified by constant and important public activity, and generous, self-denying social help on the part of both Father and Mother."[11]

The time was right for other women to recognize the need for the involvement in education of less fortunate women in order for them to advance as workers. Many became advocates for the entrance of women into the trades and professions traditionally held by men. The majority of women were already working in industry, but it was time to elevate them into "skillful, rational workers."[12] Miss Virginia Penny, in *Think and Act* (1869), advocated the introduction of women into the trades saying, "'Then the distressed needle-woman will vanish, the decayed gentlewoman and broken-down governess cease to exist.'"[13] Wheeler had observed the dependency of women upon the wage-earning capacity of men, and felt that it was time for a change. Although popular sentiment was that "women should not be wage-earners," necessity was stronger and Candace Wheeler found herself devising ways to help friends or friends of friends in their individual dilemmas.[14] To this end Candace Wheeler and many others advocated the establishment of industrial and trade schools for women.

Candace Wheeler became a friend of Peter Cooper before his idea of Cooper Union was fully developed. According to Wheeler, it was to be "the earliest public utility in New York City devoted to mental instead of physical needs."[15] In 1859, Peter Cooper, opened the institute that still bears his name, a free public institution where women could attend art classes and where the application of art to industry was emphasized. Stained glass and textiles, wallpapers and carpets were all part of the design curriculum offered to the students. The more proficient students were permitted to add to their incomes by executing orders from business firms.[16] Candace Wheeler was to consider it one of her "choicest honors" to serve on the advisory committee of the Woman's Art School of the Cooper Union.

The involvement of women in the Arts and Crafts Movement coincided with this philanthropic era. The 1876 Centennial Exhibition in Philadelphia introduced the Arts and Crafts movement of William Morris to America and to Candace Wheeler. "Although many types of embroidery were practiced in America in the nineteenth century, such as white work and Berlin wool work, after the influential exhibit of the Royal School of Art Needlework at the Philadelphia Centennial of 1876, artistic embroidery rapidly became the vogue there. Candace Thurber Wheeler was the key figure in this development."[17] The philosophy behind the designs executed for the exhibit of the Royal School was to restore "Ornamental Needlework for secular purposes, to the high place it once held among decorative art"[18] and to supply employment and benefit a class called "decayed gentlewomen." Although Wheeler rejected the phrase, she "was much taken by the idea."[19]

The pioneers of the Arts and Crafts Movement had come out in active rebellion against the degradation of the work force and the increased work loads and hours due to the introduction of mechanization in the factories. It was the basic philosophy of the movement to improve the quality of design on every level and support creative freedom. They looked back to the medieval craft guilds where the craftsman was the designer and the maker of the entire article.

Morris called for the creation of craft workshops to revive traditional crafts and craft techniques. By the early 1880s the Arts and Crafts Movement was well under way. Women involved in the Arts and Crafts Movement reflected class divisions: first, the "working class or peasant women who were organized and employed in the revival of traditional rural crafts; secondly, the aristocratic, upper- and middle-class women of comfortable means and appropriate leisure who were philanthropically engaged in the organization both of the rural crafts revivals and of the artistic training and employment of destitute gentlewomen; thirdly, there were the destitute gentlewomen themselves, the ladies forced by circumstance to make an independent livelihood. Finally, the fourth category covers the elite 'inner circle' of educated middle class women."[20]

Voluntarism had also gained momentum from the time of the Civil War. Many charitable women "whose sympathies were touched by the lives of the workers, sought to help women in many other ways. The Young Women's Christian Association of New York recognized early the necessity of educating self-supporting women in many of the skilled industries."[21] This economic need had to be balanced against society's reluctance to accept women in the workplace. Wheeler was a woman of talent and conscience and prepared to help those less fortunate than she. After the loss of her eldest daughter, she found:

when the loss came which changed my whole attitude toward life and taught me its duties, not only to those I loved, but to all who needed help and comfort, I was not unprepared.

I saw that many difficulties of existence were preventable, or at least capable of alleviation, and here came in the benefit of my Puritan childhood experience, where self-help had been the first law. There were so many unhappy and apparently helpless women, dependent upon kin who had their own especial responsibilities and burdens, and these women appealed to me strongly, for I could so easily understand their misery.[22]

For Wheeler, the Arts and Crafts Movement meant the conversion of the feminine skill and heritage women had in the use of the needle into a means of art-expression and economic reward.[23]

With her plans and her vision to work out a new commercial opportunity for women, Wheeler sought the help of her friends to make this enterprise a reality. She enlisted the help of Mrs. David Lane, who had been president of the Sanitary Commission, to act as president, and to form, on February 24, 1877, what was to be called the Society of Decorative Art. Candace Wheeler offered to serve as corresponding secretary, so that other societies could be opened across the country. With Mrs. Lane's influence, the Society had a Board of Managers and an Advisory Council that included many of the great names in New York.[24]

The Society of Decorative Art was one of many needlework groups formed at the end of the nineteenth century. It was the forerunner of the New York Exchange for Woman's Work and would offer Candace Wheeler the opportunity to work with Louis Comfort Tiffany. He and Lockwood De Forest had consented to teach a class in underglaze china painting at the Society. The objectives of the Society included the obligation to "encourage profitable industries among women who possess artistic talent, and to furnish a standard of excellence and a market for their work."[25]

It was observed that the Society was not based on "one class helping another," but rather to "eliminate the notions of philanthropy, and eradicate the traditional stigma attached to paid work for ladies. In addition, the Society of Decorative Art introduced a new and even more radical notion into their aims—that of the importance of work and creativity as a means to psychological independence for women."[26] Candace Wheeler reclaimed traditional women's art forms such as embroidery, and her reassessment of the classification of the arts imparted "a new dignity to needlework and to women as its makers," reasserting "women's right to control their own history and destiny."[27]

But the philosophy behind the Society for Decorative Art did not go far enough for Wheeler. She came to feel strongly that "philanthropy and art are not natural sisters." The Society was not liberal enough for another of the managers either. According to her autobiography, Mrs. William Choate came to her with an idea to form another society where "a woman can send a pie, if she can make a good one, even though she cannot paint a good picture; or a basket of eggs if she cannot decorate china."[28]

The original idea for a Woman's Exchange was born in 1832 when wealthy Philadelphia women established, in the heart of the city's wealthiest areas, the Philadelphia Ladies' Depository to counter the abuses of the fifty cents per day wage and the fourteen-hour workday. The economic necessities addressed by the woman's exchange movement grew at a time when various voluntary groups and movements, including the Women's Christian Temperance Union and the suffrage movement, were "opening the way to political and social reform for women. The woman's exchange movement added an economic dimension to the existing voluntary options."[29]

Candace Wheeler was among the charter members of the New York Exchange for Woman's Work. She had begun to think of the Society of Decorative Art as a failure, but in the end she saw it as "the beginning of self-help among educated women."[30] It was an important step in women's liberation in that it had given women a chance for economic independence without "losing face."

It was the difference between the Society and the Exchange that was important to Wheeler, and to those who came after:

> The "Exchange" made no such distinction; a woman of brains, industry, and opportunity might make and sell whatever she could do best, and yet not lose her place. So the bars which had kept clever but timid souls in bondage were taken away; women began to work profitably, and found in it the joy of self-help, of doing, and finally of help for the world. It was the seed of progress, sown in a fruitful and waiting soil, and it has flowered into thousands of beautiful activities which are becoming, in the stress of these evil and warring days, even great world benefits.[31]

In the 1892 annual report of the New York Exchange for Woman's Work, the remarks by Mrs. W. G. Choate demonstrate the dedication the founders and managers had for the Exchange philosophy.

> We expect to talk until people do understand it [the larger scope of our work], and as our hopes for the future are based upon what we have accomplished in the past, we do not feel that it ought to be difficult to convince any fair-minded man or woman that what we expect to do for women is warranted by the facts we have to show of what we have already done. We started to do this work fifteen years ago, and the registering of thirty articles was our first day's work. Not one piece of work had in it the slightest sign of skill. We register now between 16,000 and 18,000 articles every year, and can fill any order which a

critical and exacting customer may give to us to do. Our order books
show for the past *nine* years 88,327 orders. We have sent to consignors
during the period of our existence . . . $525,612.90. We have seen
established 74 Exchanges in different parts of this country. The last
one was established by Mrs. Jackson, in Paris, France.[32]

To the founders of the Exchanges it was important that the privacy of the
consignors be strictly kept. It was a place where women could bring their
work, and receive fair compensation for it, and where training and guidance
was offered to make their products marketable. It became a place where
business skills were developed by women who may never have considered
participating in commercial ventures, where shoppers were attracted by the
sale of homemade edibles in the tea rooms, and standard retail practices, like
seasonal sales and advertising, were also employed.[33]

In 1892, Candace Wheeler was the vice president and corresponding
secretary of the New York Exchange for Woman's Work. The annual report
by the president, Choate, exemplifies the pride that was felt for the success
of this venture.

> It gives me much pleasure to report that by comparison with earlier
> years there is a delightful air of independence and prosperity about
> some of our consignors who at first were helpless and hopeless, and
> in others a decided improvement in the more common-sense view of
> things which they now take. Foolish sentiment and false pride are a
> thing of the past. A healthy and cheerful atmosphere in our registering
> room is welcome change from the morbid and unbusiness-like de-
> mands made upon us by the same women in the beginning of their
> struggles for self-support. It is very encouraging that the marked
> improvement in the work in every department has been appreciated by
> old friends, and has secured to us the custom of many new ones. We
> have never had so important a patronage as we have had this year, and
> it is one which promises to be permanent. The education which the
> Exchange has given to so many hundreds of gentlewomen in New
> York and throughout the United States, who have been "compelled at
> once to do something for a living," yet were utterly untrained and
> unable to do any remunerative work, ought of itself to entitle the
> Society to the respect of every man and woman, who has given any
> earnest consideration to the great problem of how the untrained shall
> be made in an measure independent, or self-supporting, and not only
> self-supporting, but in many cases able to support their families and to
> so educate their children, that they shall be intelligent men and women,
> whose influence for good in the community will be the reward of those
> who have lent a helping hand in time of need, and the richest compen-
> sation to self-sacrificing and painstaking mothers.[34]

Since 1878, the New York Exchange for Woman's Work has provided
an outlet for the handiwork of thousands of people. The tales of unemploy-

ment, runaway medical expenses, and insufficient fixed incomes are as common today as they were a century ago.[35] The thirty-seven Exchanges across the country, including the ones in New York and in Brooklyn, are testaments to the continued need for this movement.[36]

The New York Exchange for Woman's Work was part of the legacy of Candace Thurber Wheeler. Her vision for a place where woman's work would have acceptance and value and where women could regain their dignity and their financial independence has made the Woman's Exchange Movement a living memorial to her. The durability of the Exchange, the path she set for women to enter the field of interior decoration, her important work defining an American style of textile and needlework, and her many books on needlework and household decoration are tributes to her upbringing and character and to her determination to right some of the wrongs done to women.

Fortunately, the philosophy behind the Exchange Movement was not static. Exchanges, consignment shops, craft fairs, and craft cooperatives have derived from Candace Wheeler's vision and goals for the Woman's Exchange Movement. For instance, for forty years, The Elder Craftsmen's program in New York City has provided a retail consignment outlet for older people to sell their handmade crafts. More recently in North Carolina, the Watermark Association of Artisans, Inc., a member-owned business, was formed to combat chronic unemployment in a poor rural area. Almost all of the members are women who earn supplemental income from their skills. The members make the products, operate the business, and even loan the trucks. Finally, the David Appalachian Crafts program began in 1971 as a non-profit organization with the goal of providing low-income Kentuckians with the facilities and training to earn supplemental income through the sale and production of authentic, high-quality, traditional Appalachian hand-crafted goods. These outgrowths may differ in locale, or in patrons, but all have become means for augmenting a family's income, ways to provide for essential needs, and venues to give women economic opportunities and personal development.

Candace Thurber Wheeler was an extraordinary woman, in extraordinary times. Drawing from her own experiences, she recognized the need to help those less fortunate. She saw the plight of women, and their need to work and earn a livelihood; she saw that the skills women possessed in the homemaking and needle arts could serve as their economic salvation. As she set up her own interior decorating business, Candace Thurber Wheeler opened up the field of interior decorating to women as a legitimate occupation. Her passion for the development of an American form of needlework led to the patenting of tapestry patterns; and to her important work with an American style of textiles and needlework, and the writing of many books on needlework and household decoration, which filled her later years. She would also go on to serve as the Director of the Applied Arts exhibit in the Woman's Pavillion and Color Director for the Woman's Building at the Chicago World's Columbian Exposition in 1893. But it was the Woman's Exchange Movement where she used her artistic talents and sense of beauty, fairness, and self worth to help women in her lifetime and beyond.

Notes

1. Candace Wheeler, *Yesterdays in a Busy Life* (New York: Harper, 1918), p. 32.
2. Ibid., p. 71.
3. Ibid., p. 73.
4. Ibid., pp. 109-10.
5. Alice Hyneman Rhine, "Women in Industry," in *Woman's Work in America, 1891*, edited by Annie Nathan Meyer (Reprint, New York: Arno Press, 1972), p. 284.
6. Ibid., p. 285.
7. Ibid., p. 285.
8. Ibid., p. 285.
9. Candace Wheeler, *The Development of Embroidery in America* (New York: Harper and Brothers, 1921), p. 106.
10. Rhine, "Women in Industry," p. 287.
11. Wheeler, *Yesterdays*, p. 33.
12. Rhine, "Women in Industry," p. 286.
13. Quoted in ibid., p. 286.
14. Wheeler, *Yesterdays*, p. 210.
15. Ibid., p. 103.
16. Rhine, "Women In Industry," p. 289.
17. Anthea Callen, *Women Artists of the Arts and Crafts Movement, 1870-1914* (New York: Pantheon Books, [1979]), p. 128.
18. Barbara Morris, *Victorian Embroidery* (New York: Thomas Nelson and Sons), p. 113.
19. Wheeler, *Yesterdays*, p. 211.
20. Callen, *Women Artists*, p. 2.
21. Rhine, "Women in Industry," p. 290.
22. Wheeler, *Yesterdays*, p. 209.
23. Ibid., p. 211.
24. Ibid., p. 215.
25. Ibid., p. 216.
26. Callen, *Women Artists*, p. 129.
27. Ibid., p. 129.
28. Wheeler, *Yesterdays*, p. 224.
29. Kathleen Waters Sander, "White Mountain Cakes and Calves'-Foot Jelly," *Advancing Philanthropy*, Summer 1994, p. 24.
30. Wheeler, *Yesterdays*, p. 226.
31. Ibid., p. 227.

32. The New York Exchange for Women's Work [*Annual Report, 1892*], in *History of Women*, no. 8564, reel 943. Microfilm, 1620 (New Haven, CT: Research Publications, Inc., 1977, p. 15.

33. Sander, "White Mountain Cakes," p. 26.

34. [*Annual Report, 1892*], no. 8564, pp. 5-6.

35. The New York Exchange for Woman's Work, *Woman's Exchange Revue. Holidays* (New York: The Exchange, 1994), p. 1.

36. See appended list of exchanges.

Appendix
The Woman's Exchange

The *Woman's Exchange* was founded in Philadelphia in 1832 and has become one of the oldest continually operating charitable movements in the United States. The Woman's Exchange of Brooklyn opened in 1854 and is still "going strong." The artists and artisan consignors derive their income to support themselves and their families from the sale of one-of-a-kind clothes, gifts and needle work. Children's wear, linens, toys, bridal accessories and gift items are all featured in the Woman's Exchange federation of stores throughout the country. Exchanges in operation in 1996 are listed alphabetically by states.

Connecticut
Fairfield Woman's Exchange, Inc.
332 Pequot Avenue
Southport, CT 06490
203-259-5138

Greenwich Exchange for Women's Work, Inc.
28 Sherwood Place
Greenwich, CT 06830
203-869-0229

Heritage Village Woman's Exchange
3 Village Street
Southbury, CT 06488
203-264-4884

The Woman's Exchange
993A Farmington Avenue
West Hartford, CT 06107
203-232-8721

The Woman's Exchange of Old Lyme
86 Hall's Road
Old Lyme Stores
Old Lyme, CT 06371
203-434-7290

Florida
The Woman's Exchange
143 St. George Street
St. Augustine, FL 32084
904-829-5064

Indiana
The Little Turtle Woman's Exchange
6374 West Jefferson Blvd.
Fort Wayne, IN 46804
219-432-6857

Louisiana
Beauregard Town Gift Shop
Woman's Exchange of Baton Rouge
201 St. Charles Street
Baton Rouge, LA 70802
504-383-7761

Maryland
The Women's Industrial Exchange
333 North Charles Street
Baltimore, MD 21201
301-685-4388

Massachusetts
Dedham Women's Exchange
445 Washington Street
Dedham, MA 02026
617-326-0627

The Hay Scales Exchange
2 Johnson Street
North Andover, MA 01845
508-683-3691

Old Town Hall Exchange
Box 44
Lincoln Center, MA 01773
617-259-9876

Port O'Call Exchange
67 Main Street
Gloucester, MA 01930
508-283-4899

The Wayland Depot, Inc.
1 Cochituate Road
Box 276
Wayland, MA 01778
508-358-5386

Missouri
Woman's Exchange of St. Louis
9214 Clayton Road
St. Louis, MO 63124
314-997-4411

New Jersey
The Depot
22 Prospect Street
Midland Park, NJ 07432
201-444-6120

The Hunterdon Exchange
155 Main Street
Flemington, NJ 08822
908-782-6229

Little Shop on the Corner
116 Elm Street
Westfield, NJ 07090
908-233-2210

Woman's Exchange of
   Monmouth County
32 Church Street
Little Silver, NJ 07739
908-741-1599

New York
Brooklyn Woman's Exchange, Inc.
55 Pierrepont Street
Brooklyn, NY 11201
718-624-3435

The Consortium for Children's Services
123 East Water Street
Syracuse, NY 13202
315-471-8331

New York Exchange for Woman's Work
1095 Third Avenue at 64th Street
New York, NY 10021
212-753-2330

Scarsdale Woman's Exchange
33 Harwood Court
Scarsdale, NY 10583
914-723-1728

North Carolina
The Country Store
University Mall
Chapel Hill, NC 27514
919-942-2855

Saint's Creations
809 Pollock Street
New Bern, NC 28560
919-638-6775

Sand Hill Woman's Exchange
Azalea Road; P.O. Box 215
Pinehurst, NC 28374
919-295-4677

Ohio
The Chagrin Valley Women's Exchange
The Sassy Cat
88 North Main Street
Chagrin Falls, OH 44022
216-247-5033

Pennsylvania
Chestnut Hill Woman's Exchange
8419 Germantown Avenue
Philadelphia, PA 19118
215-247-5911

Neighborhood League
Woman's Exchange
185 East Lancaster Avenue
Wayne, PA 19087
215-688-1431

The Old York Road Woman's Exchange
429 Johnson Street
Jenkintown, PA 19046
215-885-2470

The Woman's Exchange of Reading
720 Penn Avenue
West Reading, PA 19611
215-373-0960

The Woman's Exchange of West Chester
10 South Church Street
West Chester, PA 19382
215-696-3058

The Woman's Exchange of Yardley
47 West Afton Avenue
Yardley, PA 19067
215-493-8710

Tennessee
The Woman's Exchange of Memphis, Inc.
88 Racine Street
Memphis, TN 38111
901-327-5681

Texas
St. Michael's Woman's Exchange
5 Highland Park Village
Dallas, TX 75205
214-521-3862

Additional Works Consulted

Blair, Karen J. *The Clubwoman As Feminist: True Womanhood Redefined, 1868-1914*. New York: Holmes and Meier Publishers, 1980.

Bolton, Sarah K. *Successful Women*. Reprint, Plainview, NY: Books for Libraries Press, 1974.

Burk, Margaret. *The Woman's Exchange*. West Hartford, CT: The Exchange, n.d.

Burke, Doreen Bolger, et al. *In Pursuit of Beauty: Americans and the Aesthetic Movement*. New York: Metropolitan Museum of Art and Rizzoli, 1986.

Cott, Nancy F. *Root of Bitterness: Documents of the Social History of Women*. New York: Dutton, 1972.

Duomato, Lamia. *Candace Wheeler and Elsie De Wolfe (Decorators): A Bibliography*. Monticello, IL: Vance Bibliographies, 1989.

Edmiston, Marcene Jean. "Candace Wheeler and the Associated Artists: American Aesthetic Interiors and Their Textiles." Master's thesis, George Washington University, 1990.

Faude, Wilson H. "Associated Artists and the American Renaisance in the Decorative Arts." *Winterthur Portfolio* 10 (1975): 101-30.

Harbeson, Georgiana Brown. *American Needlework: The History of Decorative Stitchery and Embroidery from the Late 16th to the 20th Century*. New York: Coward-McCann, 1938.

Harrison, Constance Cary. *Woman's Handiwork in Modern Homes*. New York: Charles Scribner's Sons, 1882.

Hogan, Louise. *History of the Christian Woman's Exchange*. New Orleans: The Exchange, 1965.

Ideal Home 1900-1920: The History of Twentieth-Century American Craft. New York: Harry Abrams, Inc. in Association with the American Craft Museum, 1993.

Koch, Robert. *Louis C. Tiffany, Rebel in Glass*. 2d ed. New York: Crown Publishers, 1966.

Lowell, Josephine Shaw, "Charity." In *Woman's Work in America*, 1891, edited by Annie Nathan Meyer, pp. 323-44. Reprint, New York: Arno Press, 1972.

McKean, Hugh. *The "Lost" Treasures of Louis Comfort Tiffany*. New York: Doubleday, 1980.

Meyer, Annie Nathan, ed. *Woman's Work in America*, 1891. Reprint; New York: Arno Press, 1972.

Naylor, Gillian. *The Arts and Crafts Movement: A Study of its Sources, Ideals, and Influence On Design Theory*. Cambridge: MIT Press, 1971.

The New York Exchange for Woman's Work. *Serving You By Helping Others*. New York: The Exchange, n.d.

Sander, Kathleen Waters. "'Not a Lady Among Us': Entrepreneural Philanthropy and Economic Independence as Expressed through the Woman's Exchange Movement, 1832-1900." Ph.D. diss., University of Maryland College Park, 1994.

Serving You By Helping Others, pamphlet, New York Exchange for Woman's Work. n.d

"The Society of Decorative Art [New York]." *Scribners' Monthly* 22 (September 1881): 697-712.

Stansky, Peter. *Redesigning the World: William Morris, the 1880s, and the Arts and Crafts*. Princeton: Princeton University Press, 1985.

Stern, Madeleine B. *We the Women: Career Firsts of Nineteenth-Century America*, 1962. Reprint, Lincoln: University of Nebraska Press, 1994.

——. "Candace Thurber Wheeler." In *Notable American Women, 1607-1950; A Biographical Dictionary*, edited by Edward T. James, et al., 3: 574-76. Cambridge: Belknap Press of Harvard University Press, 1971.

Watson, Frank Dikker. *The Charity Organization Movement in the United States: A Study in American Philanthropy*. New York: Macmillan Company, 1922.

Wheeler, Candace. "Applied Arts in the Woman's Building." In *Art and Handicraft in the Woman's Building of the World's Columbian Exposition, Chicago 1893*, edited by Maud Howe Elliott. Paris: Goupil, 1893.

——. *Household Art*. New York: Harper and Brothers, 1893.

——. *Principles of Home Decoration*. New York: Doubleday, Page, 1903.

["The Woman's Exchange."] *The Art Interchange* 1, no. 3 (October 16, 1878): 20

——. *The Art Interchange* 1, no. 7 (December 11, 1878): iii.

21. Christine Frederick: Barometer of Conflict

Janice Williams Rutherford

"Our greatest enemy is the woman with the career," a prominent Long Island woman told the American Home Economics Association in 1913.[1] At the time she made this statement, she was forging a remarkable career as a writer, speaker, consumer advocate, and advertiser. Her daughters would remember that she inspired them to become creative, self-sufficient women, "independent of the classic roles of wife and mother."[2] Christine Frederick was a household efficiency expert who worked out of her home in Greenlawn, Long Island, New York, for three decades during the first half of the twentieth century. The early phase of her career, roughly from 1910 until 1920, coincided with the period when feminism was opening a window into the public sphere for middle-class, educated white women who had been reared in the Victorian private sphere. Frederick's life symbolized the conflict between two ideals: the movement to allow women to take their places beside men in the public worlds of education, professional accomplishment, and political participation in contrast to the nineteenth-century dictum that they should remain at home. In fact, she crafted a very public and influential career by helping to contract feminism's window; as a writer and speaker, she encouraged other women to view themselves primarily as keepers of the home.

Christine Isobel Campbell was born in Boston on February 6, 1883. Her mother was the daughter of well-to-do Scottish immigrants who had settled in St. Louis; her father was a New England Congregational minister.[3] Her parents' marriage was an unhappy one; her mother, Mimie, left her father, William Campbell, soon after Christine's birth. When Christine was two years old, Mimie fled the country to serve as governess to a wealthy Russian family outside Moscow for three years. A nasty divorce resulted in Campbell's gaining custody of little Christine from a Massachusetts court, but Mimie had returned to St. Louis where a Missouri judge gave *her* custody. Distance prevented Campbell from successfully contesting that decision.[4]

Christine was reared by Mimie and her second husband, Wyatt MacGaffey, whose name Christine assumed. They lived in Chicago where she excelled at Northwestern Division High School and graduated Phi Beta Kappa from Northwestern University in 1906.[5] While still a student, Christine had met the ambitious young advertising man, J. George Frederick. A year after she graduated, they married and moved to the Bronx in New

York City where she bore two children, a son in 1908 and a daughter two years later.[6]

After moving to the Bronx, Christine Frederick faced a dilemma. She had chosen to marry and to bear children, decisions that launched a traditional life modeled upon the nineteenth-century precept that a woman's highest duty was to care for home and children. On the other hand, she had enjoyed the advantages of the new freedom with which women could pursue higher education. Her scholastic achievements and her developing talent for writing and speaking made her long for a way to put to use the abilities she had discovered as a student.[7] As she came face to face with the realities of homemaking, confined in a small apartment and confronted by the arduous chores that she later described so often as "drudgery," she began to believe that she was not, in her own words, "doing justice to" herself.[8]

Meantime, her husband had quickly become involved with the exciting intellectual life in New York City. The latest thought on all sorts of topics "kept washing into" the Frederick house, as his daughter remembered years later.[9] Among the purveyors of modern culture that he brought home were advocates of the new "scientific management" then current among engineers who sought to improve factory output.[10] Through J. George, Christine met men such as Frank Gilbreth and Harrington Emerson, both followers of Frederick Taylor who had developed this system of managing work. Emerson's book, *Twelve Principles of Efficiency,* proved to be a guidebook to the way out of her dilemma.[11] She later wrote that as she listened to these men talk, she "had an intuition that perhaps in this new idea was the life-preserver" that would save her from her sea of drudgery.[12]

Frederick set about applying the efficiency principles to her household tasks. Thus scientific management, an area of expertise developed in the public sphere by men, was to provide the first component of Frederick's successful career as a household expert. As she "standardized" housekeeping tasks by timing motions, streamlining routes, and grouping tools, she wrote about her findings.

After four years of apartment-dwelling in the Bronx, the Fredericks bought an aging house on an old apple orchard at Greenlawn where, in 1912, Frederick established the Applecroft Experiment Station, an efficiency kitchen where she would refine the application of scientific management to homemaking.[13] Early that year, she sent a series of four articles on efficiency in the home to the *Ladies' Home Journal.*[14] The *Journal* not only accepted her articles, its editor, Edward Bok, offered her a contractual post answering individual letters about housekeeping.[15] Frederick demonstrated remarkable self-confidence in this early negotiation for her first real professional fee; when the *Journal* offered her $600 for the four housekeeping articles, she held out for more and the magazine finally agreed to $750.[16] This early relationship with the *Ladies' Home Journal* continued to provide Frederick with an outlet for her writing until 1920, by which time she was writing for many other publications and had published two books.[17]

For her first book, *The New Housekeeping: Efficiency Studies in Home Management*, Frederick added new material on the management of servants, home economics education, consumerism, and the housewife's relation to business to her four *Journal* articles. The new material that most clearly demonstrated the conflict in her advice to women dealt with the housewife's attitude. Too many women, she wrote, let housework weigh them down by focusing on the physical aspects of the work. Others lacked confidence and were inept. Too many merely tolerated housework and felt contempt for it, wishing they could do something else instead. All these attitudes, she believed, were *"poisonous and antagonistic to either efficiency or the highest personal happiness. . . ."* (italics hers). If women would simply shake off these destructive attitudes and do their housework efficiently, they would find that homemaking could be "fascinating and stimulating."[18] Frederick did not perceive, perhaps, that her own satisfaction now stemmed not from housework but from writing.

The conversion of her kitchen at Applecroft into an experiment station—Frederick's was just one among several such kitchens during this period—provided her with another creative outlet. Her writing led to product testing. By 1912, American middle-class families were buying vacuum cleaners, washing machines, electric irons, gas ranges, fireless cookers, and many other home appliances just then becoming available.[19] Enthusiasm for these products reflected the convergence of several early twentieth-century phenomena: advances in technology, increased production, the need for new markets, and an effort to preserve the home as an agent of consumption. Frederick, with an unfailing sense of modern currents, exploited these trends. She helped create the home market by using new appliances and writing about their labor-saving qualities. At the same time, she encouraged women to buy the devices and to stay at home to use them.

Acting on the common assumption that the home had been transformed from a place of production to one of consumption, Frederick took on the role of consumer advocate for the American housewife. She wrote in her first book that she considered the kitchen at Applecroft a "clearing house between the manufacturer and the homemaker."[20] In 1912, most manufacturers had not developed their own in-house testing laboratories, and they were only too happy to respond to Frederick's solicitations and send their products to Applecroft for her testimonials.[21] By the end of the 1930s, she claimed to have tested some 10,000 devices, appliances, and food products.[22]

Product testing led naturally to pamphlet writing, and Frederick enjoyed a brisk business writing advertising booklets well into the 1920s. She produced pamphlets on washing machines, chocolate, frankfurters, and enamel ware. She wrote promotional copy for the Florida Citrus Exchange, the International Nickel Company, and the League of Advertising Women.[23] Frederick believed that this kind of advertising was beneficial to both manufacturer and consumer. In her view, their interests were the same, and the pamphlets sold products while providing the housewife with important information.[24]

In another very modern attempt to disseminate homemaking information, Frederick produced a motion picture at Applecroft in 1916. She wrote the script and directed the film, the story of a young housewife who lost her servant and was delivered from the resulting chaos by a visiting housekeeper. The housekeeper not only helped the young woman systemize her house-keeping chores through scientific management but also demonstrated all kinds of laborsaving devices. Frederick's intention was to sell her film to home economics educators and women's clubs.[25] If the film was distributed, there is no evidence that it enjoyed wide circulation.

Her work with manufacturers and J. George's affiliations led to Frederick's keen interest in the field of advertising. The Fredericks helped to found one of the first advertising clubs for women in New York City. In 1912, they invited more than forty advertising women to a dinner at Reisen-weber's restaurant on Eighth Avenue. That meeting, chaired by J. George Frederick, led to the founding of the League of Advertising Women of New York, later the Advertising Women of New York. Although Christine Frederick was never a dues-paying member of the League, she was granted honorary membership and she attended meetings frequently. She was hon-ored as a founder at the group's fiftieth anniversary celebration in 1962.[26]

Advertising and consumerism presented another conflict for Frederick, though she never acknowledged it. As she advised women to ease their housekeeping burdens with the new products she had tested, she jumped into the middle of a long battle over the right of manufacturers to set prices for their products.[27] Frederick took the side of the manufacturers, arguing that most were hard-working and motivated by the desire to produce quality products. She believed that they could not maintain quality if retailers cut their suggested prices. She counseled buyers to insist on brand-named products and to refrain from patronizing dealers who cut the prices on these goods. Not only did price-cutting hurt the manufacturers, Frederick believed it demoralized women consumers who would be lured into buying things they did not need and who would gain a false sense of value through price-cutting.[28] Frederick wanted an orderly market where everyone received fair value, but her argument not only ignored the theory that the forces of supply and demand would benefit the consumer in a free market, it also denied the consumer's desire for low prices. Furthermore, she implied that women consumers were easily duped. Thus, while representing herself as an advocate for women consumers, she actually argued for legislation that might not have been to their advantage at all.

In 1919, Frederick produced *Household Engineering: Scientific Management in the Home*, a correspondence course published by the American School of Home Economics. This project suggested an alliance with the home economics movement, for it addressed a need for textbooks during a period when that field was expanding into high schools, colleges, and universities across the country.[29] Frederick's work, however, concentrated on providing information for the woman at home. She once criticized home economics educators for training women to teach the subject rather than to practice it. After 1920, Frederick's relationship with the professional home economists cooled. She lacked formal training in their field, and some of them perceived her close association with manufacturers and advertisers as exploitation of her own sex. For her part, Frederick only occasionally represented herself as a home economist and sometimes referred to them jokingly as "lima beans."[30]

Her writing about home efficiency, labor-saving devices, and consumerism launched Christine Frederick's career, but speaking made it the exciting, very public calling that it became. Soon after she published *The New Housekeeping*, Frederick was invited to give a speech before the annual meeting of the Home Economics Association in which she criticized career women.[31] Among her engagements in 1914 were presentations before the Efficiency Society in Lake Placid, New York, the House Judiciary Committee in Washington, D.C., before whom she testified on price maintenance, and the New York Advertising Men's League.[32] Her speaking schedule slowed when her third child was born in May of 1915, but three months before her confinement, she spoke before an advertising group in Lancaster, Pennsylvania.[33] Frederick met a heavy speaking schedule the next year, traveling to the Middle West for appearances in Iowa, Indiana, and Illinois and lecturing before a course on Women in Industry offered by the New York Intercollegiate Bureau of Occupations (an honor she shared with feminist Charlotte Perkins Gilman). In 1917, the year that her fourth child was born, she traveled to Washington, D.C., to testify on price maintenance two more times: once before the Federal Trade Commission and again before the House Committee on Interstate and Foreign Commerce.[34]

Her flair for the dramatic, her humor, her compelling delivery, and her modern message that could be tailored to meet wartime imperatives made Frederick a natural participant in one of the entertainment and cultural phenomena of the period. In 1918, she joined a wartime Chautauqua show that traveled from spring to fall and from South Carolina to Illinois, entertaining and educating America's small towns. Her lecture, delivered in the huge Chautauqua tent during the afternoon, was entitled "Keeping House for Uncle Sam."[35] In it, she admonished American women to use scientific management and technology to conserve food, time, and energy. Exhibiting little patience with women who participated in what she called the "band playing, flag-flying stage of war," she discounted benefits, teas, and dances for servicemen. Those activities did not measure up to wearing "a kitchen apron" to "help win the war."[36] Once again Frederick, who had left her young family for several months while on tour, was advising other women to stay in their own kitchens.

The arduous speaking schedule, added to the large volume of writing she did, underscored another conflict for Frederick. In her early writing, she often stated that she did all her own housework, but she actually required the assistance of nursemaids, laundresses, seamstresses, and cleaning women from the time her first child was born. By the time the Fredericks moved to Applecroft, her work schedule demanded a full-time secretary and a full-time nursemaid or housekeeper for the children.[37] Her experience with servants led Frederick to join in a Progressive reform movement to elevate the status of domestic work by standardizing hours and wages, offering paid vacations, and paying servants enough to enable them to live in quarters of their own. She wrote several articles on this topic and devoted an entire chapter of her second book to it.[38]

Christine Frederick began writing during a period of heady change for women. The word "feminism" was beginning to appear in the New York papers soon after she married.[39] Women such as Charlotte Perkins Gilman and Henrietta Rodman were suggesting that women would benefit by drastic changes in the traditional home.[40] The woman suffrage campaign would gain new momentum after World War I. By 1920, fifteen percent of all doctoral degrees conferred by American universities would be granted to women.[41] Educated, middle-class women were entering professions heretofore closed to them, including publishing, industrial chemistry, bacteriology, and real estate.[42] Frederick was poised to take full advantage of these developments when she graduated from Northwestern. She had attracted the notice of her professors with her writing skills and her superb speaking abilities, and she was an ambitious young woman who well understood her own capabilities.

But Frederick had been reared in nineteenth-century ideology. While in college, she had dutifully echoed the doctrine of two spheres. In a paper entitled "The Genius of Woman," she argued that the "columns of women" who had "entered into competition with man . . . were influenced by an unhealthy craving for public applause and public work. . . . Woman's true position is in her home," she wrote. "It is here that her highest development is attained; here is her greatest field of usefulness."[43]

Christine Frederick did not live by the injunctions that the young Christine MacGaffey had written to fulfill a school assignment. She nevertheless fashioned a career upon the premise that woman's place was in the home, thus resolving the educated woman's conflict, at least for herself. She was able to fulfill her need to achieve through her special talents, capitalizing on exciting trends of modernization such as technology, advertising, and consumerism. Nevertheless, she accommodated the still-prevailing view that the preservation of the single-family home depended upon woman's remaining within it. Frederick's career paradoxically exemplified the opportunities for participating in the public sphere that were newly available to women, while it flourished on the old prescription that would have them remain in their traditional roles.

The contradiction of Christine Frederick's life might suggest hypocrisy, opportunism, even duplicity. In fact, Frederick was deceiving herself. She believed that she was helping to elevate what had been drudgery into a modern, satisfying occupation. When she contrasted housework to work in the public sphere, she used office work as the measure and could write with complete conviction that homemaking was every bit as fulfilling as typing letters. She did not compare housekeeping to writing and speaking. When she told audiences that career women were her greatest enemies, she could ignore the fact that she herself had a career because she was working in the interest of the home. Her influence on the home was considerable. Frederick did, indeed, show housewives countless ways to modernize and thereby ease their traditional labors. On the other hand, her willingness to accept the nineteenth-century assumption that women were responsible for the management of the home helped to perpetuate a conflict with which many American women still struggle.

Notes

1. Christine Frederick, "Points in Efficiency," *Journal of Home Economics* (hereafter cited as *JHE*), 6 (June 1914): 280.

2. Phyllis Frederick, "The Older Woman," interview by Adele Wolkin, Hermosa Beach, CA, May 10, 1982; Jean Joyce, interview by the author, tape recording, Washington, DC, September 15, 1994.

3. Commonwealth of Massachusetts, Copy of Record of Birth of Christine Isabel Campbell, certified January 20, 1979, Christine Frederick file folder, box 36, Notable American Women Papers, Arthur and Elizabeth Schlesinger Library on the History of Women in America, Radcliffe College, Cambridge, Massachusetts (hereafter cited as Schlesinger Library).

4. *In the Matter of Christine Isabell* [*sic*] *Campbell*, no. 70851, December 7-27, 1888 (Circuit Court of the City of St. Louis, photocopies); *William R. Campbell vs. Mimie Scott Campbell*, no. 75, November 28, 1888, Superior Court, Suffolk County, Massachusetts, photocopy (Archives, Circuit Court, Missouri); [Christine Frederick],

"Only a Girl," unpublished autobiographical notes, [1969], file folder 9, Christine MacGaffey Frederick Papers (hereafter cited as Frederick Papers), Schlesinger Library.

5. Marriage certificate of Wyatt McGaffey and Mimie S. Campbell, August 7, 1894, file folder 14, Frederick Papers; "Northwestern University College of Liberal Arts Entrance Statistics," entry form, September 2, 1902, series 51/12, box 18, Alumni Biographical Files, Northwestern University Archives (hereafter cited as Northwestern Alum Files); "Phi Beta Kappa Notice of Election," May 25, 1906, file folder 14, Frederick Papers.

6. Marriage license, Justus George Frederick and Christine Isobel MacGaffey, June 27, 1907, Cook County, Illinois; wedding announcement, Christine Isobel McGaffey to Justus George Frederick, June 29, 1907, file folder 14, Frederick Papers; Joyce, interviews, September 14-16, 1994.

7. C. Frederick later described her own achievements at Northwestern in "Only a Girl," [pp. 12-16]. The college yearbook and transcripts corroborate her assessment. *The Syllabus* (Evanston, IL: Northwestern University, 1905), pp. 187, 222; 1906, pp. 187, 205, 218, 229; 1907, pp. 235; "Christine MacGaffey," copy of transcript, series 51/12, box 18, Northwestern Alum Files.

8. Christine Frederick, *Household Engineering: Scientific Management in the Home* (Chicago: American School of Home Economics, 1919), p. 7.

9. Joyce, interview, September 16, 1994.

10. C. Frederick, *Household Engineering*, pp. 7-8.

11. See Christine Frederick, *The New Housekeeping: Efficiency Studies in Home Management* (Garden City, NY: Doubleday, Page and Company, 1914), pp. 14-20; and *Household Engineering*, pp. 8-12. Emerson and Gilbreth contributed a preface and a foreword to Frederick's second book, *Household Engineering*.

12. C. Frederick, *Household Engineering*, p. 8.

13. Deed Liber 762 at pp. 251-53, photocopy, Suffolk County Clerk's Office, Riverhead, NY; C. Frederick, *New Housekeeping*, p. x.

14. S. L. Laciar to Christine McGaffey Frederick, January 29, 1912, file folder 1, Frederick Papers.

15. Karl Edwin Harriman to Christine Frederick, March 7, 1912; Edward Bok to Frederick, March 18, 1912, file folder 1, Frederick Papers.

16. Bok to Frederick, March 12, 1912; Harriman to Frederick, April 16, 1912, file folder 1, Frederick Papers. The four articles were published under the title "The New Housekeeping," in the *Ladies' Home Journal* (hereafter cited as *LHJ*), September 1912, p. 13; October 1912, p. 20; November 1912, p. 19; December 1912, p. 16.

17. In 1916, she ceased to be the *Journal*'s housekeeping correspondent. See "Ask the Ladies' Home Journal," *LHJ*, March 1916, p. 61.

18. Frederick, *New Housekeeping*, pp. 183-86.

19. Martha Bensley Bruère, "The New Home-making," *Outlook*, March 16, 1912, pp. 592-94.

20. Frederick, *New Housekeeping*, p. 256.

21. Sears, Roebuck, for example, did not install a testing laboratory in its textile division until 1919. Carolyn Goldstein, "Part of the Package: Home Economists in the Consumer Products Industries, 1920-1940," typescript, 18-19, prepared for *Rethinking Home Economics: Women and the History of a Profession,* edited by Sarah Stage and Virginia Vincenti (Ithaca: Cornell University Press, 1997).

22. Christine Frederick, "Mrs. Consumer Speaks Up," speech, New York Rotary, March 10, 1938, p. 4, file folder 10, Frederick Papers.

23. The following pamphlets by Christine Frederick can be found in file folder 12 of the Frederick Papers: *The Efficient Kitchen and Laundry* (New York: Efficiency Society, 1914); *How to Plan and Equip the Efficient Kitchen* (Philadelphia: Ladies' Home Journal, n.d.); *You and Your Laundry* (New York: Hurley Machine Company, 1920); *Woman as Bait in Advertising* (New York: League of Advertising Women of New York, 1921); *Come into My Kitchen* (Sheboygan, WI: Vollrath Company, 1922); *Tested and Recommended Household Equipment* (Springfield, MA: *Farm and Home Magazine*, n.d.); *Seald Sweet Cook Book* (Tampa, FL: Florida Citrus Exchange, n.d.); *Parties All the Year Round* (New York: Shrine Magazine, 1928); *Frankfurters As You Like Them* (New York: Stahl-Meyer, 1931); *Hershey's Favorite Recipes* (Hershey, PA: Hershey Chocolate Corporation, 1937); *Let's Bring the Kitchen Up-to-Date* (New York: International Nickel Company, n.d.).

24. For Frederick's views on the relationship between manufacturers, retailers, and consumers, see chapter 8 of *Household Engineering*, pp. 315-77.

25. "Motion Pictures of Old and New . . . Methods Are the Latest Thing in the . . . ," [November 2, 1916], fragmentary clipping, microfilm M-107, Frederick Papers.

26. "Beginnings—Formation of the League," n.d., typescript; J. George Frederick, "Notes on the Formation of the Advertising Women's Club of New York," October 1961, typescript; "Founders' Section," n.d., typescript, file folder 1, carton 2, Advertising Women of New York, Inc. Records, Schlesinger Library; Wiseman, "Christine Frederick," 17; Helen Peffer Oakley, "AWNY—An Informal History, 1912-1962," in *Advertising Women of New York, Golden Salute to Advertising* (New York: Advertising Women of New York Foundation, 1962) p. 60; Dorothy Dignam, "Some Women Have Made Good in Advertising, But As to Others—," *Printers' Ink*, April 27, 1939, p. 18, clipping, file folder 18, box 3, Dorothy Dignam Papers, Schlesinger Library.

27. For a thorough discussion of this struggle and the reasons behind it, see Susan Strasser, *Satisfaction Guaranteed: The Making of the American Mass Market* (New York: Pantheon Books, 1989), pp. 224-84.

28. Frederick, *New Housekeeping*, pp. 205-12; *Household Engineering*, pp. 320-23, 358.

29. For a study of the growth of home economics as a curriculum in the land grant colleges established by the Morrill Acts of 1862 and 1890, see Linda Marie Fritschner, "The Rise and Fall of Home Economics: A Study With Implications for Women, Education, and Change" (Ph.D. diss., University of California, Davis, 1973; Ann Arbor, MI: University Microfilms International, 1978).

30. C. Frederick, *New Housekeeping*, pp. 234-36; [Anna] Burdick to [Louise] Stanley, October 21, 1930; "Federal Board of Vocational Edu., 1929-32" file, box 564, Correspondence with other Governmental Departments, and Bureaus, 1923-37, Records of the Bureau of Human Nutrition and Home Economics (Record Group 176), General records; Joyce interview, September 15, 1994.

31. "Annual Meeting of the American Home Economics Association—June 27-July 4, Cornell University, Ithaca, New York," *JHE* 5 (January 1913): pp. 289-90. See also note 1 above.

32. "The New Housekeeping," January 18, 1914, clipping, microfilm M-107, Frederick Papers; House Committee on the Judiciary, *Hearings before the Committee on the Judiciary on Trust Legislation*, 63rd Cong., 2d sess., February 18, 1914, pp. 725-33; "Dazzling Styles Bewilder Diners," *New York Times* (hereafter cited as *NYT*), March 13, 1914, p. 11, col. 3.

33. Jean Joyce to author, January 15, 1995; "Briliant [*sic*] Banquet Planned for Dr. Wiley," *Lancaster Morning Journal*, January 30, 1915, clipping, microfilm M-107, Frederick Papers.

34. "Indiana Home Economics Association Third Annual Convention," January 13, 1916, program, microfilm M-107, Frederick Papers; Christine Frederick, "What the New Housekeeping Means to the Farm Home," speech before the Farmers' Institute, Decatur, Illinois, [February 22, 1916], file folder 10, Frederick Papers; Christine Frederick, "Household Economics," Women in Industry Lecture No. 15, February 8, 1916, file folder 16; Charlotte Perkins Gilman, "Women and Vocations," Women in Industry Lecture No. 1, October 4, 1915, file folder 3, carton 1, Bureau of Vocational Information Papers, Schlesinger Library; "Brands Needed by Consumer," October 29, 1917, clipping; "Woman Expert in Home Efficiency for Stephens Bill," n.d., clipping, microfilm M-107, Frederick Papers; Joyce to author, January 15, 1995.

35. [C. Frederick], "Only a Girl," [pp. 22-28]; "Redpath Chautauqua Program DeLuxe," August 10 [1918], flyer, microfilm M-107, Frederick Papers.

36. "Mrs. Frederick Shows How to Put Home on Conservative Basis," *Fayetteville Observer*, July 4, 1918, clipping; "Urges Women to Be 'Kitchen Soldiers,'" *Louisville Herald*, n.d., clipping; "Turn Energy the Wrong Way," n.p., n.d., clipping, microfilm M-107, Frederick Papers.

37. Joyce, interview, September 15, 1994.

38. See, for example, C. Frederick, "The New Housekeeping," *LHJ*, December 1912, p. 16; "Suppose Our Servants Didn't Live With Us?" *LHJ*, October 1914, p. 102; and *Household Engineering,* pp. 419-48. For the views of another advocate of this movement, see "Eight Hour Service," *JHE* 12 (December 1920): 548.

39. See, for example, "Talk on Feminism Stirs Great Crowd," *NYT,* February 18, 1914, p. 2, col. 4. Nancy Cott suggests that the term was first used in the American press in a 1906 article in the *Review of Reviews*. See Nancy F. Cott, *The Grounding of Modern Feminism* (New Haven: Yale University Press, 1987), p. 14.

40. For Gilman's critique of the traditional home, see Charlotte Perkins Gilman, *The Home: Its Work and Influence* (New York: McClure, Phillips and Company, 1903; reprint, New York: Source Book Press, 1970). For a discussion of an apartment hotel planned by Gilman and Rodman, see Dolores Hayden, *The Grand Domestic Revolution: A History of Feminist Designs for American Homes, Neighborhoods, and Cities* (Cambridge: MIT Press, 1982), pp 197-202.

41. June Sochen, *The New Woman: Feminism in Greenwich Village, 1910-1920* (New York: Quadrangle Books, 1972), p ix.

42. A large number of brochures on career opportunities in 1911 and 1912 can be found in file folder 4, box 1 of the Records of the Women's Educational and Industrial Union, Schlesinger Library.

43. Christine MacGaffey, "The Genius of Woman," school composition, n.d., 3, 6, file folder 14, Frederick Papers.

22. Long Island Women Go To War

Alan Singer and Christine Kleinegger

Local Newspapers Report on the Changing Roles of Women, 1941–1946
Alan Singer

World War II altered the social and economic position of women in the United States and on Long Island in fundamental ways. These changes are well documented by articles in the Long Island press from 1940 through 1946.

In January 1943, the Reverend Dr. Frank M. Kerr, pastor of Christ's First Presbyterian Church in Hempstead, told a group of local men about to be sent overseas "that those at home will accept any and all sacrifices intended to help the war effort." For Long Island women, the war meant both the sacrifices described by Reverend Kerr, and the opening up of new life possibilities. The *Valley Stream Mail* had hinted at the extent of these new opportunities in a May 1941 editorial entitled "Woman-Hours." The editorial underscored the importance of the traditional role played by women as volunteers and relief workers in wartime, but it also emphasized the emerging new role of American women as a crucial part of the nation's industrial army. According to the editorial, "Since America became the Arsenal for Democracy. . . . we know all about man-hours, but seemingly no one has yet publicized women hours. Why not? Wouldn't it be interesting to learn how many woman-hours are being worked in munition factories, in Red Cross workrooms and other war-relief organizations? . . . How many women-hours are being worked? Is the number per week increasing? How many potential women hours are not being utilized?"[1]

Other local newspapers also recognized the growing importance of women workers to the war effort. In November 1942, the *Babylon Leader* reported that the "increasing demands by war production plants in the Suffolk-Nassau area has developed a manpower problem which can only be met by the active cooperation of all employable women. . . . Women power will have to be utilized. The switching over of employed women from non-essential industries to war work has been going on for some time but has not been sufficient to meet all demands. It is necessary that women who stopped working when they married; women able to work but who are not now looking for work; and women who have never felt the necessity for it; enter the labor market to meet production needs." In September 1942, the

Republic Aviation Corporation in Farmingdale reported that 55 percent of their newly hired production workers were women. This was the first time more women had been hired at the plant than men. In another historic breakthrough, women working in the factory were being paid at the same wage rates as their male co-workers. Local newspapers proudly listed the names of these new workers. Babylon women working at the Republic plant included: W. W. Watt, Asara Jarolamo, Vivian Harris, Clara Feeley, Myra Squires, Mary Baran, Anna Gosk, and Lillian Small. Farmingdale women included: Geraldine Polcastro, Beatrice Dememco, and Frances Milano.[2]

In 1942, Republic Aviation's company newspaper declared that "A woman's place may be in the home (but we doubt it) during peace time, but under present war conditions the pretty sex is just as much at home in an aircraft factory." At Republic, women were working on the assembly line operating drill presses, putting together electrical components, and serving as quality control inspectors.[3]

On May 28, 1943, the *Port Jefferson Times* told its readers that "if enough fighters and torpedo bombers are to reach our boys in the Pacific and European fronts, their wives and mothers, sisters and sweathearts, are going to have to help build them."[4]

Women workers were not a new phenomenon to the United States. In 1940, 28 percent of United States workers were women, and 52 percent of these women workers were either married, widowed, or divorced. What the war changed was the way that American men and women saw the role of women in production and the attitudes that both men and women had towards the capabilities of women as workers. As a result of these changes, by 1944, 37 percent of the United States work force was female and 59 percent of these women workers were either married, widowed, or divorced.[5]

Wartime factory work brought about many subtle yet important changes. Women workers excelled in technical training programs—completing four week programs in as little as two and a half weeks. Women made suggestions for improving production—Kathryn Brazzell won a $25 war bond for developing a new wire identification tape dispenser at Republic Aviation. Women were frequently named as outstanding war workers, including: Mary Eldridge of Franklin Square, a policewoman in a defense plant; Beatrice Joyce of Lawrence, from the auxiliary Aircraft Warning Service; and Anna Beckvar of Valley Stream, who constructed radios for submarines and airplanes. All of these accomplishments helped challenge stereotypes about the kind of work that women were capable of doing. Men and women attended training sessions together, "adjusting themselves to the association which prevails in the shop." Because safety regulations were more important than sexual identification and stereotyping, women were required to wear standard work clothes. At Republic Aviation, guidelines included "slacks, trousers or coveralls of standard cut or style. . . . Legs of the garments should be close-fitting at the ankles. Upper clothing must be of the coat, blouse or workshirt type. . . . Low-heeled, heavy shoes are advised, preferably with reinforced toes." Women workers were so crucial to wartime production that in November 1942, the maximum hours women were legally allowed to work was temporarily raised from fifty to fifty-eight hours per week.[6]

The employment of large numbers of women in Long Island's factories meant other changes as well. The Household Finance Company directed its advertisements in local newspapers to attract women borrowers. Under pressure from the defense manufacturers, local businesses announced that they would stay open late to accommodate working women. To recruit women with young children, Republic Aviation established a "Freedom Shift" which allowed women to work every other day. Families with more than one worker in a defense plant were allowed to coordinate work hours so they could commute together, or so they could divide up household responsibilities. Federal and state funds were used to establish child care centers. In Hempstead, a child care center was opened at the Franklin School in September 1942. It accepted children six days a week from 7:00 a.m. until 7:00 p.m. and also enrolled older children in an after school program which operated all day during the summer.[7]

As Long Island women fought World War II on numerous fronts, they learned that they were capable of doing both a "woman's" and a "man's" job. Factory work did not excuse women from running households, caring for children, and dealing with wartime shortages and rationing. Women volunteers led campaigns to stockpile silk, to knit sweaters for servicemen, to recycle animal fat, to send used clothing to European refugees, and to sell war bonds. They staffed the Red Cross and the USO, visited the wounded in hospitals, acted as fire wardens, and assisted at Mitchel Field. They joined the WAVES, the WACS, and the Marines.[8]

At the end of the war, American society had to face an unexpected consequence of the vast mobilization of women as industrial work-ers—women did not want to leave the work force. In September 1944, *Newsday* reported that "Rosie the Riveter probably will change her slacks involuntarily for a postwar housedress unless an unprecedented peacetime production is achieved." According to an article focusing on the nation's automobile industry, women were scheduled to be laid-off as wartime production ebbed and as men returned from the armed forces. But the women were not happy. Eighty-five percent told union interviewers that they wanted to continue in the factories.[9] In Nassau County, 86 percent of women surveyed by the New York State Department of Labor in August 1945 said that they expected to work after the war.[10]

On Long Island, post-war jobs were deemed the "number one problem" by members of the Garden City-Hempstead League of Women Voters. By August 1945, Grumman had placed all of its employees on "leave of absence status." The company's child care centers, essential for supporting working women, were closed in Brightwaters and Freeport. The Babylon Village Board was concerned with cutbacks and lay-offs in the defense plants that it made its top priority cooperating "with the various industries and plants in the vicinity to keep as many workers in the neighborhood at work as possible."[11]

Working women realized that the closing of child care centers also meant the closing down of possibilities for women in a post-war world. The *Hempstead Sentinel* reported that fifty of the fifty-eight women with children in the Hempstead Child Care Center attended a meeting to demand that the center remain open after the war, even if it meant they had to pay increased fees.[12]

Post-war prosperity, the nurturing of delayed families, the rapid development of new communities, roads, and businesses, federal mortgage subsidies for veterans, and the evolution of a suburban consumer society, changed conditions again for women on Long Island and in the United States. Advertisements in the local press sold both a new world of electrical appliances and the image of women as brides, mothers, and contented housewives. Experts like Dr. Benjamin Spock recommended that mothers who did not have to work should stay home with their children. Spock told women that "the important thing for a mother to realize is that the younger the child the more necessary it is for him [*sic*] to have a steady, loving person taking care of him. . . . If a mother realizes clearly how vital this kind of care is to a small child, it may make it easier for her to decide that the extra money she might earn, for the satisfaction she might receive from an outside job, is not so important, after all." As a result of all of these social pressures, between 1940 and 1960, the number of single women in the United States aged twenty to twenty-nine declined from 36 to 20 percent and the American birthrate rose by 50 percent.[13]

Memories of the wartime experiences of the country's "Rosie the Riveters" and the ways that those experiences challenged traditional notions of a woman's role in society, were suppressed during the late 1940s and 1950s, but they were never completely forgotten. According to Betty Friedan, writing in *The Feminine Mystique,* these memories "lay buried, unspoken, for many years in the minds of American women. . . . Each suburban wife struggled with it along . . . she was afraid to ask, even of herself the silent question—'Is this all?'"[14]

By the late 1950s, as their children grew up, married women on Long Island and in the rest of the United States began to return to the work force in large numbers. In 1940, only 15 percent of married women held jobs outside the home. By 1960, the figure was 30 percent, and by 1980, it had reached 50 percent. This included 40 percent of the women under age thirty-five with children between ages six and eighteen. Today on Long Island, women are 45 percent of the employed work force. This includes nearly 48 percent of women with children under age six and 73 percent of women with children between ages six and seventeen. "Rosie the Riveter," her daughters, and her granddaughters have returned to the work force with a vengeance.[15]

The Janes Who Made the Planes: Grumman in World War II
Christine Kleinegger

In March 1942, three months after the United States entered World War II, six women walked on to the factory floor at Grumman's Plant No. 1 in Bethpage, Long Island.[16] They were the first female aircraft workers on Long Island. By the end of 1943, 8,000 more women were part of the "Grumman War Productions Corps." Eventually, women comprised approximately 30 percent of Grumman's wartime work force of 25,400 workers. The "Janes Who Made the Planes" built Wildcats, Hellcats, and Avengers for the Navy.[17]

Before World War II, women were considered unfit for aircraft production; however, after the bombing of Pearl Harbor, women suddenly were a perfect pool of potential workers. Once on the job at Grumman, Long Island's women were often commended for their perceived patience with repetitious, monotonous tasks, their dexterous fingers, their compliance in taking orders, and their ability to squeeze into small, awkward spots. Women soon predominated in certain departments. For example, the Electrical Department of Plant 14 had fifty-two women and only two men.

Grumman offered training to women at several "aviation schools" around Long Island. In six to ten week courses, women learned the rudiments of riveting, blueprint reading, sub-assembly, and other semi-skilled functions associated with aircraft production. Many women enjoyed learning new skills. Ethel Nelson Surprise was animated when she recalled her training: "I remember coming home and telling my father about the different things we were doing and he'd shake his head and say, 'I can never imagine my daughters riveting and working at a drill press.' We'd sit around the table and talk about things we learned that day and he couldn't get over it."[18]

College-educated women were recruited as apprentice engineers to assist male Grumman engineers in designing aircraft. These women were given crash courses in drafting, calculus, mechanics, and aerodynamics. Grumman was also the first company to hire women to test military aircraft as it came

Fig. 22.1. Recruitment display in window at Baumann's furniture store in Freeport during World War II. Photograph courtesy of the Grumman History Center.

off the line. Pilots Barbara Jayne, Elizabeth Hooker, and "Teddy" Kenyon were no doubt the most glamorous and famous of Grumman's female defense workers, and they were featured in magazine advertisements for cosmetics and cigarettes.[19]

World War II was a watershed in the history of women in the United States. A new working woman emerged: middle-class, middle-aged, and married. Although women ranged from recent high school graduates to grandmothers in their sixties, the average age of women working at Grumman was thirty-six. Management at Grumman understood that in order to recruit mothers of small children and to reduce absenteeism, consideration had to be given to the family responsibilities of working women. Wartime innovations designed to make life easier or more pleasant for harried Grumman defense workers included cafeterias, exercise breaks, and recreational sports, morale-boosting social activities and entertainment, comfortable rest rooms, a lending library, and a service for running errands. Women counselors were hired to orient new women workers to factory life and to help solve family problems that interfered with productivity.

The chief problem for many working mothers was the need for child care. Grumman operated three "war-time nurseries" in nearby communities that accommodated up to fifty children between the ages of two and five, and cost fifty cents a day. Yet with 8,000 women working at Grumman, most mothers relied on more informal forms of child care—usually relatives or neighbors. Dorothy Nelson Rabas, an inspector at Grumman during the war, had to quit her job when her neighbor would no longer take care of her daughter. When asked why she hadn't used the war-time nursery, Rabas recalled it was too far away.[20] Car pooling and gas shortages, in addition to the ten-hour work day, made child care in neighboring areas impractical for many mothers. The "war-time nurseries" were disbanded after the war, reflecting the view that child care was a war emergency measure and not an employment benefit of working parents.

Throughout the war, the Grumman newspaper, *Plane News,* printed dozens of editorials, cartoons, articles, and features on individual women that applauded women's patriotism and celebrated their skill and perseverance. In December 1942, an editorial in *Plane News* titled, "A Merry Christmas to the Ladies," even presented a feminist analysis of the war: "The place of women in the world is one of the points of issue in this war and the outcome of the war will determine whether she is to be an inferior creature according to the Nazi scheme or a free person of equal rights which she holds in the democratic way of life." The editorial went on to predict that women in the shop would have further opportunities ahead of them.[21]

Grumman management used articles in *Plane News* to motivate women and minimize male doubts about a woman's ability to do the job. Men in the shops were not wholly receptive to the idea of women joining the ranks of a traditionally male industry. Grumman women who recall male co-workers treating them with friendliness and cooperation also remember that practical jokes were played on them, such as being sent on errands for bogus tools. In an article in *Plane News* marking the two-year anniversary of the first women workers, a male foreman recalled the first day on the job for the women workers assigned to his shop: "Catcalls and whistles followed the girls from the minute they appeared that morning."[22]

Women hired specifically for the "Grumman War Production Corps" knew they were hired only for the duration of the war. As the war wound down, foremen made lists of their workers in "order of proficiency" to plan the massive lay-offs that would occur when peace arrived. Despite all of the wartime praise for their efforts, no women were deemed proficient enough to keep on after the war ended. The day after V-J Day, Grumman laid off all its employees; two weeks later, only male employees were called back and rehired. Ironically, Grumman's production manager found himself without a single riveter.[23] Riveters are essential to building planes, and certainly thousands of women were trained as riveters. Yet even when emergency telegrams were sent out to riveters to be rehired, no women were invited back.

Notes

Alan Singer's essay, "Local Newspapers Report on the Changing Roles of Women," was the introduction to a fifty-seven page booklet researched and compiled by students in a Hofstra Summer Workshop in 1995, Secondary Education (Sec. Ed.) 276. Students located articles in local newspapers and periodicals which were reprinted in the booklet, together with reviews of two movies, and an oral history interview. Students involved in the Workshop were Pamela Booth, Regina Follo, Barbara Garry, David Guerra, Stavros Kilimitzoglou, Laurence Klein, Mary Anne Langan, Patricia McGloughlin, Jeffrey Picirelli, Carol Sanders, Brenda Selmanoff, Melissa Sorgen, Patrick Sweeny, Rodica Tannenbaum, Elizabeth Uqdah, Alan Weber, and Matthew Wildes. Students involved in editing the material in Sec. Ed. 136 were Diane Tully (chairperson), Pamela Booth, Jennifer Evans, and Melissa Sorgen. Copies of the booklet were distributed to those attending the conference workshops. The booklet is available from Professor Singer in Hofstra University's School of Education or can be consulted in the Long Island Studies Institute.

Christine Kleinegger's "The Janes Who Made the Planes" was one of the articles included in the booklet; notes have been added for this publication by the author. The full article from which this was selected is scheduled for publication in the *Long Island Historical Journal.* (Editor's note.)

1. "Dr. Kerr Stresses Need for Sacrifice at Send-Off Rites," *Hempstead Sentinel,* January 21, 1943, p. 1; John N. Warren, "Woman-Hours," *Valley Stream Mail,* May 22, 1941, p. 4.

2. "Women Required to Solve Manpower Shortage," *Babylon Leader,* November 12, 1942, p. 4; "More Women than Men Hired by Republic," *Babylon Leader,* September 17, 1942, p. 1; "Women Hired Exceed Men," *Farmingdale Post,* September 17, 1942, p. 1.

3. "Real Need for Workers," *Republic Aviation,* September 18, 1942, p. 1.

4. *Port Jefferson Times,* May 28, 1943.

5. United States Department of Commerce, *Historical Statistics of the United States* (Washington DC: Government Printing Office, 1975), 1: 131, 133.

6. "Women Cut Class Time," *Farmingdale Post,* October 8, 1942, p. 1; "Women Join Parade of Idea Prize Winners," *Republic Aviation,* July 10, 1942, p. 2: "Women Taking Training Course," *Republic Aviation,* November 6, 1942, p. 1; "Women Working 58 Hours a Week," *Republic Aviation,* November 6, 1942, p. 1.

7. "Family Work on Same Shift," *Farmingdale Post,* February 25, 1943, p. 1: "Freedom Shift Gives Workers Part Time Jobs at Republic," *Farmingdale Post,* September 2, 1943, p. 1; "Child Care Film to Appear in Hempstead," *Newsday,* May 25, 1944, p. 17.

8. For some examples of activities by local women, see "Local Women Get Citations," *Hempstead Sentinel,* December 14, 1944, p. 3.

9. "See Auto Industry Dropping Women," *Newsday,* September 11, 1944, p. 18.

10. Division of Industrial Relations, New York State Department of Labor, *Survey, Women in Industry and Minimum Wage* (Albany, NY, August 1945).

11. "Jobs Discussed by Women Voters," *Hempstead Sentinel,* April 12, 1945, p. 3; "Village Board To Hold Meeting On Employment," *Babylon Leader,* August 23, 1945, p. 1.

12. "Mothers Urge Operation of Child Center," *Hempstead Sentinel,* September 13, 1945, p. 1; "Mothers Vote to Continue Child Center," *Hempstead Sentinel,* October 4, 1945, p. 1.

13. Dr. Benjamin Spock, M. D., "Baby and Child Care," in *The American Spirit,* 5th ed., edited by Thomas Bailey and David Kennedy (Lexington, MA: D. C. Heath and Company, 1975), 2: 973; Marvin Harris, *America Now* (New York: Simon and Schuster, 1981), p. 84.

14. Betty Friedan, quoted in Bailey and Kennedy, *The American Spirit,* 2: 975.

15. *Harris, America Now,* p. 88.

16. This article is based on the exhibition, "The Janes Who Made the Planes: Grumman in World War II," on display at the New York State Museum in Albany, from December 7, 1991-June 30, 1992. Joseph F. Meany, Jr., was co-curator of the exhibit. Sources for the research included interviews with nine women who worked at Grumman during the war, Grumman's employee newspaper *Plane News,* and documents, photographs, and artifacts from the Grumman History Center in Bethpage, Long Island.

17. Grumman statistics for October 1943. The title is based on a World War II song, "We're the Janes Who Make the Planes," cited in Richard R. Lingeman, *Don't You Know There's a War On?* (New York, G. P. Putnam's Sons, 1970), p. 222. Other songs that sang the praises of women aircraft workers were "The Lady at Lockheed" and the better known, "Rosie the Riveter."

18. Interview, September 6, 1991.

19. Charles Paul May, *Women in Aeronautics* (New York: Thomas Nelson and Sons, 1962), pp. 167-68.

20. Interview, September 6, 1991. See also Agnes E. Meyer, *Journey Through Chaos* (New York: Harcourt, Brace, 1943), p. 283.

21. "A Merry Christmas to the Ladies," *Plane News,* December 24, 1942, p. 4.

22. "Award Two-Year Stripes to Women Who First Invaded Men's Domain," *Plane News,* March 2, 1944, p. 4.

23. Richard Thruelsen, *The Grumman Story* (New York: Praeger, 1976), pp. 217, 220.

23. Kathryn Dudek: Breaking Barriers in the World of Sports Photojournalism

Linda Keller

Renowned photographer, the late Kathryn Dudek (1954–1992), was widely respected and recognized for her contributions to photojournalism, most notably in the world of sports. "Dudek was not only a top photographer, she was also a hard worker and an excellent businesswoman who thrived in the tough, competitive world of freelance photojournalism."[1] Knowing that at any given moment Dudek could find a part of this world to record, she was always with a camera. She had a natural instinct for capturing the peak moment in action, the gentle strength in a portrait, and the excitement of a news-breaking image. Insistent on perfection in technique and composition, her photography portrays her mastery.

Born in 1954 in Endicott, New York, to Olga and Henry T. Dudek, Kathryn was the first of five children. When she was very young, the family moved to Long Island, first to Queens and then to Floral Park, the community Dudek eventually claimed for her permanent studio and home. Her career in photojournalism evolved from diverse childhood interests. The technical and creative aspects of photography combine the two subjects at which she excelled—science and art. She began experimenting with her first camera when she was about five years old. Within a few years, with no formal training, she began recording events such as school plays and selling these images to classmates for twenty-five cents each. By about age fourteen the editor of her hometown paper, *The Gateway,* recognized her talent and began giving her assignments.

Today with auto-focus cameras, one assumes that one merely points and snaps to obtain a perfect picture; yet, behind a spectacular image is a vast technical knowledge combining physics and chemistry. Film types vary in their chemical ability to record light. Professional photographers must understand which film will achieve the finest results for different media reproduction. Specialized lenses and filters are often used. The camera's precise shutter speed freezes the movement of the subject on film. Although technical mastery may become second nature, it does not always lead to artistic achievement. Unlike a painting's composition which can be altered by the artist's stroke, a talented photographer must freeze a moment in time which cannot be erased. Dudek had mastered her equipment and technique, but she also had tremendous natural artistic instinct.[2]

Dudek learned photojournalism through practical experience. In high school, she was a photographer and a writer for her yearbook and newspaper. An accomplished athlete, she was an honor student as well. She was a member of the swimming and gymnastics teams for whom she also coached new members. She attended Nassau Community College and Towson State University, Maryland, graduating *cum laude* from each with degrees in Physical Education. Recognized as a distinguished student at Nassau Community College, she was included in *Who's Who Among Students in American Junior Colleges,* having been nominated for this honor by her classmates and teachers. Throughout her college career, she continued her work in journalism and photography, concentrating on sports. She was the Athletics Department photographer and assistant director in the Sports Information Department. She held posts such as photographer, reporter, photo editor, and sports editor on the yearbooks as well as the newspapers.

After graduation from Towson in 1976, Dudek pursued a career in photojournalism although she was certified as a teacher. She joined Maryland's *Valley Voice* newspaper where she covered local and collegiate sports and news. She was assigned as press photographer at President Jimmy Carter's inauguration and wrote the feature story. She made it a point to track Long Island athletes and personalities, following their careers and photographing them.

In 1977, Dudek joined Long Island's *Newsday* as Assistant to the Deputy Sports Editor. She wrote general interest features, covered high school sports, and became the newspaper's gymnastic coordinator. Dudek was one of the few journalists to advocate additional coverage of gymnastics, which until that time had received little attention. She corresponded with schools and organizations nationwide; she attended high school, college, and professional competitions, photographing, interviewing, and writing feature articles. Dudek's emphasis on the quality of Long Island gymnasts convinced *Newsday* to increase feature space which ultimately helped to promote this sport.

Gaining success as a freelance photojournalist, Dudek left *Newsday* but retained them as a client. In 1980, she established her own company, PHOTO NEWS PHOTOGRAPHY. Her reputation for "being there" brought her constant special assignments from major news bureaus. She photographed all aspects of life: sports, human interest, scenic, national events, and politics. She loved to capture local and international personalities who shaped our country. She recorded admirers requesting President Richard Nixon's autograph and covered President Reagan's inauguration. Her photographs of the Mondale/Ferraro campaign in 1984 include a warm image of Ferraro bending down to greet a sweetly dressed little girl. As personal press photographer for freshman Senator Alfonse D'Amato, Dudek covered political, social, and family events.

Freelance photojournalists usually hire agents to market their work, but Dudek was her own agent. She covered many different aspects of a specific subject, keeping in mind the marketability to numerous publications, from daily newspapers to academic journals to be used for covers, exclusives, advertisements, and promotions. Her work was featured with some of the most prestigious clients worldwide including ABC *Wide World of Sports*, *Life*, *Sports Illustrated*, the Associated Press, *World Tennis*, *American Turf Monthly*, *Racing Action*, *Spur*, *The Times* of London, and countless others throughout the world.

Fig. 23.1. United States Gymnastics Federation Elite Nations, at Nassau Coliseum, May 1978. Floor exercise—arch jump. Notice that the Coliseum was far from full, though top ranking gymnasts were competing. Photograph © Kathryn Dudek/Photo News.

While Dudek's output was diverse, the arena she loved most was the world of sports. Each athlete is unique in individual ability and determination for excellence. Dudek captured the soul of an athlete, the camaraderie even between competitors, the spirit among fans. A few examples of her extensive sports coverage include: the maneuvers in soccer; the excitement of the New York Islanders; the priceless expression on the face of a golf caddie; the energy of the Jets playing against the Oilers; Mets fans requesting autographs; the power of basketball; the fierce strength in Hofstra football.

Dudek never overlooked those who refused to set limits. She recorded the proud athletes at the first International Games for the Disabled held in the United States at Mitchel Field and other sites in Nassau County. She also liked to cover lower profiled athletes and events such as senior golfers, ice boating, and frisbee champions. As early as high school, Dudek was aware of attitudes toward and restrictions for women. Throughout her career, she worked to promote women in sports, including gymnastics, basketball, lacrosse, field hockey, and golf. She made a point to cover more unusual events such as girls and boys playing soccer together, or two girl punters on a boys' football team.

Dudek's photography captured the achievements of track and field from the intensity of a pole vaulter to the exuberance of a young runner. She

Fig. 23.2 The Houston Oilers vs. the New York Jets at Shea Stadium, November 23, 1980. The intense action is frozen with the football hanging in the center of the picture. As the ball sails past Pat Leahy (no. 5), after his field goal attempt, Pat Ryan (no. 4) still has his fingers where the football was positioned seconds earlier. The Jets won the game, 31–28. Photograph © Kathryn Dudek/Photo News.

covered countless women's competitions and world champions. She followed great runners in the New York City Marathon: Grete Waitz winning nine years within a single decade, Alberto Salazar winning three years,[3] and the expansive start across the Verrazano Bridge. When Dudek began her extensive coverage of this marathon, it was a relatively small, unknown event which few photographers bothered to cover. One associate, Phil Stewart, fondly remembers an early year when he and Dudek were the only press to show up, working out of the trunks of their cars. Publishing her images worldwide, Dudek helped to promote it into the major international event it is today. Some of her work graces the pages of the marathon's twenty-fifth anniversary book.

From spectators to tournament champions, Dudek photographed the subtle intensities of tennis. She captured the defeats of hopefuls, the victories of superstars, the swift ball girls, and the devoted fans. She was a fixture at the annual United States Open Tennis Championships in Queens. Her powerful images of Zina Garrison and Steffi Graff were selected for the installation of life-size posters at this event. Her memorable photograph of champion Carling Bassett published in *Tennis de France* was captioned as "one of the most spectacular in the realm of tennis."[4]

A world Dudek greatly loved was the excitement and energy of thoroughbred racing, from the power and beauty of the thoroughbred to the warmth and dignity of the people. Dudek spent much of her time at the track

Fig. 23.3. The Steeplechase, taken August 1990, in Saratoga, New York. The thrill excitement, and danger of the this race are captured from a very unique perspective. Photograph © Kathryn Dudek/Photo News.

year-round, photographing flat racing, harness racing, steeplechase, polo, and equestrian events. Dudek preferred the New York Racing Association tracks at Belmont Park, Saratoga, and Aqueduct. Yet she did not hesitate when she had the opportunity to cover the Prix du Jockey Club Lancia in Chantilly, France.

Again, one of Dudek's prime focuses was to show women's involvement and achievements, from the few legendary jockeys to the trainers, the warm-up riders, and the grooms. Capturing every aspect of racing, she also covered life beyond the tracks, including exclusive social gatherings and horse auctions. In her own words, Dudek once explained, "It's the one sport I can show the most different aspects for—the private and the public views."[5] Indeed, thoroughbred racing is a world with its own community and lifestyle.

Initially Dudek was not welcome in this exclusive world because she was a woman. Yet, in time, she became part of the track family, partly because of her genuine concern for the horses. Former *Newsday* photo editor, Tom McGuire, noted, "Kathy was always a person of quiet dignity . . . but it was obvious from her work that she had a forceful personality in the field. She'd go to the [thoroughbred] morning workouts and little by little the trainers and owners gradually came to accept her as the photographer they liked to have around."[6] Dudek "was recognized for her ability to capture the human side of racing."[7] She also gained a reputation for being respectful of people's privacy. This trustworthiness won her exclusives. For instance, jockey Angel Corderro intended to visit his father's grave upon his 6,000th win. As he reached this landmark, he allowed Dudek to be the sole photographer to accompany him, knowing that she would not divulge the location of the cemetery.

Dudek was twice the Honorable Mention recipient of the exclusive Eclipse Awards which are given to those who have made outstanding contributions to the world of thoroughbred racing. Her 1989 winning photograph was a close-up of trainer Shug McGaughey watching his horses in early workout, mist steaming from his first morning coffee. *Sports Illustrated* Director of Photography, Heinz Kluetmeier noted, "The photographs Kathryn took at dawn—with the mist on the track and the dew on the grass—have a mystical, lyrical quality. . . . Horses running in the early morning, the sun coming up, that soft, hazy light cutting through the fog."[8] National Museum of Racing Curator Field Horne stated that "Kathryn's work represents a new and higher level of artistry. The work goes beyond equine photography. The composition is the sort early nineteenth-century painters produced."[9] Dudek loved both the serene beauty as well as the colorful action. One of her favorite images was a head-on, thundering shot of Meadow Star winning at Belmont Park. Known for her passion and dedication to

Fig. 23.4. Kathryn Dudek at Aqueduct Race Track, 1991. Photograph courtesy of the Dudek family.

thoroughbred flat racing, Dudek was clearly one of the most important female action photographers in the history of this exquisite sport.

Photographing sports is unique in that it takes place within a very explosive environment filled with frenzied fans, sharp-tongued coaches, and high-charged athletes. Aware of the many risks, Dudek nonetheless refused to lose a potentially rare and exciting perspective. For instance, at a National Football League Giants game at the Meadowlands in New Jersey, she was focusing so intensely through her lens on one player that she did not have time to move out of his way and was knocked over by him. Dudek had an aggressiveness and stamina equal to the athletes. Her athletic training gave her an educated eye for the anatomy of a body in motion and a keen sense of timing. On the job she always had several cameras loaded with different film and lenses in order to switch in a split second. Hence, she would have separate images that could be utilized by various media with specific reproduction requirements. Mastering the art of photographing each sport demands extensive knowledge of the athletes, the rules of the sport, and their statistics. Yet unlike most photographers, Dudek did not limit her knowledge or her coverage to one or two sports. She not only thrived in this fiercely competitive world, she amazingly mastered an enormous range.

Beyond sharing her images, Dudek shared her knowledge and experience as a guest speaker at schools and at national women's organizations. She was a fully active member of the National Press Photographers Association from the early 1980s. In 1983, she became a member of the Long Island Chapter of the American Society of Magazine Photographers, at a time when there was decreasing membership. Knowing there were many local professionals, Dudek pushed to create a strong chapter. In 1985 and 1986, she was treasurer and from 1988 through 1991, she was president. In 1989, she also became chapter chairperson for a massive worldwide project, entitled "10,000 Eyes," which was launched by the national organization to celebrate the 150th anniversary of the discovery of photography. The exhibit was followed by an impressive book, also called *10,000 Eyes.*

Dudek was also an active member of the New York City Chapter of the American Society of Picture Professionals. She served on the Board of Directors and was treasurer (1986). For several years she was chairperson for their annual New York Photo Show, most notably the Tenth Anniversary Show. Dudek declined the presidency, because she did not have time to give the position her full attention.

Although photography was clearly one of the most important things in Dudek's life, she managed to find time for other interests, including hiking with friends, traveling, reading, enjoying country music, swimming, and cycling. In 1991, proud of her Long Island roots, she helped establish the Floral Park History Preservation Committee.

Dudek was extraordinary not merely because she kept an exhausting schedule, photographed an enormous range of subjects, or had an encyclopedic knowledge of facts. She refused to set limits because she was a woman; she was convinced that with capability and interest, she could do all that she chose. Building her career was never easy. Dudek encountered difficult situations and broke through many barriers. In the early days, she faced a strong male network of editors and cut-throat photographers who did not take her seriously: they thought she could not carry her heavy equipment and they passed her over for assignments simply because she was a woman. Yet she was a strong, determined individual who was only challenged when faced with discouragement. At top events, Dudek capably contended with many photographers who fought television crews for priority positions. In time, associates came to respect her persistence, realizing she had no intention of sabotaging their shots. Film director and former *Sports Illustrated* photo editor Donna Tsufura recognized that "Kathryn was not a cut-throat photographer. . . . She didn't look out just for herself." Tsufura further acknowledged, "She genuinely cared about the business and others. . . . It is what made her so loved and respected."[10]

On the sunny morning of May 21, 1992, in her hometown of Floral Park, Dudek died as the result of a two-car collision. She was the innocent pedestrian. News of her sudden passing was far-reaching when announced by sportscaster and friend Frank P. Dwyer on his ESPN television program. Overwhelmed with shock and grief, many relatives, friends, neighbors, and colleagues attended her wake and funeral. The New York Racing Association granted the rare privilege of allowing her funeral procession to pass through a closed Belmont Park for a final farewell to one of her favorite places.

Dudek would not have understood the enormous effect she had on others and the difference she made in their lives, both professionally and personally. She left a tremendous legacy, endearing and memorable to those fortunate to know her. She was a remarkable individual whose life has been widely celebrated. In 1992, the New York Racing Association named Belmont Park's annual "Memories of Kathryn" race in her honor. Dozens of articles have been written about her life. The Road Runner's Club dedicated the cover of the 1992 New York City Marathon issue of *Running News* with a memorable collage of Dudek's work. Still recalling her contributions after so many years, Senator Alfonse D'Amato, in 1993, read a tribute to her life into the *Congressional Record,* which stated that she was "a fine woman" and "a gifted photographer." "Kathryn Dudek," he continued, was "an enormous talent . . . a bright star whose memory will live on. She will be missed by . . . many to whom she brought joy. I salute her wonderful life and am saddened by her passing."[11]

Dudek became the first female sports photojournalist to be honored with a solo exhibition at the National Museum of Racing and Hall of Fame in Saratoga Springs, New York, in the summer of 1995. After being viewed by more than 20,000 people from the United States and abroad, the exhibit traveled to Belmont Park and then to the Floral Park Town Hall in the fall. The exhibit was also on view in March and April 1996 at Hofstra University's Lowenfeld Gallery, in conjunction with the "Long Island Women: Activists and Innovators" conference. Reviewing Dudek's work, guests wrote, "Magnificent!" "Inspiring!" "Beautiful!" "Thank you for sharing her talent!" In 1995, Eastman-Kodak named a scholarship in her honor. During the 1996 Summer Olympics in Atlanta, Eastman-Kodak paid a unique tribute to Dudek with a solo exhibition of her work covering tennis, equestrian, polo, steeplechase, and gymnastics events.

Dudek was a tremendous talent with an incredible sense of timing. Her powerful images capture the hope and determination of athletes—their anguish, joy, humor, and their intensely competitive world. She derived great satisfaction from sharing her experience and knowledge with youngsters and adults alike. She took every opportunity to help women in their pursuit of success. Her focus in life was to be a top photojournalist. She had enormous passion and self-confidence which drove her onward. She did not dwell on the barriers she faced. Her qualities and work ethics were of the highest standard. It is a testament to her fortitude and talent, notably within the world of men's competitive sports, that she became one of the most admired and respected sports photojournalists worldwide.

A master artist, Kathryn Dudek's photography never loses the excitement nor the uniqueness of the moments she exquisitely captured on film. Through her photography, part of Dudek will always remain. Combining sensitivity with assertiveness, she loved to capture life through her camera. Thus, the sadness remains that her remarkable life and talent were interrupted—her work unfinished.

Notes

1. Jenny Kellner, "Treasured Memories," *Post Parade,* July 1995.

2. Interviews with family members, 1992-1995.

3. Peter Gambaccini, *New York City Marathon: Twenty-Five Years* (New York: Rizzoli, 1994), pp. 68-71.

4. "Carling Bassett" photograph and caption, *Tennis de France,* December 1985.

5. Mary Caroline Powers, "For This Woman, Life's a Colorful Snap," *The Saratogian Pink Sheet,* August 22, 1990.

6. David Behrens, "A Photographer's Vivid Legacy," *Newsday,* June 15, 1995.

7. Karen Johnson Downey, "Hall of Fame Remembers Dudek with an Exhibition," *Daily Racing Forum,* June 7, 1995.

8. Quoted by Behrens, "A Photographer's Vivid Legacy."

9. Ibid.

10. Interview with Donna Tsufura, 1992.

11. Senator Alfonse D'Amato dedication in the *Congressional Record,* May 20, 1993.

24. Last Stop Plandome: Frances Hodgson Burnett

Bea Tusiani

Author of children's classics, Frances Hodgson Burnett lived in England, Tennessee, Washington, D.C., and traveled to New York, Paris, Canada, Boston, Newport, and Connecticut before setting foot on Long Island in 1881.[1] By that time the prolific writer was thirty-two years old and had already published seventeen books of fiction for adults.[2] She was twenty-eight when her first book was published.

It was a transition to dramatization that prompted Burnett to spend the summer of 1880 at Nook Farm near Hartford, Connecticut, which was a writers' colony and the home of Isabella Beecher Hooker, younger, half sister of Harriet Beecher Stowe.[3] Burnett's initial collaboration with Hooker's nephew, actor and playwright William Gillette,[4] on a play called *Esmeralda*, would resume the following summer at a new hotel that had opened along the newly developed oceanfront on Long Beach, Long Island.[5]

With her two young sons, Lionel and Vivian, safely tucked away at Grandmother Burnett's home in Tennessee, and her husband Swan tending to his ophthalmology practice in Washington, D.C., Burnett was free to enjoy the festive activities at the year-old Long Beach Hotel. Caught up in the gay atmosphere of what was considered a playground for the rich, the author carried on flirtatiously with both Gillette and her editor at Scribner's, Richard Watson Gilder. She also noted to a friend in a letter that she was also attracted to a member of the band and to a particularly muscular lifeguard.[6]

Of her overnight stay with Gilder she writes: "We rambled about on the beach and grubbed in the sand and then went back to the hotel . . . and dined on the immense piazza, and then went back to the beach and sat and bayed at the moon . . . and we sat in the sand again there until midnight and then went and had lemonade on the porch."[7]

She later wrote to Isabella Beecher Hooker: "I finished the *last* revision of the play yesterday and Mr. Gillette bore it back to town. . . . If this is not as perfect a letter as it should be will you kindly take with consideration the fact that I am writing in the hotel parlor with the band playing outside, my parasol up to keep the wind off and four of the most fascinating people pretending to write at the same table."[8]

Esmeralda, billed as a comedy-drama in four acts by co-authors Burnett and Gillette, opened the following fall at the Madison Square Theater in New York where it ran for a record 350 nights. The popular actress, Annie Russell, portrayed the farm girl who is sent off to Paris by her suddenly rich and ambitious mother.[9]

Twenty years would pass before Frances Hodgson Burnett returned to Long Island. Those two decades were spent crisscrossing the Atlantic Ocean a dozen times. With England as her home base, she took month-long journeys to places like Florence, Rome, the French Riveria, Belgium, Holland, and Vienna.[10] Toward the end of this period, Burnett rented and fell in love with Maytham Hall, in Kent, England. It was Maytham Hall's walled garden which inspired the author to later write her signature work, *The Secret Garden.* During this time Burnett published her first juvenile book, the widely popular *Little Lord Fauntleroy.*[11]

Another children's book, *Sara Crew,* originally published in London in 1887, was turned into a play renamed *A Little Princess* by Burnett when she rented a cottage in East Hampton in 1902. Again, the Long Island connection was her editor R. W. Gilder whose trusting wife Helena was a a member of the de Kay family who summered there since the 1890s.[12] Burnett was drawn to the household of Helena's brother's family, Charles and Lucy Edwelyn Coffey de Kay, for two reasons. The elder de Kay, a former literary critic and art editor of the *New York Times,* was a highly-regarded intellectual and poet, whose companions included the literary and international social set. The boisterous goings on of the de Kays' eight children provided rich new material for the author's juvenile stories.[13]

Burnett's biographer Anne Thwaite credits the de Kay children with inspiring Burnett to write about the poor, yet contented dolls in *Racketty Packetty House.* Burnett said of the de Kays, they "got fun out of everything. . . . They could make up stories and pretend things and invent games out of nothing. . . . They were so fond of each other and so good-natured and always in such spirits that everyone who knew them was fond of them."[14]

On a record of summer cottage rentals in East Hampton that season, the author was listed under her second husband's name, Mrs. F. H. Burnett Townsend.[15] The house she leased, owned by Mrs. A. E. Newman, was located north of Georgica Road at the intersection of Hedges Lane. The de Kays rented the residence of George A. LaMonte, a short distance away.[16]

Unlike the fanciful time she spent at Long Beach, Burnett's stay in East Hampton was to be a quiet one. The prostrated author had just spent the spring in a sanatorium at Fishkill-on-Hudson as a result of pressures from a second failed marriage and a long-standing bout with neuritis, and she sought solace in what was then considered a newly accessible (via railroad), rather lazy, seaside resort.[17] Indeed, Charles de Kay describes it that way in an article in the *New York Times Illustrated Magazine.* "Strange to say, the people who visit East Hampton as villa owners, as hirers of houses, or passing boarders, regard it as a place of rest and relaxation from city forms and customs. Dances and dinners, even driving parties and picnics, are few and far between."[18]

The setting was apparently pleasing enough to tempt Burnett back the following season. Still officially calling herself Mrs. F. H. B. Townsend,[19] she rented the residence of the Reverend E. Jewett, who lived near other clergymen on what is referred to locally as Divinity Hill.[20] This house, situated north of Georgica Road, was within walking distance to that rented by the de Kays.

Though a return address of Dune Crest appears on the letterhead of Burnett's 1903 correspondence from this residence, there is no indication that such a place existed in East Hampton that year.[21] The author herself may have given the cottage that name because it was located on a second set of dunes that was being populated by summer colonists who were not necessarily anxious to inhabit the first line of dunes that lay just beyond the surf.[22] Among the other summer residents drawn to East Hampton during that time were: John Drew, who founded the local theater; architect Cass Gilbert; Maria Victoria Torrilhon, an accomplished French pianist; Mrs. Durant Rice, founder of a pottery kiln company; and composer Mabel Wood Hill.[23]

The atmosphere must have agreed with Burnett as she went into what she herself describes as a "pen-driving" mode. In four days, she turned out a ten-thousand word adult novel, *In the Closed Room*, considered a precursor to *The Secret Garden*. In addition, she continued working on *The Shuttle*, a novel about an Anglo-American marriage that took her seven years to complete, and started to transform her previously published *The Pretty Sister of Jose* into a play.[24]

The next four years, Burnett made annual transatlantic crossings, spending most of those summers at her beloved Maytham Hall in England where much of her writing was done in the seclusion of a walled garden. Within this timespan, seven new works were published in both the United States and in London; Burnett had contracts with four different American publishers and three English publishing houses. The most popular of these novels, *A Little Princess,* was adapted from previously written stories of juvenile fiction involving the character of Sara Crewe in which Burnett utilized the trademark theme of riches-to-rags-to-riches which she herself had experienced.[25]

Writing to her then grown son Vivian Burnett from Asheville, North Carolina, in March 1904, she inquired whether he had seen the lots in Great Neck. "Who knows, but I might leave you building a house there during the summer." However, that never materialized. It wouldn't be until 1907, when her ten-year lease had run out at Maytham Hall, that Burnett's attention again turned to Long Island where she asked Vivian to find a place for her to stay during the warm weather.[26]

Vivian chose Sands Point, a location opposite the fashionable Great Neck, the West Egg of F. Scott Fitzgerald's *Great Gatsby*. It was a little furnished cottage nestled among East Egg, Gold Coast mansions. Howard Gould and William Guggenheim were two of the three dozen large property owners of note in Sands Point at the time.[27] Once again the arrival of the Long Island Railroad's direct line from Manhattan to Port Washington may have played a role in Burnett's desire to summer in this region. It was necessary for her to have access to her New York City editors and for her to be able to reach main ports-of-call and train depots for her many travels. Although the *Port Washington News* did report a list of rentals for that year, the names Burnett or Townsend were not among them.[28]

While at Sands Point, the author dramatized *The Dawn of a To-morrow*, the story of a sick, wealthy man, who is saved from killing himself by the kind attention of poor beggars. "She began after the passage of months to find the Long Island district attractive to her—albeit in a way distinctly different from the hoary and romantic way of Maytham," writes Vivian in his memoir. "Just before departing the next spring for a 'cure' at Doctor Lampe's sanitarium, in Frankfort, Germany, she purchased land at Plandome, Long Island, and gave her approval for a house to be built while she was away."[29]

In reality, years of running away from the memory of her dead firstborn child, the guilt of two failed marriages, and the pressures of meeting strict, often self-imposed deadlines, had finally caught up with the author who was now close to sixty. As a working woman, a single-parent, and the chief breadwinner for her family, she had experienced what few other women of her time had encountered. "It became obvious that the happiest plan she could devise for herself from now on would be to live near Vivian and his [future] family," said daughter-in-law Constance Buel Burnett in retrospect.[30]

The two-and-a-half acres the author purchased was part of a 1,200-acre farm, owned at the turn of the nineteenth century by United States Senator Dr. Samuel Latham Mitchell, which was being sold off in parcels at the turn of the twentieth century.[31] It was situated in a residential area along Manhasset Bay between the business districts and railroad depots of Port Washington and Manhasset. Two deeds indicate one plot and parts of two others on Bayview Road were sold to Frances Hodgson Townsend by the Manhasset Development Company on August 27, 1908; the remainder of one of those lots was purchased by F. H. Townsend (i.e., Burnett) from George and Mabel Wyeth of New York City on July 30, 1909.[32]

The design and interior decoration of "Fairseat," as Burnett called her new home, reflected the multifaceted influences of her travels. Built in the style of a sweeping Italian villa replete with a piazza and a ballustraded staircase, it was furnished with English Jacobean cupboards, a dressing-table

from Holland, and a desk surrounded by Chinese-style wall hangings.[33] The
author's garden was just as varied. By the fall of 1909, her son vividly
explained what he deemed a miracle: "The brand-new house stood on its
terraces amid green lawns, surrounded by shading trees and thickets of
flowering bushes. The 'perennial borders' were stuffed with every conceiv-
able 'hardy' plant ready to burst forth in the spring—and were even then
ablaze with a riot of hardy chrysanthemums."[34]

With the first bloom of this garden in the spring of 1910, also came the
long-birthing garden of Burnett's imagination. Though the story of a ne-
glected child and walled garden transformed by love had its roots in the
author's beloved Maytham Hall, she was actually inspired to write about it
at the height of the passionate gardening she undertook at her new Plandome
residence. The tale, written for older juveniles, was first serialized as "Mistress Mary" in *The American Magazine.* A year later, it was published in
book form under a new title, *The Secret Garden,* and thereafter it has been
regarded an enduring classic of children's literature.[35]

The year 1911 also found the author's attention turned to family affairs.
Her sister Edith's second husband, Frank Jordan, died in an automobile
accident, and Burnett took it upon herself to purchase a burial plot for him
at God's Little Acre Cemetery in Roslyn. With a businesswoman's foresight,
the family matriarch purchased one of the largest plots in the non-sectarian
cemetery, securing space for Edith and her two sons, Ernest and Archie, as
well as for Vivian and herself. The cemetery was chosen primarily for its
woodland charm.[36]

To take Edith's mind off of her lastest tragedy, Burnett had her sister
move in with her at Fairseat. She also purchased a cottage in Bermuda with
the intention of providing comfort and solace to her younger sibling during
the lonely, cold winter months.[37] Vivian, meanwhile, was left in charge of
Burnett's business correspondence and of managing the household and the
small army of gardeners at Fairseat. In November 1911, he purchased a piece
of property just across the road from his mother's and proceeded to build a
house of his own.[38]

The family compound grew in 1913 when Burnett gave her nephew,
Archie Fahenstock, $5,000 upon his marriage to Annie Prall with the
understanding that his mother (her sister Edith) could live with them in a
house they would eventually purchase next to Vivian's.[39] However, the
strings attached to this offer backfired on Burnett in a public scandal as a
result of a letter she wrote to a family member regarding Annie's treatment
of Edith. It took some time before a $50,000 libel suit filed against Burnett
by Archie's wife was finally resolved in Burnett's favor.[40]

The author seemed to have a better rapport with her neighbors. Long
Island novelist Kathleen Norris describes an encounter with the author on

Fig. 24.1. Frances Hodgson Burnett in her Plandome garden. Photograph courtesy of the Manhasset Library.

the railroad: "When I was on an afternoon train from Port Washington, Mrs. Burnett got on the same train at Plandome and we made the trip together. . . . But as we got out of the train in New York [she said], 'Oh, my luggage! I left it! It's in my room. My boat to Bermuda leaves in two hours. . . . My nightgown—my toothbrush—my bag.'" When Norris suggested Burnett could purchase those items in Macy's or Gimbel's, the Plandome author sighed with embarassment and relief and said "of course."[41]

Plandome Park resident Herbert Houston, former Vice-President of Doubleday and Company and founder of the Better Business Bureau, recounts how he was taking a cup of tea one summer afternoon in Burnett's garden when the author brought up the idea of starting a student newspaper. "Why not form Know–the World Clubs? And forthwith these clubs began to be formed. [They] grew and spread, and out of them, in the past three months has developed the plan to establish *Our World Weekly.*" Houston himself was the publisher.[42]

In addition to *The Secret Garden,* the author published half a dozen children's books and an equal amount of adult fiction during her Plandome years. She also turned five of her previously published stories into plays and wrote yet another original play, though it was never produced.[43]

Old works were never thought of as finished; the prolific author always seemed to find a way to revive or to enhance what she had already written. Twenty-two years after she published *The One I Knew Best of All,* an autobiographical account of her early years, Burnett discussed the possibility of a new edition with E. L. Burlingame, an editor at Scribner's. On a Plandome Park letterhead, dated April 12, 1915, she wrote: "I wonder from what position one would approach a new preface or an addition to the old one? I wonder also if you could take one of the numerous trains to Plandome on next Wednesday afternoon and take tea with me. . . . An excellent train leaves the 34th St. Station at 2:37 and reaches Plandome at 3:36. . . . If you will telephone to 309W Manhasset, someone shall meet you."[44]

On the author's last trip abroad just before the start of World War I, she expressed an appreciation of life in Plandome in a letter to a friend: "To live in the best suite of rooms in the best hotels in any part of Europe being strict economy in comparison to living at Plandome Park, Long Island—and as one can spend an occasional morning at home and lightly earn one's living as one goes." A family photo album portrays the author very much at peace in her surroundings at Fairseat. It depicts Burnett on a thickly carpeted lawn set off by a gravel driveway with a profusion of busyness that is typical of an English garden. Cement ballustrades lined the bay's edge; a fountain played in the center of a lilypond, and huge flower-filled stone tubs stood beside patio doors leading to the house. A circle of stone furniture to which Burnett often escaped to sit and write were enclosed in a tall bower of trees.[45]

By this point in time, 1914, thirty-two year old Vivian had married, and Burnett was delighted with his wife, Constance Buel, the twenty-one year old daughter of a former editor of *Century Magazine,* a publication which serialized many of Burnett's stories. In the following years, Burnett delighted in becoming a grandmother to Dorinda and Verity, upon whom she doted along with her books and garden. "Christmas," said Vivian, "was spent at Plandome with the fairy grand-godmother, a perfect fountain of joyous, imaginative gifts to the babies and all members of the family."[46] As they grew, Burnett played make-believe games with her grandaughters, having a host of her very own characters at the ready. Often, she would sit them down before a big Jacobean cupboard in which a doll's house was constructed watching the expressions on their faces while she, the venerable storyteller, spun and enacted enchanting tales of the inhabitants.

The last of Burnett's works, *Robin* and *In the Garden,* were written when she was in her seventies.[47] They focused on two recurring themes evident throughout the author's work, which she chose to reflect upon one last time in isolation. Critics were divided about their worth. *The Times Literary Supplement* published a scathing review of *Robin*: "lush sentiments flow from her pen with a sweetness that suggests syrup rather than plain ink," whereas the *Boston Transcript* chose to defend the author: "Burnett not in her best mood is far better than the average storyteller of the day."[48]

After suffering for most of her life from what was referred to as nervous indigestion, neuritis, and even a bizarre diagnosis of "osteoperinestitch," Burnett was ultimately driven from her garden to the upper floor of her home. "In brief excursions from her bed into her writing-room, she was able to . . . look at the abundance of the side garden below . . . the overflowing beds of white and pink petunias; colonies of white lilies . . . roses in the glory of their autumn perfection . . . gladiolus filling in the chinks everywhere with brave, erect spikes of red, white and pink," recalls Vivian of his mother's last days.[49]

Author and playwright Marguerite Merington was staying at Fairseat when the end came. She and Burnett's sister Edith were in the house and Vivian was down the road when the nurse aroused them in the early morning hours of October 29, 1924, with the news that Burnett was fading. It was one month shy of the author's seventy-fifth birthday. Edith fainted and had to be put to bed while Vivian and the servants waited and prayed. "I dressed and went downstairs. . . where the spacious rooms were void and chill. Outside a pall of fog blotted out the bay, the lights of Great Neck and Port Washington . . . only a white birch and tall white rose loomed wraith-like—fog impenetrable, and acrid with the pungence of dead leaves," said Merington.[50]

The obituary in the *Port Washington News* revealed that Burnett had been ailing with intestinal troubles during the last three weeks of her life. She died on a Wednesday and funeral services were held in her home the following Saturday. Many of the mourners who attended traveled by train to Plandome. Hers was the third body to be placed in the family plot she had purchased years before in the cemetery on Northern Boulevard in Roslyn. She and her nephew Ernest B., Edith's younger son who died of pneumonia at the age of forty-two, were interred in a large in-ground vault; Frank Jordan's remains lay in a separate, adjacent plot.[51]

A unique feature of the gravesite is a statue of a young boy that many people mistakenly identify as Little Lord Fauntleroy. The young boy dressed in knickers, waistcoat, and bowtie is actually a likeness of Burnett's older son, Lionel, who died at the age of fifteen in Paris and was buried in a cemetery at St. Germain.[52] "Parlor statuary was in vogue in those days and Frances Hodgson Burnett derived comfort from this likeness of her dead son. After his mother's death, Vivian had to dispose of her things. He felt the only place for the statue was in the cemetery where she herself had been laid to rest," recalled Vivian's wife, Constance Buel Burnett.[53]

In 1991, the Burnett gravesite, together with those of poet and editor William Cullen Bryant and writer Christopher Morley, in addition to graves of other important persons of the late nineteenth and early twentieth centuries, was considered of such historical significance that the Roslyn Cemetery was included in the National Register of Historic Places.[54] Although Burnett's grave is overrun with haphazard growth, a former groundskeeper said it was the author's intentions to keep it in its natural state.[55]

While the Roslyn gravestone remained Long Island's only monument to the female author, in 1925, a drive to erect a memorial statue to honor Burnett in New York City's Central Park was headed by her former Plandome neighbor and admirer, Herbert Houston. The inscription on a plaque near the bronze statue of two children that was dedicated in 1936 reads: "Fountain group given to the children of the city in the name of Frances Hodgson Burnett."[56]

Burnett left the greater part of an estate worth $150,000 to her son Vivian; she bequeathed all of her clothes and her house in Bermuda to her sister, Edith. Thereafter, the local legacy of Frances Hodgson Burnett's heirs remained as dramatic as many of her stories. In 1927, Edith Jordan purchased Fairseat from Burnett's estate and upon her death in 1931, it passed to her son, Archie. He renamed it "Archways" and lived there with his second wife, Fanny, who was a former Plandome neighbor.[57]

In 1935, a fire ripped through and destroyed "Archways," causing an estimated $100,000 worth of damage to priceless books, antiques, and furniture. Among the highly prized articles saved were a William Merritt Chase portrait of actress Elsie Leslie as *Little Lord Fauntleroy* and a slightly scorched manuscript of *T. Tembarom*.[58]

In 1937, Vivian Burnett died in a valiant attempt to rescue four people from a sinking boat on Long Island Sound. Hailed as a hero, he was finally able to shed the Fauntleroy image that plagued him all his life.[59] His ashes were buried next to his mother, aunt, uncle, and two cousins, not far from the statue of his older brother—together again, though hardly noticed, along one of Long Island's most heavily traveled roads.

Notes

1. Ann Thwaite, *Waiting for the Party: The Life of Frances Hodgson Burnett, 1849-1924* (New York: Charles Scribner's Sons, 1974), p. 248.

2. Phyllis Bixler, *Frances Hodgson Burnett* (Boston: Twayne, 1984), pp. 137-38. The titles of her books were: *Earlier Stories: First Series; Earlier Stories: Second Series; A Fair Barbarian; Haworth's; Jarl's Daughter and Other Stories; Kathleen; That Lass o' Lowrie's; Louisiana; Miss Crespigny; Natalie and Other Stories; Our Neighbor Opposite; Pretty Polly Pemberton; A Quiet Life and The Tide on the Moaning Bar; Surly Tim and Other Stories; Theo; Through One Administration;* and *Vagabondia.*

3. Harriet Beecher Stowe wrote *Uncle Tom's Cabin* in 1852.

4. Thwaite, *Waiting For the Party,* p. 72. Both Burnett and Gillette had made the acquaintance of Mark Twain who had a house at Nook Farm.

5. The Long Beach Hotel opened on July 17, 1880, exactly two months after the Long Island Railroad reached Long Beach. The posh hotel, which accommodated 800

guests, was destroyed by fire on July 29, 1907. See Edward Graff, *The History of Long Beach, 1880–1961* (Privately printed: Association of Zone A & B Home Owners, n.d.), pp. 3-5.

6. Vivian Burnett, *The Romantick Lady* (New York: Charles Scribner's Sons, 1927), pp. 123-24.

7. Ibid., pp. 123-24. This letter was written on Long Beach Hotel letterhead to Julia Schayer who was living in Washington, D. C. It revealed Burnett's coquettish philandering with her editor after his wife gave him permission to stay overnight with his star author, primarily because she was safely married.

8. Letter dated August 23, 1881, courtesy, Stowe-Day Foundation, Hartford, Connecticut.

9. Bixler, *Frances Hodgson Burnett*, p. 22; V. Burnett, *The Romantic Lady,* pp. 124-25.

10. Constance Buel Burnett, *Happily Ever After* (New York: Vanguard Press, 1965), p. 126. Her daughter-in-law indicates that the author needed a constant change of environment in order to forget the pressures of work and poor health and to stimulate the desire to write.

11. Bixler, *Frances Hodgson Burnett*, p. 136. Fauntleroy was published in 1886 in New York by Scribner's.

12. *The First Fifty Years of the Maidstone Club, 1891–1941* (East Hampton: Maidstone Club, 1941), p. 164.

13. "Charles de Kay Dies: Novelist, Poet and Critic," undated clipping, [May 24?] 1935, *Herald Tribune,* Pennypacker Long Island Collection, East Hampton Public Library.

14. Thwaite, *Waiting for the Party*, p. 229.

15. "Cottage List," *East Hampton Star*, May 30, 1902, p. 1. The author divorced Swan Burnett in 1898 and married another physician (turned actor), Stephen Townsend, in 1900. However, she separated from him in 1902.

16. Locations depicted on the *Atlas of Suffolk County, N.Y.* (Brooklyn: E. Belcher Hyde, 1902), vol. 1.

17. Thwaite, *Waiting for the Party,* pp. 203, 207.

18. Charles de Kay, "East Hampton The Restful," *New York Times Illustrated Magazine,* Oct. 30, 1898. He noted "the railway now gives access to thousands."

19. Though Burnett publically announced a separation from Townsend in 1902, she did not divorce him until 1907.

20. *East Hampton Star*, June 5, 1903, p. 8; *Fifty Years of the Maidstone Club,* p. 65.

21. Mention of it appears in V. Burnett's *Romantick Lady*, p. 305 and in Thwaite's *Waiting for the Party*, p. 205.

22. "Summer Homes at East Hampton, L.I.," *The Architectural Record,* January 1903, p. 29.

23. V. Burnett, *The Romantick Lady,* p. 305. Vivian Burnett later married Maria Victoria Torrilhon's daughter.

24. Ibid., p. 306-7.

25. Thwaite, *Waiting for the Party*, pp. 249, 251. *A Little Princess* was written as a play before it was made into a novel. The other six titles were: *In the Closed Room;*

The Dawn of Tomorrow; The Troubles of Queen Silver-Bell; Racketty Packetty House; The Cozy Lion; and *The Shuttle.*

26. V. Burnett, *The Romantick Lady*, pp. 311, 323. Vivian, widely known as the model for Fauntleroy, was Burnett's second son by her first husband, Swan. Her firstborn, Lionel, died of consumption at age fifteen in Paris.

27. Guggenheim was a capitalist, Gould a financier and railroad magnate. A 1906 *Map of Long Island* (Brooklyn: E. Belcher Hyde, 1906) depicts thirty-two property owners in addition to the United States government, a golf club, and hotel.

28. The railroad extension reached Great Neck in 1867 and Port Washington in 1898; the Port Washington station was the closest train station to Sands Point. A *Sands Point Civic Association Handbook* explains, "City people first came to Sands Point to enjoy their summer vacations," some of them "recognized the accessible train route and chose to reside [here] year round." *Port Washington News,* May-September 1907.

29. V. Burnett, *The Romantick Lady*, p. 323.

30. C. Burnett, *Happily Ever After*, p. 157. Burnett may have realized that if she settled down, perhaps her son would too. As it turned out, he did marry in 1914.

31. Beatrice A. Tusiani, "A Complete History of Plandome Manor," *The Long Island Forum* 44 (July 1981): 132-33. Dr. Samuel Latham Mitchell was elected to the United States Senate in 1804.

32. The Office of Nassau County Clerk: Liber 163, p. 392; Liber 195, p. 31; V. Burnett, *The Romantick Lady*, p. 333. The author continued to use the name Townsend for business purposes; she never used it to indicate authorship.

33. V. Burnett, *The Romantick Lady*, pp. 328, 332.

34. Ibid., p. 327.

35. "This is the first instance I have ever known of a child's story being published in an adult's magazine," said Mrs. Burnett (Thwaite, *Waiting for the Party*, p. 222). *The Secret Garden* was published in New York and London in 1911.

36. Roslyn Cemetery Deed Book, Field Chart Section, vol. 5 plot nos. 176, 177, 183, 184; purchased July 14,1911 and August 9, 1911 (copy in Local History Collection, Bryant Library, Roslyn). The woodland charm comment was made by Constance Buel Burnett in a conversation with Roslyn librarian Helen Glannon, October 30, 1961 (typescript of notes in Burnett Collection, Bryant Library, Roslyn).

37. V. Burnett, *The Romantick Lady,* pp. 351, 345. Burnett also had another younger sister, Edwina and two older brothers, John George and Herbert, none of whom are mentioned beyond their early years in the author's biographies.

38. Nassau County Clerk's Office, Deed no. 276.

39. A genealogy of the Fahnestock family identifies Archer Pleasant and Ernest Benjamin as the two sons of Edith's first marriage to Pleasant Andrew Fahnestock.

40. V. Burnett, *The Romantick Lady*, pp. 351-52.

41. Kathleen Norris, *Family Gathering* (New York: Doubleday, 1959), pp. 144-45.

42. Tusiani, "History of Plandome Manor," pp. 135-36; Herbert S. Houston, "Burnett Our Fairy Godmother," *Our World Weekly,* undated [1925]; written three months after Burnett's death.

43. Children's novels: *The Good Wolf; Barty Crusoe and His Man Saturday; The Land of the Blue Flower; The Lost Prince; The Spring Cleaning;* and *The Way to the House of Santa Claus.* Adult novels: *T. Tembarom; The White People; Little Hunchback Zia; The Head of the House of Coombe; Robin;* and *In the Garden.* Plays: *Dawn of a*

To-morrow; Racketty-Packetty House; The Making of a Marchioness; The Shuttle; T. Tembarom; and *Judy O'Hara* (not produced).

44. *The One I Knew Best of All* was published in 1893 by Charles Scribner's Sons; letter to E. L. Burlingame in Scribner's Collection, Princeton University Library. According to Dr. Barbara M. Kelly, Curator of the Long Island Studies Institute, Hofstra University, the "W" at the end of Burnett's telephone number indicates a party-line.

45. V. Burnett, *The Romantick Lady,* p. 348; Kenneth Fahnestock Photo Album, Frances Hodgson Burnett Collection, Manhasset Public Library. K. Fahnestock was Ernest's son, Burnett's sister Edith's grandson.

46. V. Burnett, *The Romantick Lady,* pp. 386-87.

47. *Robin* was published in 1922; *In The Garden* was published posthumously in 1925.

48. Thwaite, *Waiting for the Party,* p. 240.

49. Ibid., p. 207; V. Burnett, *The Romantick Lady,* p. 408.

50. Marguerite Merington, "The Garden of the Children's Story Teller," *McCall's Magazine,* April 1928.

51. "Mrs. F. H. Burnett Dies at Her Plandome Home," *Port Washington News,* October 31, 1924. In years to come, Edith and Archie Jordan would be buried along with Frances Hodgson Burnett and Ernest Jordan in the vault; Vivian Burnett and Archie Jordan's second wife, Cecilia (Fanny) Fahnestock were interred nearby in separate graves.

52. V. Burnett, *The Romantick Lady,* p. 381.

53. Helen Glannon's notes of conversation with Constance Buell Burnett, October 30, 1961 (Bryant Library, Roslyn). The statue (and Burnett's plot) is located northwest of the restored toll house in the cemetery on the north side of Route 25A.

54. United States Department of the Interior, National Park Service, National Register of Historic Places, Roslyn Cemetery, August 21, 1991: no. 1024–0018. See also Peter D. Shaver, *The National Register of Historic Places in New York State* (New York: Rizzoli, 1993), p. 92.

55. Jane Gerard, "Three Giants Rest in Tiny Cemetery," *Newsday,* August 23, 1961, p. 20.

56. Letter to Charles Scribner from the Frances Hodgson Burnett Memorial Committee, August 1, 1925, Scribner's Collection, Princeton University Library. "Mayor Dedicates Bird Bath in Central Park," *New York Times,* undated [1936]. A small statue of a child was dedicated in memory of Burnett on May 16, 1987 at the Manhasset Public Library.

57. "Famous Woman Author Leaves $150,000 Estate," *Nassau Daily Review,* November 15, 1924. Fanny was the nickname of Cecilia Schotte. Her tombstone in the family plot reads: "Fanny C. Fahnestock." Archie Jordan's first wife, Annie Prall, is not buried in the Roslyn Cemetery

58. "Relics Rescued As 'Fauntleroy' Building Burns," *New York Herald Tribune,* December 30, 1935; "Fahnestock Blaze Damage $100,000," *Manhasset Mail,* January 2, 1935.

59. F. J. Handler, "The Real Fauntleroy—Lived in Plandome," *Great Neck Newsmagazine,* February 1977; Tom McCarthy, "The Real Lord Fauntleroy," *American Heritage,* February 1970, p. 50.

25. Marianne Moore and the Brooklyn Dodgers

Joseph Dorinson

Marianne Moore is an enigma to this prosaic Brooklynite, a plodding historian who gets no Cole Porter kick out of poetry. To this meat and potatoes man, reading verse evokes a political question: where's the beef? In focusing on the thoroughly modern Ms. Moore, almost involuntarily, elusiveness easily slips into obscurity. Why then do I write about maid Marianne? Because at the core she not only shares my birthday, November 15, but we also have another vital element in common, namely, a love for Brooklyn.

Her residence in our beloved borough was no strange interlude. The inseparable Moores, mother Mary and daughter Marianne, moved into Brooklyn as the Great Depression engulfed America. Their abode, a five-story brownstone, offered a bright view. Ever observant, Miss Moore loved the sunny space and the beautiful churches that graced her Fort Greene neighborhood. After considerable wandering, the Moore family needed stability and Brooklyn offered the "tame excitement on which I [Marianne Moore] thrive."[1]

One of America's great poets in this century, Marianne Moore was born near St. Louis in 1887. Hailing from Ohio, her father John Milton Moore was an engineer; her mother Mary was an English teacher and the daughter of a Scotch-Irish Presbyterian minister. The marriage, shrouded in mystery, unraveled when John broke down after the failure of his design for a smokeless furnace. He moved back to Ohio and, despite his efforts for reconciliation, was rejected by his wife. He was allowed no further contact with her and their two children: his son John, and daughter Marianne, who was seventeen months younger than her brother. Mary Moore took her children home to her father with whom they lived until he died in 1894. She had served as her father's housekeeper. Fiercely independent and morally rigid, Mrs. Moore refused all offers of financial assistance from her husband's family.

After her father's death, Mrs. Moore moved to Pennsylvania; she settled first in Pittsburgh, and later in Carlisle where she taught English at a school for girls. Marianne Moore attended this school and subsequently entered Bryn Mawr College in 1905. Here, she made several friends who would play significant roles in her future. Graduating with a B.A. in 1909, Moore showed a practical bent by opting for training in secretarial skills instead of pursuing graduate work in literature, her *bereuf* (calling). She used her newly acquired skills to teach Native Americans. Among her students at Carlisle were two outstanding athletes whom Moore likened to Greek gods, Jim Thorpe and Chief Bender. Sportswriter Robert Cantwell has suggested that this experience sensitized Moore to sports and to the positive impact it had on her Native American students.[2]

Moore and her mother left Carlisle, Pennsylvania, for Chatham, New Jersey, to keep house for her brother John Warner Moore, a recently ordained Presbyterian minister. (Mrs. Moore preferred to call John by his middle name, Warner, rather than his given name which was that of her husband. A psychotherapist could tease deep-seated truths from such transpositions.) When John joined the United States Navy one year later, the Moore women moved to New York City's Greenwich Village to be near him.

During this important period, Moore found her poetic voice and burst into print in 1915 with poems published in *The Egoist* and *Poetry* journals. Her brilliant mind was much admired by literary giants William Carlos Williams, Kenneth Burke, Wallace Stevens, Conrad Aiken, Ezra Pound, and T. S. Eliot. Williams, for example, remembered Moore's red hair, brilliant conversation, and saintly innocence.[3]

Her first collection of poetry appeared in 1921, published by the Egoist Press. A second book, *Observations,* in 1924, confirmed Moore's reputation as a poet, a true avant-guardist. Wider recognition came from her work for *The Dial,* a magazine for which she was both contributor and editor. Indeed, this modernist magazine awarded her their $2,000 literary award in 1924. She became *The Dial's* managing editor in 1925 and its editor-in-chief in 1926, a position she held until the periodical's demise in July 1929. Editing had limited Moore's time for writing, so when *The Dial* folded, Moore was able to turn back to her writing.[4]

Moore moved to Brooklyn with her mother to be nearer to her brother who was stationed at Brooklyn's Navy Yard. The Moores moved into a five-story building on 260 Cumberland Street, part of a still elegant Fort Greene section. Brooklyn provided a much needed respite from Manhattan and the period from 1929 to 1965 in New York's second borough sparked Moore's return to high poetic creativity.

"Decorum marked life on Clinton Hill in the autumn of 1929 when my mother and I came to Brooklyn to live. . ." begins Moore's remembrance of things past for *Vogue* in 1960. She speaks of "an atmosphere of privacy with a touch of diffidence": surely a projection of her solitary self. In a most revealing phrase, Moore praises "anonymity, without social or professional duties after a life of pressure in New York, we found congenial."[5] In subsequent portions of this essay, Moore offers a funny valentine for Brooklyn. She concentrates on churches and trees. Of the latter, she singles out tanager, magnolia, elms, and oaks. In deference to spirituality, a legacy shared by mother and brother, Moore cites S. Parkes Cadman, Phillips Packer Elliott, George L. Knight, and Henry Ward Beecher. She touts schools: Erasmus, Packer, Polytechnic, Brooklyn Tech, Pratt, Brooklyn Institute. She praises the Brooklyn Museum, Prospect Park, Botanic Garden, Brooklyn Bridge, the view from the promenade, and the Brooklyn Dodgers.

Among the prominent figures mentioned in this curious article are Seth Low, W.H. Auden, Jennie Jerome, John Ericsson, and Dr. Edward Robinson Squibb. Moore offers homage to animals, to street names, and to local scenery.[6]

Moore's Brooklyn evokes Edith Wharton's New York, but Moore adored baseball. This rural game played in urban parks linked Moore with America's mass culture. Not only did she write in adoration of Brooklyn's Dodgers; she also waxed poetic over New York's Mets and Yankees. The Dodgers, however, remained her first love.

When the Dodgers abandoned Brooklyn in 1957 for the sunnier California clime and the bigger bucks that beckoned, team owner Walter O'Malley, whose cupidity prompted the move, drove a dagger deep into the heart of its loyal fans, fans that included Moore. Baseball in Brooklyn went back to the Excelsiors, a local amateur club in 1854. Success invited emulation: the Atlantics in 1861 and the Eckfords in 1862 joined the competition for regional loyalty. Only one team turned professional in 1884, the team with an apt moniker, the Trolley Dodgers, a reference no doubt to an imperative survival skill in a busy burg blessed with modern transportation. The Dodgers switched from the American Association to the National League and celebrated the decade of the gay nineties in 1890 with a pennant victory and an anomalous tie for the world title.

Fortune eluded the Dodgers thereafter despite the construction of a new park, Ebbets Field, in 1913. Despite an occasional pennant in 1916 and 1920, they failed to win the world title. They became a team of "characters"—as eccentric as Moore with her tricorn hats, billowing capes, and mannered discourse, but with considerably less class. They stumbled and fumbled earning the name, the "Bums." Babe Herman, not Ruth, once doubled into a double play sliding into third base with two Dodgers already on the "hot corner." He also once fielded a fly ball after it caromed off his shoulder nearly decapitating him, though his detractors may have questioned whether he had a head to lose. On another embarrassing occasion, Herman lost a ground ball in the sun.[7] Catcher/Manager Wilbert Robinson, testing his macho on a dare, caught a grapefruit dropped from an airplane and was sent sprawling, saturated in exploding juice. Despite prohibition, many players were permanently "juiced." Some pitchers like the belligerent Burleigh Grimes and the bibulous Hugh Casey "juiced" their pitches, i.e., throwing the illegal "spitball." One such spitball cost the Dodgers a crucial World Series game in 1941 in the ninth inning of game four. The Dodgers were down in the Series two to one, but they were ahead in the game four to three. Two outs and two strikes: Casey faced Tommy Henrich, the Yankees' last hope. Suddenly, Henrich swung at strike three. Game over? No, the ball caromed wildly to the backstop. Catcher Mickey Owen could not recover in time. Henrich, the last out, was perched safely at first. The great DiMaggio followed with a single. Then Keller smashed a double off the right field screen. Dickey walked. Gordon doubled. Yanks won seven to four.[8] In 1951, Casey committed suicide. A few of the fanatic Dodger faithfuls quipped that this tragic event came ten years too late.

Generally, Dodger players generated more laughter than tears. Brooklyn produced a bumper crop of zanies, more colorful than grey. Even their names conveyed their uniqueness. Ebbetts Field attracted Casey Stengel, Van Lingle Mungo, Dazzy Vance, Dixie Walker, Goody Rosen, Eddie Stankey, Pete Reiser, Pee Wee Reese. Dodger fans kept the faith. Thirty-five thousand Brooklyn faithful packed into their secular shrine to root, toot, and pray for victory. Elfin leader Shorty Laurice conducted a band of music illiterates while Hilda Chester, resident eccentric with a voice composed of steel, added cow-bells and cacophony to the mix.[9]

Dodger fortunes improved under General Manager Branch Rickey who came to Brooklyn in 1943. He inspired conflicting emotions and labels: "Mahatma" for his wisdom and "El Cheapo" for his parsimony. Rickey consistently mined the Dodger farm system and repeatedly found baseball gold. His most glittering prize, Jackie Robinson, revolutionized baseball. Facing a traditional taboo, Rickey chose Robinson to break the color barrier for all sports. As an officer and gentleman, a junior college graduate, a solid family man, and a magnificent athlete, Jackie Robinson was the logical choice for this noble experiment. In his brilliant ten-year major league career, Robinson led a stellar cast—celebrated in Moore's famous poem "Hometown Piece for Mssrs. Alston and Reese"—to glory in Brooklyn. Under his fiery aegis, the Dodgers won six National League titles, three second places (two on the last day of play) and one—the first ever—world championship in 1955.[10]

Win or lose, the Dodgers played a crucial role in the civic life of Brooklyn, which by 1940 eclipsed Manhattan as the city's most populated borough. Half of Brooklyn's adults at that time were foreign born.[11] As a microcosm of America, an ethnic, religious, and cultural pastiche, Brooklyn lacked homogeneity. Clearly, the Dodgers provided a unifying force for the Jews, Blacks, Irish, Italians, Poles, Norwegians, and native-born Americans like Marianne Moore. The "Bums" fostered the ideals of community, equality, and careers open to talent. They even inspired exquisite poetry.

Baseball and writing are both exciting, Moore observed, because "You can never tell with either / how it will go / or what you will do."[12] After writing in relative obscurity, acclaimed by the cognoscenti and ignored by the masses, Moore copped a Pulitzer Prize for poetry, a National Book Award for poetry, the Bollingen Prize, an honorary degree from Dickinson College, and a Youth Oscar Award from Brooklyn's Youth United for a Better Tomorrow in 1952.[13] That same year, the Brooklyn Dodgers blew a golden opportunity to win the coveted World Series. They were leading those "damned Yankees," three games to two and ahead two to zero late in game six when Yankee lightning struck. Yogi Berra hit a home run for their first run, and Vic Raschi singled to tie the game which was won by Mickey Mantle's four bagger, with a score of three to two to send the series to a deciding seventh game. The Yanks won again, three to two; the Dodgers continued as "Bums."[14]

In 1953, Moore added a Gold Medal for Poetry from the National Institute of Arts and Letters; an honorary degree from Long Island University; a visiting lectureship at her alma mater, Bryn Mawr; and the M. Carey Thomas Award to her laurels. In that year, the Dodgers lost their fifth attempt to unseat the champion Yankees. Finally, in 1955 the Bums shed their skin and loser image: they beat the Yankees in seven games. When they tried to repeat in 1956, Moore exhorted them in the poem "Hometown Piece for Messrs. Alston and Reese," which appeared in the *New York Herald Tribune* on October 3rd.

> You've got plenty: Jackie Robinson
> and Campy and big Newk, and Dodgerdom again
> watching everything you do. You won last year. Come on.

With an almost strident urgency, Moore exhorted the Dodgers to repeat their world series victory of 1955 in the coda of this poem. She begins with a lullaby associated with Southern, perhaps Negro folklore.

> "Li'l baby, don't say a word: Mama goin' to buy you a mocking-bird . . ."

There is an abrupt transition to

> "Millennium," yes; "pandemonium"!

Roy Campanella, the great Dodger catcher, enters leaping like a young lord followed by Johnny Podres, hero and Most Valuable Player of the 1955 Series. Then, the brass—Buzzi Bavasi, the General Manager, Sandy Amoros, an unlucky Cuban except for game seven in 1955 when he robbed Yogi Berra of a sure triple and two runs batted in. ". . . 'Everything's / getting better and better . . .'" for

> "'Hope springs eternal in the Brooklyn breast.'"

Moore offers an obscure reference to the IRS in the section that housed Dodger Symphoney in section 8, row 1: "Why Not Take All of Me—All of Me, Sir?" Duke of the round-tripper sends a 400 foot blast to the wall. Jim—not Junior here—Gilliam drops "a neat bunt"; Campy is on deck, a "stylish stout" squatting for pleasure where pay is the measure. He's a rock. (That's my metaphor, not Moore's.) She wishes that Willie Mays would join the Dodger pantheon with Roger Craig and Clem Labine on the Dodger nine. (Fat chance.) In the wings is Peewee Reese. "Ralph Branca has Preacher Roe's number. . . ." Why? And Don Bessent with a fast ball that faded into obscurity.

Gil Hodges—of the great glove and home run swing—"in custody of first" (as policeman?) stretches into the stands where "He defeats / expectation by a whisker." A perfectionist, Hodges "The modest star, / irked by one misplay, is no hero by a hair." Is this a reference to the Biblical Samson? In an earlier series with the Yankees, Hodges went for the collar: zero for twenty-one including several Ks (strikeouts) in clutch moments. The local parish priest offered prayers for the Bedford Avenue hero, but nothing helped at that time, October 1952. Now, four years later, Hodges recovered his stroke. Perhaps the penitential worked, belatedly. He emerged from "strike-out slaughter" with a mighty blast (or smight) to the scoreboard which Moore idiosyncratically calls "the signboard" and "changed the score." Furillo follows in "his nineteenth season" (actually he had joined the Dodgers in 1946 so it was his tenth season). Rifle-armed Carl, nicknamed "the Skoonj" after a favorite Italian dish, scungilli, is identified as the "big gun" who "almost dehorned the foe."

Moore turns to Jake Pitler, an elderly, white-haired Jewish coach who gets a night "made heartier by a harrier / who can bat as well as field—Don Demeter." This name certainly conjures up Greek lore. Here, Moore's judgment errs. His god-like name notwithstanding, Demeter quickly descended into mediocrity. Moore earns redemption, however, with a switch in time to Carl Erskine, twirler of shut-outs and that wicked curve. A good hitting pitcher (almost an oxymoron), he left "Cimoli nothing to do." In an uplifting coda, Moore exhorts the faithful:

> Take off the goat-horns, Dodgers, that egret
> which two very fine base-stealers can offset.
>
> You've got plenty: Jackie Robinson
> and Campy and big Newk, and Dodgerdom again
> watching everything you do. You won last year. Come on.[15]

The Dodgers left Brooklyn forever in 1957. Moore would follow in 1966. Her biographer Charles Molesworth observes that after 1960, Moore's Brooklyn had become a scary place with break-ins and people sleeping in front of her apartment building. The *New York Times* covered Marianne Moore's 1965 move to Manhattan in an article. Columnist Michael Stern pontificated that with Moore's departure, "Brooklyn had lost its last gem."[16]

Baseball did not lose its glitter in Moore's eyes. She continued to root passionately and write elegantly on this popular subject. Her marvelous poem "Baseball and Writing" rewards careful scrutiny.[17]

> Fanaticism? No. Writing is exciting
> and baseball is like writing.
>
> You can never tell with either
>   how it will go,
>   or what you will do;
> generating excitement—
> a fever in the victim—
> pitcher, catcher, fielder, batter.
>   Victim in what category?
>
> *Owl*/man watching from the press box?
>
>   To whom does it apply?
>   Who is excited. Might it be I?

Wow! What writer could match this imagery? Moore goes on to describe a " . . . pitcher's battle all the way—a duel." Cat-like, she pounces on a personal favorite, Elston Howard, the catcher/outfielder "with cruel / puma paw, Elston Howard lumbers lightly / back to plate." Having hit a gaudy .348 to win the batting title in 1961, Howard helped the Yankees to repeat in 1962, minus the hitting crown. He is "very satisfied" because "We won." The Yankees took the San Francisco Giants in another seven game thriller.

The Yankees who earned Moore's loyalty after the Dodger departure hailed the versatile Bronx team which had " . . . three players on a side play three positions / and modify conditions." Here, she could be referring to a trinity of Yankee catchers—Howard, Berra, and Blanchard who were diverted from the backstop to outfield and first base in order to get their heavy lumber into the daily lineup.

Marianne Moore echoes announcer Mel Allen—"'Going, going . . .' Is / it?" Then Roger Maris makes a catch that no one can match. Mickey Mantle's fielding skill invites more attention from Moore than his vaunted hitting and destructive drinking. "Mickey, leaping like the devil" snares, one-handed, "the souvenir-to-be / meant to be caught by you or me." Yogi Berra is consigned to Secretary of Defense as it were, because "he could handle any missile." Fielding again catches Moore's eagle eye. Cletus Boyer makes two magnificent saves from the knee. Whitey Ford has three kinds of pitches (including a wicked spitball) "with pick-off psychosis." Moore astutely observes that a crafty pitcher like Ford "can learn to / catch the corners."

Aggressive pitchers aim at Mickey Mantle's knees. Vulnerable, not unlike the fleet-footed Achilles and plagued with "Muscle kinks, infections, spike wounds," the Mick stands tall in the box, not Pandora's, and concentrates on victory. He needs ". . . food, rest, respite from ruffians (Drat it! / Celebrity costs privacy!)." Moore also prescribes health food, *"Cow's* milk, 'tiger's milk,' soy milk, carrot juice, / brewer's yeast (high-potency) . . . sped by Luis Arroyo . . ." the roly-poly relief pitcher from Puerto Rico with a screwball or "scroogie" and Hector Lopez, who is " . . . deadly in a pinch." Led by Manager Houk and Coach Sain, the Yankees win again: a galaxy of nine with each contributing. In the end, the sage Moore counsels Yankee brass:

> if you have a rummage sale,
> don't sell Roland Sheldon or Tom Tresh,
>   Studded with stars in belt and crown,
>   the Stadium is an adastrium.
>   O flashing Orion,
>   your stars are muscled like the lion.

On June 14, 1967, eighty years of stardom earned Marianne Moore an honorary degree from New York University. The citation read: "Native of Missouri, daughter of Bryn Mawr, neighbor in Greenwich Village, fan of the Brooklyn Dodgers, laureate of the Brooklyn Bridge." Two out of five—a hefty .400 batting average in any league—links Moore to Brooklyn. The honorary doctorate goes on to describe Moore as "lover of the vital, the exact, and the genuine, fastidious poet of candor and restraint, distinguished and beloved lady of literature."[18] Still rooted to her former place, Moore remembered the trees. One of her last best poems, "The Camperdown Elm" evokes time and place and vulnerability. Her favorite elm, found in Prospect Park, is losing ground in the struggle for survival. Moore contrasts this endangered species with another elm as imagined in Asher Durand's painting of William Cullen Bryant and Thomas Cole, *Kindred Spirits.* To be sure there are lindens, sycamores, maples, oaks, and horse-chestnuts, but Moore favors the Camperdown elm which needs tree-food and props. " . . . It is still leafing; / still there; *mortal* though. We must save it. It is / our crowning curio."[19]

In this signature poem, Moore captures her former borough: mortal, imperiled, abandoned, but still leafing. The obituaries of Brooklyn penned in the decade of Moore's death in 1972 were—like the reported demise of Mark Twain—premature. It is clear that Moore found an appropriate metaphor for Brooklyn's resurrection in the local elm. Inspired, she wrote some of her best poetry and prose while living in Brooklyn. And many literary critics miss her message because they comprehend neither our borough nor our baseball. Both served as Muses for Marianne Moore.

Notes

1. This observation first appeared in *Vogue* 136 (August 1, 1960): 143 and is quoted from *The Complete Prose of Marianne Moore,* edited by Patricia C. Willis (New York: Elizabeth Sifton Books/Viking, 1986), p. 547.

2. Robert Cantwell, *Sports Illustrated,* February 1960.

3. Bernard F. Engle, *Marianne Moore* (New York: Twayne Publishers, 1964), pp. 32-33.

4. Ibid., pp. 34-36.

5. Marianne Moore, "Brooklyn From Clinton Hill," *Vogue* 136 (August 1, 1960): 82-83, 140 as reprinted in Willis, *Complete Prose,* pp. 539-40.

6. Ibid., pp. 540-47.

7. For Floyd "Babe" Herman's antics, see Richard Whittingham, *Los Angeles Dodgers: An Illustrated History* (New York: Harper and Row, 1982), pp. 33-45. Other Dodger lore can be found in a variety of sources. Among the best are: Donald Honig, *The Brooklyn Dodgers* (New York: St. Martin's Press, 1981); Harvey Frommer, *New York City Baseball: The Last Golden Age: 1947-1957* (New York: Macmillan 1980); and Peter Golenbock, *Bums: An Oral History of the Brooklyn Dodgers* (New York: G. P. Putnam's Sons, 1984). Gene Schoor, *The Complete Dodgers Record Book* (New York: Facts on File, 1984) provides vital statistics.

8. Joseph Dorinson, oral interview, "New York: The Way It Was—the Brooklyn Years," first telecast on WLIW, Channel 21, Spring 1996; also see Golenbock, *Bums,* p. 74.

9. John Durant, *The Dodgers: An Illustrated History of Those Unpredictable Bums* (New York: Hastings House Publishers, 1948), pp. 139-42.

10. Jules Tygiel, *Baseball's Great Experiment: Jackie Robinson and His Legacy* (New York: Random House, 1985) provides the most insightful narration of this pivotal period in baseball history.

11. Ron Miller, Rita Seiden Miller, and Stephen J. Karp, "The Fourth Largest City. A Sociological History of Brooklyn," in *Brooklyn USA: The Fourth Largest City in America,* edited by Rita Seiden Miller (Brooklyn: Brooklyn College Press, 1979), pp. 26-29.

12. Marianne Moore, *The Complete Poems of Marianne Moore* (New York: Macmillan/Viking Press, 1967), p. 221.

13. Engel, *Marianne Moore,* p. 14.

14. Golenbock, *Bums,* pp. 320-25.

15. Moore, *Complete Poems,* pp. 182-84.

16. Charles Molesworth, *Marianne Moore: A Literary Life* (New York: Atheneum, 1990), pp. 425-26.

17. Moore, *Complete Poems,* pp. 221-23.

18. Sister M. Therese, *Marianne Moore: A Critical Essay* (New York: William B. Eerdmans Publishing, 1969), p. 11.

19. Moore, *Complete Poems,* p. 242.

Additional Works Consulted

Costello, Bonnie. *Marianne Moore: Imaginary Possessions.* Cambridge: Harvard University Press, 1981.

Hall, Donald. *Marianne Moore: The Cage and the Animal.* New York: Pegasus, 1970.

Nitchie, George W. *Marianne Moore: An Introduction to the Poetry.* New York: Columbia University Press, 1969.

Sargeant, Winthrop. "Humility, Concentration and Gusto," in *The New Yorker* 32 (February 16, 1957):38-73.

Tomlinson, Charles, ed. *Marianne Moore: A Collection of Critical Essays.* Englewood Cliffs: Prentice-Hall, 1969.

26. Alicia Patterson and the Shape of Long Island

Robert F. Keeler

She was born into a wealthy, influential family in America's heartland, endowed with riches, a restless intelligence, raw charm, and a bountiful store of courage that grew from her awkward role as a daughter forced to act like a son. But in the early years of Alicia Patterson's life, it seemed doubtful that she would ever amount to anything. She attended the best private schools in America and Europe, but she managed to get herself kicked out of two of them. She made her society debut at an expensive coming-out party in a Chicago hotel, but a few months later, making another debut—as a reporter for her father's newspaper, the *New York Daily News*—she fouled up one of her first stories so badly that her own father fired her.

Returning home ignominiously to Chicago, a sad failure before the age of twenty-one, she soon married a department store executive's son and dashed off for a long honeymoon in the horse country of England. That marriage, which began disintegrating in a series of arguments on the honeymoon, lasted only a year. She traveled the world, became a record-setting pilot and an experienced hunter, and married a man who shared her interests in flying, hunting, and fishing.

Her second husband, Joseph W. Brooks, a fishing buddy of her father, was fifteen years older than she. At first, they were quite happy, living in a house that her father had rented to her for $1 a year in Sands Point. She loved Brooks for his courage, his sportsmanship, and his engaging personality, but in less than a decade, she had decided that her second marriage was simply too frivolous. "As the years went on, I began to feel restive about a life based on sports," she later wrote. "Joe and I grew apart."[1]

With this shaky, seemingly purposeless start, she could very easily have become the stereotypical poor little rich girl, living a life of great leisure and little impact, but by the time she died in 1963 at the age of fifty-six, Patterson had in many ways shaped the growth of her adopted home, Long Island. What turned her around and molded her into someone who helped shape her community, physically and socially? What made the poor little rich girl into a Long Island power, the editor and publisher of one of the most successful new newspapers of the postwar era?

To begin with, she had something restless in her personality, a burning will to show the world that she could be as good a journalist as her father, one of the most influential newspaper executives of the century. When Alicia Patterson arrived in the world on October 15, 1906, Joseph Medill Patterson already had one daughter and was ready for a son. His response to his second daughter's birth was to slam the door, walk out, and stay away for days.

"He had wanted a boy, instead of three daughters in succession, and that meant one of the Patterson girls would have to be his substitute son," Miss Patterson wrote later.[2] So, as she grew up, her chief desire was to please her father, to hunt with him, to fish with him, and to show all the physical courage that any son would have showed. "Father seemed to get a kick out of having me do dangerous things," she said to an interviewer from *The New Yorker.* "In fact, what with one thing and another, I kept getting so scared that finally I wasn't scared of anything anymore."[3]

In her youth, she watched her father increase in stature, first as one of the leaders of the family business, the *Chicago Tribune,* then as founder of America's first successful tabloid, the *New York Daily News,* which opened in 1919 and reached a circulation of one million by the end of 1925.[4] During those years, even as she struggled with the unruly instincts that made school a difficult adventure, she began aspiring to follow her father into journalism.

The other crucial element in her conversion from playgirl to woman of substance was her third marriage to one of her Sands Point neighbors, Harry Frank Guggenheim. Guggenheim was sixteen years older than Patterson, but that was not the most important difference between them. For one thing, there was the matter of life experience. At the time they met, she had done little of substance beyond writing a few articles for *Liberty,* a magazine that her father had established, and setting a few women's flying records. In sharp contrast, Guggenheim was a man of immense accomplishment.

Guggenheim grew up in a wealthy Jewish family that had come to America to flee anti-Semitism in Switzerland and had made a fortune in mining and smelting. He had been an executive of one family-owned business, Chile Copper, had become one of the first naval aviators in World War I, and had helped his father, Daniel Guggenheim, to establish a foundation that would help develop the American aviation industry. Among other things, Guggenheim money in those years established a model airline, paid for a cross-country tour by Charles Lindbergh after his Paris flight, arranged for the first-ever instruments-only flight, and bankrolled Robert Goddard's rocket experiments. In addition, Harry Guggenheim had served as American ambassador to Cuba from 1929 to 1933 and built his own thoroughbred racing stable, Cain Hoy.

Their personalities and political beliefs, too, were sharply different. She was liberal. He was conservative. She was impulsive and fun-loving. He was serious and earnest. She had little sense of the value of money, because her father had always supplied her with whatever she needed. He was prodigiously careful with a dollar.

When they married in 1939, one of Guggenheim's primary concerns was to keep his new wife busy and out of trouble. Patterson believed that her father would someday leave her in a position of power at the *News*. Guggenheim felt that she should prepare for that opportunity by running a small newspaper of her own. To find the right newspaper, they sought the help of her father's friend, Max Annenberg, the circulation director at the *News*.

In the summer of 1939, while they were on their honeymoon at Goddard's rocket-testing site in New Mexico, Annenberg telegraphed them that he had found a good opportunity. The *Nassau Daily Journal,* a small paper located in a former auto dealership in Hempstead, had opened on March 1, 1939, and closed on March 10th. The paper's equipment was still sitting in the building, unused.

"On the arrival of Max's telegram, Alicia balked," Guggenheim later wrote. "She wanted, at that moment, to give up the whole idea."[5] But Guggenheim was adamant. He insisted that they go through with the deal, and she finally agreed. At that critical turning-point in her life, Guggenheim had supplied the wisdom and determination to push her into the first step toward her own life of accomplishment. The result was the establishment of *Newsday* on September 3, 1940. Not long after that, Guggenheim returned to active duty in the Navy and was assigned to command a naval air station near Trenton. That left Patterson running the paper solo in its early, formative years.

Her first contribution to Long Island was to bring competition to a newspaper market dominated by one party and one newspaper, the *Nassau Daily Review-Star*. Its publisher, James Stiles, was not only a member of Nassau County's dominant Republican Party, but he was also a committeeman. He was generous to the Republicans, publishing "thousands of dollars' worth of political advertising as a contribution to the party, and to individual candidates he wanted to help."[6] And the party was generous to Stiles, placing county legal ads—a profitable form of advertising—with his paper.

In 1941, only a few months after *Newsday* opened, Patterson launched a campaign to wrestle the legal advertisements away from the *Review-Star*. In addition to arguing its merits before the county's board of supervisors, *Newsday* campaigned in the newspaper itself, accusing Stiles of running up the cost to the taxpayers by setting the legal ads in a larger-than-normal typeface, surrounded by white space. *Newsday* argued that it could provide this service to the taxpayers at much lower cost.

The campaign finally succeeded when the county awarded the ads to *Newsday* in 1944. That was the first serious challenge to the monolithic dominance of the Nassau County Republican Party. Three years later, the two papers took opposing positions on an issue that was pivotal to the future growth of Long Island.

With the end of World War II, millions of veterans streamed back to the United States, ready to put the war behind them and start their families. What they found was a cruel housing shortage. Veterans ended up living with in-laws or in such substandard forms of housing as quonset huts and trolley cars. In consequence, wrote suburbia expert Kenneth T. Jackson, "the great American land rush after 1945 was one of the largest mass movements in our history."[7]

In the metropolitan area, much of New York City itself had already been developed. So the wide-open spaces of Long Island became the natural target for new home construction. Even before the war ended, *Newsday* had carried a five-part series in 1944 on the need for cheap, mass-produced homes.[8] The inspiration for the series was apparently a letter from Patterson's neighbor, Albert Wood, stressing the need for houses that would cost under $5,000. Wood had been the construction engineer for the Ford subsidiary that built inexpensive housing for Ford employees in Dearborn, Michigan. In that project, workers moved from house to house, performing the same functions on each, to speed construction.

That sort of assembly-line construction was exactly what the firm of Levitt & Sons had in mind for postwar Nassau County. Before the war ended, the Levitts had already begun to buy up the land and put together the needed materials that they later used in mass producing homes that they could rent to returning veterans at reasonable prices. On May 7, 1947, the lead story in *Newsday* detailed those plans, under the headline: "2,000 $60 Rentals Due in L.I. Project."

The problem with their plan was that they hoped to build on concrete slabs, without basements, and heat the houses with radiant heating pipes imbedded in the slab. But the Town of Hempstead's building code required cellars. *Newsday* jumped on the issue with both feet, citing Wood's expertise as evidence that cellarless homes were the wave of the future, and arguing strongly in an editorial that nothing should stand in the way of the Levitt plan. "The Island Trees project is big, practical, and ideal enough to make national news," the editorial said. "If it were prevented by the code it would make Long Island a national laughing stock."[9]

But Nassau County Republicans had their doubts. The expressed reasons had to do with the viability of the radiant heating plan. But the unspoken subtext was apparently a fear that thousands of veterans moving to Long Island from New York City would be Democrats. If the Republican Party was cautious, so was James Stiles, the publisher of the *Review-Star*. "If a revolutionary change in home construction is in process we will have to recognize it and reconcile ourselves to it," the *Review-Star* editorial said. "But we should be extremely cautious not to permit the existing shortage of houses to stampede us into junking all the precautions that have been adopted to protect individual purchasers and the standard of entire communities."[10]

During the interval between the announcement of the Levitt plan and the town board meeting at which the proposed ordinance change would be discussed, *Newsday* hammered relentlessly at the issue. Finally, confronted with a large crowd and an emotional appeal for housing, the town board unanimously approved the code change that allowed Levitt & Sons to build what later became Levittown.[11]

The key *Newsday* operative in this Levitt campaign was not Patterson herself, but her managing editor, Alan Hathway, an old-fashioned, hard-drinking, crude, rowdy, go-for-the-knees newspaperman who had learned his trade in the brawling era of Chicago journalism in the 1920s and who later worked as an editor at Joseph Medill Patterson's *Daily News*. From the time Patterson made him managing editor in 1944, she allowed Hathway wide latitude to set the gutsy tone that she wanted for *Newsday's* aggressive reporting of local politics.

She occasionally had to rein him in, as she did soon after the war, when he actually used *her* typewriter to help a veterans' group craft a response to an expected attack by the Nassau Republicans over some garden apartments that the group wanted built. Once Hathway had helped them write the response, he put it in the paper. The Republicans found out and complained to Guggenheim, who relayed the complaint to Patterson. She had to warn Hathway never to do that again, but he kept his job.[12] Patterson also had to rein Hathway in during the early 1960s, when he put the paper's resources behind a plan by master builder Robert Moses to build a highway the length of Fire Island. Hathway was not a disinterested observer; he owned property on Fire Island and stood to benefit by construction of the road.

The road's opponents considered it a potential environmental disaster and advocated instead that the area become a national seashore. One of them, an environmentally conscious developer named Murray Barbash, met with Patterson and arranged a meeting between her and Secretary of the Interior Stewart Udall in Washington. The visit with Udall and his aide, Walter Pozen, helped convince her that *Newsday* should abandon the road and push exclusively for the national seashore. That change of heart was crucial to the creation of the Fire Island National Seashore. "So *Newsday* was incredibly important in that respect," Barbash said.[13]

Though Hathway required occasional throttling back, he was the driving force behind the investigation of William DeKoning, a corrupt union boss who was able to control much of the Long Island construction industry. That investigation of DeKoning won for *Newsday* its first Pulitzer Prize, in 1954. It also set a pattern for a *Newsday* tradition of aggressive investigative reporting.

One of the keys to the success of that investigation was a young reporter named Robert W. Greene, who is now leading the development of the journalism program in Hofstra's School of Communications. Hathway hired Greene from the New York City Anti-Crime Committee, where he was an investigator. At *Newsday,* Greene turned his skills to the DeKoning investigation.

In the years that followed, Greene pioneered a new level of investigative reporting. Before Greene, most investigative reporting relied on friendly sources inside government agencies to drop copies of investigative reports into the laps of reporters. Greene pioneered and developed journalistic techniques that allowed the newspaper to construct its own investigative reports by aggressive and intelligent use of raw documents.

In later years, investigative projects led by Greene focused on such targets as widespread land corruption in Suffolk County. Of all *Newsday* investigations, perhaps none had greater impact than a two-year probe of the LILCO Shoreham nuclear plant. The reporter was a Greene disciple named Stuart Diamond. His 1981 series fundamentally changed the political atmosphere and ultimately led to the decommissioning of the plant before it had even opened.

It was Patterson who established the overall atmosphere in which Bob Greene flourished and helped to change in lasting ways the face of Long Island. Though she delegated much of the detail work to Hathway, there were matters that she handled very much on her own, especially presidential politics.

Soon after the war, she began arguing in *Newsday* that General Dwight D. Eisenhower should run for the presidency. In 1952, *Newsday* heavily promoted a Garden City rally that served as a preliminary to a larger rally at Madison Square Garden, aimed at persuading the general to run. Later, *Newsday's* circulation department actually gave out "WE LIKE IKE" buttons. Patterson herself interviewed Eisenhower in Europe and reported back rhapsodically. "It was a blessed relief at long last to talk to a man who appears to be above the slime of our present-day politics," she wrote in a full-page report. "I am more convinced than ever that I LIKE IKE."[14]

But she soon found herself on the horns of a dilemma when the Democratic opponent to Eisenhower turned out to be her close friend, Illinois Governor Adlai Stevenson. Patterson had known Stevenson in Chicago in the 1920s, and some friends say he may even have proposed marriage to her then. In 1946, when he moved to New York to work at the United Nations, they renewed their acquaintance. From then until her death in 1963, they kept up a constant correspondence. Most of her letters are lost to history, but Stevenson's letters are filled with terms of endearment almost adolescent in their intensity and with admiration for her toughness and talent.

"So you've made it—you indomitable little tiger," he wrote her after *Newsday* passed the 100,000 circulation mark in 1949. "I could bite your ears with savage joy."[15] Stevenson also relied on her judgment as he wrestled with the question of whether to run for the presidency. It was in a letter to Patterson that he first hinted he might accept a draft by the Democratic convention.[16] Even as she pushed for Eisenhower, she worked to persuade Guggenheim's nephew, Roger W. Straus, Jr., of Farrar, Straus & Giroux, to publish a Stevenson campaign biography, which Straus did. "It was an enormous seller," he recalled.[17]

Once Stevenson decided to run in 1952, Patterson had to do an agile dance on the editorial pages. While not backing down from her support for Eisenhower, she made it clear that Stevenson would also be an excellent choice, for those inclined to vote Democrat. She even hosted a supper for Stevenson at Manhattan's prestigious River Club to introduce him to newspaper publishers.

Of course, Eisenhower beat Stevenson easily in 1952. Stevenson ran against him again in 1956. This time, Patterson, instead of endorsing the incumbent Republican, endorsed Stevenson. This stunned Guggenheim, who had told a Republican friend that *Newsday* would back Eisenhower. This surprise endorsement was one of the central reasons for a marital disagreement in 1957 that nearly resulted in divorce, as Guggenheim tried to assert editorial control of the paper, and his wife resisted. Patterson went so far as to type a letter of resignation.[18] But in the end, they stayed together. She could not bear the thought of losing *Newsday*.

The bitter conclusion to the 1956 campaign planted the seeds of a bizarre arrangement in 1960. Guggenheim, the arch-conservative, was a firm supporter of Richard Nixon. Patterson initially supported Stevenson but Senator John F. Kennedy met with her and her staff for lunch on Long Island, and he charmed her. She promised him that he would be her second choice for the nomination. At the convention, when it became clear that Kennedy would be the nominee, Patterson deputized Bob Greene to meet with Robert Kennedy and try to get a promise that the senator would make Stevenson his secretary of state, in exchange for Stevenson's support at the convention. That ploy failed, and she came around to support Kennedy.

Newsday endorsed Kennedy, but it was not simple. Over the endorsing editorial was an editor's note with Patterson's signature: "The opinions of this newspaper are expressed in the editorial column. Today we endorse John F. Kennedy for President of the United States. The reasons for our choice are set forth below. In a column on the opposite page my husband, Harry F. Guggenheim, president of *Newsday*, states his personal endorsement of Vice President Richard M. Nixon for President."[19]

Between that time and election day, Guggenheim took several more opportunities to sound a pro-Nixon counterpoint to his wife's pro-Kennedy editorials—surely one of the strangest juxtapositions of political opinion ever to appear in a major newspaper. The last laugh, however, belonged to Patterson. Not only did Kennedy win, but he was grateful enough for her support that he acceded to her request for a White House lunch. It was at that lunch that she made her pitch for his help on an issue that shaped the face of Long Island.

The issue was a struggle over the future use of Mitchel Field, a former military air base. A group of businessmen wanted it converted to a general aviation airport. Though she was herself a pilot, Patterson felt that the area around the base was so heavily developed that any aviation use was unsafe. There were plenty of other potential uses for the base, including space for Hofstra University and Nassau Community College.

At Patterson's White House lunch with Kennedy, the issue came up. With little hesitation, Kennedy picked up the phone and called Najeeb Halaby, the administrator of the Federal Aviation Administration. In a brief conversation, Kennedy instructed Halaby to close Mitchel Field down. Bill Woestendiek, one of Patterson's key aides, recalled: "Then he turned around, put the phone down. He said: 'It's closed. . . .' That was very impressive."[20]

Of course, the saga of Mitchel Field has been anything but uncomplicated since then. It has been the center of hundreds of stories, as politicians fought over its use. If it had not been for Alicia Patterson, however, Mitchel Field might very well have become a general aviation airport, which would certainly have altered the way this corner of Nassau County eventually developed. Though she grew up in Chicago, Patterson was a strong partisan of the community that her newspaper served. "She really did represent Long Island," said her friend, Phyllis Cerf Wagner. "She felt so fiercely about it, as if she'd grown up there. . . . It was her child, as the newspaper was her child."[21]

To protect her child, *Newsday,* she stayed in a marriage that had gone sour. Over the years, that dedication to *Newsday* had an impact on her adopted community that went beyond merely a road not built on Fire Island and an airport not operating in the center of Nassau County. She was an early advocate of women's equality, filling her newsroom with female reporters from the start. She was a voice of sanity standing up to the abuses of the McCarthy era. She nurtured an aggressive style at the newspaper that provided a vigilant watchdog over Long Island's dominant one-party culture. Her newspaper helped create a Long Island identity for a fragmented community that had been little more than a collection of small villages separated by trees.

Alicia Patterson had her pet causes and her favored friends, her blind spots, and her odd quirks. But when you add it all up, she created *Newsday,* an institution that has lasted more than a half century, and she significantly influenced the development of Long Island, the shape of its demography, and the expansion of its major centers for higher education in Nassau County. By any rational measure, that is a substantial epitaph for someone who could have remained just a poor little rich girl.

Notes

1. Alicia Patterson and Hal Burton, "This is the Life I Love," *Saturday Evening Post,* February 21, 1959, p. 45.

2. Ibid., p. 44. Despite her three marriages, people at *Newsday* always called her Miss Patterson or Miss P.

3. John M. Flagler, untitled, unpublished manuscript about Alicia Patterson written for *The New Yorker,* 1963, part 1, pp. 14-15, in the Alicia Patterson papers at Newsday.

4. Leo E. McGivena, *The News: The First Fifty Years of New York's Picture Newspaper* (New York: News Syndicate, 1969).

5. Harry F. Guggenheim, *Newsday,* "Silver Anniversary Edition," September 10, 1965.

6. Edward Uhlan, *Dynamo Jim Stiles: Pioneer of Progress* (New York: Exposition Press, 1959), p. 96.

7. Kenneth T. Jackson, *The Crabgrass Frontier: The Suburbanization of the United States* (New York: Oxford University Press, 1985), p. 282.

8. *Newsday,* September 28-29, October 2-4, 1944.

9. *Newsday,* May 8, 1947.

10. *Nassau Daily Review-Star,* May 22, 1947.

11. *Newsday,* May 28, 1947.

12. Interview with Paul Townsend, December 9, 1987.

13. Interview with Murray Barbash, March 8, 1988.

14. *Newsday,* May 22, 1952.

15. Letter, Adlai Stevenson to Alicia Patterson, March 8, 1949, in Alicia Patterson papers at Newsday.

16. Letter, Adlai Stevenson to Alicia Patterson, March 13, 1949; Porter McKeever, *Adlai Stevenson: His Life and Legacy* (New York: William Morrow, 1989), pp. 182, 187-88.

17. Interview with Roger Straus, May 20, 1987.

18. Draft of resignation statement, December 1957, in Alicia Patterson papers at Newsday.

19. *Newsday,* October 25, 1960.

20. Interview with Bill Woestendiek, February 24, 1988.

21. Interview with Phyllis Cerf Wagner, September 16, 1987.

27. Barbara McClintock: An Overview of a Long Island Scientist

Janice Koch

It might seem unfair to reward a person for having so much pleasure over the years, asking the maize plant to solve specific problems and then watching its responses.

—Barbara McClintock, upon receipt of the Nobel Prize, 1983[1]

Barbara McClintock (1902-1992) is one of the ten women scientists in the world who have been awarded the Nobel Prize. Born in Hartford, Connecticut, she moved with her parents, her younger brother, and two older sisters to the Flatbush section of Brooklyn in 1908, where she received her elementary and secondary education. As McClintock pursued her academic interests in science, specifically genetics, she did not return to Long Island to live until 1942, when she took up residency and a research position at the Cold Spring Harbor Laboratory where she lived and worked until her death in September 1992.

During her fifty years at the Cold Spring Harbor Laboratory, McClintock gained national, and then international, recognition for her research on transposable elements as controlling factors for gene expression in the cells of the maize plant. This essay explores the historical and social contexts of Barbara McClintock's work, work that was honored with the Nobel Prize in Physiology or Medicine in 1983. It addresses the way McClintock saw herself in the larger context of professional science and the ways in which feminist scientists analyze her research style and assign their own meaning to it.

Finding the Answer

Barbara McClintock's solitary life was rooted in her childhood. As a child, she was happiest in her solitary experiences: reading, exploring, intensely absorbed just "thinking about things."[2] Her biographer reports that, even as a little girl, McClintock had an uncanny capacity to be alone and to entertain herself. McClintock's parents were supportive of their children's interests and encouraged their daughter's musings and her love of sports activities; however, her mother was concerned when McClintock did not outgrow her tomboy interests by adolescence.

As a student at Erasmus Hall High School in Brooklyn, McClintock discovered science and the profound pleasure of solving problems. She later recalled: "I loved information. I loved to know things. . . . I would ask the instructor, 'Please, let me . . . see if I can't find the standard answer' and I'd find it. It was a tremendous joy, the whole process of finding that answer, just pure joy."[3]

Mrs. McClintock feared that Barbara's intense intellectual interests and her desire for a college education would lead her to become a college professor and make her unmarriageable, so she opposed Barbara's wish to attend college until she was out of high school for one year. During that time, McClintock worked for an employment agency and taught herself in the library in the evenings. Her mother relented in 1919, and McClintock began her undergraduate career at Cornell University's College of Agriculture. McClintock majored in botany, and when she earned her undergraduate degree in 1923, 74 of the 203 Bachelor of Science degrees that Cornell awarded were earned by women.[4]

By her junior year, McClintock had become fascinated with genetics and was invited to take graduate courses in the subject while she was an undergraduate. She continued her graduate work at Cornell; she earned her master's in botany in 1925 and her doctorate in 1927. It was only twenty-one years since the rediscovery, in 1900, of Gregor Mendel's principles of heredity, and Cornell faculty pioneered in the field of plant genetics, particularly in investigating maize, or Indian corn. McClintock explored the morphology of the ten maize chromosomes and established the correlations between the visible genetic traits and the cytological markers. Much of this work was done with graduate students Marcus Rhoades and George Beadle and they produced nine published papers. For all of them, corn cytogenetics became a passion that would last their entire lives.

A Capacity for Total Absorption

McClintock emerges, through her recollections in her biography, as a deeply-absorbed scientist whose capacities for total absorption were evident as a child. What was exceptional, according to her biographer Evelyn Fox Keller, was the "extent to which she maintained her childlike capacity for absorption throughout her adult life."[5]

McClintock remained at Cornell after completing her doctorate to continue her research on the relationship between chromosomes, genes, and other aspects of cytogenetics. She learned to cultivate her own corn plants and, by 1931, she published a landmark paper with Harriet Creighton. The paper provided evidence for genetic exchange between chromosomes, or crossing over: that chromosomes exchange genetic information and physical material when they cross over in early meiosis (cell division resulting in the number of chromosomes being reduced by half).[6] In 1931, she received a National Research Council Fellowship which funded her until 1933. During that time, she traveled from Cornell to the California Institute of Technology and to the University of Missouri, to study with and to collaborate with scholars at those institutions. She even traveled to Germany in 1933, on a Guggenheim Fellowship, but she returned abruptly, shocked and traumatized by the rise of Nazism.[7]

Despite her rising acclaim as a geneticist, her gender prevented her from being appointed to a faculty position at Cornell, and she watched as less capable males were accorded faculty status. By 1936, she secured employment at the University of Missouri at Columbia where she remained until 1941. She worked on the process by which broken chromosomes fuse, continuing her work with maize plants and continuing to publish. As a woman and as an independent thinker, she often demonstrated non-traditional behavior that left her on the margins of academia. She did not conform to the "lady scientist" role; she did what was expedient to advance her work. The culture of the university may have demanded a more politically astute professor than McClintock; after five years, still an assistant professor, she left the University of Missouri in 1941. She spent that summer working with her lifelong friend and colleague Marcus Rhoades, who had secured a position for her at Cold Spring Harbor Laboratory on Long Island. After a one-year temporary position, Milislav Demerec, Director of the Department of Genetics of the Carnegie Institution of Washington at Cold Spring Harbor, offered her a permanent position.

Cold Spring Harbor Laboratory, 1942–1992

McClintock's permanent position at Cold Spring Harbor gave her the stability to pursue the research which ultimately led to the discovery of the transposable elements for which she received the Nobel Prize in 1983. In 1944, she was elected president of the Genetics Society of America and became the third woman named to the prestigious National Academy of Sciences. In that same year, she was listed among the 1,000 top scientists in the United States by the new edition of *American Men* [*sic*] *of Science*.[8]

In 1951, when Barbara McClintock presented her theory of transposable genetic elements at Cold Spring Harbor Laboratory, it was neither understood nor accepted. She was later quoted in *Time* as saying, "They thought I was crazy, absolutely mad at times."[9] At that time in genetics, the central principle was the elucidation of the structure of DNA, the master molecule which encodes the genes, and was viewed as immovable beads on a string.

> In McClintock's system, the controlling elements did not correspond to stable loci on the chromosome—they moved. In fact, this capacity to change position, *transposition* as she called it, was itself a

property that could be controlled by regulator, or activator genes. This feature made her phenomenon a more complex one, and, in the minds of her contemporaries, less acceptable.[10]

In the 1970s, a series of genetic engineering experiments performed by molecular biologists demonstrated that pieces of bacterial DNA do "jump around" on the chromosomes; other research documented that transposition occurs not only in maize and bacteria, but in viruses, insects, and higher organisms.[11] When time caught up with McClintock's research on transposition, she became showered with awards. In 1970, she received the National Medal of Science, followed by the Albert Lasker Basic Medical Research Award in 1981. She also received the MacArthur Foundation Lifetime Annual Fellowship in 1981, and in 1982, she shared Columbia University's Horwitz Prize with Susumu Tonegawa.

By the time she received the Nobel prize in 1983, it was considered long overdue by both her colleagues and the general public. The media capitalized on some of the circumstances of McClintock's work and promoted her image as a loner, a recluse, a woman scientist who worked without the benefit of high tech equipment, and one whose work was ignored for over thirty years.[12] She was constantly described as a loner and captured the attention of the media as a counterpart to Gregor Mendel, a scientist who worked alone with plants and without complicated equipment in the nineteenth century. *Time* reported:

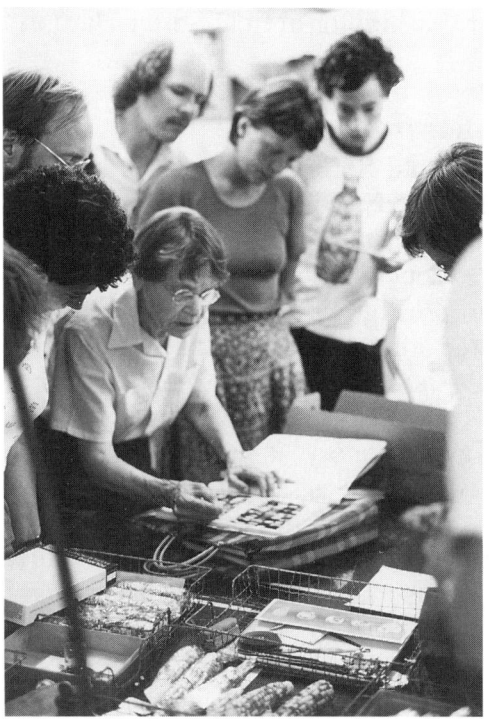

Genetics is a science founded by a monk, 19th century Augustinian Gregor Mendel—and McClintock is in every sense his disciple. For half a century she has labored in almost monastic solitude over her patch of Indian corn, or maize, much as Mendel did in his famous pea patch. In an era when most scientific work is done by large research teams, McClintock did not even have a laboratory assistant.[13]

Fig. 27.1 Barbara McClintock teaching at Plant Course at the Cold Spring Harbor Laboratory, 1981. Photography courtesy of Cold Spring Harbor Laboratory Archives.

The media was frustrated in its attempts to portray McClintock as "womanly." *Newsweek* called her the "Greta Garbo of genetics. At 81, she has never married, always preferring to be alone." The *New York Times* covered McClintock in a long feature article which began by saying that "she is well known for baking with black walnuts."[14] Typically, women scientists have been lauded by the press for being able to be feminine and motherly as well as scholarly. McClintock did not meet this media-driven criteria. She preferred, instead, a life filled with the joys of discovery and of investigation. In fact, it is just this pleasure that her biographer, Evelyn Fox Keller, captures so well.

"A Feeling for the Organism"

McClintock's views of nature inform much of the story of her life and her work. Her affection for and intimate knowledge of her maize plants was necessary in order for her to understand and make meaning of their complexity. McClintock believed in getting close to her objects of study, in listening to the material, and in hearing what is said about how it worked. It was an approach that was at odds with the dominant principles of objectivity and distance that undergird professional science.

To McClintock, nature was infinitely more complex than we could imagine; anything you can think of you will find: "No two plants are exactly alike. They're all different, and as a consequence, you have to know that difference. I start with the seedling and I don't want to leave it. I don't feel I really know the story if I don't watch the plant all the way along. So I know every plant in the field. I know them intimately, and I find it a great pleasure to know them."[15] As one of her colleagues described it, she could write an autobiography of every plant she works with.

When McClintock describes the state of mind that allowed her to identify chromosomes which she had earlier not been able to distinguish, she explained:

> I found that the more I worked with them, the bigger and bigger [they (the chromosomes)] got, and when I was really working with them I wasn't outside, I was down there. I was part of the system. I was right down there with them, and everything got big. I even was able to see the internal parts of the chromosomes—actually everything was there. It surprised me because I actually felt as if I were right down there and these were my friends. . . . As you look at these things, they become a part of you. And you forget yourself.[16]

McClintock's method was to listen to the material. Over and over she told her biographer that "one must have the patience to 'hear what the material has to say to you.' . . . Above all, one must have 'a feeling for the organism.'"[17]

In her own image of herself, Barbara McClintock was a maverick in all respects—as a woman, as a scientist, even as a woman scientist. She disclaimed any analysis of her work as woman's work as well as any suggestion that her views of nature represent a woman's perspective. Despite this, it has been very tempting for feminist scientists and feminist critiques of science to use McClintock's methodologies to represent the productive marriage between gender and science. Conceptualizing her "feeling for the organism" as uniquely integrating female intuition and affect, feminist scientists claim her way of thinking as an example of a feminist scientist's work. To McClintock, however, science was not a matter of gender, but the place where "the matter of gender drops away." Her rejection of female stereotypes seemed to have been a prerequisite for her becoming a scientist at all. In fact, her very commitment to science represented the part of her lifelong wish to transcend gender altogether.[18]

Because of the congruence between McClintock's views of nature and a feminist epistemology for science, some feminist scientists continue to cite her work as being carved from the fabric of her gender. Ruth Bleier remarked that McClintock's attitude towards this "object" nature gives new meaning to the relationship of objectivity and subjectivity and explodes them as rigid dichotomies. In fact, Bleier continued, had it not been for her extraordinary accomplishments, her views of nature would be dismissed as a romantic, poetic involvement with the natural world, a woman incapable of maintaining a proper distance from her object of study.[19] Feminist critiques of science argue that women, because of the ways that they are socialized, have privileged access to an alternative view of nature. While McClintock's alternative view of nature fits nicely into a feminist epistemology, McClintock disapproved adamantly of a feminist label for her work or her life.

McClintock's more holistic, less heirarchal conception of nature and her view of the connection between scientist and the object of study as essential is reminiscent of Rachel Carson's view of nature, her reverence for it, and her slow, plodding, deliberate struggle toward the publication of *Silent Spring* in 1962.[20] Feminist critics point to the centrality of the sense of oneness with nature as informing both McClintock and Carson's work. McClintock advised that we approach nature with humility and warned about the scientists who just accumulate data without taking time to look, and who apply technology before thinking about consequences. She said, "We've been spoiling the environment just dreadfully and thinking we were fine, because we are using techniques of science. . . . We were making assumptions we had no right to make."[21]

Because what it means to be "scientific" and "feminine" have been perceived as being in opposition to each other, a "woman scientist" suggests a contradiction in terms. McClintock's work appears to deny that contradiction and women scientists read into her Nobel Prize the possibility of an alternative to the classical scientific dichotomies. McClintock's story is compelling because it suggests the viability of difference in the world of science as we know it. The Nobel Prize invites both mainstream scientists and feminists to claim her as one of their own.[22] The reality of Barbara McClintock's life is that she rejected categories and labels and lived her own scientific life having fun with the maize plants by making their differences understandable.

The Final Years

In 1990, Lori Rosendale, a graduate student in my course in science education, interviewed Dr. McClintock to fulfill a course requirement. She convinced a reluctant McClintock to allow her a few minutes of her time which developed into a two-hour conversation that Rosendale recorded and summarized in an unpublished paper. This is the first opportunity to explore McClintock's thoughts from Rosendale's 1990 interview.

When Rosendale interviewed her, Barbara McClintock was living in a residence facility on the grounds of the Cold Spring Harbor Laboratory. After many years of renting a small house on Route 25A, she moved to the Laboratory campus because she could "no longer outrun the cars."[23] She explained that she had never wanted to buy her own home for fear that it would distract her from her work by consuming too much of her time. She shared the story of her feeling pressure in the 1940s to buy her own home when most researchers at Cold Spring Harbor were doing so. Everyone thought she was foolish to rent, but McClintock never regretted her decision,

and she referred to her dormitory living as "living on the reservation."[24] Behind the laboratory building that bears her name, there is a pale grey building with a lab and a small office with a large adjoining room. In this office, Lori Rosendale interviewed Barbara McClintock on an autumn day two years before her death.

Fig. 27.2. Barbara McClintock, 1990. Photograph courtesy of Cold Spring Harbor Laboratory Archives.

In the course of the conversation, McClintock spoke of the burden of being a public person and the demands that were made on her after receiving the Nobel Prize in 1983.

> I am considered public property . . . the same kind of property that entertaining people are, but they [entertainers] have to have it. That is for their benefit. They are entertainers; they are part of the public domain, and I'm not. It's quite an imposition. Sometimes, it's beyond belief. People will write and ask you questions—very intimate questions—even questions about your sex life. Or they'll ask you for money.[25]

McClintock unabashedly reported that her life "had been ruined by the Nobel—just ruined. Just one request after another request." Although curiously gracious to Lori, worrying about whether the sun was in her eyes, and apologizing for being so harsh about the requests, she seemed conflicted about her fame. Clearly, she wanted to be left alone to continue her work and to consult with other scientists; however, she did not want to seem ungracious about the public demands.

When Rosendale talked to McClintock about her education, and specifically her love of science, McClintock affirmed the stories about her education that had been reported by her biographer. She expressed her love of learning: "I loved any kind of learning. I could get absorbed in doorknobs and how they worked and their designs. It could just be fascinating . . . The best thing I could have was intellectual pleasure. Understanding, analyzing, and thinking through—it was very stimulating."[26]

One soon finds out that all issues come down to an individual level with Dr. McClintock. Rosendale explained that McClintock would not speak of the general experience of being a female scientist. "Each scientist must eek out his/her own life. If they're female; they're female. Get on with the business at hand," seemed to be McClintock's feeling as Rosendale summarized it. The notion that each person must do what is right for him or her was the philosophy by which she lived her life.

The most intriguing aspect of the interview for Rosendale was the sheer joy with which Dr. McClintock discussed science. The ways she spoke of science were almost sensual. It was the thing you could wrap your life around and fall in love with, this wonderful life experience. Before concluding the interview, Rosendale asked McClintaock if she could complete the sentence, "science is . . ." "Science is pure investigative pleasure," she answered warmly, "pure pleasure."[27]

Notes

The DNA Learning Center on Main Street in Cold Spring Harbor has an exhibit on Barbara McClintock which recreates her laboratory; call 516-367-7240 for directions and hours. (Editor's note.)

1. Barbara McClintock, "The Significance of the Responses of the Genome to Challenge," (Stockholm: Nobel Lecture, 1983).

2. Evelyn Fox Keller, *A Feeling for the Organism: The Life and Work of Barbara McClintock* (New York: W. H. Freeman and Co., 1983), p. 22.

3. Ibid., p. 26.

4. Ibid., p. 29.

5. Ibid., pp. 35-36.

6. Sue V. Rosser, *Biology and Feminism: A Dynamic Interaction* (New York: Twayne Publishers, 1992), p. 6.

7. Keller, *Feeling for the Organism,* pp. 70-72.

8. Rosser, *Biology and Feminism,* p. 8.

9. Barbara McClintock, "Jumping Genes," *Time,* November 30, 1981, p. 84.

10. Keller, *Feeling for the Organism,* pp. 8-9.

11. Rosser, *Biology and Feminism,* p. 8.

12. Ibid., p. 9.

13. *Time,* October 24, 1983, pp. 53-54.

14. Dorothy Nelkin, *Selling Science* (New York: W. H. Freeman and Co., 1987), p. 20.

15. Keller, *Feeling for the Organism,* p. 198.

16. Ibid., p. 117.

17. Ibid., p. 198.

18. Evelyn Fox Keller, *Reflections on Gender and Science* (New Haven: Yale University Press, 1985), p. 173.

19. Elizabeth Fee, "Critiques of Modern Science," in *Feminist Approaches to Science,* edited by Ruth Bleier (New York: Pergamon Press, 1986), p. 48.

20. Linda Jean Shepherd, *Lifting the Veil: The Feminine Face of Science* (Boston: Shambhala Publications, 1993), p. 232.

21. Keller, *Feeling for the Organism,* p. 205.

22. Evelyn Fox Keller, "The Gender/Science System," in *Feminism and Science,* edited by Nancy Tuana (Bloomington: Indiana University Press, 1989), p. 39.

23. Lori Rosendale, "Thoughts of a Research Scientist: A Conversation with Dr. Barbara McClintock," unpublished paper for Education course, Hofstra University 1990, p. 7.

24. Ibid., p. 7.

25. Ibid., p. 4.

26. Ibid., p. 6.

27. Ibid., p. 10. The quotes are from Rosendale's 1990 interview of McClintock, as reported in her paper.

28. Lee Krasner "From There to Here"

Helen A. Harrison

The life and career of the painter Lee Krasner (1908–1984) exemplify the crusading, indomitable spirit of the modernist vanguard which established New York as the international art capital following World War II. Among the first generation of the New York School, Krasner, a native of Brooklyn whose most innovative work was done on eastern Long Island, is now recognized as the only female artist on a par with her most esteemed male colleagues, including her husband Jackson Pollock. Testifying to the growing acceptance Krasner's art has achieved since her death, the playwright and art patron Edward Albee wrote in 1990 that she "is not only the finest woman painter the U.S. has produced in this century but—since sex is really not the vital matter here—is right in the top of the pile of great 20th century American artists, period."[1] In this essay, I will examine the personal, artistic, and environmental factors that validate Albee's claims.

Those who knew Krasner almost always describe her in terms that reflect her forceful personality. Her admirers, such as the art dealer John Bernard Myers, emphasize her intelligence, her dynamic energy, and her commitment to people and things she believed in.[2] Her detractors call her opinionated, temperamental, and tough to the point of ruthlessness. Such attitudes have deeply influenced the interpretation of Krasner's work. Indeed it seems almost impossible for anyone familiar with Krasner to separate her from her art, for in her work they see reflected the traits, good or bad, that they associate with her character and behavior. She once told an interviewer that initially she did not agree with Pollock's "conviction that art and life are one," but later came to appreciate the truth of his claim that "you cannot separate me from my paintings—they are one and the same,"[3] as well as its application to herself. In another interview she insisted that her painting was autobiographical, "if anyone can take the trouble to read it."[4]

One of Krasner's fundamental qualities, remarked on by friends and enemies alike, was her tenacity. She took charge of her life at an early age and pursued her professional and personal development with single-minded devotion. The child of Russian-Jewish immigrants, she was neither encouraged nor discouraged in pursuing an art career; as an adult, she could never pinpoint what had prompted her to become an artist. Once she determined her course, however, nothing prevented her from following it. Whatever doubts or misgivings she may have had, especially as an art student entering a male-dominated educational system, she suppressed beneath an outer shell of self-confidence that was sometimes interpreted as arrogance.

At the National Academy of Design, where she studied from 1928–1932, her grade report noted: "This student is always a bother—insists on having her own way despite school rules."[5] But in Krasner's case, assertiveness was not so much disrespect for her teachers as it was a hunger to excel and an unorthodox openness to new ideas. Later, in classes at the more innovative Hans Hofmann School of Fine Arts, she would impress fellow students as an "intense, serious person who didn't go in for small talk or nonsense" and who was "seeking the most advanced ideas in art."[6]

During the Depression, when Krasner was employed on the WPA's Federal Art Project, she was a vigorous supporter of the social and political causes that united hard-line Communists with less committed fellow travelers and left-leaning liberals like herself. She read *Partisan Review,* debated the merits of Trotsky versus Stalin, joined the Artists Union and took part in its demonstrations against WPA layoffs. Abram Lerner, director emeritus of the Hirshhorn Museum, who knew Krasner on the WPA, described her as intensely vivacious and deeply involved in the group activities that laid the foundations of the New York School. "She often stood right in front of me on the paymaster's line—she was K and I was L," he recalled. "She always seemed to have a petition for us to sign or a notice of a meeting or rally we were supposed to attend. She was a real live wire."[7]

Notwithstanding her political activities, Krasner continued ardently to pursue her artistic development. As an early member of the American Abstract Artists, she was among the small but active avant-garde adapting European precedents to an American context. But it was not long before she turned away from what she perceived as the group's rigid adherence to non-objective formalism,[8] preferring to experiment with several modernist strategies, including Surrealism, Cubism, and nature-derived abstraction inspired by the flat, high-key colors of Matisse. Already a mature artist of twenty-nine when she entered Hofmann's school in late 1937, she demonstrated an unusual willingness to reconsider her artistic position coupled with an extraordinary capacity for self-renewal. Contrary to her image as a formidably self-assured individual, a characterization that persisted as the years passed and she occupied a more prominent position in the art world, Krasner periodically rejected earlier modes of expression and found new direction as her internal needs, rather than outside expectations, dictated.

The apparent contradiction between Krasner's uncompromising personality and her artistic uncertainty make a superficially biographical reading of her work highly suspect. Although she subscribed to the notion of art as self-expression, she was acutely aware that what appears on the canvas cannot always be located in conscious impulses. Her most telling example of the rift between outward manifestation and underlying truth is the series of paintings she created after Pollock's death (August 1956) while she was on her first trip to Europe. The trip came at a paradoxical moment in her life. She had a breakthrough in her work that resulted in a well-received New York exhibition and signalled a promising new direction in her creative development, but it was a time of crisis in her private life when she was contemplating divorce.[9] Having left Pollock to wallow in chronic alcoholism and the attentions of a young mistress, Krasner returned from Paris to face the humiliating circumstances of his drunken car crash which injured his mistress and killed her friend who was along for the ride.

In spite of her grief, Krasner returned to her own work not long after Pollock's death. By the following spring she had moved into his old studio and was rapidly developing along the lines suggested by her work of the previous year, when convoluted shapes—part human, part plant— studded with eyes and overflowing with vital fluids had made their appearance. Given the ambiguous nature of this imagery, it might readily have accommodated the shock, sorrow, anger, and guilt that Krasner was experiencing; indeed, such themes might have been expected to appear in her work as a visual equivalent of exorcism. On the contrary, her canvases of the 1957–1959 period, collectively known as the Earth Green series, are joyous rather than sad, bright instead of subdued, filled with voluptuous forms suggesting fertility, growth, and regeneration, not death, loss, or tragedy. When she later discussed them with the poet Richard Howard, she remarked how improbable it was that *Listen,* a work of 1957, should be "such a happy painting," when she was in the depths of mourning. "I can remember that when I was painting it I almost didn't see it," she told Howard, "because tears were literally pouring down."[10]

Three years later, however, when according to Howard she was "exultant" about her work and she herself confirmed that she was far from depressed, her imagery was stark, hostile, and filled with what Howard described as "great possibilities of not only depression but even despair." Such phenomena caused Krasner to develop an acute awareness of the "disparity between what you feel and what's happening or what you're doing. . . . What I feel at the moment is not necessarily what's being brought forth in the painting." She sought actively to engage those feelings that lay below the conscious level and to explore the territory toward which they directed her. In spite of what she perceived as an emotional upswing in her life, she acknowledged that the work of the late 1950s and early 1960s was a "night journey," on which she went "deep down into something which wasn't easy or pleasant."[11] And this was by no means the first time that Krasner had undergone such a re-evaluation.

When first confronted by Pollock's work in late 1941, when he was synthesizing influences from Picasso and the Mexican muralists to Surrealist automatism and Jungian symbolism, Krasner recognized his potential and sensed that he was "ahead" of her. "I couldn't have felt that if I hadn't been trying for the same goal myself," she told the writer Eleanor Munro.[12] Consequently, in spite of the strides she had made in Hofmann's class, Krasner virtually jettisoned her career and devoted herself to promoting Pollock's as she struggled to absorb the lessons she believed he could teach her, not least of which was how to gain access to the wellspring of unconscious creativity. Her habitual strategy became a series of concentrated bursts of productivity followed by periodic re-evaluations which often led her to destroy entire bodies of work. Eventually this method yielded handsome dividends, first in the beautiful mid-1950s collages made from her own rejected paintings and scraps of Pollock's discarded canvases and drawings, and later in her audacious re-use of Hofmann School drawings in a stunning series of large collages that pay oblique homage to Matisse's cutouts, as well as to the Cubist principles of formal analysis that were the foundation of Hofmann's curriculum.

Thus Krasner's primary creative method, the one that yielded the most innovative and idiosyncratic results, capitalized on her tendency toward periodic re-evaluation. In her perceptive introduction to the recently-published catalogue raisonné of Krasner's work, the art historian Ellen G. Landau points out that Krasner's obsessive "destruction, refocus, recapitulation and revision" were byproducts of her deeply-rooted belief that "change is the only constant."[13] They are also a direct consequence of the lifelong activism that led Krasner to tackle issues head-on and face problems defiantly, as if the force of her will were enough to resolve them.

Interestingly, although they were very different personality types, she and Pollock shared that approach to art-making. Although in his case the results superficially appear to be more spontaneous and unrevised, there is in fact considerable re-working in many of his canvases. "I have no fears about making changes, destroying the image, etc., because the painting has a life of its own," he wrote in 1947,[14] an attitude he reiterated three years later in his narration for Hans Namuth's famous film of the artist at work. In Krasner's case, she referred to this impulse as responsiveness to an "inner rhythm" that dictated both the direction of an individual painting and the development of whole bodies of work. In an interview with the journalist Gaby Rodgers, she insisted that the inner rhythm was inviolate. "I know it is essential for me," she told Rodgers. "I listen to it and I stay with it. I have always been this way."[15]

Attentiveness to internal factors—whether the forms and colors organized on canvas or the unconscious emotional impulses underlying those aesthetic choices—was an essential ingredient in Krasner's creativity. Yet she was aware that her development was profoundly influenced by external factors as well. Her artistic training is an obvious example, but here again it is clear that her temperament played a major role in leading her to reject academic limitations and seek out more advanced modes of expression. When the Museum of Modern Art opened in 1929, Krasner's view of art's potential was radically altered. She later described her first visits to the museum as "an upheaval, . . . an opening of a door," without being able precisely to identify why she responded so intensely.[16]

In retrospect, it appears likely that an innate interest in experimentation was already proving decisive, even before Krasner became aware that, as she put it, "for me all the doors are open."[17] Experimentation meant rethinking and even destroying work in progress, abruptly abandoning previous work to move in a new and challenging direction, or exhuming the past to discover its hidden potential for the future. As she once remarked to the Whitney Museum curator Marcia Tucker, "my own image of my work is that I no sooner settle into something than a break occurs. These breaks are always painful and depressing. . . . All my work keeps going like a pendulum; it seems to swing back to something I was involved with earlier, or it moves between horizontality and verticality, circularity, or a composite of them."[18]

Krasner pursued such strategies without regard for their impact on her career. Her unwillingness to compromise was demonstrated, for example, in 1959, when she abruptly canceled an exhibition arranged for her by Clement Greenberg, the enormously influential art critic who had championed Pollock. There are several versions of the incident,[19] but the most likely explanation is that Greenberg disapproved of the new direction Krasner's work had taken when the lyrical, "happy" Earth Green series gave way to the angry, slashing imagery of the Night Journeys. Greenberg planned to select the show and he wanted the earlier work; Krasner insisted on making the choices and she intended to expose her most recent material. "Thus," as Tucker later observed, "she retained her independence at the cost of the much needed and deserved visibility such a show would have given her."[20]

For Krasner, the inevitability of change, whether it came as a result of an abrupt break, a pendulum-like swing, or an evolutionary cycle, meant that her work did not follow a consistent path of aesthetic development. Yet there is an underlying coherence engendered by an inborn sensitivity to nature, not as a subject *per se* but as a generative force analogous to the creative process itself. While it is true that many of Krasner's paintings and collages refer to nature motifs and natural phenomena, those elements are seldom literal. Even in her earliest extant painting, a 1929 self-portrait, the flower she holds in her right hand and the potted fern on a table behind her are deliberately symbolic. The red blossom recalls her childhood delight in the gardens and wildflowers of her native Brownsville, where, she recalled, "there were beautiful flowers. I loved it. A back yard with irises. . . . And roses on the fences, and in all the back yards. I would walk to school through the lots filled with buttercups."[21] The fern, resting on an overturned wooden pail, represents the miraculous unfolding of form that occurs organically in nature and art alike, the way Pollock would later describe painting as "a natural growth out of a need."[22] Behind the fern, a basement window opens onto the family's own backyard, affording a glimpse of the plantings that so enriched the aspiring painter's imagination.

Fig. 28.1. Lee Krasner, *Self-portrait,* c. 1930. Oil on canvas, 30"x15". The Pollock-Krasner Foundation, Inc., courtesy of Robert Miller Gallery, New York City.

Soon after the self-portrait was painted, Krasner's parents moved to Huntington, Long Island. By that time young Lenore, as she was then known, was sharing a studio with friends on Fifteenth Street in Manhattan and attending classes at the National Academy. At the age of twenty or twenty-one she was already manifesting the self-confidence that led her teachers to question whether she could adhere to the discipline of traditional art training. Another self-portrait, painted the following summer, seemed to confirm their misgivings while simultaneously demonstrating Krasner's innate talent. (See fig. 28.1.) "I spent that whole summer out in Huntington . . . with a mirror nailed to a tree doing a self-portrait," she related in an interview with the writer Cindy Nemser. In the fall she submitted the painting as evidence that she deserved promotion to the Academy's life drawing class, but she was charged with faking the pose. "My new instructor accused me of playing a dirty trick by pretending to have painted the picture outdoors when I had really done it inside. No amount of explanation helped,"[23] she recalled ruefully. This unjust accusation was all the more hurtful because of Krasner's intense honesty, a quality that is apparent in the portrait itself. Falsifying her position *vis-à-vis* her surroundings would have been anathema to her. Moreover, her deep identification with nature, tentatively examined in the previous self-portrait, had found overt expression in this work, where the artist's boldly handled figure is depicted as analogous to the sturdy upright trees behind her. Decades later, reconsidering the meaning latent in this image, she concluded that it heralded a lifelong preoccupation with self as subject matter, with "truths contained in my own body, an organism as much a part of nature and reality as plants, animals, the sea, or the stones beneath us."[24]

As a student of Hans Hofmann, Krasner subscribed to his definition of an artist as "an agent in whose mind nature is transformed into a new creation." According to Hofmann's teaching, "whether the artist works directly from nature, from memory, or from fantasy, nature is always the source of his creative impulses."[25] Hofmann's approaches to formal analysis, color relationships, and compositional structure, based on the Cubist precepts developed in Paris during his sojourn there in 1904–1914, could be applied to a wide range of pictorial styles, from representation to non-objectivity. For this reason, and because he served as a direct link to the most advanced currents of European modernism, the German-born Hofmann, who immigrated to the United States in 1930, became a popular and highly influential teacher for two generations of American artists. From 1933–1958, his classes on Eighth Street in Manhattan and his summer school in Provincetown were meccas for fledgling members of the New York avant-garde. Hofmann's

Fig. 28.2. Lee Krasner at the Hans Hofmann School of Art, New York, c. 1940. Photograph courtesy of the Archives of American Art, Smithsonian Institution.

insistence on working from nature was legendary, but in his studio this meant still life and figure study, essentially formal exercises designed to sharpen the student's technical and analytical skills. Nevertheless Krasner's achievements under his direction were considerable, including not only the figure drawings that would later be recycled in her collages of the 1970s, but also a series of colorful still-lifes that established her as one of the most advanced young painters of the day. Compared to the anecdotal, picturesque canvases of Mark Rothko, Adolph Gottlieb, and Franz Kline, to name just three of the male artists who would later be hailed as leading lights of the New York School, Krasner's paintings were audaciously modern.

Exhibiting with the American Abstract Artists and working for the Federal Art Project with the rank of Senior Artist, Krasner seemed destined for recognition. Indeed, she was one of a handful of Americans selected for inclusion in "American and French Paintings," an exhibition organized by the artist and respected connoisseur John Graham for the McMillen Gallery in 1942. Here, in an evident affirmation of Graham's high regard for her work, she would be grouped with Picasso, Braque, Matisse, and Bonnard. Krasner did not recognize the name of another American invitee, Jackson Pollock, and decided to visit his studio to preview the unknown paintings. As she later told the writer John Gruen: "To say that I flipped my lid would be an understatement. I was totally bowled over by what I saw."[26] That was the beginning of her relationship with Pollock. Her immediate surroundings, in the form of the avant-garde milieu in which she was developing, had therefore provided Krasner with the solid foundation on which to build an artistic life, but it had not liberated the inner wellspring of original creativity that she sensed was awaiting discovery. She had recognized that quality in Pollock's work, although he had not yet fully realized its potential. For Krasner, that liberation would be a long and difficult process. Initially it entailed a nearly three-year period of intensive re-evaluation, during which she created a series of so-called Grey Slab paintings which she later destroyed.[27] For Pollock, a radical break with his familiar environment would prove to be the decisive factor.

The break came in November 1945, when the newly-married couple left their Greenwich Village walk-up and relocated permanently to The Springs, a hamlet some five miles from the center of East Hampton, Long Island. Having spent the month of August with friends in a beach shack on nearby Louse Point, they realized that they could live quite cheaply in the area where the Depression and wartime gas rationing had taken their toll on the tourist trade and fishing industry alike. At first they considered renting a house for the winter, but Pollock was determined to buy property and settle down. A loan from his dealer, Peggy Guggenheim, enabled them to purchase a rather rundown and fairly primitive homestead on Fireplace Road. Among its attractions, which did not include central heating or plumbing, were a small barn which Pollock soon converted into a painting studio and a spectacular view across the salt marsh to Accabonac Creek, a narrow harbor, and Gardiners Bay beyond.

It is unlikely that either artist anticipated the profound influence this property would have on their creative development. The move clearly had other advantages, chiefly to distance Pollock from surroundings that were limiting his productivity. Although his work had begun to attract critical attention and the Museum of Modern Art had bought one of his paintings, Pollock was unable to cope with even limited success, and he expressed his discomfort by drinking heavily. The New York art world, small and close-knit in those days, was for him a metaphorical fishbowl in which he felt himself to be on display—simultaneously admired and trapped. Whatever misgivings Krasner may have had about leaving the scene of all the latest vanguard developments, her devotion to Pollock was sufficient to convince her that getting him away from what he called the city's "wear and tear"[28] was worth any personal sacrifice she would make. And the move was initially traumatic for Krasner. As she later recalled, "it was hell, to put it mildly, for me. For instance, it was during the war period so that you couldn't get a supply of fuel. Cold water, no hot water, no bathroom—no, it was a rough scene. It [wasn't] like most artists know today."[29]

However uncomfortable their physical circumstances were, both artists responded enthusiastically to the natural environment. Neither of them painted views of the scenery, but the landscape was a fruitful source of raw material for compositions that evolved the way Krasner's fern unfolded its fronds. Her earliest East Hampton canvases, of which only two survive, illustrate her transition from a traditional figure-ground approach to imagery, in which forms are expressed as objects occupying implied space, to an all-over approach to composition. In works such as her untitled painting of 1946, the entire surface is equally activated, with no foreground or background to simulate illusionistic space. The picture creates its own internal reality, adhering to Hofmann's precept that "the picture plane must be preserved in its two-dimensionality throughout the whole process of creation until it reaches its final transformation in the completed picture."[30] To achieve this crucial synthesis, Krasner had to transcend Hofmann's teachings by internalizing his method and applying it to imagery derived from her own perceptions. That stimulus was provided by her surroundings—the natural phenomena that she and Pollock observed literally in their own back yard.

"I remember," she told John Gruen, "sitting with Jackson on our country porch—sitting there for hours, looking into the landscape, and always at dusk, when the woods ahead turned into strange, mystifying shapes. And we would walk in those woods, and he would stop to examine this or that stone, branch, or leaf."[31] Speaking to Eleanor Munro, Krasner reaffirmed their shared fascination with nature: "One thing Jackson and I had in common was experience on the same level, . . . feeling the same things about landscape, for instance, or about the moon. . . . Very often I would get up at two or three [in the morning] and come out on the porch and just sit in the light here."[32] Among the paintings from her early days in East Hampton, *Shellflower* and *Night Life* bear titles that reflect this fascination with nature as an inspiration rather than a source of specific subject matter. Like Pollock's contemporaneous Sounds in the Grass series, these paintings fill pictorial space with colors and gestures that analogize the environment instead of depicting it. Their reality is all the more real because it expresses the artist's inner responsiveness to external stimuli, combining observation and feeling in abstract, non-illusionistic imagery.

Articulate and outspoken, Krasner often referred to her desire to work organically, relying on her highly developed intuition to generate and govern creative growth. In one of her most poetic statements, she summarized the ideal approach she struggled to achieve: "Painting, for me, when it really 'happens,' is as miraculous as any natural phenomenon—as say, a lettuce leaf. . . . [T]he painting I have in mind, in which inner and outer are inseparable, transcends technique, transcends subject and moves into the realm of the inevitable—then you have the lettuce leaf."[33]

To promote that inevitability, Krasner opened herself to nature's influence without preconceptions. This allowed her to produce life-affirming images as antidotes to her grief following Pollock's death, to express her pent-up rage years after she believed it to be safely buried, and to return periodically to sources in the East Hampton landscape, from which she distilled the essences of leaves, flowers, seed pods, and grasses, sometimes interwoven with human and animal allusions. Throughout the 1960s, having completed her dark, introspective Night Journeys, Krasner harnessed nature's regenerative forces to sustain her after a near-fatal illness. Recuperating from a brain aneurism that struck her in late 1962, she embarked on a series of bright, upbeat canvases and paintings on paper that hark back to her breakthrough all-over works of the mid-1940s. With titles like *Flowering Limb, August Petals,* and *Chrysalis,* they confirm her conviction that art, like natural growth, is a cyclic process.

As she entered the final decade of her career, Krasner had so fully assimilated the lessons of nature that she carried the landscape within her as a perpetual frame of reference. She also carried her own past, not as an encumbrance but as a fruitful source of inspiration. Her last major series, begun in 1979, deals with the solstice, the turning point of the seasons. True to its theme, the imagery revolves on itself in arabesques of interwoven forms. Several of these paintings and collages are re-workings of canvases begun as much as twenty-five years earlier, again illustrating Krasner's compulsive need to retrieve and integrate earlier achievements as a means of advancement. She sometimes joked that she was not to be trusted around her work because she continued to find new possibilities in what had once seemed completed. In truth, her so-called breaks—similar to the experiences of several of her male colleagues—were less decisive than her own appraisal indicates. They more closely resemble the convolutions that play such a prominent and consistent role in her imagery.

Judged in its totality, Krasner's *oeuvre* justifies Albee's assertion that she ranks with the foremost twentieth-century American artists. From its beginnings in self-scrutiny and formal analysis to its culmination in a 1983 collage painting, in which a 1950 canvas is overlaid with fragments of her 1938–1940 drawings and unified by new gestures in translucent paint, Krasner's aesthetic journey took her along an idiosyncratic path. Yet her direction paralleled that of her foremost contemporaries, including Pollock, who also sought to harmonize inner and outer realities. Krasner's singular contribution, too long overlooked or underrated, was to demonstrate that covering the distance "from there to here"[34] is a cumulative rather than a progressive process.

Notes

1. Edward Albee, "Considering Krasner," *Lee Krasner: Paintings from 1965 to 1970* (New York: Robert Miller Gallery, 1991), n.p.

2. John Bernard Myers, *Tracking the Marvelous* (New York: Random House, 1983), p. 103.

3. John Gruen, *The Party's Over Now* (New York: Viking Press, 1972), p. 232.

4. Cindy Nemser, "The Indomitable Lee Krasner," *Feminist Art Journal,* Spring 1975, p. 9.

5. Jeffrey D. Grove, "Chronology," in *Lee Krasner: A Catalogue Raisonné,* edited by Ellen G. Landau (New York: Harry N. Abrams, 1995), p. 300.

6. Michael Loew, quoted in Jeffrey Potter, *To A Violent Grave: An Oral Biography of Jackson Pollock* (New York: G. P. Putnam's Sons, 1985), p. 64.

7. Interview with the author, August 1993.

8. Eleanor Munro, *Originals: American Women Artists* (New York: Touchstone/ Simon and Schuster, 1979), p. 110.

9. Andrea Gabor, *Einstein's Wife: Work and Marriage in the Lives of Five Great Twentieth-Century Women* (New York: Viking, 1995), pp. 76-77.

10. Interview between Richard Howard and Lee Krasner, *Lee Krasner: Paintings, 1959-1962* (New York: Pace Gallery, 1979), n.p.

11. Ibid.

12. Munro, *Originals,* p. 112.

13. Landau, *Lee Krasner,* p. 13.

14. Jackson Pollock, "My painting," *possibilities* 1 (Winter 1947/48): 79.

15. Gaby Rodgers, "She Has Been There Once or Twice," 1977, quoted in Robert Hobbs, *Lee Krasner* (New York: Abbeville Press, 1993), p. 100.

16. Munro, *Originals,* p. 106.

17. Ibid., p. 119.

18. Interview with Marcia Tucker, July 1973, quoted in Tucker, *Lee Krasner: Large Paintings* (New York: Whitney Museum of American Art, 1973), p. 8.

19. See, for example, the summary account in Gabor, *Einstein's Wife,* pp. 81-83.

20. Tucker, *Lee Krasner,* p. 12.

21. Munro, *Originals,* p. 103.

22. Jackson Pollock, narration to *Jackson Pollock,* 16 mm. film, 10 minutes, color, Hans Namuth and Paul Falkenberg (distributed by Museum at Large, Ltd.), 1951.

23. Cindy Nemser, *Art Talk: Conversations with Twelve Women Artists* (New York: Charles Scribner's Sons, 1975), p. 84.

24. John Bernard Myers, "Naming Pictures: Conversations Between Lee Krasner and John Bernard Myers," *Artforum* 23 (November 1984): 71.

25. Sara T. Weeks and Bartlett H. Hayes, Jr., eds., *Search for the Real and Other Essays by Hans Hofmann* (Cambridge: M.I.T. Press, 1967), p. 70.

26. Gruen, *The Party's Over Now,* p. 230.

27. Landau, *Lee Krasner,* p. 97.

28. Pollock discussed his transition in an interview with Berton Roueché in "The Talk of the Town," *The New Yorker* 26 (August 5, 1950): 16.

29. Statement in *Jackson Pollock: Portrait,* 16 mm. film, 54 minutes, color, Cort Productions (distributed by Direct Cinema, Ltd., Los Angeles), 1982.

30. Weeks and Hayes, *Search for the Real,* p. 64.

31. Gruen, *The Party's Over Now,* p. 233. Their property is now the Pollock-Krasner House and Study Center, a National Historic Landmark and research center open to the public by appointment.

32. Munro, *Originals,* p. 114.

33. "Statement by Lee Krasner," in *Lee Krasner: Paintings, Drawings and Collages* (London: Whitechapel Gallery, 1965), n.p. (following illustrations).

34. Munro, *Originals,* p. 118. Describing her return to earlier work, Krasner reiterated her lifelong strategy of facing an issue head-on, "dealing with it. Not ignoring, hiding it," as well as her delight in the possibilities offered by reappraisal: "I'm saying, here it is in another form. This is where I've come from: from there to here. . . . It renews my confidence in something I believe. That there is continuity."

29. Reflections on Long Island Women

Marilyn Goldstein

Our hair might have been teased and our skirts might have been mini, we may have baked our share of chocolate chip cookies, and sometimes, some of us revolutionaries had to be home by three p.m. for the kids, but, though you might find this hard to believe now, Long Island was, in the 1970s, a veritable hotbed of feminism.

Some of the great changes for women in society, changes that affected the entire nation, came out of such unlikely places as Farmingdale, Babylon, Hicksville, and Garden City. They were heady times. They were successful times. They were times we thought would end only when all the goals women were fighting for had been met. They are times I take great pleasure in recalling for you today.

So for me, this invitation to open the Hofstra University Long Island Studies Institute Conference on Long Island Women is an honor and a delight. But it *is* a little disconcerting when you stop to think you've been asked to view your own life and times as history. I feel the way I did on the day I was introduced as "a pioneer in the women's movement." I wondered if the audience expected me to come out in ankle-length skirts, bloomers, and a placard demanding votes for women.

But it is true that I was there, as a journalist and as a woman, when the second wave of feminism burst upon the scene after Betty Friedan's *The Feminine Mystique* was published in 1963. And it is true that to recount the years I will speak about today, I didn't need to refer to many historical texts. All I had to do was reread some of my old stories in *Newsday*, recall some of my speeches, and phone some old friends. Do you think that is what they mean by the phrase "living history"?

Oh, how lucky I was to be in the right job at the right time and in the right place. And I do want to emphasize right place. While the world was still believing—wanted to believe?—that women in suburbs like Long Island were interested only in backyard barbecues and diaper services, I was reporting stories of a Long Island where teachers in Farmingdale were suing for the right to work through pregnancy.

I was writing about a Long Island where, at the State University of New York at Old Westbury, the Feminist Press started to roll, and under Professor Florence Howe, was turning out new and reprinted material that helped clear the scales from the eyes of long-blinded women.

In one of the glory years of the women's movement, 1973, women ran in so many local political races that I was called on to do a story about the phenomenon. Photos of women running for all sorts of offices rolled across two pages of Part II of *Newsday*. All of the women were Democrats, by the way. And some of them actually won.

Pearl Weill, who ran and won as a councilwoman in Long Beach, recalls that when she attended a League of Women Voters candidates' night, every one of the candidates who showed up were women. The men, of course, didn't have to show up. They were members of the GOP and assured victory. Or so they thought.

In fact, one of the reasons so many Democratic women won spots as candidates, is that most Democrats in Nassau County were sure losers. It always has been easier for women to get nominations for unwinnable spots. But that year the conventional wisdom was turned on its head. Some women did win. Not many, but some. One of the victors was Hannah Kaminoff, elected supervisor of the city of Long Beach. Along with her, came Councilwoman Weill, who I must tell you, still serves.

I interviewed Hannah at the time and asked her what her election meant for women in politics, and Hannah answered that although she thought it was great that her constituents had elected a woman supervisor, she did not think it was time for other women to run. Too much, too fast, she told me. Well, I maintain the 1970s were good, not perfect.

The year before, in 1972, Nassau County had elected another woman, both the first female and the first Democrat from Long Island to go to the state senate—Karen Burstein. Karen, who came a hair's breath away from being New York State's Attorney General in 1995, came in along with what was referred to as the women's Mafia: Carol Bellamy, now heading UNICEF, and Mary Ann Krupsak, who went on to become Lieutenant Governor under Hugh Carey. Those were the people and the years that led to the influx of women on the political scene in the next decade.

In 1974, another young woman, Eileen Brennan, of Hicksville, the daughter of a police officer, started making women's history too. She sued the Nassau County Police Department because she wanted to be a cop like her dad. She tried to enlist as a police cadet, which then was a police training program. But she was only nineteen, and a woman had to be twenty-one and a college graduate to become a cadet; men qualified at eighteen, with a high school diploma. Steven Hyman argued the case in front of the Civil Service Board. Steve and Eileen won; the rule for having different criteria for each sex was cast aside, setting precedent within the Civil Service system,

Hyman remembers cross-examining Lt. Marty O'Connor of the Nassau County Police, and asking him to explain the two standards for the different sexes. Hyman can still quote O'Connor word for word. O'Connor said:

"Putting a woman on the street is like having a product with a latent defect. You never know when it will explode."

Of course, when she finally won, Eileen made known to a reporter what I had heard so often from women who had personally gained by standing on the backs of feminists, that although she wanted to be a cop, she was no "women's libber." Eileen Brennan is a "women's libber" now. She's a captain in New York City, and she is taking on the Police Department again. Her staff of men complained in 1995 that she was showing favoritism to the one female detective under her supervision. As a result, the women were both transferred. The men stayed. The women have filed a complaint with the Department.

Even the venerable suburban institution of the Little League was taken on by Long Islanders. In one of the first challenges to the boys-only baseball teams, Steven Hyman, who lived in Great Neck, represented a Great Neck girl who wanted to play ball. And Jenny Leeds became a shortstop in Little League.

In Farmingdale, teachers were required to inform the administration when they were three months pregnant and required to leave at four months. The reason given was the fear that something might happen to the fetus and the teacher would sue. That, of course is a non-issue, because in law, the fetus is not a person. But the women did indeed sue—on behalf of themselves. What was really behind the issue, said Linda Lamel, one of the named plaintiffs in the case, was sex. If you were pregnant, you had obviously "done it," and were thereby setting a bad example for the students. Not only did you have to leave in your fourth month, you could not come back to work until six months after the child was born or September 1, whichever was later. This could prevent a woman from working nineteen months.

The case was won in the New York State Division of Human Rights. Thus the decision wasn't precedent setting until the district went into the New York State Court of Appeals to appeal the decision. That court ruled for the teachers, this time setting precedent in New York—which often sets national precedent. Linda told me that one of those involved in the case, a high school English teacher named Cyla Allison, was due to have her baby in July. She refused to say yes or no when asked if she was pregnant. She was finally fired in June and ordered not to appear on the premises, but she was teaching a Regent's class, so in order not to let her students down, she continued holding classes at her home so she could take her kids through the Regents.

On another front, a young woman from Babylon named Ellen Cooperman went to court in 1976 to change her name to Ellen Cooperperson. Ellen told me recently, "I was conscious of sexist language. Language is a reflection of people's attitudes and attitudes . . . drive people's behavior. If we could change the language, we could change people's perceptions." So, while others of us were insisting writers use "he" and "she," not just "he" when they meant both genders, Ellen was doing it her way. Now in most cases, changing a name is routine; you fill out an application, pay a fee, and a judge approves the application. Not with Ellen. A Suffolk County Supreme Court Justice John Scileppi turned down this routine request with a nineteen-page decision. The decision read that the name change would "have serious and undesirable repercussions perhaps throughout the entire country . . . for example, those named 'Jackson' would want to become 'Jackchild' and 'Manning' might have to be changed to 'Peopleing' . . . furthermore, this precedent might then be expanded to other areas of language usage, with the result that clergyman would be changed to 'clergyperson,' and . . . 'mankind' to 'personkind.'"

If only his fears had come true.

He also wrote that "the anatomical differences between those whom God created to become fathers and those whom he made mothers necessarily impose certain limitation on both sexes which prevent complete equality. I consider it ludicrous to ignore this. After all, males have their right to identity too." And he goes on to admit in his decision he "may not personally approve [of] a married woman's adoption of a name different from her husband's in order to delineate more clearly her own personal identity."

You can imagine the media reaction to that one. Ellen said her aunt read about it in Milan.

Suffolk lawyer Susan Lebow appealed to the Appelate Division, which refused to take the case. She instituted a new name change petition in the New York Supreme Court and Justice Leon Lazer granted it. And, as Ellen told me a few months back, now she's stuck with the name Cooperperson. But she had made her point.

It was not only in the courts where women were having their day. In living rooms in every town and village, women were meeting week after week in what was called consciousness-raising sessions, talking about their lives from a brand new perspective, that of feminism. For many of us, the women's movement wasn't, to paraphrase football coach Vince Lombardi, the most important thing; it was the only thing.

Hundreds would turn out for meetings of the National Organization for Women (NOW) in the Unitarian Fellowship in Garden City. Betty Schlein, who was president of NOW from 1973 to 1975, told me that the membership of Nassau NOW increased from 75 to more than 500 during her tenure, making the Nassau chapter the third largest in the United States.

In her history of NOW, Betty Schlein wrote: "Long Island NOW's leaders spoke to groups in churches, schools, clubhouses, community rooms, living rooms and kitchens, disseminating information about the newly developing women's movement and the issues it raised. By 1975, there were four other Long Island NOW chapters, all in Suffolk."[1]

This is not to say that getting there was easy. In the 1960s, letting people know you were a feminist was guaranteed to make you the entertainment at local parties. What most people couldn't understand about me was how could a married woman be a feminist. Everyone knew women's libbers were either angry divorced women who weren't getting their alimony, or worse, lesbians. Society at large was hostile to women's liberation. They liked to call it "women's lip."

And there were very few of us in the late 1960s. It was lonely out there then. When I started covering the women's movement in 1969, I was sure there were only four feminists on Long Island: the president of NOW, which did have a president but I think no members; Karen Burstein, then a lawyer, Selma Greenberg, a professor of education at Hofstra; and myself. But we made it look like there were a lot of us.

Karen would make a statement about an issue; Selma would validate it with her imprimatur, since a professor must be listened to, and I would write the story. If we kept up the shuffle fast enough, we made it seem like we had an army of feminists out there. And soon we did.

I learned just recently, in doing research for this speech, that there were three other women, two from Long Island, who were playing the same game up in Albany. They were Linda Lamel, of the Farmingdale pregnancy suit, Barbara Shack, who headed the Nassau Civil Liberties Union and who went on to direct the New York Civil Liberties Union Women's Rights Project, and a Manhattan lawyer whose name neither Linda nor Barbara could remember.

The three would go up to Albany to try to get legislation passed. That wasn't easy. Prior to 1972, there were only two women serving in the legislature: Rosemarie Gunning, a right-wing Republican and Connie Cook, an upstate progressive Republican. Connie Cook was their only ally, Barbara Schack said. They asked her to carry a bill that would make pregnancy-related illnesses a disability—not the pregnancy per se, mind you, just unexpected illnesses resulting from pregnancy, like cesareans, edema, high blood pressure, and the like. Cook told them, Barbara said, "you'll never get anything done if you don't get the women together to come up here."

Of course, they had no women to organize, so they would introduce themselves to lawmakers as the New York Women's Lobby, the group that "represented the women of New York State," when in fact they represented the three of them. Barbara recalls they even held awards ceremonies for legislators who rated 100 percent on the bills the three women were pushing.

One of their biggest victories was legislation to prohibit discrimination based on sex in courses of instruction in public schools. This was a time when girls had to take home economics and boys had to take shop, and no cross fertilization was allowed. The boys in many schools got the first open spots in driver's education; the girls were admitted if there were spots left over.

The women had to eliminate sports in that bill because the legislators were terribly worried about women's poor, frail bodies in contact sports. Or, Barbara's favorite argument, that equal access to sports programs would lead to co-ed skinny dipping. So only sports that were part of the curriculum, in gym, were covered.

Once Carol Bellamy, Marianne Krupsak, and Karen Burstein joined the Senate, there really were organized women in the state. The groups they represented included the State Women's Political Caucus, the NOWs, the Trade Union Women, the National Association of Social Workers, the Women's Equity Action League, the National Black Feminist Organization, the Progressive Household Technicians, the Women Officer Workers, and the Civil Liberties Union.

Barbara Shack said "I used to sit on the floor of the Senate chamber between Karen Burstein and Carol Bellamy's desks with the backup material for the debate."

Karen pushed a bill to allow girls to deliver newspapers. She was a sponsor of the New York State Equal Rights Amendment (ERA), which went through the legislature but went down in a referendum. And she was instrumental in pushing a bill to eliminate so-called protective labor laws, such as one that did not allow women between sixteen and twenty-one to work after 10 p.m. There went all the good waitressing jobs.

I know Karen does not want to be remembered mostly for this one, but it was important. She introduced and passed the pay-toilet bill which outlawed charging for women's toilets when men's were free. You may laugh, but there were times when life seemed to hang on having a quarter in your purse.

In 1973–1974, hundreds of women's rights bills were introduced. Unfortunately, the leadership, Governor Malcolm Wilson, Senate Majority Leader Warren Anderson, and Assembly Speaker Perry Duryea, were not friends of women, and most bills either went down or never got out of committee. The attempt to end the automatic exemption of females from serving on juries was never approved by the legislature; it took the United States Supreme Court to change that. Nor did the pregnancy disability bill pass. But the New York State Court of Appeals did find that pregnancy should be considered a disability.

One great victory was the repeal of the requirement for corroboration of a victim's testimony in rape trials. It was nice to know that someone no longer had to see the rape and testify to it to get a conviction. And the legislature did outlaw discrimination in giving credit.

One of the bills they could not get through in 1974 was the effort to repeal restrictions on the sale of contraceptives. How quaint in this day and age when condom ads appear on television.

I am jumping a little ahead of myself. I want to go back to the days before any of these laws existed, to the late 1960s, when the second wave of feminism was still in its infancy. The resistance I got at *Newsday* in the beginning was symptomatic of the world view of feminism then. In 1969, I wrote an impassioned three-part series explaining this new phenomenon, Women's Liberation. Women, I explained, are total human beings, and can't exist only as sex partners, housewives, and mothers. I got only one query from the editor after he had read the entire series. It was in the form of a note that said: "Isn't this all because of the pill and labor-saving appliances?" Yes, as he saw it, the women's movement was something the "girls" were doing because they had a little free time.

I think we surprised some people when they realized we really were not out to make some changes in our lives, we were out to entirely change life.

And I and my women colleagues started to make those changes where we worked. It was in Garden City, at *Newsday*, Long Island's newspaper, in 1973, that reporters, editors, telephone operators, secretaries, telephone-ad solicitors, and clerks filed one of the earliest and largest class-action suits in federal court charging sex discrimination under Title VII of the Civil Rights Act of 1964.

What a ride that was. When we started organizing there was not one woman in a management position. There was not one woman working nights as an assistant editor, which is the traditonal path to an editorship. When I arrived at *Newsday* in 1966, there were exactly three women reporting news stories; the rest of the women reporters were where females belonged: on the women's page.

There was one woman who seemed to be doing well. Her name was Marilyn Berger and she was covering the United Nations. She even got herself to cover Henry Kissinger's peace talks in Paris. Years later, when she had left *Newsday* and I called her to interview her concerning her experiences for the lawsuit, Marilyn Berger told me her career indicated *Newsday* did not discriminate against women. All you had to do was work hard, she said. Then she explained how she had covered her regular beat, the exciting city of Glen Cove, all day, and then, on her own time, for no extra pay, went into the city each night and covered the United Nations. Her coverage was a free gift to *Newsday*. If ever there was an example of how women had to work twice as hard as men to get half as far, this was it. Yet even Marilyn Berger herself was unable to view her situation in feminist terms back then.

Things changed slowly at *Newsday* from 1968 to 1972. But too slowly for us. We decided to investigate the situation and to file charges, first with the Equal Employment Opportunity Commission (EEOC) and then, because of the backlog at the EEOC, in federal court in Brooklyn.

One of my colleagues, Annabelle Kerins, went through months and months worth of *Newsdays* and came up with a statistical analysis showing that women were rarely assigned to major news stories, appeared on the front five pages much less often than their numbers of the staff would indicate they should, and rarely got prestigious out of town or overseas assignments.

And we women certainly made less money than men with similar experience. And had very few positions of power. Kerins counted the names on the masthead. Thirty-three. Each a male. She counted those with the title Manager. Twenty-one. Three were women, and to quote our federal complaint, "These three are office managers with mainly clerical duties." She counted those with the title Editor. Forty-seven. Six were women. And again to quote from our court papers, "Only one of the twelve senior editors appearing [under] the *Newsday* masthead is a woman, and that position was not opened to women until after . . . charges were filed with the EEOC."

There was another problem the court papers did not identify. That lone woman under the masthead was named Blake Femrite. Now, was Blake the name of a man or a woman? Here was *Newsday* trying to make a show with a woman senior editor and their readers didn't even realize it because of her androgynous first name.

The biggest splash was made in the tenth count of the complaint, dealing with sexist attitudes of top-level males such as William Atwood, the publisher at the time. You could not get more top level than he. The complaint quotes a memorandum that he sent to his assistant, who was in charge of hiring personnel, stating "Female Ph.D.s . . . are usually insane."

The charge that made the biggest splash was the one in which a woman who had applied for a job had given Atwood's name as a reference. She had met him when she was living in Italy. In a written note to the editor doing the hiring, Atwood recounted their meeting, told how he had gone up to her apartment where he plied her with grappa, and then, when he made his advances, was turned down. He wrote that she was "a frosty dish." Need I say she didn't get hired.

In another citation, a Suffolk County editor wrote an evaluation of a reporter coming off her six-month probation, which he sent to editor David Laventhol. The evaluation said that this reporter: "has a very nice pair of legs. She should be kept." Another of the named plaintiffs, Marian Leifsen, said she was denied a position as copy editor, then a night job, because, one of the managing editors told her "working nights would ruin her sex life."

Sylvia Carter, another named plaintiff, said that she had been asked to run errands for her bosses. In the winter of 1971–1972 the complaint reads, the Suffolk day editor, "assigned her tasks such as picking up paint swatches at a local paint store for him." When art critic Amei Wallach, then a feature writer, went to an editor to discuss a problem she had with her work, she said he told her not to bother herself about it and go buy him an ice cream cone. He also asked her whether she kissed with her eyes closed.

The *Newsday* class action dragged on and on. Deposition after deposition was taken. *Newsday* hired statisticians; we hired statisticians. *Newsday* hired fancy lawyers; we hired fancy lawyers. *Newsday* had deep pockets; we did not.

We had been funding our suit with donations from the women, by holding fundraisers, and with some money from our union, the Graphic Communications Workers. But most important, we got the free support of a not-for-profit federal agency called the National Law Employment Project. But by 1982, with Ronald Reagan in the White House and a change in attitude pervading the land, we knew the employment project wasn't long for this world, nor was a judicial climate sympathetic to women's rights.

We were tired, broke, and going to lose our lawyers, so we settled out of court on the eve of trial. For our efforts we got an affirmative action program promising advancement for women in all areas of the paper. For a couple of years, we saw progress. But in fact, the greatest changes at *Newsday* were made during the years the suit was on the table, between 1973 and 1981—the years the women's movement was being taken seriously by friend and foe. Women were made editors; women were sent to the major political bureaus like Albany and Washington; women were given major assignments. And we expected the tide would become a tidal wave.

Instead, as the 1980s progressed, the tide turned.

Management felt it could ignore the affirmative action plan and discontinue some of the gains made. They were right. As the situation started to revert, the women seemed to shrug it off. Those of us who had driven so hard were exhausted; the new women, hired due to our efforts, didn't seem to know how to organize for themselves. They would try to organize around a complaint and the effort would fade like a rainbow.

But it was not only at *Newsday* that the needs of women—as well as the needs of labor and minorities and the poor—were now on the back burner, or worse, ridiculed and demeaned, or made vulnerable by backlash. No, the malaise was nationwide. It threatened not only future progress but past gains. Never again would the women's movement have the strength and breadth it did in the 1970s. We are still feeling the backwash of the 1980s today. And now in the 1990s we must face a new threat—a threat of women who call themselves feminists yet who disavow just about everything feminists have stood for.

I would like to take a few minutes to talk about a phenomenon, which I call neo-feminism. It is represented by women like Camille Paglia, who said,

"It is the patriarchal society that has freed me as a woman." Katie Roiphe claims date-rape is over stressed because none of her friends told her they had been date-raped in college. Ariana Huffington, the immigrant from Greece, rails against immigration; Christina Hoff Sommers's *Who Stole Feminism? How Women Have Betrayed Women* was financed by two right-wing think tanks; and Lisa Birnbaum, who claims feminists like me are out of touch and says that, philosophically, her feminist friends from Brooklyn Heights have everything in common with Phyllis Schlafly except class. Yes, these are the women who call themselves feminists today.

What is common to all these women is that they claim their movement has been hijacked by left-wing sore losers who don't know when they've already won. Sore losers like me. These neo-fems concede that women were discriminated against once, yes, but that is past, and those who think there is still a way to go are just whiners, or, to use their phrase, victim feminists.

And what is also common to these neo-fems, is that they are allied with the radical right. I see them as instruments of the radical right who are being used as women historically have been used—to promote other people's agendas. They may call their organizations by names like Independent Women's Forum, the Freedom Network, and Network for Empowering Women, but in truth they are limbs of the conservative tree, hiding under the word feminist to destroy everything we won in the 1970s and tried to maintain in the 1980s. It's difficult enough keeping our gains without a Trojan horse in our midst.

What exactly was it that broke our balloon, stopped progress in its tracks, and then opened the doors to revisionists like Paglia, Roiphe, and crew?

To Betty Schlein, the NOW president I spoke of, who in later years was a political operative in the state Democratic Party, the defeat of the ERA in the late 1970s marked the end of the glory years for the second wave of feminism. With this symbol fell a movement. Others believe it was the election of Ronald Reagan in 1980—representing not only a backlash to the growing rights of women, but to the rights of all the have-nots in society. We were drowning in the conservative tide. Others say that once women had made progress and had something to lose, they were afraid to rattle their cages any longer, especially where their careers were concerned.

My theory is that the swell of the women's movement receded because the second and third generation of feminists we expected to materialize in our wake and take over the helm did not emerge in large enough numbers. Why? Quite possibly because young women today grew up with the advances we had won and cannot believe they were not always there, that they had to be fought for, and have to continue to be fought for lest they become eroded. To them, life without a credit card of their own; quotas on women in colleges; newspapers with ads that read Help Wanted Male, Help Wanted Female, with

Fig. 29.1. Marilyn Goldstein.

all the good jobs in the male columns, are no more immediate than
the Spanish Inquisition. That's history.

When I think of the 1970s, I
think of all the energy we had.
There seemed always to be scores
of women interested in working on
whatever project was necessary.
And maybe all the energy came
from the fact that we gained so
much ground. We saw things
change right before our eyes. When you start from zero, everything is up.
We could see the differences we made so distinctly.

One day you could not get into an Ivy League university and the next
day you could. One day you could be escorted out of the men-only Oak Room
of the Plaza and the next day you could have lunch there. One day you could
not get a mortgage based on both a husband's and wife's salary and the next
day you could. One day you could not get a legal abortion, the next day you
could. One day there were no lawsuits involving discrimination due to
gender, the next day there were. One day there was no such concept as sexual
harassment, the next day it was illegal. One day American Express could
deny you a credit card, the next day you were allowed to overextend yourself
just like men. One day the idea of women politicians was a dream and now
even Republicans run women.

Besides, these aims were specific; much could be changed by changing
the law. Now it gets a little harder. It is attitudes that need to be changed now,
not laws. And it's easier to legislate than change thinking.

Men and women, for example, still do not equally share the domestic
load. So for too many, Women's Liberation means only the right to hold two
full time jobs, one at home and one at work.

Fathers claim they take half responsibility for their children today, but
show me one father who actually went out to find and hire the nanny or
day-care provider. Show me more than one father who actually took his
hard-won right to child-care leave. (The one I know, I am proud to say, is
my son-in-law.) And show me the father who actually stays home from work
when the baby is sick.

While no man, except maybe Patrick Buchanan, will insist women are less capable than men these days, show me the man who considers a female college classmate one of the old boys' network. Show me the voters who, while never condemning all incompetent white male politicians because one fails, do not still brand all women when any woman fails.

And while you're at it, count the number of women on the *Newsday* masthead.

Notes

1. "Nassau Now Herstory: The First Ten Years," p. 1 (copy in Hofstra University, Long Island Studies Institute vertical files). The early records (1970-1974) of the Long Island National Organization for Women, Nassau County Chapter are in the Department of Special Collections, Melville Library, SUNY Stony Brook, M.C. 248. (Editor's note.)

Suggested Reading

Epstein, Cynthia Fuchs and William J. Goode, eds. *The Other Half—Roads to Women's Equality.* New York: Prentice Hall, 1971.

Hole, Judith and Ellen Levine. *Rebirth of Feminism.* New York: Quadrangle Books, 1971.

Morgan, Robin, ed. *Sisterhood is Powerful: An Anthology of Writing from the Women's Liberation Movement.* New York: Vintage, 1970.

Strainchamps, Ethel Rees, ed. *Rooms With No View. A Woman's Guide to the Man's World of the Media.* New York: Harper and Row, 1974.

30. On the Frontiers of Feminism:
The Life and Vision of Letty Cottin Pogrebin

Linda F. Burghardt

Power, love, work.

Parenting, God, equality.

For the internationally known author, lecturer, and feminist activist Letty Cottin Pogrebin, these issues form the substance of her life's work. While her ideas have crossed the generations, circled the world, and leaped the barriers of gender, her kaleidoscopic vision developed slowly over many years of deep introspection which first began to find shape during her restless childhood on Long Island. Born in Jamaica, Queens, in 1939, Pogrebin grew up in a quiet, suburban neighborhood with tree-lined streets and white-washed fences, but inside her home roiled the conflicts that would fire her intellectual powers in years to come, and in her heart hid the rage that would fuel her activist energy.[1]

Pogrebin is fond of saying she grew up aspiring to her mother's character and her father's achievements.[2] Both her parents alternately supported and damaged the future activist and innovator in their own individual ways. For her primary and high school education, they sent her to a private Jewish day school where she received an excellent education in ethics, art, and academics—and patriarchy. The ego-destroying paternalism that was fully supported by her father, Jacob, became the central locus of a full-fledged adolescent rebellion in later years. But as a child, she was carefully schooled in the power of female secrecy by her mother, Ceil.

Living under the thumb of a domineering man, Ceil nurtured her daughter's sense of independence by teaching her the value of having her own money as she squirreled away nickels and dimes from her household allowance.[3] Yet at the age of twelve, Pogrebin discovered a betrayal: both her parents had lied to her about their previous marriages and their two other daughters, one entirely unknown to her, the other passed off as a full sister when she was really another man's child.[4]

Pogrebin was changed forever by these discoveries, pledging a silent oath to herself to spend her life uncovering the subtext in the interaction between individuals, families, and groups so she would never again be hurt by the truth.[5] Carol Gilligan had not yet written *In a Different Voice,* but Letty Cottin Pogrebin had already determined she would speak in it. As an adult, she would value relationships over individual rights, and she would master the delicate art of balancing her needs rather than striving for the high level of autonomy that embraces a value system which engenders lies.[6]

At thirteen, her father prepared her for a bat mitzvah ceremony that would enable her to take her place among the adult Jews in their Conservative congregation in Jamaica.[7] Yet two years later, when her mother died, he did not allow her to join the minyan of ten adult Jews who gathered to say Kaddish for her, the prayer for the dead.[8] Yes, technically she may have been an adult, he argued, but she was not a man, and thus could not be included. Deeply hurt, bereaved, and flooded with feelings of abandonment, she turned from him, from Judaism, and from the traditional patriarchal society she saw as the embodiment of all these imprisoning forces.[9]

This painful and alienating experience set her on the course much of her future life would follow, not only giving her an emotional context from which to view society, but also providing her with a focus for her intellectual powers and her budding activist energy.[10] Feminist author Maureen T. Reddy wrote in *Sisters in Crime,* "Feminist values show subjectivity superior to pretenses of objectivity, involvement more valuable than distance, and compassion more important than justice."[11] These are the major values Pogrebin would espouse in her own writing when her feminism had the chance to flower from these early seeds planted during her Long Island girlhood.

At sixteen, Pogrebin left her childhood home, her father, and New York to begin her college education at Brandeis University in Waltham, Massachusetts.[12] She took along the nourishing self-love with which her mother had infused her life, the Jewish ethical foundation she had absorbed in school, and the iron will she had developed by both simultaneously emulating and defying her father. These gifts continued to serve her when she entered the glittering world of book publishing on the cusp of a new decade of change in New York City after her college graduation in 1959.

Through her writing and activism, Pogrebin has helped improve the status of women throughout the world and aided the acceptance of women's accomplishments through the advancement of feminist ideals. She has grappled heroically with the difficult task of reconciling feminism and Judaism and battling religious sexism in a general feminist framework.[13] But as Pogrebin herself puts it, a funny thing happened on the way to the typewriter.[14] How did she metamorphose from an apolitical Long Island girl into one of the most visible leaders of the women's movement?

Part of the answer lies in the fact that the road from a Queens row house to global activist ran through some of the most fertile fields in contemporary history, collectively known as the 1960s. Like many other young innovators who came of age in that catalytic cauldron, Pogrebin spent the early years of her career channeling her activist energy into women's organizing and general feminist consciousness raising.[15]

The resulting richness came together in 1971 with the publication of the first issue of a new magazine, founded on a new concept, put together by a new group of editors. Together with Robin Morgan, Andrea Dworkin, and Gloria Steinem, who was just beginning to achieve national stature, Letty Cottin Pogrebin founded *Ms.* magazine. In the next two and a half decades, Pogrebin would spread the gospel of feminism through her stories in *Ms.*, her column in *The Ladies Home Journal*, her articles in such diverse publications as the *New York Times, Tikkun*, and *Working Woman*, in her books, and in her lectures around the globe.

In an interview, Pogrebin said she believes she has been able to reach the minds and hearts of so many people because she is "a radical woman who leads a very conventional life. This has made all the difference in the level of trust I am able to engender in ordinary people, who might otherwise not listen to a bona fide feminist."[16]

At the time she helped found *Ms.*, Pogrebin was already leading this conventional life, married to New York City lawyer Bertram Pogrebin, and the mother of three children, twin daughters, and a son. She recalls she was the only one at an early editorial meeting of *Ms.* who had children, so when the editors decided they needed an article on non-sexist child rearing, she was the natural choice to write it.[17] As it turned out, researching that article changed her life, and also the lives of countless other parents who would read her theories in *Growing Up Free: Raising Your Child in the 80's*, the highly successful book that grew out of her research for that article.[18]

Five years previous, in 1975, she had published *Getting Yours; How to Make the System Work for the Working Woman*. This very popular book, which was selected by three major book clubs, hit the market at a time when many young women were opting to enter the job market instead of joining the ranks of park-bench mothers. Women's employment was rising dramatically, particularly in areas like management, which had long been considered part of the male domain, and someone had to show the new recruits how to succeed. Pogrebin took the challenge to heart.

In doing so, she became one of the strongest voices of a generation of women who were determined not to relive their mothers' lives. Pogrebin knew from first-hand experience how to use her talents and integrate family and work. And in *Getting Yours*, she showed other women the way.

Yet, although she dedicated *Getting Yours* "to my marvelous children, who know how to live with a working mother,"[19] she had not yet discovered for herself how to raise her son and her daughters as equals. Perhaps it should have been a short leap from envisioning herself as a professional woman equal to the men with whom she worked to providing parity in the home for all her children. But in theory, while reform in the workplace may have been at the forefront of the feminist revolution, in reality reform in the home was to lag behind for many years. This largely unexamined attitude formed the unspoken bias in the way boys vs. girls were raised.

When she published *Growing Up Free* in 1980 after nine years of research, Pogrebin posited this simple statement as the basic tenet of her book: "Non-sexist childrearing is good for your child."[20] Along with Drs. Spock, Brazelton, and Balter, her book became the bible of a generation of anxious parents looking for a better way to raise their kids. In explaining the thesis for her book, Pogrebin states, "For the non-sexist parent raising children in the here and now, the idea is to find an alternative to paranoia and paralysis and to bring a heightened consciousness into one's dealings with 'the system.'"[21]

Yet to fully comprehend what she means by "the system," it is crucial to define two vital terms that appear with frequency in her work: feminism and sexism. Pogrebin explains that by feminism she means, "An ideological commitment to the legal, economic and social equality of the sexes. It does not replace male supremacy with female supremacy or patriarchy with matriarchy. Rather, a feminist is any person, female or male, who envisions and works toward equal rights, opportunity and human dignity."[22] In the ideal re-vision of childhood laid out in her book, all people would be free of sexism, which she defines as "a bias, prejudice or discrimination based on gender, offering stereotyped expectations of what women and men or girls and boys are like."[23]

Growing up Free does not make much of religion, devoting only five pages out of 548 to a discussion of its value in the life of children. In 1980, when it was published, Pogrebin had not yet incorporated into her family life a pivotal event that had occurred nearly a decade before. When that experience finally hit home, as she recounts in *Deborah, Golda and Me,* it came with the force of a comet, leaving no surface of her life unmarked. Like the early years that shaped the philosophy she was to embrace, this event, too, grew out of her deep roots on Long Island.[24]

Since 1968, Pogrebin and her family had been spending summers on Fire Island. Although they did not consider themselves observant Jews, they joined with other families in the resort community to observe the Jewish holy days in early fall of 1970. Pogrebin was able to reconstruct sufficient knowledge from her childhood education at the Jewish day school to volunteer as the cantor.[25]

She experienced a deep spiritual awakening from this event, and continued to serve as the cantor for the next thirteen years.[26] During this time, her heightened religious identity was directly challenged at two United Nations-sponsored international conferences that forced her to confront the existence of anti-Semitism in the women's movement. The result of this double trauma

Fig. 30.1. Letty Cottin
Pogrebin. Photograph
courtesy of Crown Publishers.

was a deep self-examina-
tion, and finally, in 1991,
*Deborah, Golda and Me;
Being Female and Jewish
in America.*

Always seeing herself
as the outsider looking for
a way in, Pogrebin had
made significant improve-
ments in the status of
women in the workplace
and the home. In this book, she now explained how she came to do the same
with Judaism, historically a male preserve where women, though honored
for their contribution, were not perceived as full members of the group.
Pogrebin determined that it was not enough for individual women to be
accepted, as she had been as cantor at Fire Island services; it was mandatory
for the door to be opened to everyone. "Unless women band together to
challenge the principles underlying our exclusion," she wrote, "our individual advances will never add up to permanent progress for Jewish women."[27]

Demonstrating once again the old feminist maxim that the personal is
political, the book illustrates her struggle to integrate her two identities,
feminism and Judaism. She calls it "living with a feminist head and a Jewish
heart"[28] and describes her journey from alienation to reconciliation in a way
that enables her readers to conceive of taking the trip themselves.

Before she was able to tell this deeply personal story, Pogrebin published
Family Politics; Love and Power on an Intimate Frontier in 1983 to a chorus
of powerful comments from such diverse critics as Phyllis Theroux, Phil
Donahue, and Senator Bob Packwood. In this book Pogrebin explores "the
legitimate dignity of the diverse marital, sexual, racial and economic family
configurations flourishing in America today," explaining that it was written
for what she calls "the transitional generation, a group of contemporary

people who are critical of many aspects of traditional family life but also recognize its virtues."[29]

This book gives voice to the subtext that dominates much of the more powerful interactions between individuals in a family, thus enabling family members to deal with their feelings openly and more effectively. Pogrebin's childhood oath to herself to never again be surprised by the truth is in evidence here, coupled with her strong interest in empowering others to avoid the same pain.

Like all innovators, Pogrebin keeps writing. Her book, *Getting Over Getting Older; An Intimate Memoir,* appeared on bookshelves in spring, 1996. Once again, Pogrebin is shedding light on a situation that is a current feminist issue and important to a wide range of people. But activism, of course, does not end with simply publishing a new volume.

"What is most important to me is to be a bridge builder," Pogrebin says of herself today,[30] speaking about how she has contributed to society and how she plans to continue. "I have been able to do this in two contexts: first, between family women and more radical women, and second within the Jewish community.

"It's important to understand how it's possible for me to reach such a wide audience. First, it matters that I'm comfortable with motherhood, and second, it's important that I didn't have to leave my husband to speak my thoughts. Thus I am able to represent feminism to women who might otherwise not be able to hear about it, because the very concept of it threatens their family life.

"Next, I have built a bridge within the Jewish community for Jewish identified women to be feminists and feminist women to take part fully in Jewish life. My prominence in the women's movement has let me bring light into the Jewish world for women with 'special Jewish sorrows,' the sadness of being excluded from their own tribe as full members.

"Finally, I have played a role not possible for others to play," Pogrebin says of her global influence on contemporary ideas today. "Sometimes I have been part of a legion of women working for change; sometimes I have been a special voice."[31]

But despite the fact that her words have reached around the world, helping to mold contemporary thought and projecting into the lives of future generations, Letty Cottin Pogrebin will always be a part of the home-grown history of Queens, with her roots buried deep in the soil of Long Island and her branches growing always toward the light.

Notes

1. Letty Cottin Pogrebin, *Deborah, Golda and Me; Being Female and Jewish in America* (New York: Crown Publishers, 1991), p. 5.

2. Ibid., p. 82.

3. Ibid., p. 13.

4. Ibid., p. 5.

5. Ibid., p. 8.

6. Carol Gilligan, *In a Different Voice* (Cambridge: Harvard University Press, 1982), p. 49.

7. Pogrebin, *Deborah, Golda and Me,* p. 33.

8. Ibid., p. 42.

9. Lore Dickstein, "Counting Herself In," *New York Times Book Review,* October 20, 1991, p. 16.

10. Midge Decter, "Engendering Judaism," *Commentary,* January 1992, p. 62.

11. Maureen T. Reddy, *Sisters in Crime* (New York: Continuum, 1988), p. 67.

12. Pogrebin, *Deborah, Golda and Me,* p. 148.

13. Dickstein, "Counting Herself In," p. 15.

14. Letty Cottin Pogrebin, *Growing Up Free; Raising Your Child in the 80's* (New York: McGraw-Hill, 1980), p. 1.

15. Decter, "Engendering Judaism," p. 62.

16. Personal interview by author with L. C. Pogrebin, October 20, 1995.

17. Pogrebin, *Growing Up Free,* p. 1.

18. *National Review,* April 3, 1981, p. 369.

19. Letty Cottin Pogrebin. *Getting Yours: How to Make the System Work for the Working Woman* (New York: David McKay Company, 1975), dedication page.

20. Pogrebin, *Growing Up Free,* p. 8.

21. Ibid., p. 519.

22. Ibid., p. xi.

23. Ibid., p. x.

24. *Publishers Weekly,* August 2, 1991, p. 58.

25. Pogrebin, *Deborah, Golda and Me,* p. 93.

26. *Publishers Weekly,* August 2, 1991, p. 58.

27. Pogrebin, *Deborah, Golda and Me,* p. 150.

28. Ibid., p. 273.

29. Letty Cottin Pogrebin, *Family Politics; Love and Power on an Intimate Frontier* (New York: McGraw-Hill, 1983), p. ix.

30. Interview of Pogrebin.

31. Ibid.

Additional Works Consulted

Bird, Caroline. *The Two Paycheck Marriage; How Women at Work are Changing Life in America.* New York: Rawson, Wade, 1979.

Eagle, Dr. Carol J., and Carol Colman. *All That She Can Be.* New York: Simon and Schuster, 1993.

Morgan, Robin. *The Anatomy of Freedom; Feminism, Physics and Global Politics.* Garden City: Anchor Press/Doubleday, 1982.

Steinem, Gloria. *Outrageous Acts and Everyday Rebellions.* New York: Holt, Rinehart and Winston, 1983.

Tannen, Dr. Deborah. *You Just Don't Understand; Women and Men in Conversation.* New York: William Morrow and Co., 1990.

31. Significant Moments in the Evolution of the Southern Suffolk NOW Chapters

Linda Lane-Weber

The South Suffolk chapter of the National Organization for Women (NOW) rolled into being on the new wave of feminism in America. I was there at its beginning. The starting up of a NOW chapter is always an exciting event. Besides attracting women of proven abilities, new chapters hold the promise of being a training ground where budding activists can develop talents in communication and leadership. The memory of our first meeting is a vivid one. On a bitterly cold January 22, 1985, twelve of us gathered around a circular wooden coffee table in the meeting room of the Unitarian Universalist Society in Bay Shore. I had the pre-convening kit that Mary Ann Page, Membership Task Force Chair of NOW-NYS (New York State) had sent me, because I was the one who protested most vehemently the official dissolution of the former South Shore NOW chapter the previous November. Joy Wowak, long-time South Shore member, had the bookkeeping skills necessary to be treasurer. Without hesitation we all put our dollars on the table to cover the $25 cost of a convening kit from the State, and we had all we needed to start a chapter.

One month later, on February 26, 1985, twenty-four people came to a publicly advertised start-up meeting in the same room, where Jane Seitz-McGuire, who would be in charge of programming, Joy Wowak, who would be treasurer, and I, who agreed to be first president, became the three conveners. South Suffolk NOW was born.[1]

Between 1986 and 1988, Wowak was elected president twice. I served a second term and Carole Delisa, Camille Cono, Jean Howard, and, in 1994, Barbara Celona followed, who was succeeded in 1996 by Peggyann McGee. While the chapter's purpose remained the same as that of its predecessor, the type of women, focuses, and activities were a little different from the old South Shore chapter.[2]

South Shore NOW had been founded in 1972, when a group of southern Suffolk women led by Irene Wolf, who had previously been attending Nassau NOW's meeting, decided there were enough women to start their own chapter. Back then, in the 1960s and 1970s, female sexuality, a new area of exploration for women, was as important a focus as reproductive rights. Feminists were avidly concerned with public education providing equal opportunity for girls in careers, in vocations, and in sports.

Like other chapters on Long Island, South Shore NOW established a committee for employment compliance that helped women with work-related complaints. We promoted public awareness about sexist language, particularly that which perpetuated sex-role stereotypes. Job titles ending with "man" were cited, rejected, and replaced with titles that were receptive to both sexes. Feminism was still a novel idea, and feminist boutiques replete with bumper stickers, T-shirts, coffee mugs, and buttons abounded. We returned from our conferences and conventions with message-bearing souvenirs for our less progressive friends and relatives.

A woman in our chapter named Ellen Cooperman sought and won, on appeal, the right to change her name to "Cooperperson." The change, first viewed as frivolous by some, became recognized as a personal, political statement indicative of her deep commitment to changing society. Cooperperson, who had played an important role in producing a slide show that explained how the various committees in the chapter functioned, went on to a position in the Women's Studies program at SUNY Farmingdale and later started her own management consultation corporation. Before that happened, however, a dispute arose between factions in the chapter over credit for the copyrights to the slide show. It became one of the issues that contributed to the resignation of members and to the ultimate demise of South Shore NOW.

NOW was an operating arena where women denied power elsewhere in society could have a voice and be influential; some were very possessive of this empowerment and competed even among themselves. Faction disputes and heatedly-contested elections characterized the functioning of the higher level NOW organizations (state and national), as well as local chapters. Among other issues were the role of men in the organization and whether the numbers of highly-visible lesbians would damage our "image." Bisexual women were bringing us horror stories of their becoming "defendants" at hearings to obtain child support money from "dead beat dads," when judges as well as respondents used their sexual and affectional preferences against them to deny their petitions for support. We listened with sympathy rather than anger. It took changes throughout all the levels of NOW (national, state, and local chapters) to finally embrace lesbians as sisters, to equally defend them as citizens, and to recognize that we are all women with freedoms and civil rights at stake. It took time to develop trust.

In 1974, several South Shore chapter members became aware that girls elsewhere were suing for the right to play Little League ball. In May, Marian Kent, a chapter activist whose daughter Laurie had been denied the opportunity to join a Little League team, filed a complaint with the New York State Division of Human Rights. None of us went with her. We all feared appearing too radical and that we might damage her case! We waited; she filed; we worried; she won. Laurie finally played. We cheered!

Domestic relations was another major issue in the 1970s and 1980s. Divorce laws were unfair to women and NOW-NYS was pushing for reform, monitoring pending legislation, and distributing position papers on specific bills for chapter letter writing campaigns. The state level activity actually started with two women, Lillian Kozak and Joan Anderson, from the Nassau and Mid-Suffolk chapters.[3] Equitable distribution laws were finally passed, and NOW grieved the absence of "presumption of equal" and other legal flaws. With the advent of common joint custody awards and the end of maternal stereotyping, non-paying fathers used custody threats to dissuade women's attempts to gain child support payments.

Rape victims were also abused by the system and often treated callously by both the police and the judiciary. Instead of attempting to remove officers and judges viewed as unfit for their professions, NOW chapters initiated sensitivity training. South Shore NOW did not have its own active rape task force; however, three women from Huntington NOW's Rape Task Force, Susan Saltz, Sue McGrath Graham, and Cathy Hazel, got together and started Victims Information Bureau of Suffolk (VIBS) to help women who were victims of violence. Securing funding was impossible without an established, seasoned board of directors, so the women had to allow the board of a Suffolk hotline called Response to oversee the operation, and they did not, themselves, serve on the VIBS board. South Shore NOW utilized these women as resources and made referrals to the agency they had founded.

Spouse abuse was coming out of the closet in the 1970s and the domestic violence committees of the NOW chapters were not adequate to address all the needs of battered women. Domestic violence was an issue which spanned liberal, conservative, and radical interests. In 1975, the Long Island Women's Coalition (LIWC) was a loose, unincorporated collection of groups including NOW chapters concerned with injustices against women, primarily, nonsupport. I gathered the groups and formed the Coalition in response to a request from the Suffolk branch of a group called FOCUS (For Our Children and Us), that wanted better enforcement of child support laws. We demonstrated outside of Suffolk Family Court in 1975, and received favorable press coverage; the Court acquiesced in a few of our points, such as opening some of the proceedings to an advocate.

During the winter holiday season, our NOW phones never stopped ringing with calls from victims of domestic violence seeking help—advice, legal or psychological referrals, and sometimes shelter. Grace Welch, South Shore chapter president at that time, telephoned me to say that we had to do something to house women who had left violent domiciles with their children and had no place to go. Some had left literally in their nightgowns and had called from phone booths on the Long Island Expressway.

I invited the interested LIWC groups' representatives for a meeting, and we decided to start a volunteer safe-homes network (which we did that year) and to incorporate LIWC as a not-for-profit corporation (1976). Two other women and I had crisis hotlines in our homes, and I had the freezer for a food-lending bank in my den! We were all unpaid volunteers. The first three member organizations were South Shore NOW, the Islip Women's Center at Oakdale, and Huntington NOW. Their representatives became board members, and we later expanded the board to include other NOW chapters and organizations as well as individual members.[4] We laid the groundwork for opening a central shelter facility in addition to operating the safe-homes.

LIWC, like NOW, was a not-for-profit organization, but contributions to either of them were not tax-deductible. Realizing the LIWC needed a tax-deductible status to ensure sufficient grantors to purchase a facility and operate a shelter, Marsha King, the first LIWC treasurer, and I drove down to Washington, D.C. on a very hot summer day in 1977 to convince the Internal Revenue Service to grant us a 501(c)3 charitable deduction status.[5]

I can still see us, seated around a large conference table. Selig Rosen-zweig, our attorney, was to my left, the hearing officer to my right, and Marsha King across from me. The hearing officer objected to our having demonstrated outside of Family Court in 1975 and to several of our other early activities. LIWC was "suspect" because of its origins with NOW members. Rosenzweig responded that we were only seeking enforcement of existing laws, not legislative changes. I insisted that we devoted all of our board meetings, most of the time, to the domestic violence project. King and I had an "ace in the hole," a brown paper grocery bag filled with cassette tapes of our meetings for the past year. I had a cassette player in a shoulder bag, and Marsha and I dumped the tapes on the table. I said, eagerly, "Here, let me show you. We have been working on a shelter!" The hearing officer drew back a little and declined, saying, "No. No, thank you. That's all right." We had our charitable status. This opened the gates to big funding grants which gave me the opportunity to develop some skill as a grant writer, much of which I learned from Susan Saltz, the member of the Huntington NOW Rape Task Force who was one of the three founders of VIBS.[6]

LIWC ultimately phased out the court reform project, the food-lending bank, and some other early activities which were not allowable under the tax code for a 501(c)3 organization.[7] We were now focused on the domestic violence project, and members of South Shore and Huntington NOW were actively involved.

Raising money was, and always is, difficult for not-for-profit groups designed to help women. LIWC's first grants which ranged from $900 to $3,000 were from IBM, Citibank, and the Presbytery of Long Island (Pres-byterian churches in Nassau and Suffolk). By 1979, there was plenty of community support for a central shelter house, but still not enough money. Our bank balance on February 28, 1979, was only $3,620.54. Then we got a break! As volunteer Executive Director, I submitted a proposal to the North Shore Unitarian Veatch Program, which awarded us a renewable, amendable $25,474 grant to hire a full-time services coordinator and a part-time housing specialist. By 1983, we had office space donated by Southside Hospital, a central shelter facility, and a $200,000 operating budget. Despite this success, competition among not-for-profits for awards from the same funding sources was intense, and LIWC board and staff suffered chronic, annual anxiety over whether there would be enough money next year to pay salaries.

Through these initial years of development, the NOW chapters in Suffolk County continued to be a source of volunteers for LIWC's services and activities. Some of the victims, in turn, when no longer in crisis, joined consciousness raising, or "CR" groups, which were sponsored regularly by the chapters.

Consciousness raising in the 1970s and 1980s consisted of small groups of women who got together weekly to discuss topics of interest to themselves. While the subjects often included discrimination they had experienced in their own lives, the groups were unstructured, leaderless, and often continued for years. Since successful CR continued indefintely, and the women, who had formed a bond, were bound by confidentiality, new women rarely had the opportunity to join a group. Our old South Shore chapter, therefore, was not revitalized by new members through CR. Consciousness raising had long been recognized as a means of introducing women to feminist philosophy, helping them tie in to a support group, and bringing them in as chapter activists.

By 1985, the inception of the South Suffolk NOW chapter, National NOW had developed printed guidelines for "Ten Session Feminist Political Consciousness Raising." This was a structured series of discussions on a list of feminist topics related to NOW issues. Each topic moved from the "personal" to the "political" and had a suggested action ending. There was a leader who stayed with and participated in each group. For years, I was one such leader. Camille Cono, our fourth chapter president, joined the chapter through a CR group, became a member, and later was elected president of South Suffolk NOW. The composition of the new chapter was different. It was not comprised primarily of victims, so-called "fringe radicals," and charismatic leaders, as South Shore had been; indeed, non-traditional ideas, personalities, and lifestyles were already being assimilated into the mainstream, and these mainstream women who were fed up with lack of opportunity and unequal protection under unequal laws came seeking "know-how," encouragement, and funding to educate themselves and develop their potential. Many had, themselves, been liberated from oppressive interpersonal, domestic, and employment situations. All the women in the new chapter were ready to work with and to befriend other women of different ages with varied economic backgrounds, educational experiences, sexual and affectional preferences, and personal styles.

The abortion issue, which had served as a rallying point to polarize society in the United States, was, and continues to be, a major issue. Violent assaults on abortion clinics and harassment of women visiting them resulted in the mobilization of national and state NOW, as well as local chapters, to defend these victims against such groups as Operation Rescue. South Suffolk NOW participates in these defenses, with volunteer members ready at a moment's notice. Some have attended formalized training sessions and learned how to escort and to protect women seeking medical care at these facilities when they are under siege by violent, anti-choice radicals. These "war" activities are scheduled along with routine chapter tasks such as newsletter preparation, public information programs, fundraising, and committee meetings. Our chapter members are engaged in unconventional combinations of activities. Single mothers of young children are attending law school; women working on genteel and intellectual feminist projects (book clubs and newsletters) are also guarding the doors of abortion clinics; chapter leaders and planners are stuffing envelopes and marching at the front of feminist demonstrations.[8]

I remember a chilly spring dawn several years ago when Camille Cono was South Suffolk chapter president. A group of us responded to an emergency contact telephone warning that anti-choice demonstrators were scheduled to block the entrance to a clinic in Lindenhurst. About eight of us, including Camille's husband, Joe Ettari, and Sandra Jelnicky, a long-time South Shore as well as South Suffolk member, gained access to the doorway first and seated ourselves on the cold steps and stoop. We arranged ourselves in such a way as to open a pathway for patients and staff to enter the building which contains an ophthalmologist's office and other businesses, as well as the clinic. The police finally arrived; there were no confrontations this time. The crowd dissipated, and we left, too.[9]

The abortion issue, the need to elect pro-choice candidates for public office, the threats against affirmative action, and the plans to cut funding from women's programs pushed the new wave of feminism forward and prompted NOW chapters, including South Suffolk, to focus on political activities. Following State, and National guidelines, NOW began holding workshops on the election process and began preparing and running women for office.

In 1987, realizing that supporting the political campaigns of feminist candidates who would advocate our issues is an expensive proposition, several NOW women got together and formed the Long Island NOW

Alliance PAC (Political Action Committee) under the guidance of Karen Perlman, from the Huntington chapter, who became the PAC's first president. All five Long Island chapters—Nassau, Huntington, South Suffolk, Mid-Suffolk, and East End—are members, and send delegates to meetings at local libraries. They review chapter recommendations to endorse or support specific candidates, and they plan the annual PAC fundraiser, so that selected candidates can receive financial contributions, as well as physical help for their campaigns. The guest speaker at the PAC's first fundraiser, which was held at Touro Law College in Huntington, was Gloria Steinem. Lucille Divona was second PAC president, immediately following Karen Perlman.

According to Arlene Goscinski, third PAC president, tens of thousands of dollars have been raised over the years which have been given to hundreds of candidates who support feminist causes. The president in 1996 was long-time activist Carol Traynor, who was succeeded by Melissa Bishop-Morgan from East End NOW, who is also a vice-president for NOW-NYS. As the PAC's recognition and influence grow, veteran feminists with leadership ability are drawn to participate in it, as well as to take positions in NOW-NYS, because they see these larger operations as viable means to make changes. Their commitment to the PAC or NOW-NYS sometimes causes some inner conflicts for them and some ambivalent feelings for other activists in their local chapter.

The experiences of the previous two decades taught feminists of the 1990s that as well as insufficient funds for feminist politics, there were also financial needs for charitable, educational, and health-related projects for women and girls. Betty Schlein, a past Nassau NOW president, and three other forsighted women got together in 1992 and founded the Long Island Fund for Women and Girls. The four women—Betty Schlein, Emily Berkowitz, Barbara Strongin (a director of Planned Parenthood), and Suzy Sonenberg (Director of the Long Island Community Foundation)—all experienced fundraisers, decided to establish a permanent endowment, the income from which could be used to support community-based efforts by women and girls to achieve their agendas and to support services and advocacy that address critical women's issues.[10] Since its inception, the Fund has given grants to thirty-nine, primarily 501(c)3 groups, totaling $70,000 (in three grant-awarding cycles).

On November 30, 1995, I attended the Fund's first annual awards breakfast, "Women Achievers Against the Odds," at the Melville Marriott. There were four hundred present and among the eleven grantees were: East End NOW, LIGALY (Long Island Gay and Lesbian Youth), and a domestic violence agency alliance which included Long Island Women's Coalition and Victims Information Bureau of Suffolk. I see the Long Island Fund for

Women and Girls and the NOW Alliance PAC as the two most significant developments for women on Long Island in the past decade.

LIWC is now a United Way organization whose hotline received 6,140 calls in 1996. That year, shelter was provided to 289 women and children, support to 185 persons in 249 group sessions, advocacy for 1,768 women, and community education for more than 5,235 adults and children.

Our South Suffolk NOW chapter still holds monthly, public meetings at the Bay Shore-Brightwaters Library. It has grown from seventy members to about 150, with an additional 150 at-large NOW members in our area. As with our CR groups, its focus has changed largely from the "personal" to the "political." The nature of the feminist movement in southern Suffolk has changed because women are developing their potential and are on the move, but NOW is alive and well, and chapters like ours still offer women—and men—the opportunity to develop leadership and other skills and to work productively with like-hearted others who share their belief in equality.

Notes

1. Sources for the data in this paper are my recollections and copies of documents I retained from the time I served as President of South Shore NOW, President of South Suffolk NOW, and President and volunteer Executive Director of the Long Island Women's Coalition, Inc. The following people provided input to substantiate my memories and gave me permission to use their names: Barbara Celona, Camille Cono, Arlene Goscinski, Marian Kent, Marsha King, Lillian Kozak, Gloria Rosenblum, Don Sallah, Barbara Strongin, Grace Welch, and Joy Wowak.

2. According to the NOW Statement of Purpose, adopted October 29, 1966, at the organizing conference in Washington, D.C., "The purpose of NOW is to take action to bring women into full participation in the mainstream of American society now, exercising all the privileges and responsibilities thereof in truly equal partnership with men."

3. Lillian Kozak, a CPA and member of Nassau NOW, shared her expertise on the financial aspects of divorce with lawyers and legislators, testifying regularly at hearings and working tirelessly for divorce reform. For years, at NOW-NYS's council meetings attended by South Shore delegates every other month in Albany, Kozak, as Domestic Relations Task Force Chair, presented reports and planned strategies and activities.

4. The first LIWC board of directors was comprised of three lawyers: Don Sallah, Gloria Rosenblum (who was affiliated with our South Shore NOW chapter), and Selig Rosenzweig (an acquaintance of Don's); and Fred Saunders, an IBM marketing executive, whose wife Genevieve belonged to Huntington NOW. Fred became first Chair of the LIWC board. I was President and first Executive Director, Barbe Maxwell was vice-president, Isobel Weider was secretary, and Marsha King was treasurer. Don Sallah did the legal work to incorporate us and provided prototype papers for me to write our first by-laws. Don Sallah and Gloria Rosenblum are still practicing law in Suffolk County, and Marsha King is now a supervisor at ARINC (Aeronautical Radio, Inc.) and owns a travel agency, The Travel Shoppe, in Islip.

5. Don Sallah arranged for Selig Rosenzweig to fly down and meet us in the IRS building lobby. Marsha was a radio operator for Aeronautical Radio, Inc. (ARINC). I figured if pilots listened to her with respect, the hearing officer would certainly have to do the same.

6. I first met Susan Saltz in the late 1970s. In addition to the Huntington NOW Rape Task Force, she worked for an HMO at the time. Susan showed me how to write grant applications and guided me through a functional understanding of the Comprehensive Employment Training Act (CETA) and other government programs and agencies we needed to operate LIWC's housing and supportive services. She knew more officials and had more connections than I, and without her help, I seriously doubt that our central shelter facility would have opened in 1983. Saltz has since finished law school and opened her own law practice in Huntington.

7. We stopped the Search and Serve Squads, which served legal processes on "dodgers," and were viewed as "dangerous" by some LIWC members. We also totally abandoned a project to reform paternity proceedings in Family Court to allow women to use inclusionary blood grouping tests to prove filiation and ultrasound to prove conception date for petitioners who had not yet delivered. In order to promote the project, I had published an article on the issue in the *New York Times* (September 26, 1976, Long Island Weekly Section, p. 22), which the editors had lasciviously titled "On the Track of the Unwed Father."

8. The immediate past South Suffolk Chapter president, Barbara Celona, is raising her seven-year-old daughter, Molly, and attending law school; she was elected a vice-president of NOW-NYS.

9. Since that morning, Jelnicky has passed the bar exam. Cono, who stays in touch, became a training executive for Fortunoff's; she began maternity leave in 1996 to care for her son, Benjamin Joseph.

10. As Barbara Strongin tells it, beginning in January 1992, the four founders of the Long Island Fund for Women and Girls met regularly for carp salad lunches, where they discussed the expected impact of forthcoming governmental budget slashes on women's programs. Women's programs, at the time, were receiving only four cents of every foundation dollar and even less of corporate contributions. The Long Island Community Foundation generously provided start-up management, as well as office space and equipment to the Fund. By a Veatch grant, the Fund was able to hire two outreach people to assess needs at grassroots levels. Recently, the Fund completed a "Youth in Philanthropy" project where young people learned how to raise money.

32. Women on the Job:
Long Island's Grassroots Action for Pay Equity

Charlotte M. Shapiro

Women on the Job was conceived as a women's equal employment project to address sex discrimination in employment. The project began with just two women who conducted a feasibility study to determine what were the most important employment issues for women on Long Island. They learned that the overwhelming issue was women's undervalued wages, a consequence of women's concentration in sex-segregated, low paying occupations. There were sexist assumptions about "women's work" and "men's work." And, despite the rising need for women to support themselves and their children, the myth persisted that women were only supplemental or secondary wage earners.[1]

Pay Equity: Social and Economic Climate

Women on the Job's initiation depended upon its activist founders, but it could not have been organized without the special conjunction of conditions that encouraged this singular women's equal employment rights project. In 1979, women who worked full-time earned fifty-nine cents for every dollar earned by men.[2] The Equal Pay Act of 1964 had had little to no impact on women's average wages. The long-accepted tradition that women be paid less than men persisted because women were "trapped in female occupational ghettoes."[3] At a time of a great influx of women into the labor market, that tradition came under increased scrutiny as a condition that deprived women of fair compensation for their work; it was sex-based wage discrimination.

The concept of pay equity, equal pay for work of equal value, or "comparable worth" gained increasing recognition in 1979.[4] Essentially, it was an effort to assess the real value of wages by applying job evaluation methodologies to occupations in which women predominated.[5] The idea of comparable worth grew out of the realities of "pink ghettos." Women accounted for eighty percent of the workers in eight of the lowest paying occupations.[6] To achieve equal pay for work of equal or comparable value in skills, effort, and responsibilities would require job evaluation studies—well established wage-setting methods used by management consultants and personnel directors.

Congresswoman Barbara Mikulski was quoted in the *New York Times* repeating the complaints she heard from women in her blue-collar district in Baltimore: "I'm not one of those women libbers, but I sure want to earn the same salary as the guy next to me."[7] Women who gave voice to the cause of pay equity were those most affected by gender-based wages, women who wished to be identified as "feminine," not "feminist." Yet pay equity was soon attacked as just another feminist plot.

Opposition to comparable worth from Reagan administration officials did not discourage the considerable interest and support for pay equity action on Long Island. Women on the Job and its coalitions successfully challenged sex discriminatory wages of women, primarily in public employment. Women who worked in the offices of schools and county and town governments were the cutting edge of the local pay equity movement .

Origins of Women on the Job

Several important conditions supported Long Island's efforts to launch a local pay equity project. There was national attention to the great influx of women in the workplace. Wage discrimination litigation under Title VII of the Civil Rights Act of 1964 was meeting with some success in the federal courts.[8] Feminist pressures were building within organized labor causing the AFL-CIO to support the idea of comparable worth.[9] Reports with significant prestige, such as the study performed by the National Academy of Sciences, gave indirect support to the idea of comparable worth to remedy disparate wages.[10] And, locally, there was financial support from the North Shore Unitarian Universalist Society Veatch Program, a Long Island foundation committed to the extension of equality. Long Island was fortunate to have Veatch because, unlike most national foundations, it provided seed money to community groups that would work locally to improve economic and social conditions for women and minorities.

Veatch's confidence was placed with a civic leader whose track record for successful community projects was impeccable. Lillian McCormick, founder and director of Women on the Job since 1982, had started her career as a human services professional and activist twenty years earlier when she marshalled local money and support for a community center for domestic workers in Great Neck. Among McCormick's more prominent initiatives to improve the social fabric of Long Island communities were a group home for young runaway and abused boys that became part of Children's House, a safe home for victims of family violence (a service still offered by the Coalition Against Domestic Violence), and the historic preservation and transformation of a closed school building into affordable senior housing and community center. As an innovator for the advancement of human services for more than thirty years, McCormick has been the recipient of many awards and honors from her peers.

Partner and co-founder of Women on the Job was Charlotte Shapiro. As former teacher and author, she contributed her skills in research, writing, and program development as well as her special experience in legislative lobbying on feminist issues. Her experience in community organization, local government, and leadership training had been a product of her activism in the League of Women Voters over a period of twenty-five years.

Long Island was fortunate to have a large number of highly skilled community leaders, women and men. Those who joined the Board of Directors of Women on the Job lent their prestige and expertise to the project. The Board, in 1982, consisted of three attorneys who had worked with well-established community agencies for many years, a regional administrator with the Office of Federal Contract Compliance Programs, the editor of a women's monthly newspaper, a leader in the League of Women Voters, and the executive directors of the Day Care Council, the Education Assistance Center (EAC), and PREP, an affirmative action recruitment and training program.[11]

Among the men who inspired Women on the Job's growth and achievements were Veatch's program director, Ed Lawrence; Veatch's assistant director, David Di Rienzis, who previously had been the director of the local CAP anti-poverty program; the late Winn Newman, the attorney who initiated pay equity litigation in the state of Washington on behalf of the American Federation of State, County, and Municipal Employees (AFSCME); and Sam Lynn, the regional director for the federal affirmative action Office of Federal Contract Compliance Programs.

A One-of-a-Kind, Local Employment Rights Project

Searching for a similar local project in other communities which it could replicate, Women on the Job could find no comparable model. Other local women's employment groups were training women to re-enter the workplace or helping women to overcome entry barriers to nontraditional occupations. Women on the Job had some affinity and contact with women's equal employment groups in the cities of Philadelphia, Chicago, Boston, and Cleveland, but each of them differed from Women on the Job in important respects, particularly their sponsorship by labor. Philadelphia's group, Women's Alliance for Job Equity, was tied to local labor unions rather than to community groups. Chicago's Women Employed was a statewide project engaged in advocacy and litigation. Boston and Cleveland were large city projects with ties to a national organization, the National Association of Working Women, 9 to 5. Women on the Job's support came from a strong coalition of local community organizations, individual members, and the Veatch Foundation. Its project design would have to stand alone.

The issue of pay equity was supported by the fledgling National Committee on Pay Equity (NCPE) founded in 1979.[12] NCPE has kept pay equity advancement on the national agenda by providing resources to local and state organizations and lobbying Congress. Commissions on the status of women, some of which supported pay equity, had been appointed by governors and mayors in many states and large cities. The major players in the pay equity movement could be seen in NCPE's roster of member organizations. Labor unions had the greatest representation, thirty-five percent; professional, civic, and women's organizations, twenty-five percent; civil rights and religious groups, ten percent each; and commissions, five percent.[13]

Advancing Strategies: Coalition Building

Social and political change require a large constituency. Out of that need came the broad coalition of community groups and professional associations, the Women on the Job Task Force. Task Force membership made it advantageous to broaden the project's program to include related equal employment issues: affirmative action and sexual harassment prevention.

Twelve women representing a broad range of ten community groups met for the first Task Force meeting in April 1983.[14] Before the year was out, seven more groups had come aboard, making for a total of nineteen organizations. They ranged from the League of Women Voters, the American Association of University Women (AAUW), Older Women's League, and two union locals to professional women's groups in business, school administration, law, social work, and science.[15] The Task Force met monthly in order to set advocacy goals, to act as a forum for women who had discrimination complaints, to join in action to redress sex discrimination, and to give direction to the work of Women on the Job. In ten years, the Task Force grew to fifty-nine organization members.

The Task Force was the first coalition to be established. The second coalition consisted of the women working in sex-segregated occupations. Established in 1983, it was an essential part of the project's organizational strategy. Its purpose was to provide leadership development, to document disparate treatment for women, to push for pay equity through contract negotiations, and to facilitate networking among many small groups of clerical employees who were isolated in their respective places of employment. The coalition grew to include representatives from sixty-two of the 126 school districts on Long Island.[16]

Known as the Educational Support Staff Association (ESSA), the coalition included women with varied job titles: clerk, aide, secretary, or school nurse. Cutting across school district lines, ESSA increased communication, provided mutual support, pressured employers and unions, and, in cooperation with the Task Force, carried out advocacy campaigns for the public.[17]

Technical Assistance and Advocacy

Women who had to negotiate for pay equity with their employers needed to understand job evaluation methodology to be aware of their rights under Title VII of the Civil Rights Act, and to know how to gain support from co-workers, school board members, community leaders and legislators. Technical assistance from Women on the Job empowered the women in pressing for pay equity in contract negotiations. The first order of business was usually sensitivity training to help the women recognize and stop sex discriminatory behavior to which they had accommodated for so many years. Many were shocked to learn that the sexual harassment and hostile work environment they had experienced on a daily basis was actually illegal behavior.

The most popular training program was called "Working Smarts." It was so successful that ESSA urged Women on the Job to write a comparable program for high school students. The four annual conferences called "Narrowing the Wage Gap," in which ESSA and the Task Force joined forces, were especially exciting. National and state leaders were invited to meet with all the women in order to "feed the fires," to promote growth, and to publicize pay equity progress.[18] Other pay equity advocacy was accomplished with how-to publications, press articles, television interviews, rallies, and a "Raises Not Roses" survey to profile school support staff. Lastly, Women on the Job monitored enforcement agencies, particularly the State Division of Human Rights, and advocated greater responsiveness to wage discrimination complaints.[19]

Setting Precedents for Pay Equity:
School Secretaries and Public Health Nurses

Among those who came to Women on the Job with complaints of wage inequities were two groups of women: clerical workers in the Glen Cove School District and public health nurses employed by Suffolk County. They represent two of the many pay equity cases addressed by Women on the Job.

In 1984, 103 clerical workers and aides, members of the Glen Cove Educational Secretaries Association (GCESA), under the leadership of their president, Marianne Stanton, went en masse to the Hempstead office of the New York State Division of Human Rights to file 103 sex discrimination complaints.[20] This group of respectable, far-from-radical women caused quite a stir in the press because of their unprecedented action. A phone call to Marianne Stanton revealed the group was totally unarmed. They had no union, no attorney, no documentation of disparate treatment, no advocates. What GCESA had, however, was a soft-spoken, intelligent, and determined president who had rallied her co-workers to protest their unfair wages.

Fig. 32.1. Pay equity rally in Glen Cove, 1986 by women employed in school offices from all over Long Island. Liz Abzug is speaking; May Newburger is seated to her left. Photograph courtesy of Women on the Job.

Women on the Job set the wheels in motion to ensure that Glen Cove's complaints would get the legal support necessary to set a precedent in the Division of Human Rights and to win their case. Women on the Job enlisted Winn Newman, the attorney who had won the first round of AFSCME's wage discrimination case in the state of Washington, acquired additional funding from Veatch, and helped the women document the wide range of gender discriminatory practices they experienced. At the same time, the advocacy component of the project, the Task Force, was put into action.[21] We used to say Glen Cove was "the tip of the iceberg." The iceberg consisted of 126 school districts on Long Island.

Over the succeeding years, Marianne Stanton's increasingly strong leadership was a valuable asset to ESSA, the coalition of school support personnel in Nassau County. Changes occurred. The women no longer allowed themselves to be called "girls," no longer smiled at degrading remarks, no longer feared negotiating contracts. To Glen Cove's horror, the women signed on with the Teamsters Union, the union's first and only school clericals local in Nassau County. In 1987, the women in GCESA won $270,000 in retroactive pay increases, professional advancement benefits, recognition for their demands that wage equity be part of contract negotiations, and the respectful treatment they deserved.[22]

Another case that set a precedent was that of public health nurses in Suffolk County who bridled under salaries that deprived them of civil service rank and pay equal to the county sanitarians (food inspectors), all male. In 1985, the Suffolk County Association of Nurses (SCAN), led by their president Jane Corrarino, met with the Women on the Job Task Force to request assistance with their lobbying for a civil service upgrade. The Task Force evaluated the merit of their sex discrimination complaints and the potential impact they could have on other women employed by the county.

Over the next eighteen months, the Task Force met with SCAN to provide technical assistance and to train its members in pay equity advocacy. Statements were made at legislative hearings, legislators were lobbied, and county data were collected on the disparities of wages in women's occupations compared to occupations held predominantly by men. Pay equity pressures were needed not only for the employer in this instance, but also for the county union to which the nurses belonged. Union leaders feared the floodgates would open up with complaints from other women in job titles held predominantly by women. And they did! We pressed on. The nurses received two civil service upgrades and salary increases to give them parity with male sanitarians.[23]

Jane Corrarino was a founding member of SCAN and its first president. Her leadership in the nurses' association, her effectiveness in educating opposing constituencies in the union, and in skillful lobbying of Suffolk County legislators were crucial to the success the nurses achieved. SCAN's pioneering efforts, with Women on the Job's assistance, paved the way for the appointment of a county government comparable worth commission, two Suffolk County job evaluation studies for all civil service workers, and the county's subsequent contractual commitment to compensatory wage gap payments.

The public health nurses' success set a precedent in Suffolk County and helped other women employees, but the financial straits of county government has made the achievement of pay equity a constant struggle in contract negotiations. It is played out in fits and starts, dependent upon the politics of changing administrations and union leadership.

Barriers to Pay Equity and Achievement

Initially, local unions rejected Women on the Job for stirring up unrest in the rank and file, for encroaching on their turf, and for threatening competion for membership. Pay equity advocacy, in many instances, was divisive—it caused internal conflict in the union from male members who frequently had a larger membership representation in the parent union than the clerical workers. The women's message was that pay inequity was a problem not only for women, but for the majority of families that depended upon two full paychecks, not one and two-thirds paychecks. The message was not always heard.

The multiplicity of governmental jurisdictions on Long Island (more than 230) presented advocates with a surfeit of resistant employers who maintained that women's lower pay was a consequence of the market, not gender. Pay equity was a hard sell. It did require a modest increase in school and municipal budget expenditures, causing the women to propose that the wage gap be closed gradually over a period of several years.

Opponents of the pay equity theory gave no credence to job evaluation as an objective methodology and ridiculed "comparable worth." They declared that comparing women's job titles to men's job titles was like comparing apples and oranges. Some, like Phyllis Schlafly, gave comparable worth the full anti-feminist treatment.

Successes

In 1983, the issue of pay equity was nonexistent in school district contract negotiations. By 1989, Women on the Job found that forty percent of the fifty support staff associations in their survey had achieved some success in narrowing the wage gap.[24] Women had succeeded in winning pay equity adjustments in twenty-five public jurisdictions over a period of seven years. Support staff in the Central Islip School District had also mounted a successful test case in the New York State Division of Human Rights in tandem with Glen Cove. The clerks in the Town of North Hempstead received civil service upgrades and raises as a consequence of unpublicized meetings with the Town Supervisor. Suffolk County's legislature appointed a Comparable Worth Commission and instituted job evaluation studies for county personnel.[25]

Grassroots action had achieved significant success. Union leaders became more responsive to the women's pay equity demands. The Civil Service Employees Association (CSEA), and the National Education Association (NEA), developed job evaluation models for school support staff positions to be used in contract negotiations. The New York State United Teachers (NYSUT), passed a resolution in support of pay equity, initiated by its members on Long Island.

Women on the Job's monitoring of the New York State Division of Human Rights' enforcement of state and federal civil rights law had some remedial influence on its investigative and administrative processes, in that class action complaints were accorded special status.

The real heroes in the grassroots pay equity campaign were the women who worked in the offices of Long Island's schools, municipal governments, and colleges. They were on the front lines. The women had to endure months, even years, of difficult contract negotiations, the contempt of bosses, the many years of waiting for a discrimination complaint to make its way through the New York State Division of Human Rights, and, too often, challenges to their dignity and integrity. For the community organizations in the Task Force, it was activism on behalf of the "pay equity movement"; for women working in offices, it was the anguish of seeking wage justice, employer by employer by employer.

Success had come from linking two coalitions: one of community leaders, the other of women working in underpaid "women's" occupations. Advocacy for pay equity built bridges that connected women of different incomes and lifestyles. The linkage effectively maximized pressure for the recognition of women's wage inequities and the adoption of job evaluation studies in the public sector. Task Force members were more credible advocates because they were advocating for their sisters, not themselves. Public employers on Long Island continue to be aware of the female employee wage gap. Because the current political and economic climate discourages pay equity action, the movement is temporarily dormant, not deceased.

The Women on the Job project model became the basis for its 1990 publication, *Working for Pay Equity: A Blueprint for Local Community Action,* with national distribution.[26] Women on the Job also received considerable recognition for its work from the National Committee on Pay Equity and with invitations to address conferences in Albany and Washington, D.C.

The Women on the Job project continues to have an impact on equal rights for women in the Long Island workplace since its founding in 1982. The 1990s have seen substantial gains (i.e., affirmative action) in women's advancement to management positions in local and county governments and to administrative positions in Long Island's school districts. For now, success is greater in Women on the Job's programs for sexual harassment prevention education and training. However, the upturn in Long Island's economy bodes well for renewed progress in achieving pay equity for women who are still underpaid in "pink ghetto" workplaces.

Women on the Job's distinction was that it proved that community grassroots action for pay equity could succeed at local levels of government and independent school districts. And it proved that well-organized activists, working in their communities, could accomplish social and economic change for women.

Notes

1. Women on the Job, *Long Island Women in the Economy: Excerpts from Findings of a Feasibility Study* (Port Washington, NY: Women on the Job, 1982).

2. Joy Ann Grune, ed., *Manual on Pay Equity: Raising Wages for Women's Work* (Washington DC: Conference on Alternative State and Local Policies, 1980), p. 13.

3. Ibid., p. 16.

4. Leslie Bennetts, "The Equal Pay Issue: Focusing on 'Comparable Worth,'" *New York Times,* October 26, 1979.

5. Donald J. Treiman and Heidi Hartmann, eds., *Women, Work and Wages: Equal Pay for Jobs of Equal Value* (Washington, DC: National Academy Press, 1981), chapter 4.

6. Bernard Weinraub, "Feminists Turn to Economic Issues for '80," *New York Times,* October 23, 1979.

7. Ibid.

8. Winn Newman and Jeanne M. Vonhof, "'Separate But Equal' Job Segregation and Pay Equity in the Wake of Gunther," *University of Illinois Law Review,* vol. 1981, no. 2 (1981): 269-331.

9. "The New Pay Push for Women," *Business Week,* December 17, 1979, p. 66.

10. *Comparable Worth Issue* (Washington, DC: Bureau of National Affairs, 1981).

11. Women on the Job's Board of Directors was incorporated as Resources for Program Development. Members in 1982 included Lillian McCormick, President; Winifred Freund, Vice-President; Leonard Weintraub, Esq., Secretary/Treasurer; Craig Shields, Esq., Assistant Secretary; Directors: Cheryl Smyler-George, Director of PREP (the initials stood for Preparation, Recruitment, Education Programs), a local affirmative action program funded by the United States Secretary of Labor; Jane Gitlin, Editor, *Women's Record;* Dr. Lorence Long; Samuel Lynn, Regional Director for Federal Contracts Compliance Program; Jill Sheinberg, Esq.; Gloria Wallick, Director of Nassau County Child Care Council; and Marjorie Weinstein.

12. National Committee on Pay Equity, *A Decade of Working for Economic Justice* (Washington, DC: National Committee on Pay Equity, 1989).

13. Ibid.

14. Women on the Job, minutes of April 21, 1993. Attendance included Adelphi School of Social Work Women's Project (Susan Parato), American Association of School Administrators Women's Caucus (Susan Kaye), American Business Women's Association (Dorothy Cicchetti and Terry Derasmo), Council of Nursing Practitioners (Dianne Mackey), League of Women Voters of Nassau County (Judy Schmertz), Long Island Coalition for Full Employment (Carolyn Martocchia), Nassau NOW (Judy Sanford Guise), National Association of Social Workers (Ivory Holmes), North Shore Unitarian Women's Group (Eunice Nichols and Dorothy Prunhuber), Older Women's League (Marion Donner). As the year progressed, seven more groups joined the Task Force: American Association of University Women, North Shore Branch (Virginia Hansen and Roxee Joly); Coalition of Labor Union Women (Elaine Kennedy); Displaced Homemakers (Phyllis Borger); Womanspace in Great Neck (Florence Rapoport); Women's Bar Association (Jan Weissman); Women in Electronics (Ann Kennedy); and Women in Science (Matilde O'Conner).

15. Women on the Job, minutes of April to December 1983.

16. Women on the Job, *Pay Equity in Contract Negotiations* (Port Washington, NY: Women on the Job, 1989), Appendix 1-A.

17. Women on the Job, *Working for Pay Equity: A Blueprint for Local Community Action* (Port Washington, NY: Women on the Job, 1990), p. 19.

18. Ibid., Appendix H-1

19. Ibid., p. 43-46.

20. New York State Division of Human Rights, April 12, 1985 memo, Case no. 2-e-s-84-96059E.

21. Women on the Job, *Working for Pay Equity,* Appendix G.

22. Anemona Hartocollis, "Women Settle Bias Suits in Two LI School Districts," *Newsday,* May 6, 1987; and National Committee on Pay Equity, "Pay Equity," *Newsnotes,* Summer 1987.

23. Women on the Job, *Working for Pay Equity,* p. 11 and Appendix G-13.

24. Women on the Job, *Pay Equity in Contract Negotiations.*

25. Women on the Job, *Working for Pay Equity,* passim.

26. See note 17 above.

33. Long Island's Nationally Notable Women

Natalie A. Naylor

Adams, Maude (1872-1953), Ronkonkoma. Actress; donated estate to the Cenacle.

Alexander, Hattie Elizabeth (1901-1968), Port Washington. Pediatrics professor and medical researcher (microbiology) at Columbia Presbyterian Medical Center.

Ayres, Sister Anne (1816-1896), Queens and Kings Park. First women in America to become an Episcopal sister; began religious order; worked with the Reverend Dr. William Augustus Muhlenberg.

Bancroft, Jessie Hubbell (1867-1952), Brooklyn and Queens. Physical education teacher and administrator, Brooklyn and New York City school systems.

Bayer, Adèle Parmentier (1814-1892), Brooklyn. Pioneer Catholic welfare worker; known as the "Guardian Angel of the Sailors" for her work with merchant seamen.

Belmont, Alva Erskine Smith Vanderbilt (1853-1933), Sands Point and East Meadow. Socialite and leader in women's suffrage movement.

Blatch, Harriot Eaton Stanton (1856-1940), Shoreham. Leader in women's suffrage movement.

Boole, Ella Alexander (1858-1952), Brooklyn. Temperance leader; president, New York Woman's Christian Temperance Union (WCTU) for twenty years, and national WCTU, 1915-1933.

Bremer, Edith Terry (1885-1964), Port Washington. Leader in immigrant social service work; founder, International Institute movement.

Brownscombe, Jennie Augusta (1850-1936), Bayside. Painter specializing in genre and historical scenes.

Burchenal, Elizabeth (1876?-1959), Brooklyn. Folk dance educator; founder of American Folk Dance Society, 1916; head of Folk Arts Center in New York City.

Burnett, Frances Hodgson (1849-1924), Plandome. Author *Secret Garden* and other popular books, including *Sara Crewe or A Little Princess*.

Burns, Lucy (1879-1966), Brooklyn. Leader in militant wing of women's suffrage movement; worked with Alice Paul; chief organizer in Congressional Union and National Woman's Party.

Campbell, Persia Crawford (1898-1974), Queens. Economics professor, Queens College, 1939-1965; consumer advocate in New York State government and United Nations; a director of Consumers Union, 1959-1974.

Cary, Elisabeth Luther (1867-1936), Brooklyn. First full-time art critic of the *New York Times* (1908-1936); writer on art and literature.

Castle, Irene (1893-1969), Manhasset. Fashion-setting dancer; with husband, Vincent, popularized the tango, Castle Polka, Hesitation Walk, and Castle Walk in the 1910s.

Crosby, Fanny (1820-1915), Brooklyn. Hymnwriter; author of more than 5,500 hymns.

Dennett, Mary Coffin Ware (1872-1947), Astoria. Suffrage leader; active advocate of birth control and sex education who challenged Comstock and other restrictive laws.

Doubleday, Neltje Blanchan De Graff (1865-1918), Locust Valley. Author of bird and garden books under pen name, Neltje Blanchan.

Dreier, Mary Elisabeth (1875-1963), Brooklyn. Headed New York Women's Trade Union League, 1906-1914; active in suffrage and peace movements and in labor reform.

Earle, Alice Morse (1851-1911), Brooklyn. Author of *Home Life in Colonial Days* (1898) and numerous books on colonial artifacts, childhood, dress, domestic life, and social history.

Fedde, Sister Elizabeth (1850-1921), Brooklyn. Founder Lutheran nurses' training center and hospital in Brooklyn (now Lutheran Medical Center).

Folger, Emily Clara Jordan (1858-1936), Brooklyn and Glen Cove. Collaborator with husband assembling Shakespeare collection and founding Folger Shakespeare Library in Washington, D.C.

Frederick, Christine McGaffey (1883-1970), Greenlawn. Household efficiency expert, author, lecturer, and businesswoman; operated Applecroft Home Experiment Station.

Garnet, Sarah J. Smith (1831-1911), Brooklyn (roots in Hempstead). Teacher and civic worker; first black principal in New York City public schools; active in suffrage organizations.

Hunton, Addie D. Waites (1875-1943), Brooklyn. Black leader and Young Women's Christian Association (YWCA) official.

Keller, Helen (1880-1968), Forest Hills (1917-1939). Author; advocate, role model, and fundraiser for the deaf and blind.

Kober, Alice Elizabeth (1906-1950), Brooklyn. Classical scholar; professor, Brooklyn College, 1930-1949; deciphered Minean script, Linear B.

Levine, Lena (1903-1965), Brooklyn. Gynecologist and psychiatrist; active in birth control movement; marriage and sex counselor.

Libbey, Laura Jean (1862-1925), Brooklyn. Author of popular romance novels.

Matthews, Victoria Earle (1861-1907), Brooklyn. Social worker and clubwoman. Founder of White Rose Mission, 1897; active in Negro women's clubs.

Miller, Olive Thorne (1831-1918), Brooklyn. Nature writer and author; wrote popular books on birds and children's books.

Moody, Lady Deborah (c. 1583-1659?), Gravesend. Founder and chief patentee of Gravesend in 1643, the first English settlement on western Long Island.

Moore, Marianne (1887-1972), Brooklyn. Poet, literary critic, editor.

Moran, Mary Nimmo (1842-1899), East Hampton. Painter and prominent etcher.

Morgan, Helen (1900?-1941), Brooklyn. Popular singer and actress; played Julie in *Show Boat* on stage and film.

Mosher, Eliza Maria (1846-1928), Brooklyn. Physician and educator; promoted health services and physical education for college women.

Ovington, Mary White (1865-1951), Brooklyn. A founder and officer of the NAACP.

Palmer, Frances (Fanny) Flora Bond (1812-1876), Brooklyn. Artist and lithographer; one of the most prolific artists for Currier & Ives firm; some of her lithographs are Long Island scenes.

Patterson, Alicia (1906-1963), Sands Point. Founder (1940), co-publisher, and editor of *Newsday*.

Plummer, Mary Wright (1856-1916), Brooklyn. Head of Pratt Library School, 1894-1911 and New York Public Library School, 1911-1916; advocated better training for librarians.

Post, Marjorie Merriweather (1887-1973), Brookville (estate now C. W. Post College). Philanthropist and businesswoman (General Foods).

Powdermaker, Hortense (1896-1970), Queens. Anthropology professor, Queens College, 1938-1968; author *Hollywood: The Dream Factory* (1950) and *Stranger and Friend: The Way of an Anthropologist* (1966).

Powell, Maude (1868-1920), Great Neck. Concert violinist.

Preston, May Wilson (1873-1949), East Hampton. Artist and popular illustrator; member of the "Ashcan School"; exhibited at the 1913 Armory Show.

Rathbone, Josephine Adams (1864-1941), Brooklyn. Teacher, Pratt Library School from 1893; head of Pratt Library School, 1911-1938.

Ray, Charlotte (1850-1911). Brooklyn and Woodside, Queens. First African American woman lawyer; taught in Brooklyn public schools.

Roosevelt, Edith Kermit Carow (1861-1948), Oyster Bay. Married Theodore Roosevelt in 1886; "a most impressive First Lady," 1901-1909.

Sabin, Pauline Morton (1887-1955), Southampton. Republican party official; leader in prohibition repeal; founder Women's Organization for National Prohibition Reform.

Sage, Margaret Olivia Slocum (1828-1918), Lawrence and Sag Harbor. Philanthropist.

Sangster, Margaret Elizabeth Munson (1838-1912), Brooklyn. Magazine editor *(Christian Intelligencer* and *Harper's Bazar);* author of articles and verse.

Smith, Elizabeth Oakes Prince (1806-1893), Patchogue. Author and reformer; poet and novelist; writer and lecturer on women's rights (e.g., *Woman and Her Needs,* 1851).

Sullivan, Mary Josephine Quinn (1877-1939), Brooklyn and Astoria. Art collector; a founder of the Museum of Modern Art; operated art gallery, 1932-1939.

Thursby, Emma Cecilia (1845-1931), Brooklyn. Concert singer and vocal teacher.

Tyler, Julia Gardiner (1820-1889), East Hampton. Second wife of President John Tyler and First Lady, 1844-1845.

Wheeler, Candace Thurber (1827-1923), Brooklyn and Jamaica. Textile designer (embroidered tapestries) and interior decorator; member Tiffany's Associated Artists (1879-1883); formed own Associated Artists, an all-woman firm (1883-1890).

Whitney, Gertrude Vanderbilt (1875-1942), Westbury. Sculptor, art patron, and founder of the Whitney Museum of American Art.

Wolfson, Theresa (1897-1972), Brooklyn. Labor economist; professor, Brooklyn College, 1928-1967; specialized in labor relations; active in workers' education.

Note

Limited to women who lived or worked on Long Island for extended periods (including their years of achievement) who appear in the standard scholarly reference works: *Notable American Women, 1607-1950: A Biographical Dictionary,* edited by Edward T. James, Janet Wilson James, and Paul S. Boyer, 3 vols. (Cambridge: Belknap Press of Harvard University Press, 1971); and *Notable American Women: The Modern Period,* edited by Barbara Sicherman and Carol Hurd Green (Cambridge: Belknap Press of Harvard University Press, 1980). These volumes include women who died before 1976. See Natalie A. Naylor, "Long Island's Notable Women," *Long Island Forum* 47 (June and July 1984): 104-9, 135-41. On African American women, see also entries in *Black Women in America: An Historical Encylopedia,* edited by Darlene Clark Hine, Elsa Barkley Brown, and Rosalyn Terborg-Penn, 2 vols. (Bloomington: Indiana University Press, 1993). Additional information on these women is in these sources which also include bibliographic references.

34. Bibliography on Long Island Women*

Natalie A. Naylor

Amato, Dennis J. "America's First Women's Open Golf Championship." *Long Island Forum* 53 (Winter 1991): 15-18.

Avenoso, Karen. "Saluting the Hers in Island History." *Newsday,* March 17, 1992, sec. 2, pp. 47, 68.

Bailey, Paul. "Famous L. I. Women." *Long Island Press,* July 29 and August 3, 1961.

Baxandall, Rosalyn and Elizabeth Ewen. "Picture Windows: The Changing Role of Women in the Suburbs, 1945-2000." *Long Island Historical Journal* 3 (Fall 1990): 89-108.

Berbrich, Joan. "All About Mad Nan, Hannah Hawk and a Revolution." *Newsday,* July 13, 1971.

Berkow, Ita G. "Last of the Mount Family Artists: Evelina Mount (1837-1920)." *Long Island Historical Journal* 9 (Spring 1997): 245-51.

Biemer, Linda. "Lady Deborah Moody and the Founding of Gravesend." *The Journal of Long Island History* 17 (1981): 24-42.

Bland, Sidney R. "'Never Quite So Committed as We'd Like': The Suffrage Militancy of Lucy Burns." *The Journal of Long Island History* 17 (1981): 4-23.

Buck, Sarah. "An Inspired Hoax: The Antebellum Reconstruction of an Eighteenth-Century Long Island Diary." *Long Island Historical Journal* 7 (Spring 1995): 191-204. Re Lydia Post.

____. "Response to an Uninspired Hoax: Judith E. Greenberg and Helen Carey McKeever, *Journal of a Revolutionary War Woman." Long Island Historical Journal* 9 (Fall 1996): 120-21.

Bunce, Mildred. "A Cold Spring Harbor Childhood." Parts 1-4. *Long Island Forum* 29 (August-October 1966): 153-55, 169-72, 191-93, 211-13.

Capozzoli, Mary Jane. *Three Generations of Italian American Women in Nassau County, New York, 1925-1981.* Detroit: Garland, 1990.

Carpenter, Angelica and Jean Shirley. *Frances Hodgson Burnett: Beyond the Secret Garden.* Minneapolis: Lerner, 1990. For younger readers.

Cash, Floris Barnett. *Black Women of Brooklyn.* Brooklyn Historical Society, 1985. Exhibition catalog.

____. "Long Island's African-American Women." In *Exploring African-American History,* 1991, edited by Natalie A. Naylor, pp. 53-57. Rev. ed. Hempstead: Long Island Studies Institute, 1995.

Cooper, Victor. *A Dangerous Woman, New York's First Lady Liberty: The Life and Times of Lady Deborah Moody (1586-1659?).* Bowie, MD: Heritage Books, 1995.

Crawford, Eugene. *The Daughters of Dominic on Long Island: The Brooklyn Sisters of Saint Dominic.* 2 vols. New York: Benziger, 1939-1953.

Currie, Catherine. *Anna Smith Strong and the Setauket Spy Ring.* Privately printed, 1990. For younger readers.

Custead, Alma. "Elizabeth Oakes-Smith, Period Piece." *Long Island Forum* 4 (Feb. 1941): 27-28, 38.

*See also references in the articles in this book.

Dilliard, Leona M. "Three [Wright] Sisters of Oyster Bay." *Long Island Forum* 40 (May 1977): 88-92.

Dobson, Meade C. "Fire Island's Historic Shipwreck." *Long Island Forum* 4 (August 1941): 185-86.

Doty, Robert, ed. *Jane Freilicher: Paintings.* New York: Taplinger Publishing, 1986.

Druett, Joan. *Captain's Daughter, Coasterman's Wife: Carrie Hubbard Davis of Orient.* Orient, NY: Oysterponds Historical Society, 1995.

___. *Hen Frigates: Wives of Merchant Captains Under Sail.* New York: Simon and Schuster, 1998.

Druett, Joan and Mary Anne Wallace. *Sailing Circle: 19th Century Seafaring Women from New York.* Cold Spring Harbor Whaling Museum and Three Village Historical Society, 1996.

Dwyer, Norval. "Susan B. Anthony In Riverhead." *Long Island Forum* 24 (February 1961): 29-30.

___. "A Wading River Childhood, 1878-1888." Parts 1 and 2. *Long Island Forum* 28 (May and June 1965): 89-91; 117-19.

Dyson, Verne. *The Human Story of Long Island.* Port Washington: I. J. Friedman, 1969. Includes Lady Deborah Moody, Anna Harrison, Julia Gardiner Tyler, Jacqueline Kennedy, and Margaret Fuller.

Falco, Nicholas. "The Ladies Employment Society of Flushing." *Long Island Forum* 48 (June 1985): 107-9.

___. "Sigrid Undset, Nobelist of Brooklyn Heights." *Long Island Forum* 52 (Spring 1989): 48-50.

Flick, Alexander. "Lady Deborah Moody: Grand Dame of Gravesend." *Long Island Historical Society Quarterly* 1 (July 1929): 69-75.

Floyd, Candace. "Legend vs. History: Raynham Hall Redirects Interpretation [of Sally Townsend] from Romance to Documentary." *History News* 36 (September 1981): 14-15.

Funnell, Walter S. "'General' Jones, A Real Fighter." *Nassau Daily Review,* April 10, 1936.

Gordon, Edith L. "Title IX, A Catalyst for Change, Women and Education Since 1972: Long Island a Case History." *Long Island Historical Journal* 8 (Fall 1995): 83-102.

Griffing, Eugene S. "That Fanny Bartlett [Homan] Station." *Long Island Forum* 17 (June 1954): 117-18.

___. "Grandma Mallison." *Long Island Forum* 20 (January 1957): 10-13.

Hand, Julia. "Teen-Age Diary of '86." Parts 3-4. *Long Island Forum* 24 (January and February 1961): 9, 14, 18-20; 33, 36, 38-39. See Chester G. Osborne 1960 entry for parts 1-2.

Hicks, Rachel. *Memoir of Rachel Hicks,* 1880. Quaker minister (1789-1878).

Homire, Marion Hunt Berg. *Grandmother Burned Peachpits.* New York: Privately printed, 1972.

Horne, Field, ed. *The Diary of Mary Cooper: Life on a Long Island Farm, 1768-1773.* Oyster Bay: Oyster Bay Historical Society, 1983. Excerpts in *Domestick Beings,* edited by June Sprigg (New York: Knopf, 1984).

Horton, H. P. "Fire Place Lodge on Gardiner's Bay" (girls' summer camp). *Long Island Forum* 5 (April 1942): 67.

___. "America's First Woman Patentee" (Lady Deborah Moody). *Long Island Forum* 8 (January 1945): 9-10.

___. "Long Island Girl (Mary Farmer) Sailed To Good Health." *Long Island Forum* 29 (December 1966): 235-36.

Huguenin, Charles A. "The Cenacle, Maude Adams' Gift." *Long Island Forum* 21 (January 1958): 3-4, 9-10.

Kay, Sally. "Yaphank's Famous Daughter" (Mary Louise Booth). *Long Island Forum* 5 (November 1942): 203, 212.

Keeler, Robert. "Alicia Patterson." In *Dictionary of Literary Biography, American Newspaper Publishers, 1950-1990,* edited by Perry J. Ashley, pp. 225-35. Detroit: Gale Research, 1993.

Keller, Evelyn Fox. *A Feeling for the Organism: The Life and Work of Barbara McClintock.* New York: W. H. Freeman, 1983.

Kestler, Frances R. "Faith Baldwin: America's First Lady of Romantic Fiction." *Long Island Historical Journal* 7 (Spring 1995): 243-52.

Kittredge, Mary. *Barbara McClintock, Biologist.* New York: Chelsea House, 1991. For younger readers.

Kleinegger, Christine. "The Janes Who Made the Planes: Grumman in World War II." Forthcoming in *Long Island Historical Journal.*

Koppelman, Lucille L. "Lady Deborah Moody and Gravesend, 1643-1659." *de Halve Maen* 67 (Summer 1994): 38-43.

Krieg, Joann P. "Walt Whitman's Long Island Friend, Lisa Seaman Leggett." *Long Island Historical Journal* 9 (Spring 1997): 223-33.

Landau, Ellen G., ed. *Lee Krasner: A Catalogue Raisonné.* New York: Harry N. Abrams, 1995.

Lee, Josette. "Our Founding Mothers . . . an Exercise in Domestic Feminism." *The Quarterly of the Huntington Historical Society* 16 (Fall/Winter 1986): 7-28.

Leoniak, Mallory and Jane S. Gombieski. *To Get the Votes: Woman Suffrage Leaders in Suffolk County.* [Brookhaven: Town Historian], 1992.

Libby, Valencia. "Marian Cruger Coffin, The Landscape Architect and the Lady." In *The House and Garden,* exhibition catalog. Roslyn: Nassau County Museum of Fine Art, 1986.

Lockwood, Estelle D. "The Lady Known as '355.'" *Long Island Forum* 55 (Winter 1993): 10-15. See also Harry Macy's article.

Lynn, Joanne. "'Women's Cradle of Aviation': Curtiss Field, Valley Stream." In *Evoking a Sense of Place,* edited by Joann P. Krieg, pp. 85-95. Interlaken: Heart of the Lakes Publishing/Long Island Studies Institute, 1988.

Lyons, Maritcha R. "Sarah J. S. Garnet" and "Susan S. McKinney Steward. In *Homespun Heroines and Other Women of Distinction,* 1926, edited by Hallie Q. Brown, pp. 110-16, 160-68. Reprint, New York: Oxford University Press, 1988.

Macy, Harry, Jr. "Robert Townsend, Jr., of New York City" (identity of Townsend's mother and the alleged "Lady 355"). *New York Genealogical and Biographical Record* 126 (January 1995): 25-34.

Mathews, Jane. "The Woman Suffrage Movement in Suffolk County, New York, 1911-1917: A Case Study of the Tactical Differences Between Two Prominent Long Island Suffragists: Mrs. Ida Bunce Sammis and Miss Rosalie Jones." M.A. thesis, Adelphi University, 1986. (Copy in Long Island Studies Institute, Hofstra University.)

___. "'General' Rosalie Jones, Long Island Suffragist." *Nassau County Historical Society Journal* 47 (1992): 23-34.

McDermott, Charles J. "M. Louise Forsslund, Novelist." *Long Island Forum* 21 (October 1958): 187, 194. See also Elizabeth Farley's letter, *Long Island Forum* 22 (January 1959): 14.

McGee, Dorothy Horton. *Sally Townsend, Patriot.* New York: Dodd, Mead, 1952. Fictionalized biography for younger readers.

McKay, Ann, ed. *She Went A-Whaling: The Journal of Martha Smith Brewer Brown, 1847-1849.* Orient: Oysterponds Historical Society, 1993.

___. "Getting it into Print: The Journal of Martha Smith Brewer Brown from Manuscript to Book." *Long Island Forum* 56 (Spring 1994): 12-16.

Metz, Clinton. "Sarah Ann Baldwin Barnum." *Long Island Forum* 57 (1984): 167-73.

Morris, Sylvia. *Edith Kermit Roosevelt: Portrait of a First Lady.* New York: Coward, McCann and Geoghegan, 1980.

Naumann, Anne. *The Junior Partner: Edith Loring Fullerton, Long Island Pioneer.* Las Vegas, NV: Scrub Oak Press, 1997.

Naylor, Natalie A. "Long Island's Notable Women." Parts 1 and 2. *Long Island Forum* 47 (June and July 1984): 104-9, 135-41.

___. "Long Island's Mrs. Tippecanoe and Mrs. Tyler Two" (Anna Symmes Harrison and Julia Gardiner Tyler). *Long Island Historical Journal* 6 (Fall 1993): 2-16.

___. "Mary Steichen Calderone." In *Women Educators in the United States, 1820-1993,* edited by Maxine Schwartz Seller, pp. 86-94. Westport, CT: Greenwood, 1994.

___. "'In Deeds of Daring Rectitude': Winning Votes for Women in Nassau County and the Nation." *Nassau County Historical Society Journal* 50 (1995): 31-45.

___. "A New Incarnation of Lyndia Minturn Post's *'Personal Recollections'* of the *American Revolution:* A Review Essay." *Long Island Historical Journal* 9 (Fall 1996): 109-19.

___. "Harriet Quimby, Aviation, and the Suffrage Movement." *Harriet Quimby Research Conference Journal* 2 (1996): 79-90.

Nicholas, Fontine Z. "The Trial of Goody Garlick." *Long Island Forum* 49 (April 1986): 77-81.

Pollard, Clarice Fortgang. "Of War, The WAC and Camp Upton." Parts 1 and 2. *Long Island Forum* 52 (Winter-Spring 1989): 25-33, 72-78.

Osborne, Chester G. "Teen-Age Diary of '86." *Long Island Forum* 23 (November and December 1960): 247-48, 258-59, 262; 279, 283-84, 286. See Julia Hand entry for continuation.

___. "Mrs. Bartlette's School." *Long Island Forum* 24 (May 1961): 109, 116-17.

___. "Young Ladies' School in Brooklyn." *Long Island Forum* 24 (September 1961): 199-200.

___. "Patty [Martha Smith] Heathcote." *Long Island Forum* 27 (February and March 1964): 37-38, 59-61.

Overton, Marion F. "Frances Matilda White Overton's Diary." Parts 1-4. *Long Island Forum* 8 (July-October 1945): 125, 135-36, 145-56, 167, 173-74, 187, 193-94.

___. "A Brooklyn Churchgoer of 1862." *Long Island Forum* 9 (February 1946): 24-34.

___. "Brooklyn's Greenleaf Female Institute." *Long Island Forum* 9 (June 1946): 103-4, 121-22.

___. "Romance and Marriage of 1722." *Long Island Forum* 18 (May 1955): 83-84, 93-94.

___. "Sarah Rapelje, Islander." *Long Island Forum* 18 (September 1955): 169.

Post, Lydia. *Personal Recollections of the American Revolution,* 1859, edited by Sidney Barclay. Reprint, Port Washington: Kennikat, 1970. On lack of authenticity, see articles by Buck and Naylor (1996).

Postal, Maxine. "Politics as a Career for Long Island Women." *Long Island Historical Journal* 4 (Fall 1991): 74-78.

Quinn, Sr. Margaret. "Sylvia, Adele, and Rosine Parmentier: Nineteenth Century Women of Brooklyn." *U.S. Catholic Historian* 4 (1986): 345-54.

Roith, Jo. *A Five Year History of the Women's Forum of Nassau County.* Nassau Daily Review: 1949. Pamphlet in Vertical File, Nassau County Museum Collection, Long Island Studies Institute, Hofstra University.

Ross, Alice. "Ella Smith's Recipe Collection, Smithtown, 1889-1910." *Long Island Historical Journal* 1 (Spring 1989): 147-57.

Shepherd, Edith. "Miss Cornelia's Secret Legacy." *Long Island Forum* 48 (September 1985): 171-74.

Shiel, John B. "The Trials of Mollie Fancher." *Long Island Forum* 48 (March 1985): 53-57.

Schluter, Mildred Burr. "New Netherland's First-Born White Girl." *Long Island Forum* 12 (May 1946): 82, 86.

Schneider, Louis H. "Diary [1865-1871] of a Quaker Girl" (Anna Pearsall Willets). *Long Island Forum* 28 (February 1965): 31-32.

Seversmith, Herbert F. "The Valiant Mrs. [Keziah] Leek." *Long Island Forum* 11 (October 1948): 191-92.

Singer, Alan, ed. *Long Island Women Go to War: The Changing Roles of U.S. Women, 1940-1946.* Hempstead, NY: Hofstra University, School of Education, 1996. Curriculum booklet.

Simonson, Franklin E. "Elizabeth Powell, 1788-1878: Her Dutch Ancestry." *Long Island Forum* 35 (August 1972): 182, 184.

Smith, Elinor. *Aviatrix.* New York: Harcourt Brace Jovanovich, 1981. Autobiography.

Smith, Harvey Garrett. "Widow Avery Called the Militia [1814]." *Long Island Forum* 31 (November 1968): 205.

Smith, Mildred H. "The Remarkable Mrs. Stewart." *Garden City News,* April 19, 1985.

Smith, Renville Silleck. "Downing-Vernon Nuptials of 1875." *Long Island Forum* 12 (August 1948): 153-54.

Spinzia, Raymond E. "In her Wake: The Story of Alva Smith Vanderbilt Belmont." *Long Island Historical Journal* 6 (Fall 1993): 96-105.

Starace, Carl. "The Two Lady Elizabeths [Cateret]." *Long Island Forum* 31 (December 1968): 224-25.

____. "The Most Powerful Woman in Long Island's History" (Lady Deborah Moody). *Long Island Forum* 56 (Winter 1994): 30-32.

Stone, Gaynell. "Women's Work: Native and African American Women of Long Island. Exhibition leaflet. Stony Brook: Suffolk County Archaeological Association, 1992.

Strasser, Susan. *Never Done: History of American Housework.* New York: Pantheon, 1982. Re: Christine Frederick, pp. 214-19, 246-50.

Strong, Kate W. "Nancy's Magic Clothesline." *Long Island Forum* 2 (November 1939): 13; reprinted in 15 (March 1952): 49, and 39 (July 1976): 142-43. See also Strong's, "In Defense of Nancy's Clothesline," *Long Island Forum* 32 (July 1969): 138-39; and "Nancy's Clothesline Code," *Long Island Forum* 38 (April 1975): 79-80, reprinted 39 (July 1976): 142-43. Kate Wheeler Strong (1879-1977) published more than 300 articles in the *Long Island Forum;* included here are a sample of those dealing with women and domestic life.

___. "Down to the Sea in Ships" (Mary Satterly Rowland's voyage). *Long Island Forum* 4 (August 1941): 181-82.

___. "Witchcraft in Setauket." *Long Island Forum* 8 (July 1945): 131-32.

___. "Seven Sisters of Long Ago." *Long Island Forum* 10 (November 1947): 213.

___. "More of Madame Martha [Smith]'s Recipes." *Long Island Forum* 11 (January 1948): 7.

___. "Marriage Vows and Agreements." *Long Island Forum* 13 (February 1950): 29.

___. "Petticoats, Hoops, Bustles and Clothespin Dolls." *Long Island Forum* 28 (September 1965): 181-82.

___. "Madam Martha Smith: 'The Perfect Woman.'" *Long Island Forum* 36 (November 1973): 218-20.

Strong, Lara M. and Selcuk Karabag. "Quashawam: Sunksquaw of the Montauk." *Long Island Historical Journal* 3 (Spring 1991): 189-204.

Suffolk County Archaeological Association. Forthcoming poster series on Long Island women.

Tarzia, Ann. "Elizabeth Oakes Smith: A Woman Not of Her Time." B.A. thesis, St. Joseph's College, Patchogue, 1984. Copy in Hofstra University, Long Island Studies Institute Vertical Files ("Women").

Tuomey, Douglas. "The Death of Margaret Fuller." *Long Island Forum* 23 (December 1960): 277-78, 285.

Valentine, Harriet G. "Great-grandmother Sarah Bunce." *Long Island Forum* 11 (January 1948): 14, 18, 20.

___. *The Window to the Street: A Mid-Ninteenth-Century View of Cold Spring Harbor, New York, Based on the Diary of Helen Rogers,* 1981. Reprint; Cold Spring Harbor Whaling Museum, 1991.

Van Santvoord, Peter Luyster. "Did Sally Townsend Save West Point?" *Long Island Forum* 26 (March 1963): 53-54, 69-70.

Weigold, Marilyn. *Silent Builder: Emily Warren Roebling and the Brooklyn Bridge.* Port Washington: Associated Faculties Press, 1984.

___. "1911 Crop of Female Farmers." *Long Island Forum* 43 (June 1980): 116-24.

___. "Montauk's Angels: The Women's War Relief Association at Camp Wikoff [1898]." *Long Island Forum* 48 (October 1985): 191-95.

Wilhelm, Arlene. "Quaker Women of Westbury and Jericho." Senior project, SUNY College at Old Westbury, 1981. Copy at Historical Society of the Westburys, Cottage, Westbury Library.

Wittenburg, Joy. "Excerpts from the Diary of Elizabeth Oakes Smith." *Signs* 9 (Spring 1984): 534-48.

Wood, Clarence A. "Stella Prince, Lighthouse Keeper." *Long Island Forum* 11 (July 1948): 125, 135.

___. "Riverhead Boasts First Lady, Too." *Long Island Forum* 13 (August 1950): 149-51.

Wortis, Helen Zunser. *A Woman Named Matilda and Other True Accounts of Old Shelter Island.* Shelter Island: Shelter Island Historical Society, 1978. Matilda was a slave manumitted in 1795.

Yeager, Edna H. "Long Island's Unsung." *Daughters of the American Revolution Magazine* 109 (October 1975): 908-14.

___. "Woman, Her Role in an Earlier Age." Parts 1 and 2. *Long Island Forum* 37 (November-December 1974): 214-19, 234-38.

___. "Long Island Women in the Revolution." *Long Island Forum* 40 (January 1977): 10-11.

About the Editors and Contributors

Cynthia J. Bogard is a sociology professor at Hofstra University. She previously taught sociology and women's studies at the State University of New York (SUNY) at Stony Brook, where she also was involved in a number of projects on homelessness conducted by the Institute for Social Analysis. Her article, "Rhetoric, Recision and Reaction: Homelessness and the Clinton Administration," is in *Social Policy and the Conservative Agenda* (1998).

Linda F. Burghardt is a journalist whose articles and columns have appeared in newspapers across the country, from the *New York Times* and *Newsday* to the *Chicago Tribune,* the *San Francisco Chronicle,* and *USA Today.* She is president of Burgardt Communications, a corporate and marketing communications consulting firm. Currently at work on a book about first-generation Americans, she is a native of New York City and has made her home on Long Island since 1978.

Floris Barnett Cash is an assistant professor in the Africana Studies Program at SUNY, Stony Brook. She curated an exhibition at the Brooklyn Historical Society on *Black Women of Brooklyn* (1985). Dr. Cash is the author of "African-American Whalers: Images and Reality," in the *Long Island Historical Journal* (1989); "Radicals or Realists: African American Women and the Settlement House Spirit in New York City," in *Afro-Americans in New York Life and History* (1991); and "Long Island's African American Women," in *Exploring African American History* (rev. 1995).

Norma A. Cohen has been executive director of the Smithtown Arts Council since 1985. She has curated many exhibitions at the arts council's headquarters at the historic Mills Pond House in St. James and has organized numerous presentations in various disciplines. Ms. Cohen is also a painter who exhibits regularly in New York and Paris.

Kathryn M. Curran teaches art in the Connetquot School District. She was guest curator of the conference exhibition, *"To Blush Unseen": Nineteenth-Century Long Island Women,* and previously curated an exhibit at the Cold Spring Harbor Whaling Museum, *Maritime Themes in Long Island Folk Art* (1992). She is currently completing a Ph.D. at New York University in American folk art. The topic of her dissertation is "Crafting Eel Spears on Long Island, 1840-1940: Form, Use and Variation in the Utilitarian Art of Blacksmithing."

Mildred Murphy DeRiggi is an historian with the Nassau County Museum Services at the Long Island Studies Institute. Her Master's thesis at the University of Delaware was, "The Settlement of Muskito [Glen] Cove, 1668-1700" and her Ph.D. dissertation at SUNY Stony Brook was, "Quakerism on Long Island: The First Fifty Years, 1657-1707." Dr. DeRiggi's article, "A Tradition of Toleration: The Dutch, the English and the Quakers," appeared in the *Nassau County Historical Society Journal* (1995).

Joseph Dorinson is a professor in the history department (which he chaired, 1985-1997), at the Brooklyn Campus of Long Island University. He has published numerous articles, including "Brooklyn: The Elusive Image" in the *Long Island Historical Journal* (1989), and "The Suburbanization of Brooklyn: Persistence Without Plan" in *Long Island: The Suburban Experience* (1990), as well as articles on humor and ethnicity. He has organized conferences at his college on Jackie Robinson (1997), Paul Robeson (1998), and Brooklyn: U.S.A. (1998), and is currently editing the Jackie Robinson conference volume.

Marilyn Goldstein writes the biweekly "50 and Up" column for *Newsday.* In her thirty-year career at *Newsday,* she often covered women's issues as a feature writer, news reporter, assistant editor, and columnist. In her twice weekly "(516)" column in *Newsday* (1987-1995), she reported and analyzed Long Island political, social, and women's issues. She is the recipient of numerous awards from women's organizations, journalism associations, and other groups for her newspaper features and columns.

Bernice Forrest Guillaume is professor of American History at Benedict College in Columbia, South Carolina. She wrote her dissertation on "The Life and Work of Olivia Ward Bush (Banks), 1869-1944," a native of Sag Harbor, and compiled *The Collected Works of Olivia Ward Bush-Banks* (1991). Dr. Guillaume has done field work on Native American ethnohistory at the Poosepatuck and Shinnecock Indian Reservations, and is preparing a monograph on the Poosepatuck (Unkechaug) Native Americans.

Helen A. Harrison is Director of the Pollock-Krasner House and Study Center in East Hampton and an art reviewer for the Long Island section of the *New York Times.* She is an art historian, specializing in twentieth-century American art, and was formerly Curator of Guild Hall Museum and the Parrish Art Museum. Her article, "From Dump to Glory: Robert Moses and the Flushing Meadow Improvement," appeared in the Institute's conference volume, *Robert Moses: Single-Minded Genius* (1989).

Joanne Lynn Harvey is the Audiovisual/Adult Services Librarian at the Bryant Library in Roslyn. A graduate of Hofstra University who received her M.S. in Library Science from the Palmer Library School at C. W. Post Campus of Long Island University, she is a founder and first president of the Media Services Division of the Nassau County Library Association. She is the author of "'Women's Cradle of Aviation': Curtiss Field, Valley Stream," in the Long Island Studies Institute's conference volume, *Evoking a Sense of Place* (1988).

Henry M. Holden is an aviation consultant and the author of nine books on aviation, including *Ladybirds: The Untold Story of Women Pilots in America* and *Hovering: The Whirly-Girls: International Women Helicopter Pilots*, as well as a biography of Harriet Quimby, *Her Mentor Was an Albatross*. Mr. Holden is a former Quality Consultant to the NYNEX Corporation. He is the founder of DC-3/Dakota Historical Society and publishes the *DC-3/Dakota Journal*.

Robert F. Keeler is currently a religion writer for *Newsday;* his series on life in St. Brigid's parish received a Pulitzer Prize for Newsday in 1996. During more than two decades at Newsday, he has had a variety of responsibilities, including lead reporter for Brookhaven Town and Suffolk County beats, Albany bureau chief, national correspondent, editor of the *Newsday Magazine*, state editor, and projects reporter. He is the author of *Newsday: A Candid History of the Respectable Tabloid* (1990) and *Parish! The Pulitzer Prize-Winning Story of a Vibrant Catholic Community* (1997).

Linda Keller has been a fashion/costume designer and historian in New York City for more than ten years. Her work has included projects in Seventh Avenue fashion, film, theatre, cruise ship entertainment, as well as couture for individuals. Ms. Keller's previous career was as a city planner. She is also a self-trained artist, creating decorative and conceptual art.

Christine Kleinegger is Senior Historian at the New York State Museum, Albany, New York. She specializes in the history of women, and nineteenth and twentieth-century cultural and social history. She was co-curator of the Museum's exhibition, *The Janes Who Made the Planes*, which focused on women at Grumman during World War II, as well as the exhibition, "Mirrors: Reflections of Society and Self." She is currently researching a social history of sleep.

Janice Koch teaches science education at Hofstra University and does research on women's experiences in science. She has been a consultant to school districts and universities across the country. Dr. Koch has published many articles and given numerous presentations. Her most recent books are *Gender Equity Right from the Start* (1997) and *Science Stories, Children and Teachers as Science Learners* (1998).

Martha Kreisel is a reference librarian in the Axinn Library at Hofstra University. She has been working in public and university libraries for two decades. Her publications include *Photography Books Index: Subject Guide to Photo Anthologies* (1980, 1985) and *Papercutting: An International Bibliography and Selected Guide to U.S. Collections* (1994).

Linda Lane-Weber has been a local activist with the National Organization for Women, having served as president of each of the southern Suffolk chapters. She is also a founder and was president and executive director of the Long Island Women's Coalition. Ms. Lane-Weber is a former teacher who personally has been successfully involved with a sex discrimination suit. She is a graduate of C. W. Post College of Long Island University and received an M.S. from Hofstra University.

Lucinda A. Mayo, a former director of the Amagansett Historical Association, is co-author of *Images of America: Amagansett,* a photographic history (1997). A long-time textile artist and conservator, she is currently working on commissioned art quilts, as well as researching and studying history in Mexico.

Sister Edna McKeever, CSJ, Archivist of the Sisters of St. Joseph of Brentwood, previously had spent many years teaching in secondary education. She has a B.A. and an M.A. in French from St. Joseph's and Brooklyn Colleges respectively, as well as a Certificate in Archival Management from Long Island University. She is currently on the boards of several archival organizations: locally, the Long Island Archives Conference; regionally, Archivists of Religious Institutions; and nationally, Archivists of Congregations of Women Religious. She also belongs to the Society of American Archivists and the Middle Atlantic Regional Archives Conference.

Eunice (Telfer) Juckett Meeker, born in East Hampton, and educated at Russell Sage College, the University of Southern California, and the University of Colorado (Journalism) has spent a lifetime researching early South Fork history. She became interested in LVIS activities as a teenager, has served on LVIS committees for fifty years, and has been secretary, publicity chairman, and editor of *Cooking Wisdom* (1996). She is both a charter and an Honorary Marco Polo member of the Society of American

Travel Writers. Her Long Island feature stories, especially on the Hamptons, have been published in the *New York Times* and other national newspapers.

Maureen O. Murphy is professor of Curriculum and Teaching in Hofstra University's School of Education. She has edited two books on Irish women, Sara Hyland's *I Call to the Eye of the Mind, A Memoir* (1996) and Maire MacNeill's *Maire Rua: Lady of Leananeh* (1990), and is co-editor of *James Joyce and His Contemporaries* (1989) and *Irish Literature: A Reader* (1987). She edited *A Guide to Irish Studies in the United States* for several years, is past president of the American Conference for Irish Studies, and on the board of the American Irish Historical Society. Dr. Murphy is currently working on a study of Irish domestic servants in the United States.

Natalie A. Naylor is director of the Long Island Studies Institute with responsibility for conferences and publications. She is also professor and teaching fellow in New College of Hofstra University, where she teaches American social history. Dr. Naylor has published articles on Long Island history and the history of education, and edited or co-edited several Institute publications, including *Theodore Roosevelt: Many Sided American* (1992); *Roots and Heritage of Hempstead Town* (1994); *Exploring African American History* (rev. 1995), and *To Know the Place: Exploring Long Island History* (1995).

Alice Ross is the director of Alice Ross Hearth Studios where she conducts historical food workshops. Her doctoral dissertation at SUNY Stony Brook was, "Women, Work, and Cookery, Suffolk County, N.Y., 1880–1920." Dr. Ross has taught at Queens College, CUNY and for the Suffolk County Organization for the Promotion of Education (S.C.O.P.E.). She formerly taught home economics in the Sachem Central School District in Holbrook. She often conducts demonstrations, is a consultant for museums and living history museums, and has published a number of articles on historic foodways.

Dorothy B. Ruettgers taught for many years in the Farmingdale Public Schools. More recently, she taught writing and children's literature at Hofstra University. She is a graduate of Douglass College of Rutgers University and did graduate work at Columbia University and Hofstra University where she completed an M.A. She was a Fulbright Exchange teacher in Newcastle-upon-Tyne in England. She edited two Long Island Studies Institute books for younger readers and has spoken at several Institute conferences.

Janice Williams Rutherford teaches United States and Public History at Washington State University. She previously taught at Eastern Washington University, Louisiana State University, and Georgia State University. Dr. Rutherford's other experience includes historic preservation work in Oregon and Washington. She was also Director of the Louisiana Associations of Museums and Program Director, Southeastern Museums Conference. Her doctoral dissertation at Louisiana State University was "'Only a Girl': Christine Frederick, Efficiency, Consumerism, and Woman's Sphere."

Charlotte M. Shapiro has worked for community organizations as program administrator, lobbyist, publications editor, and education consultant. She was a co-founder of the Women on the Job project which is described in her article. Ms. Shapiro has been very active in the Nassau County League of Women Voters and is a past president. She is a former high school social studies teacher. Her publications include *Working for Pay Equity: A Blueprint for Local Community Action* (1990) and *Practical Guide to Women's Job Rights* (1988).

Alan Singer is a social studies educator in the Department of Curriculum and Teaching of Hofstra University. He previously taught in New York City secondary schools. He has published several articles on multiculturalism and other curriculum and educational issues. His most recent projects with students are *Immigration Stories* (1997) and *The Civil Rights Movement on Long Island: A Local History Curriculum Guide for Middle School and High School* (1997); each booklet is distributed by Hofstra Social Studies Educators.

Arlene B. Soifer joined the League of Women Voters in 1956, after hearing Eleanor Roosevelt speak at a League meeting in Levittown. Recently, she has been active in the League as director of public relations for the County League and has also held presidencies in several organizations. She retired from her twenty-five year career as an education executive with Nassau BOCES, and is now in charge of community relations for the Nassau County Museum of Art.

Geri Solomon is the University Archivist at Hofstra. She is Education Coordinator and a past president of the Long Island Archives Conference and has chaired the Documentary Heritage Program and Preservation Committees for the Long Island Libraries Resource Council. Her previous archival experience was at Cornell University and New York University.

John A. Strong is professor of History and American Studies and director of the Social Sciences Division at the Southampton Campus of Long Island University. He has published numerous articles and given many presentations on Long Island Indians. Dr. Strong is the author of two books recently published under the auspices of the Long Island Studies Institute: *"We Are Still Here!": The Algonquian Peoples of Long Island Today* (1996), and *The Algonquian Peoples of Long Island from Earliest Times to 1700* (1997).

Bea Tusiani is a freelance writer who has contributed frequently to the Long Island section of the *New York Times* and *Newsday*'s viewpoints pages. Her essays have appeared in numerous magazines. Locally, she has written historical accounts of Plandome Manor in the *Long Island Forum* and of Manhasset, in *Manhasset, the First Three Hundred Years*. Her interest in Frances Hodgson Burnett's ties to Manhasset led her to establish the Burnett Collection at the Manhasset Public Library.

Sister Lois Van Delft, F.M.M. is Assistant to the President for Pastoral Care at St. Francis Hospital. She graduated from St. Mary's Hospital School of Nursing in Waterbury, Connecticut, and has a B.S. in Nursing and an M.S. in Community Health Nursing from Boston College. She did Clinical Pastoral Education Studies at Interfaith Ministries of Brown University and Rhode Island Hospital. She is a member of the Franciscan Missionaries of Mary and is certified by the National Association of Catholic Chaplains.

Norma White was the Historian of the Sayville Village Improvement Society and a past president, former treasurer, and long-time board member of the Sayville Historical Society. She taught elementary school for twenty-two years and had been president of the Suffolk Reading Council. She was also a charter member of Wet Paints Studio Group, a local group of practicing artists. Unfortunately, she died on February 17, 1996, a few days after she had submitted her article. Her paper was presented at the conference by Suzanne Robilotta, president of the Sayville Historical Society and a vice president of the Sayville Village Improvement Society.

354

Index

References are to page numbers; references to illustrations are in *italics*.

The Long Island Studies Institute

The Long Island Studies Institute is a cooperative endeavor of Hofstra University and Nassau County. This major center for the study of local and regional history was established in 1985 to foster the study of Long Island history and heritage. Two major research collections on the study of Nassau County, Long Island, and New York State are located in the Special Collections Department on the University's West Campus, 619 Fulton Avenue, Hempstead. These collections—the Nassau County Museum collection and Hofstra University's James N. MacLean American Legion Memorial collection—are available to historians, librarians, teachers, and the general public, as well as to Hofstra students and faculty. Together, they offer a rich repository of books, photographs, newspapers, maps, census records, genealogies, government documents, manuscripts, and audiovisual materials.

The Long Island Studies Institute is open Monday-Friday (except major holidays), 9–5 (Fridays to 4 in the summer). For further information, contact the Institute, 516–463–6411. The Institute also houses the historical research offices of the Nassau County Historian and Division of Museum Services (516–463–6418).

In addition to its research collections, the Institute sponsors publications, meetings, and conferences pertaining to Long Island and its heritage. Through its programs, the Institute complements various Long Island Studies courses offered by the University through the History Department, New College, and University College for Continuing Education.

Long Island Studies Institute Publications

Heart of the Lakes Publishing/Empire State Books:

The Aerospace Heritage of Long Island, by Joshua Stoff (1989).

The Algonquian Peoples of Long Island from Earliest Times to 1700, by John A. Strong (1997).

The Blessed Isle: Hal B. Fullerton and His Image of Long Island, 1897-1927, by Charles L. Sachs (1991).

Evoking a Sense of Place, edited by Joann P. Krieg (1988).

From Airship to Spaceship: Long Island in Aviation and Spaceflight, by Joshua Stoff (1991). For younger readers.

From Canoes to Cruisers: The Maritime Heritage of Long Island, by Joshua Stoff (1994). For younger readers.

Long Island and Literature, by Joann P. Krieg (1989).

Long Island Architecture, edited by Joann P. Krieg (1991).

Long Island: The Suburban Experience, edited by Barbara M. Kelly (1990).

The Long Island Studies Institute

The Long Island Studies Institute is a cooperative endeavor of Hofstra University and Nassau County. This major center for the study of local and regional history was established in 1985 to foster the study of Long Island history and heritage. Two major research collections on the study of Nassau County, Long Island, and New York State are located in the Special Collections Department on the University's West Campus, 619 Fulton Avenue, Hempstead. These collections—the Nassau County Museum collection and Hofstra University's James N. MacLean American Legion Memorial collection—are available to historians, librarians, teachers, and the general public, as well as to Hofstra students and faculty. Together, they offer a rich repository of books, photographs, newspapers, maps, census records, genealogies, government documents, manuscripts, and audiovisual materials.

The Long Island Studies Institute is open Monday-Friday (except major holidays), 9–5 (Fridays to 4 in the summer). For further information, contact the Institute, 516–463–6411. The Institute also houses the historical research offices of the Nassau County Historian and Division of Museum Services (516–463–6418).

In addition to its research collections, the Institute sponsors publications, meetings, and conferences pertaining to Long Island and its heritage. Through its programs, the Institute complements various Long Island Studies courses offered by the University through the History Department, New College, and University College for Continuing Education.

Long Island Studies Institute Publications

Heart of the Lakes Publishing/Empire State Books:
The Aerospace Heritage of Long Island, by Joshua Stoff (1989).

The Algonquian Peoples of Long Island from Earliest Times to 1700, by John A. Strong (1997).

The Blessed Isle: Hal B. Fullerton and His Image of Long Island, 1897-1927, by Charles L. Sachs (1991).

Evoking a Sense of Place, edited by Joann P. Krieg (1988).

From Airship to Spaceship: Long Island in Aviation and Spaceflight, by Joshua Stoff (1991). For younger readers.

From Canoes to Cruisers: The Maritime Heritage of Long Island, by Joshua Stoff (1994). For younger readers.

Long Island and Literature, by Joann P. Krieg (1989).

Long Island Architecture, edited by Joann P. Krieg (1991).

Long Island: The Suburban Experience, edited by Barbara M. Kelly (1990).

Long Island Women: Activists and Innovators, edited by Natalie A. Naylor and Maureen
O. Murphy (1998).
Making a Way to Freedom: A History of African Americans on Long Island, by Lynda
R. Day (1997).
Robert Moses: Single-Minded Genius, edited by Joann P. Krieg (1989).
Roots and Heritage of Hempstead Town, edited by Natalie A. Naylor (1994).
Theodore Roosevelt: Many-Sided American, edited by Natalie A. Naylor, Douglas
Brinkley, and John Allen Gable (1992).
To Know the Place: Exploring Long Island History, edited by Joann P. Krieg and Natalie
A. Naylor (rev. ed., 1995).
"We Are Still Here!" The Algonquian Peoples of Long Island Today, by John A. Strong
(1996; 2d ed. 1998).

Long Island Studies Institute:

*The Calderone Theatres on Long Island: An Introductory Essay and Description of the
Calderone Theatre Collection at Hofstra University,* by Miriam Tulin (1991).
Cumulative Index, Nassau County Historical Society Journal, 1958-1988, by Jeanne M.
Burke (1989).
Exploring African-American History, edited by Natalie A. Naylor (1991, 1995).
To Know the Place: Teaching Local History, edited by Joann P. Krieg (1986).
Vignettes of Hempstead Town, 1643-1800, by Myron H. Luke (1993).

Greenwood Press:

Contested Terrain: Power, Politics, and Participation in Suburbia, edited by Marc L.
Silver and Martin Melkonian (1995).
Suburbia Re-examined, edited by Barbara M. Kelly (1989).

The Institute collections and reading room are on the second floor of the Library
Services Center on Hofstra's West Campus, 619 Fulton Avenue, Hempstead, NY.